Historians on Housewives

Historians on Housewives
Fashion, Performance, and Power
on Bravo Reality TV

· ·

EDITED BY
KACEY CALAHANE
JESSICA MILLWARD
MAX SPEARE

The University of North Carolina Press Chapel Hill

This book was published with the assistance of the Anniversary Fund of the University of North Carolina Press.

© 2025 The University of North Carolina Press
All rights reserved
Set in Charis by Westchester Publishing Services
Manufactured in the United States of America

Library of Congress Cataloging-in-Publication Data
Names: Calahane, Kacey, editor. | Millward, Jessica, editor. | Speare, Max, editor.
Title: Historians on housewives : fashion, performance, and power on Bravo reality TV / [edited by] Kacey Calahane, Jessica Millward, Max Speare.
Description: Chapel Hill : The University of North Carolina Press, 2025. | Includes bibliographical references and index.
Identifiers: LCCN 2024044994 | ISBN 9781469686271 (cloth) | ISBN 9781469686288 (paperback) | ISBN 9781469683263 (epub) | ISBN 9781469687827 (pdf)
Subjects: LCSH: Bravo Cable Network. | Real Housewives television programs—Social aspects. | Reality television programs—United States. | Housewives—History. | Women in popular culture. | United States—Social life and customs—21st century. | BISAC: HISTORY / United States / 21st Century | SOCIAL SCIENCE / Ethnic Studies / American / General
Classification: LCC PN1992.8.R32 H57 2025 | DDC 791.45/6543—dc23/eng/20241030
LC record available at https://lccn.loc.gov/2024044994

Cover art: abstract gold background © rangizzz / Adobe Stock.

*Dedicated to all the Bravolebrities who shaped us,
and the Bravodemics who gave us community.*

Contents

List of Illustrations, ix

Acknowledgments, xi

Introduction, 1
Scholars Do Bravo Too!
KACEY CALAHANE, JESSICA MILLWARD, AND MAX SPEARE

Part I
Self-Fashioning Identities and Performing Real Housewives, 21

1 I'm Being Nailed to the Cross Like Jesus Was, 25
Martyrdom and Suffering in Medieval History and Modern Real Housewives
JENNIFER C. EDWARDS

2 From Sumptuary Laws to Glam Squads, 46
Clothing and Identity in the Spanish Empire and The Real Housewives of Beverly Hills
HALEY SCHROER

3 Drama Queens, 65
The Politics of Performance in the Early Modern Royal Court and the Housewives Franchise
EMILIE M. BRINKMAN

4 The Real Housewives of Medieval France, 83
Feminism, Domestic Drama, and the History of the Household
NOAH D. GUYNN

Part II
Consuming Bravo, 105

5 The Bravo Brand, 107
Andy Cohen, Bravolebrities, and the Bravoverse
MARTINA BALDWIN

6 Domestic Lives as Commodity, 123
   *The History of Housewifery as a Consumer Good from
   Early America to Bravo's* Real Housewives
   SERENITY SUTHERLAND AND JENNIFER M. FOGEL

7 Behind the Scenes, 145
   *Housewives' Strategies for Reclaiming Control
   in Intimate Partner Violence Narratives*
   ROSEMARIE JONES

8 Politics and *The Real Housewives*, 168
   *The 2016 Election and the Increase in
   Political Conversations on Bravo*
   NICOLE L. ANSLOVER

   Part III
   The Realities of Race and Space in Historical Memory, 191

9 Old Money and Champagne Taste, 193
   The Real Housewives of Potomac *and the
   History of Black Philanthropy*
   TANISHA C. FORD

10 Charleston and *Southern Charm*, 216
   A Drinking Town with a History Problem
   KRISTALYN SHEFVELAND

11 *Real Housewives*, Black Capitalism, and the New South, 233
   *The Franchise History Behind Dennis "The Hot Dog King
   of Atlanta"*
   MARCIA CHATELAIN

   Bibliography, 247
   Contributors, 263
   Index, 267

Illustrations

2.1 Dorit Kemsley, 58

4.1 Aquamanile featuring Aristotle and Phyllis, 87

4.2 Casket with scenes from romances, 87

4.3 *Cucking Stool*, 88

4.4 *Scold's Bridle or Branks*, 88

Acknowledgments

The authors wish to thank Barbara and Marc Speare for the financial support of the *Historians on Housewives* (*HonH*) project; Christina Hinkle, Pete Murray, Christina Ghanbarpour, and other Saddleback College colleagues for their encouragement with the initial launch of the podcast; Dr. Joaquin Galarza for composing our *HonH* theme song, and Megan Galarza for her unwavering vote of confidence, and Larry; Lara Loper, and Kim Betterndorf for their merch marketing and technical assistance; Molly Calahane for emotional support; Lewis Osio-de Dios for his continuous enthusiasm about all things *HonH*; the Millwards in Utah for smart jokes and merchandise purchases; and the Agyepongs in Ghana for smart jokes, radiating light, and believing in freedom and justice. As this project was born at UC Irvine, we would like to thank Annabel Adams—formerly at UC Irvine and now at UCLA—for marketing assistance; Marc Kanda for facilities troubleshooting; Tyrus Miller and Amanda Swain for asking questions that clarified the project vision; Judy Wu for providing our initial recording space and a training ground for managing large editorial projects; and Sharon Block for teaching the "paragraph" skill.

A special round of applause, snacks, and gifts of appreciation are extended to our editor at UNC Press, the fabulous Dawn Durante. Dawn has believed in this project since we first pitched it to her in the middle of the book display at the 2019 meeting of the Organization of American Historians in Philadelphia. Unbeknownst to us at the time, Dawn was an encyclopedia of Bravo TV knowledge. Dawn has since been a featured guest on the *Historians on Housewives* podcast. Thank you, Dawn, for championing this project and our ability to bring this volume to life. Thank you to "Coach" Daina Ramey Berry, who, in all her wisdom, suggested that we meet with Dawn, and obviously, she was right.

We would like to thank all the Bravodemics included in this volume for their patience, contributions, and wit, and all the current Bravodemics who contributed to the *Historians on Housewives* podcast as well as guests yet to come. These include Tikia K. Hamilton, Tanisha C. Ford, Dawn Durante, Emily Ryalls, Jen Edwards, Nora Lessersohn, Marcia Chatelain, Nicole

Anslover, Martina Baldwin, Kumi Silva, Haley Schroer, Rachel Silverman, Catherine Koonar, Rosemarie Jones, Allison Madar, Brett Rushforth, David Yontef, Jason Herbert, Gwendolyn Fowler, Noah Guynn, Emily Baum, Sowande' Mustakeem, Sean Gallagher, Adam McNeil, Kristalyn Shefveland, Kate Flach, Allison Tait, Mary Klann, Carly Silver, Suzanna Krivulskaya, Emilie Brinkman, Serenity Southerland, Jennifer Fogel, Jay Shelat, Vicki Ruiz, Garrett Saleen, Cristina Rosetti, Jennier McCutchen, Olivia Stowell, Marissa Fenley, and Nikki Gallegos. Mary Ann Lieser improved the final version with on-point and on-call proofreading, as well as constructing the index.

The final round of applause and Friday bagels go to Kelly Bear Calahane-Speare, who arrived during the pandemic, sat through numerous shows intently listening (mostly), and has constantly brought us joy, kept us sane, and entertained us ever since; to Charlie Bee Calahane-Speare, who energized us to the finish line and arrived in tandem with the finalization of this book; and to Ella and Maggie, without whom life beyond the book would not be complete.

Historians on Housewives

Introduction

Scholars Do Bravo Too!

....

KACEY CALAHANE, JESSICA MILLWARD, AND MAX SPEARE

In 2023, *Real Housewives* cast member Vicki Gunvalson received the first ever Wifetime Achievement Award to a standing ovation at BravoCon, the third annual convention celebrating Bravo's slate of television programming. Executives wanted to honor Vicki, who had been a major draw for the network since its flagship show *The Real Housewives of Orange County* (*RHOC*) debuted in 2006. No longer a regular cast member, Vicki had nevertheless remained relevant to *RHOC* history more than seventeen years later, not something many stars of any franchise can claim. Vicki was quick to remind the audience of that fact, stating, "I did not take a family van to get here" and "I've never been with multiple partners in my life." If these uncontextualized quotes make sense, then this book is for you. For everyone else, these quotes represent some of Vicki's most iconic moments on television. In the first instance, Vicki admonished a car rental agency for sending a six-seater van to take her family of four to the airport. In the second, Vicki was denying a rumor that she had participated in a ménage à trois, something that fellow castmate and presenter of the Wifetime Achievement Award, Lauri Peterson, had shared with the group.[1]

Vicki's speech resonated not only with fans who celebrate the chaotic and bizarre episodes that viewers have come to expect from Bravo original programming but also, as this book will show, with some historians who have found the Housewives franchise a productive site for intellectual inquiry. Vicki took the time to "thank my sisterhood of all my housewives . . . cast members that we filmed with season 1. I love you all."[2] Perhaps unknowingly, Vicki borrowed the language of idealized female friendship common among affluent New England women in the late eighteenth through the mid-nineteenth century to reference the community that she and the other Housewives had built together over the past eighteen years. Historically, women's development of a group consciousness through a shared "sisterhood" was predicated on what historian Nancy Cott called "the appearance of women as a discrete class," bound together in early America by the difficult experience of domesticity and housewifery. Such a connection, Cott argued, provided the conceptual foundations for the nascent women's rights movement in the United States.[3] The sisterhood Vicki imagined likewise offered an idolized view of her friendships with her sisters, specifically Lauri, though she was quick to point out, "It has not been easy!" Joining this sisterhood brought out "something in me that I didn't see myself," including a sense of belonging and identity.[4] Taking seriously the relationship between Bravo's world of unscripted television and history is the focus of this book.

In 2019, the *Historians on Housewives* podcast launched from a shared passion for Bravo network's *The Real Housewives* (*TRH*) programming and for using these shows as vehicles for popularizing history. Far from mindless and meritless viewing, as some scholars and cultural critiques would have you believe, Bravo franchises including *The Real Housewives*, *Below Deck*, and *Southern Charm* offer primary source snapshots of the way that different groups of people, both affluent and working class, have navigated histories in the United States and globally. These shows offer windows into broader ideas about historical memory and serve as time capsules to how history has changed over time. *Historians on Housewives* and our fellow "Bravodemics" engage with the Bravo phenomenon intellectually and how it can translate to a popular audience. Ultimately, this book is an extension of that podcast project.

The Real Housewives franchise capitalizes on the regional diversity of the United States by strategically selecting filming locations that aid in the mythologizing of suburban and metropolitan histories. At the time of writing, Bravo had produced TRH in ten U.S. cities: Miami, Washington, D.C., Potomac, New Jersey, New York, Atlanta, Dallas, Salt Lake City, Beverly Hills, and Orange County. Housewives from these different programs are chosen as representatives of their unique communities. In more recent years, Bravo has expanded the Housewives' reach into international markets, adding additional franchises in eighteen countries.

As the flagship franchise to launch the *Real Housewives* brand, Orange County has a reputation for being youthful, wealthy, conservative, and a world-class beach destination. In 2006, Bravo's cameras brought viewers behind the gates of some of the wealthiest communities in the United States. Just an hour north (without traffic), those on *The Real Housewives of Beverly Hills* (*RHOBH*) drip extreme wealth deriving from Hollywood and Los Angeles's music, restaurant, and real estate industries. Despite their proximity to each other, there is little historic overlap between the social circles of *RHOC* and *RHOBH*, which are now in their eighteenth and twelfth seasons, respectively. Beverly Hills alum Taylor Armstrong joined the OC cast in 2022, while her OC costar, actress Heather Dubrow, has Hollywood and plastic surgery industry connections to the Beverly Hills cast. The newest OC cast member Katie Ginella met her costars through RHOBH's Sutton Stracke, and former Beverly Hills star Teddi Mellencamp's podcast venture *Two Ts in a Pod* with OC's Tamra Judge resulted in securing screen time as a guest in Orange County. However, Dubrow's place in Orange County remains an outlier due to the exorbitant wealth she and her plastic surgeon husband, Terry, have compared to her other castmates. To be sure, the women of Orange County have disposable income to varying degrees, but nowhere near the money Dubrow or the Beverly Hills cast have on display from episode to episode. As on the West Coast, housewife franchises on the East Coast capture the regional divides between new money and old money. For instance, *"The Real Housewives of New York"* (*RHONY*) women like Sonja Morgan share familial connections to the robber barons of the late nineteenth and early twentieth centuries. Countess Luann married into the de Lesseps family, known for funding the constructions of the Suez and Panama Canals. Just across the Hudson River, the ladies of *The Real Housewives of New Jersey* (*RHONJ*) trace their ancestries back to the largely impoverished Italian, Irish, Jewish, and Turkish immigrants who came to the United States over the last 150 years.

Fan appeal for *The Real Housewives* is part aspirational and part hate voyeurism, following cast members' lives as they brag about and one-up each other over their homes, businesses, and glamorous fashions; it is the modern soap opera centered on the conspicuous consumption of wealthy women. The shows can suspend viewers in a fantastical world that imagines the thrill of spending time in these customized mansions, dining on five-star meals, or relaxing on a luxury vacation. But the cast members also provide fans an outlet for venting anger and frustration about social problems, where the Housewives become stand-ins representing issues of white privilege, disaster capitalism, homophobia, sexism, toxic masculinity, class inequality, religious evangelism, and colonialism.[5]

Further capitalizing on viewer investment in their luxurious lifestyles, *RHOC* began a practice of cast trips in the early seasons, featuring family and semi-cast vacations to more local West Coast destinations like Lake Havasu, Bass Lake, and Puerto Vallarta. This quickly launched the *Real Housewives* formula of annual extravagant and explosive luxury getaways all over the world, complete with cast members' traveling glam squads. In vacation check-in and shopping scenes, viewers watch the Housewives drop more money on a room, a purse, or a pair of sunglasses than most Americans make in an entire year of work while taking in the subtle horrific (and sometimes overt) reinforcement of American empire and colonial dynamics as the women traverse the globe.

Some of the most prominent evangelizers of American empire on the network, the ladies of *RHONY* embodied this dynamic when they visited Morocco in 2011. Countess Luann greeted Moroccan workers with "Bonjour," harking back to the country's history as a French protectorate, purposefully eschewing local customs of Arabic greetings and insisting on workers referencing her by her royal title. Ramona Singer, possibly the most notorious Housewife colonialist, joked about how "native" Luann looked when she welcomed them to the hotel before requiring riad workers to personally fold and store her clothing (which was enough for seven women by her own admission) upon arrival.[6] Contrast those racial, ethnic, and class dynamics with *The Real Housewives of Atlanta*'s (*RHOA*) trip to Jamaica in 2022.[7] Organized by Kingston-born Housewife Sanya Richards-Ross, cast members made seemingly genuine attempts to understand aspects of the island's people, culture, and cuisine. In other words, the women of *RHOA* did not seem to reinforce U.S.-centric values of cultural superiority and self-identity, but this perception may have been the result of both the cast's and production's careful curation of audience perceptions of these Americans abroad.[8] Moreover, unlike the *RHONY* trip to Morocco, *RHOA*'s ladies were indeed more familiar with the cultural landscape of Jamaican society. In short, settler colonialism remains a consistent theme of the Bravo franchises that is both challenged and reinforced by the racial and ethnic biases held by Housewives and production.

What seemed like a documentary in early *RHOC* seasons quickly evolved into cast members' awareness of the cameras and an understanding of how their potential storylines would be edited. Housewives more carefully curate their fights and reunions. Producers also craft the plots they think will lead to greater viewership. Critics rebuking the "fakeness" of unscripted television usually question the likely inaccurate presentation of subjects' situations and the lack of substance in the characters.[9] Given this climate of apathy and sometimes outright hostility toward this genre, it can be hard to vocalize interest in unscripted television shows—or even obsession, as in our case. The "realness" of unscripted conflicts aside, the content portrayed on Bravo's original programming provides examples for translating seemingly dense academic concepts and, more importantly, delivers a template for teaching popular histories to the public. As our project aims to accomplish, historians can use the language of reality television to create more open access to knowledge and undermine the intellectual gatekeeping separating academia from the general public.

Our understanding of the efficacy of reality television can best be understood through what historian Dipesh Chakrabarty terms a "time knot," a recorded event that is edited, consumed, and learned about from multiple perspectives.[10] Content on Bravo follows this similar formula: stories are shaped in the filming, post-production, and release by the content creators and the audiences that consume this media. The events taking place on these shows may be contrived through production, but the subjects presented are offering real responses to these moments. During the finale for *The Real Housewives of Salt Lake City*'s (*RHOSLC*) fourth season, Heather Gay revealed at a Bermuda Triangle–themed dinner party that rookie Housewife Monica Garcia deceived her fellow castmates in the most stupefying manner. According to Gay (who learned this from mutual friend Tenesha), Garcia created a social media account prior to joining the show that was "dedicated to annihilating and exposing" Jen Shah, a former Housewife who had been federally convicted of running a fraudulent telemarketing scheme against the elderly. Garcia harassed other cast members from this account too.[11] But then Gay provided the most shocking revelation: Garcia had infiltrated the show, secretly working for Shah under the pseudonym Monica Fowler. Garcia was seen on security footage witnessing the iconic moment when Shah's other assistant shoplifted a clutch from cast member Meredith Marks's boutique, which Marks seemed to know about. How much did production contrive this fight or the events leading up to the blowup? How much did Jen Shah help in producing the theft for viewers to consume? These events were learned about at different times and places, and the multiple stories that spanned multiple seasons leading to the conflict on the Bahamian beach not only reshaped audiences' perspectives on stories from years prior but also required a different eye with which to view these older episodes given the new pieces of information. When *Real Housewives* story arcs are laid out like this, conceptualizing Chakrabarty seems like a walk-in-the-park in comparison.

Bravo programming offers more sobering entry points into historical methodologies and perspectives on the past too. Producers revealed that episodes from *Southern Charm*, a show that follows the lives of socialite descendants of some of the nation's most prominent enslavers, had been edited to remove "racially insensitive" material.[12] In one moment, cast member

Thomas Ravenel's father tells his son that he likes to get rid of five-dollar bills because Abraham Lincoln is pictured on them. He then breaks the fourth wall and smiles at the camera. In another scene, Kathryn Dennis (the direct descendant of statesman John C. Calhoun—one of the nation's most notorious proslavery advocates and enslavers) gives a tour of her family's Lewisfield Plantation and, more specifically, the slave cemetery on the grounds before sharing a mint julip with a guest.

Both of these instances are examples of what anthropologist Michel-Rolph Trouillot calls "history 1" and "history 2," or "what happened, and what was said to have happened in the past."[13] What we know about the past is shaped by powerful forces that are rooted in complex relationships, such as the limited information that Dennis shared about the enslaved men, women, and children buried beneath her feet. We can know a little bit more about the lives of the enslaved from studying estate inventories. In a ledger titled "Slaves at the Lewisfield Plantation of Keating Simons, Berkeley, SC, 1835," we find a list of 182 names, including Hannah, Billy, Susey, George, and Dolly. The plantation at Lewisfield was a larger estate.[14] We do not know the ages of these men, women, and children, nor much else about their biographies. Perhaps thumbing through other digitized databases would yield a few fugitive slave advertisements with the names of some of those making attempts to escape bondage. There is also likely some evidence of slave sales records—documents that offer a window into how families were torn apart. Enslaved people's perspectives are largely left to the writings of the men and women who participated in their enslavement. In other words, what has happened was directly curated first by the enslavers, then by Dennis herself, and finally by production in their decision to remove this evidence from future airings of the episode. Similarly, Ravenel's disgust for President Lincoln's visage reinforced the Lost Cause mythology, which—through a Southern elite lens—claims that slavery was not the cause of the American Civil War, but instead that the conflict began over the issue of states' rights and Northern aggression.[15] "What happened" and "what was said to have happened" are unconnected to each other, but Ravenel's riddance of legal tender attempted to present a claim on the collective memory of Lincoln's role in ending the institution of slavery. History is a form of power that historians and the public take part in producing both inside and outside academia, just as creators and cast members of unscripted television attempt to influence modern interpretations of the past.

While Bravo is a fruitful space for discussing historical concepts, the Housewives themselves are the result of longer histories around constructions of womanhood in America. One of the major conceits of *The Real Housewives,* particularly in earlier seasons, is that Housewives' successes on unscripted television is tied to their exaltations of motherhood, protection of the family unit, and leveraging of their power as women-of-means for political and moral influence over the public. These ideas echo mid-nineteenth century middle and wealthy white women's sentiments in particular, who were itinerants of the cult of domesticity, a practice that emphasized women's roles as mothers and wives in the home and supported the division of men and women in the public and domestic spheres, respectively.[16]

Four main attributes defined the cult of domesticity in the nineteenth century: piety, purity, submissiveness, and domesticity. Upper-class white women vested with practicing these virtues wielded morality as a form of social power to reform, not just in their homes but also in society through notions of moral uplift. Nancy Cott argues in the *Bonds of Womanhood* that the home came to represent hierarchical privilege and safety while building the middle-upper class collective consciousness of the cult of domesticity, helping white women organize to combat gender discrimination by accentuating their differences to men. White women were not victims to the creation of the women's sphere but rather active participants in its construction, even though domesticity was constraining as well as liberating.[17] The logics of white women's reform efforts in the nineteenth and early twentieth centuries conflated femininity and morality while anchoring activism in a class-based language that was Christian, moral, female, and synonymous with whiteness.

The cult of domesticity was underscored by the racial dynamics of activism. Wealthy white women's interest in moral reform resulted in social control measures for poor whites, immigrants, and women of color. Remember that time Countess Luann de Lesseps descended on the local YMCA to lecture Black children on the importance of maintaining a slim figure to become a model? White moral reformers championed the morality of sobriety and abstention from alcohol. Consider Kyle Richards's sobriety journey and dismissal of Sutton Stracke for her alleged morning consumption of vodka. White moral reformers of the nineteenth century championed Christian education to "civilize" nonwhite communities during America's colonization of Indigenous communities in North America, Australia, and Asia.[18] We see similar attempts to discipline historically colonized people in Lisa Vanderpump's work to end the dog meat trade in China and establish a dog rescue foundation on season 8 of *RHOBH*. Juxtapose this focus of reform with African American moral reformers of the same period. Toward the end of the nineteenth century, African American women who had achieved some level of economic stability in the Jim Crow period fancied themselves the vanguard of their race and sex in the fight against the rampant white supremacy of the period through campaigns to give Black men voting rights and to end lynching of Black men. A similar dynamic has emerged on *The Real Housewives* too. Black women's reform activism on *RHOA* and *The Real Housewives of Potomac* (*RHOP*) focuses largely on reforming systemic police brutality and advocating for criminal justice reform.

By the twentieth century, women's activists were interchangeably making arguments for social change based on sex equality and on women's differences linked to nineteenth-century ideas about white womanhood. As such, antifeminist and feminist logic operated alongside each other, shaping women's relationships with one another and with American society. Television embraced complex and contentious portrayals of feminist and antifeminist women, the housewife, and housewifery, transforming the way we consume American womanhood in pop culture. There was never a full media transition from the June Cleaver image of the 1950s to the bra-burning feminist protesting the Miss America pageant in 1968 or from the conservative Phyllis Schlaflys of the late twentieth century to the third-wave "boss bitches" of the Gen X and millennial generations. As feminism was celebrated and villainized in U.S. society, women navigated competing images of womanhood, femininity, and women's roles. The women of Bravo routinely espouse both antifeminism and an array of feminist viewpoints on every franchise precisely because, as sociologist Roxane Gay argues, the "franchises allow women to be their truest selves."[19] Moreover, each franchise demonstrates how completely useless the term "housewife" is; it imposes a mental image and definition that is simultaneously being redefined or outright rejected by the cast members, which speaks to a long history of feminist and antifeminist battles over the home and women's private and public lives.

The franchises present an almost exclusively heteronormative space, yet in addition to the queerness constantly bubbling between the women, there is a queering of the heteronormativity from the audience's perspective. Gender and sexually diverse audience members consume these shows with an element of queer desire that manifests in various ways. Viewers express a spectrum of desires: wanting to look like a certain cast member, to ooze age-defying sexuality that transcends monogamous heteronormativity, and to celebrate and imitate the loving intimacy formed in female friendships (and the bromance of househusbands).

Using scenes from *The Real Housewives* (and unscripted television more generally) to contextualize historical events, ideas, and methods creates a vehicle for meeting the public where we mutually share time and space. Our overall goal with this book is not just to act as a compendium for *Historians on Housewives* but, more importantly, to serve as a teaching tool for students of history and as a time capsule for those consuming American pop culture in the twenty-first century and beyond. It is important to note that we are not the first academics to consider unscripted television a worthwhile framework for analysis. Among scholarship, media studies academics have truly been leaders for taking this genre (and Bravo specifically) seriously in pursuit of truth about American society and society abroad.[20] Where this volume diverges from previous work, however, is in our insistence on *doing history*. We incorporate unscripted television into discussions about historical methods, events, and people to consider the longer historical contexts that inform our present moment. For professional historians, this is unorthodox to say the least. This insistence on validating histories in certain forms also guarantees that historians often discover trends much later than other disciplines. *Historians on Housewives* began at a time when it was difficult to find institutional support and resources on college campuses. Frustrated, we wanted to channel Luann and tell everyone, "Don't be all, like, uncool." To our mind, this seemed like an apt comparison to this Housewife's declaration about the virtues of "girl code" when sleeping with anonymous men.[21]

As this volume shows, bringing unscripted television to discussions of academic history is anything but "uncool." Our podcast guests turned contributors to this volume skillfully use their unscripted television obsessions as lenses to reflect on and interrogate the relationships between the past and the present. Engaging this genre and taking seriously its place within pop culture helps us imagine futures not yet seen and pasts not yet fully explored. Historians do not get to pick what forms of entertainment become cultural mainstays; however, because of the critical acclaim and attention given to Bravo's *Real Housewives* franchise, these shows deserve to be understood and contextualized both as forms of escapism and aspiration, and as a generative source from which to pose productive historical questions. Unscripted television is a tool that can be used to dismantle the elitism of the university and bring more people to history who would otherwise not engage with more academic forms of analysis.

Moreover, in our experience, *The Real Housewives* has served as an icebreaker among academic colleagues in an otherwise isolating industry and provided a method for making community between scholars. We can simultaneously dish about the latest Bravo scandals while discussing the significance of our own research projects. The project has become an exciting way to make meaning out of seemingly niche subjects, including the collective grief of millions of viewers—across the racial, gender, and class spectrum—when *RHOA* house-husband Gregg Leakes died after a long battle with colon cancer in 2021, or the various threads, memes, and gifs as fans responded to Garcelle Beauvais's many unsuccessful confrontations with *RHOBH* castmate Dorit Kemsley over her "colorblind" bigotry, or the social impact of Shannon Beador's embarrassing DUI before her ex-boyfriend John Janssen gave fellow *RHOC* cast member Alexis "Jesus Jugs" Bellino a promise ring. Unscripted television has produced its own community of fans well-versed in deep analysis, and we aim to meet them where they are to broaden historical discussions to as many people as possible.

Taken together, therefore, Bravo's unscripted programming should be considered a legitimate vehicle for popularizing history. The edited volume before you is the culmination of our work since the *Historians on Housewives* podcast began. This work demonstrates how historians across the spectrum of fields and disciplines can interact with the public in culturally relevant and accessible ways while also exploring new avenues for student engagement. If you have trouble categorizing this book, you're not alone. It could easily sit alongside works in new media, public history, and historical pedagogy, as well as in a variety of other study areas. Our authors represent a diversity of fields, including African American history; modern American culture; medieval Europe; histories of empires, hagiography, and consumption; gender and sexuality; and personal histories.

● ● ● ● ● ●

RHOBH Erika Girardi's pop star alter ego Erika Jayne proclaimed her "kitty's like a python. Tick-tickin' like a timebomb" in her hit single "XXPEN$IVE." She basks in her wealth, sexuality, and defiance of a submissive suburban housewife existence, declaring: "You like these Georgia peaches / You mad you can't compete with / I changed the game, now say my name / Hi bitches, nice to meet ya / I take shit off the runway / My money origami / I'm Haute couture, on a world tour / From Tokyo to Bombay."[22] While it certainly was and continues to be expensive for Erika Girardi to maintain her lifestyle amid an embezzlement scandal she finds herself connected to through ex-husband Tom Girardi, her song is nonetheless the perfect background track to the essays found in part 1. These essays examine the medieval period through the early modern royal court and the rise of the European empires. Authors delve into the ways consumption of fashion, theater, sexuality, and hagiography (the writing of saints' lives) shape the public image of individuals and social groups and displace social norms through the spectacle of performance.

In chapter 1, Jennifer Edwards examines the similarities between *The Real Housewives of Orange County* and medieval hagiography to demonstrate how the drama of martyrdom and suffering builds a loyal audience from ancient Rome to modern day Coto de Caza. Next, Haley Schroer discusses Housewives, history, and self-fashioning through comparative analysis of the parallel relationship between clothing and identity found in the early-modern Spanish Empire and *RHOBH*. As Schroer notes, Spanish imperial subjects and *RHOBH* stars used clothing to project their perceived belonging to the elite sphere. Building on themes from Schroer's work, Emilie Brinkman's chapter moves us to the English court of the late seventeenth century. Focusing specifically on female courtiers and present-day Housewives, Brinkman argues that fashion and accessorizing contextualized women's relationships to the court and one another as they laid the foundation for their identities within the royal circle. Finally, in chapter 4, Noah Guynn analyzes medieval farce alongside *The Real Housewives of Atlanta*. Guynn argues that the farce, a comedy of highly exaggerated and improbable situations, shows how much continuity exists between medieval and modern mass entertainment, as well as what we can learn about the gender politics of our own household fictions through this deeper history.

The Real Housewives and pop culture overlap in a multitude of ways, as *RHOA* star Kandi Burruss—of Xscape and TLC "No Scrubs" fame—reminds us with her season 5 tagline: "I may be small, but my empire keeps on growing."[23] On the show we get an insider's look at her music career and *RHOA*, as well as the business ventures that emerge from this synergy. Expanding on these themes, Martina Baldwin focuses on Andy Cohen's not-so-hidden hand in the success of the Bravo brand in chapter 5. Baldwin argues that the synergistic relationship between Andy Cohen's *Watch What Happens Live*, viewers, and Bravolebrities signals a winning combination for the network that has also driven major changes in television's history. In considering the evolution of the housewife on television, Serenity Southerland and Jennifer Fogel argue in chapter 6 that the ideal housewife is and always has been part of gendered mythmaking about women's roles in society.

A culture of consumption is pivotal to understanding the construction of the ideal housewife in media and in public memory.

The shows in the Housewives franchise are filled with pithy one-liners, verbal roasts, and epic battle cries that are known throughout various segments of society. Whether or not the speaker knows the context matters little. Rather, these women shape our collective consciousness in daily life and have real impacts on how sexual and gendered violence and current politics is understood today. In chapter 7, Rosemarie Jones provides layered case studies of intimate partner violence (IPV) as showcased across the Housewives franchise and other Bravoverse series. Jones takes a closer look at the ways that Bravo shows can be used as a site of consciousness raising to better support survivors and challenge the social systems and stigmas that contribute to IPV. Examining Housewives' successes in shaping both subtle and overt politics in recent history, Nicole Anslover wades into the murky waters of the current political moment as it manifests on Bravo in real time in chapter 8. Anslover presents a sobering chapter, beginning with the 2016 election and ending with Bravo's treatment of the murder of George Floyd in 2020. By discussing the varying ways that individual Housewives express their political views and how they participate in politics, Anslover exemplifies an important point of this volume, suggesting we use these shows not just as an archive to understand the past but as an avenue for engaging current social, cultural, and political struggles.

Editing magic can leave us with skewed perceptions of the spaces cast members inhabit in their franchise cities—until, that is, these eclipses are made apparent, like when Alex McCord reminded us of the spatial and class divides that underscore some of the conflicts on *TRH*. Sparring with costar Jill Zarin, Alex declared: "I don't want to hear what you think is wrong with my husband. . . . You are in high school. You are a mean girl, and you are in high school. And while you are in high school, I am in Brooklyn trying to survive in this economy, working."[24] In a similar vein, the last section unravels persistent myths in popular culture, highlighting the historical complexities shaping our relationship to race and space in the past and present in America. In chapter 9, Tanisha Ford looks at the world of philanthropy and social uplift in *The Real Housewives of Potomac* and *The Real Housewives of D.C.* Specifically, Ford asks, "What does it mean to be Black, a woman, and philanthropic while also trying to fit into a *Real Housewives* brand that was not initially modeled to reflect the lived experiences of an all-Black cast?" Ford answers this question by arguing that the "*Real Housewives* gospel of wealth" paradigm describes Bravo's newest formula in branding for African American casts. Next, Kristalyn Shefveland analyzes *Southern Charm* and the historical memory surrounding Charleston. By paying particular attention to the city's relationship to the Lost Cause myth, Shefveland uncovers the dark history related to Charleston and lays out the stakes for seeming to forget the ways that the legacies of slavery and systems of white supremacy shaped Charleston before it rebranded itself as a foodie travel destination. Finally, Marcia Chatelain, concludes this volume with an analysis of *RHOA*, Porsha Williams, and Dennis "the Hot Dog King" McKinley within the longer history of post–Civil War Atlanta and African Americans' experiences with capitalism.

· · · · · ·

As we prepared this volume for press, we felt it necessary to "mention it all" in true *RHONY* meltdown fashion, as everything is still about Tom. Although instead of Tom D'Agostino, the Bravoverse has been focused on Tom Girardi's ongoing embezzlement scandal since 2020 and, as of March 2023, the *Vanderpump Rules* (*VPR*) #Scandoval of Tom Sandoval's at least nine-month affair with Rachel "Raquel" Leviss, while his Tom Tom business partner, Tom Schwartz, worked to cover it up. True flashpoints in modern cultural history, both scandals went outside the limits of the Bravo fan base and made their way into the broader American consciousness. #Scandoval, in particular, became a subject of mockery during the 2023 White House Correspondents Dinner, suggesting that even President Joe Biden had heard of what Tom and Rachel did behind Ariana's back.[25] We are still not entirely sure how #Scandoval made national news for several months, since so much of *VPR* is predicated on cast members cheating on each other. It begs the question, Is water wet? And finally, *RHOSLC*'s Heather Gay delivered an Emmy-worthy monologue exposing fans' plot to infiltrate the *RHOSLC* and outing co-star Monica Garcia as Reality Von Tease in the show's season 4 finale. Her documentation of "receipts, proof, a timeline, screenshots" was so noteworthy that California representative Robert Garcia quoted Heather into the *Congressional Record* just a few days later (January 11, 2024).[26]

Since it debuted in 2013, the cast of *VPR* has always represented the gentrification and the straight co-optation of West Hollywood, transforming this gay neighborhood into a space for wealthy white heterosexual tourism. In fact, the cast and their matriarch, Lisa Vanderpump, have repeatedly used allyship and LGBTQ+ rights as an empty platform as they ostracized and bullied the only trans cast member, Billie Lee. After the Orlando nightclub shooting in 2016, the cast split over what allyship to the West Hollywood community should look like, with many of them voicing statements along the lines of "I'm an ally, but . . ." So it was really no surprise to watch the cast's fractures deepen well before Scandoval, alongside the sexual, gender, and racial politics surrounding the strengthening of the conservative movement under Donald Trump and the international Black Lives Matter uprisings in 2020.

Politically labeling Bravo cast members is fraught, not only because so many of them are not politically active but because many also lack any desire for political engagement, especially among white casts. For the most part, the same cast members who supported Billie Lee and who continued to participate in the LA Pride weekend in the hours after Orlando became an alliance facing off against the other half of the cast. Former lovers Stassi Schroeder and Jax Taylor led the show's more politically conservative faction. Stassi hails from a wealthy New Orleans family and consistently ends up on apology tours for "racist actions."[27] Jax and his soon to be ex-wife Brittany Cartwright asked a "family friend" pastor to officiate their televised wedding despite public backlash around his anti-LGBTQ+ views.[28] Despite the network's reputation for attracting LGBTQ+ fans and being "progressive" (we absolutely question the reality of this claim), the network didn't fire Jax and Brittany over this episode. Even Andy Cohen put them in the hot seat for their politics, but Andy maintains that fans are both conservative and liberal (without interrogation of what those terms mean in practice), and therefore the shows need to maintain a balance among the cast so as not to alienate viewers and advertisers.

So when Andy and Bravo symbolically fired Stassi, Jax, and Brittany (and a few other cast members, including longtime fan favorite Kristen Doute) in June 2020 for past racist and homophobic actions, it marked what viewers hoped would be a major transition for the network in terms of supporting a more progressive vision for programming, fueled by public support for the Black Lives Matter uprisings and viewers' demands for network accountability. In fact, Nina Parker hosted a few special episodes about systemic racism titled *Race in America*. On *Watch What Happens Live*, Andy welcomed Porsha Williams (*RHOA*)—the granddaughter of civil rights activist Josiah Williams, to educate white cast members and viewers on racial inequality and allyship. The appearance of white cast members was entirely performative, largely divorced from active political engagement, and geared toward attracting an anti-Trump, pro–Black Lives Matter viewership. Appearances on this Bravo special coupled with hollow social media statements helped remaining cast members publicly distance themselves from former *VPR*, *RHONY*, *Southern Charm*, and *Real Housewives of Dallas* (*RHOD*) cast members who had recently been fired for racist controversies.

One way to conceptualize the performative allyship that has developed over the last several years is found in a comparison of how the network has handled racism-related controversies as they relate to women of color. Among the cast members fired was *RHOSLC*'s Jennie Nguyen, the show's first Asian American Housewife, who was fired after her first season for blatantly racist and anti–Black Lives Matter statements made on social media. Shortly thereafter, fans denounced costar Whitney Rose for distancing herself from a friend on the show who participated in the January 6 insurrection but not from Jennie "for making fun of black [people] being killed by the police. . . . Fake ally," as one commentator argued.[29] Whitney was seen photographed with Jennie in the wake of the incident, something which she has since said she regrets. Like Jennie, Eboni K. Williams was the first African American woman to integrate *RHONY*'s historically majority-white cast in 2020. Eboni was not fired but instead "put on pause" after her debut because fans resented her for challenging the anti-Black bigotry of her fellow cast members, particularly Mar-a-Lago partygoer Ramona Singer. Ramona, however, was not publicly reprimanded until years later, when she was recorded seemingly using a partial racial slur and was summarily disinvited from BravoCon 2023.[30] Similarly, Bravo introduced Dr. Tiffany Moon to further integrate *RHOD*'s majority-white cast, but the series continued to suffer criticism because cast members repeatedly disparaged Chinese and Mexican people. Rather than reboot the series, executives canceled the show in 2021. In all three of these case studies, white cast members succeeded where women of color were stigmatized. Jennie, Eboni, and Tiffany received zero tolerance for fan disapproval, while Whitney, Ramona, and the entire cast of *RHOD* were given numerous opportunities to perform for the network.

The setting of each Bravo show changes the acceptable range of politics presented on camera. *RHOA*, *RHOP*, *Southern Charm New Orleans*, and *Married to Medicine* are all majority or exclusively African American casts living in southern cities. These episodes frequently focus on issues related to colorism, systemic racism in America, medical missionary work, disaster relief, activism and organizing, speaking with policymakers, and hosting community action events. Aside from one episode dedicated to chiding *VPR*'s Jax Taylor and Randall Emmett for a tone-deaf arrest prank on Tom Sandoval or Eboni Williams's interrogation of Ramona Singer during that *one* season, similar conversations around race are hardly the focus of majority-white casts on the network. All of this brings new meaning to the term "performative activism."

It goes without saying that this edited volume offers analysis of only a portion of the Bravo programs and personalities that have generated so much rich historical discussion. For instance, shows such as *Shahs of Sunset*, *Texicanas*, and *Family Karma* are ripe for considering Iranian, Mexican, and Indian immigrant narratives in the twentieth century. Historians of labor, deindustrialization, and the American economy would likely have a lot to say about *Million Dollar Listing*'s portrayal of the real estate industry following the Great Recession of 2008. We also would be remiss to neglect mentioning that *Below Deck*'s focus on the luxury yacht industry offers an incredible entry point into investigating popular ideas about sailing culture and the histories that are made on the sea. If each of the bobby pins that lined Teresa Giudice's beehive hairdo on her wedding day represented a story that *Historians on Housewives* could tell, the proposition for historical engagement would be endless. But alas, publications have timelines, and sometimes those timelines do not line up with academic vision. Nonetheless, we hope that this volume contributes to a growing space for Bravodemics and reality television fans to enter into this intellectual middle ground together. With any luck, we hope that we can respond to the call issued by Sutton Stracke in season 13 of *RHOBH* to "name 'em," and that this will be just one of many volumes to come.

Notes

1. Ingrid Vasquez and Dave Quinn, "Vicki Gunvalson Honored with Bravo's 'Wifetime' Achievement Award: 'I Love You All,'" *People*, November 4, 2023, https://people.com/bravocon-2023-vicki-gunvalson-honored-with-bravo-lifetime-achievement-award-8385926.

2. Vasquez and Quinn, "Vicki Gunvalson Honored with Bravo's 'Wifetime' Achievement Award."

3. Cott, *Bonds of Womanhood*, 194.

4. Vasquez and Quinn, "Vicki Gunvalson Honored with Bravo's 'Wifetime' Achievement Award."

5. Danesha Ferguson, "The Molten Center of *The Real Housewives* Multiverse," interview by Brittany Luse, host, *It's Been a Minute*, NPR, March 3, 2023, transcript, https://www.npr.org/transcripts/1160697394; Carly Thomas, "Andy Cohen Says *Real Housewives* Gave Women over 50 a Platform to Express Their Sexuality: 'Great Feminist Tableau,'" *Hollywood Reporter*, February 19, 2023, https://www.hollywoodreporter.com/tv/tv-news/andy-cohen-the-real-housewives-franchise-sexuality-success-1235330077; J. Peterson, "Inside *The Real Housewives of Sydney* Reboot as Producers Ditch 'Toxic' Cast and Fake Drama for 'Fun and Glamorous' Women in

a Desperate Bid to Save the Australian Franchise," *Daily Mail*, June 30, 2023, https://www.dailymail.co.uk/tvshowbiz/article-12237115/Inside-aspirational-Real -Housewives-Sydney-reboot.html; Jennifer Wilson, "The Real Message of *The Real Housewives*," *New Yorker*, September 22, 2023, https://www.newyorker.com /culture/cultural-comment/the-real-message-of-the-real-housewives.

6. *RHONY*, season 4, episode 8, "Misfortune Teller," aired May 26, 2011, on Bravo.

7. *RHOA*, season 14, episode 14, "Montego Baes," aired August 14, 2022, on Bravo.

8. Said, *Orientalism*.

9. Louis Staples, "The *Real Housewives* Shows Are in the Midst of an Authenticity Crisis," *Rolling Stone*, February 22, 2023, https://www.rollingstone.com/tv -movies/tv-movie-features/real-housewives-series-authenticity-crisis-bravo-robyn -dixon-heather-gay-lisa-rinna-1234683210; Jennifer O'Brien "*Vanderpump Rules*: Why Fans Complain about Ariana's Contrived Storyline," *Screen Rant*, January 10, 2022, https://screenrant.com/vanderpump-rules-ariana-madix-tom-sandoval-forced -storyline; Allisun Talley, "Report: Kyle Richards and Mauricio Umansky's Separation Is for a 'Juicy Storyline' on *RHOBH*," *Reality Tea*, October 17, 2023, https:// www.realitytea.com/2023/10/17/report-kyle-richards-and-mauricio-umanskys -separation-is-for-a-juicy-storyline-on-rhobh; AATT Staff, "*Real Housewives of Beverly Hills* Producers DRAGGED on Twitter for Manipulating Drama!," *All about the Tea*, September 1, 2020, https://allaboutthetea.com/2020/09/01/real-housewives -of-beverly-hills-producers-dragged; Rose Meacham, "Critic Jerry Saltz on Bravo's *Work of Art*: This Isn't 'The Real Artists of Bushwick,'" *GQ*, June 16, 2010, https:// www.gq.com/story/this-isnt-the-real-artists-of-bushwick.

10. For a more extensive discussion of historical time knots, see Chakrabarty, *Provincializing Europe*, 112.

11. Maggie Kreienberg, "*RHOSLC* Women Claim Monica Garcia 'Deceived All of Us' in Shocking Season 4 Finale Confrontation," *People*, January 2, 2024, https:// people.com/rhoslc-recap-monica-garcia-trolling-account-exposed-season-4-finale -8421154.

12. Tyler Aquilina, "Bravo Temporarily Pulls *Southern Charm* Episodes Due to Racially Insensitive Moments," *Entertainment Weekly*, August 21, 2020, https://ew .com/tv/bravo-southern-charm-episodes-temporarily-pulled.

13. Trouillot, *Silencing the Past*, 29, 2, 24.

14. "Slaves at the Lewisfield Plantation of Keating Simons, Berkeley, SC, 1835," January 1835, South Carolina Estate Inventories and Bills of Sale, 1732–1872, Charleston, South Carolina Department of Archives and History, https://www.fold3.com /memorial/283365239/slaves-at-the-lewisfield-plantation-of-keating-simons -berkeley-sc-1835/stories#ca044380-e065-11df-1e04-68405a637b51. This source was brought to our attention by the TikTok account @the.christina_chronicles.

15. For more on the American Civil War in historical memory, see Blight, *Race and Reunion*.

16. For a discussion of white womanhood, housewifery, and the cult of domesticity in nineteenth-century America, see Boydston, *Home and Work*; Cott, *The Bonds of Womanhood*; DuBois, *Feminism and Suffrage*; DuBois, *Woman Suffrage and Women's Rights*; Epstein, *Politics of Domesticity*; Ginzberg, *Women and the Work of*

Benevolence; Ginzberg, *Women in Antebellum Reform*; Isenberg, *Sex and Citizenship in Antebellum America*; Martin, "'A Star That Gathers Lustre,'" 274–92; McGarry, "Spectral Sexualities," 8–29; Pascoe, *Relations of Rescue*; Stanley, *From Bondage to Contract*; Stansell, *City of Women*; Welter, "Cult of True Womanhood," 151–74; Wright, *"The First of Causes to Our Sex."*

17. For a fuller discussion of hierarchical privilege in the domestic sphere, see Cott, *The Bonds of Womanhood*, 1977.

18. Wu, "Interchange," 678; Jacobs, *White Mothers to a Dark Race*.

19. Brian Moylan, "Gloria Steinem Hates It—but Is *The Real Housewives* Secretly a Feminist Triumph?," *Guardian*, June 8, 2021, https://theguardian.com/tv-and-radio/2021/jun/08/gloria-steinem-hates-it-but-is-the-real-housewives-secretly-a-feminist-triumph.

20. Silverman, *Fantasy of Reality*; Andrejevic and Colby, "Racism and Reality TV"; Dubrofsky, "Surveillance of Women on Reality TV," 111–29; P. Orbe, "Representations of Race in Reality TV," 345–52; Lee and Moskowitz, "'Rich Bitch,'" 1–19; Cox and Proffitt, "Housewives' Guide to Better Living," 295–312; Alison Brzenchek and Mari Castañeda, "*The Real Housewives*, Gendered Affluence, and the Rise of the Docusoap," 1–15.

21. *RHONY*, season 7, episode 15, "Don't Be All, Like, Uncool," aired July 14, 2015, on Bravo.

22. Erika Jayne, "XXpen$ive," Pretty Mess Records, 2017, digital distribution.

23. For an example of this tagline, see *RHOA*, season 5, episode 0, "Hairstylists Tell All," aired October 28, 2012, on Bravo.

24. *RHONY*, season 3, episode 10, "Leap before You Look," aired May 7, 2010, on Bravo.

25. Emily Tannenbaum, "Ariana Madix Attends the White House Correspondents Dinner as Host Roasts Tom Sandoval," *Glamour*, April 30, 2023, https://www.glamour.com/story/vanderpump-rules-white-house-correspondents-dinner-ariana-madix.

26. Armando Tinoco, "Congressman Robert Garcia Goes Viral Channeling *Real Housewives* Star Heather Gay as He Made a Case against Donald Trump," *Deadline*, January 10, 2024, https://deadline.com/2024/01/congressman-robert-garcia-real-housewives-heather-gay-donald-trump-1235713943.

27. Kate Aurthur and Elizabeth Wagmeister, "*Vanderpump Rules* Fires Stassi Schroeder and Kristen Doute for Racist Actions," *Variety*, June 9, 2020, https://variety.com/2020/tv/news/stassi-schroeder-kristen-doute-fired-vanderpump-rules-1234629172; Bruce Haring, "Former *Vanderpump Rules* Star Stassi Schroeder Explains the Racial Misconduct That Got Her Fired," *Deadline*, September 17, 2020, https://deadline.com/2020/09/stassi-schroeder-vanderpump-rules-explains-racial-misconduct-that-got-her-fired-1234579351.

28. Michele Corriston, "*Vanderpump Rules*: Tom Sandoval Accuses Jax Taylor of Waiting to Fire Homophobic Wedding Pastor," *People*, February 18, 2020, https://people.com/tv/vanderpump-rules-tom-sandoval-accuses-jax-taylor-of-waiting-to-fire-homophobic-wedding-pastor.

29. Mad Beefs (@MadBeefs), "It's revolting how Whitney denounced her friend she filmed with for being apart of January 6th but never condemned Jennie for making fun of black ppl being killed by the police. It's almost like she waited for everyone to forget to invite her to her event. Fake ally #RHOSLC pic.twitter.com /A9oGVghOyo," Twitter (now X), September 23, 2023.

30. Savannah Walsh, "Ramona Singer Axed from BravoCon after Alleged Racist Remark," *Vanity Fair*, November 1, 2023, https://www.vanityfair.com/hollywood /2023/11/ramona-singer-axed-from-bravocon-after-alleged-racist-remark.

Part I **Self-Fashioning Identities and Performing Real Housewives**

∙∙

This first part emphasizes the ways that scholars and students can use *The Real Housewives'* (*TRH*) archive to explore moments of historical continuities. These chapters examine how cast members wield the power of performance to shape narratives in their favor and amass an individual following. From martyrdom and suffering in medieval hagiography, to the ways that fashion shapes the politics of identity, belonging, and empire, to the parallels between medieval French farce and *TRH* as mass cultural sites of domestic household contradiction and resistance, the following chapters analyze the relationships between self-promotion, consumption, and performance in the past and present. These authors demonstrate that we can analyze material culture and verbal sparring on *TRH* to garner new insight into historical dynamics and to highlight historical resonances in our own work and classroom discussions. *TRH* serves as an important reminder of the power of material culture for situating identity and self-representation throughout time and space, whether performing sainthood, claiming a particular social status, or staging acts of domestic upheaval.

Jennifer Edwards traces the parallels between the accounts of Roman noblewoman Vibia Perpetua and Saint Radegund of Sainte-Croix Abbey in Poitiers, France, and Vicki Gunvalson's self-proclaimed crucifixion in season 10 of *The Real Housewives of Orange County* (*RHOC*). Gunvalson serves as an entry point to discuss martyrdom, stigmata, and other forms of imitatio Christi in medieval hagiographies, or texts serving as holy propaganda to depict a person's sanctity to promote a saint's cult. Edwards argues that both saints and cast members on *RHOC* use suffering to change narratives as a means of self-promotion. Whereas saints' suffering denoted selflessness to glorify God, *RHOC*'s Housewives invoke suffering as a method for battling one another on screen. Despite this difference, these texts can still inform each other, especially because of the mindfulness with which Housewives and saints perform their self-fashioning narratives. Ultimately, Edwards argues that Housewives are their own hagiographers.

While subjects in the sixteenth- and seventeenth-century Spanish Empire navigated sumptuary laws dictating permissible fashions to denote racial, ethnic, and class statuses, *The Real Housewives of Beverly Hills* (*RHOBH*) offers a parallel avenue for exploring the continuities and divergences between materiality and belonging in both the modern fashion industry and the past. Haley Schroer argues that individuals in the Spanish Empire and cast members on *RHOBH* conceptualized the relationship between clothing and identity in similar ways; clothing can be used as a form of surveillance to define or confine certain groups and to signal an extravagance of wealth and social power, or lack thereof. Both used fashion performatively to shape perceptions of their place in society and to claim certain kinds of belonging. Schroer contends that garments acquired transformative meanings as performative markers of inclusion and exclusion that individuals across centuries could consume to alter or solidify their self-fashioned identities.

Lest we need more convincing about the historical resonances of clothing making history through the power of material culture as tools of self-representation and identity, Emilie Brinkman traces the lineages of various housewives to sixteenth- and seventeenth-century royal courts. Whereas Schroer discusses the ways people navigated fashion in the context of daily life within the Spanish Empire, Brinkman examines fashion as a form of politics and agency for female courtiers within the early modern English royal court. While *RHOBH* viewers remember Erika Girardi's "Pantygate" scandal, Brinkman explores the English "Pantygate" of 1662 to highlight how elite women used garments and material wealth to communicate their individual power, to make political statements, and to promote and perform their position within the court. The use of fashion and handbags as a form of self-promotion echoes themes of both Schroer's and Edward's essays, as courtiers and housewives employ material culture to signal their value to other political elites or to the Bravo and *TRH* fandom, respectively.

Moving from Brinkman's analysis of women navigating seventeenth-century royal courts, Noah Guynn looks to theatrical depictions of the household as a political space to analyze domestic drama. Guynn suggests that both medieval French farce and *The Real Housewives of Atlanta* (*RHOA*) are forms of mass culture that act as sites to both reinforce patriarchy and offer women the space to imagine and enact resistance. Guynn analyzes moments of feminist fantasies within sexist genres using oppositional readings of sources to show how female farce characters and *RHOA* cast members transform tropes for self-invention and self-display. In comparing *Le galant qui a fait le coup* (The cad who pulled a fast one) from 1535 and NeNe Leakes's haranguing of Peter Thomas on *RHOA*, this chapter shows us the importance of performing submissiveness, defiance, respectability, and ratchetness as strategies for women to navigate historical agency within domestic spaces.

1 I'm Being Nailed to the Cross Like Jesus Was

Martyrdom and Suffering in Medieval History and Modern *Real Housewives*

JENNIFER C. EDWARDS

Suffering is a key expectation of a saint's vita, a biographical text designed to demonstrate a holy person's sanctity. Some medieval saints endured martyrdom, literally dying as witnesses for their faith; some experienced the stigmata, the wounds of Christ; some lived as ascetics in an imitatio Christi, or imitation of Christ, by denying themselves material comforts, conducting self-mortification, and performing extraordinary service to others, such as attending the dangerously ill. Saints' vitae linger over the details of this suffering in order to demonstrate that the text's holy subject truly earned sanctity. Saints' cult institutions used these stories to encourage patrons, pilgrims, and devotees to visit and make donations to saints' shrines. Suffering was good for cult business.

Likewise, the women of Bravo's *Real Housewives* franchise know that suffering makes for riveting television. Savvy Housewives display their pain in order to stay on the show, be the center of its drama (and season title card), and earn the coveted power seats next to executive producer and former Bravo network executive Andy Cohen at the reunion, a series of episodes in which Housewives review the season and confront one another. In key plotlines, Housewives have displayed the misery of a divorce, the estrangement of a child, a medical challenge, bankruptcy, alcoholism, or legal troubles to keep the audience's focus and to win sympathy. Typically, Housewives emphasize their suffering in complex friendships with fellow castmates. Whether by accusing other Housewives of bullying them, suggesting that they have been misrepresented, or claiming that a friend has hurt them unfairly, women such as Vicki Gunvalson, Lisa Vanderpump, Jill Zarin, Lee-Anne Locken, Luann de Lesseps, Phaedra Parks, and many others have claimed martyr-like victimhood and suffering in attempts to win sympathy and shift narratives in their favor. In *Real Housewives* episodes, Vicki Gunvalson can lie about a partner's cancer, broadcast a friend's worst secrets, and then assert that she is "being nailed to the cross like Jesus was" when criticized for her actions.

As a medievalist, I was reminded of imitatio Christi in medieval saint narratives after witnessing Vicki's defense. Hagiography, which might include saints' biographies, miracle tales, and art, had clear purposes within a saint's cult: to publicize the holy person, depict their sanctity, and encourage devotion to the saint. These are holy propaganda, and following Jesus's demonstration of holiness in his Passion, narratives of suffering demonstrated sanctity. Hagiographers knew that painful martyrdom in the arena, vicious self-mortification of a saint's flesh, and dramatic charitable care for those suffering from the most notorious diseases were narrative strategies that made saints memorable, proved their holiness, and drew supporters. While saints' cults were not jockeying for position on a reunion couch or season title card, they were competing for pilgrims and patrons who had to travel farther than their own living room or twitter stream to engage them. Winning their way into compendia of vitae such as the *Golden Legend*—a medieval bestseller of saintly stories—was the hagiographical equivalent of syndication.

This chapter will examine claims of suffering and martyrdom in the Housewives genre through the lens of suffering narratives in hagiography. While such narratives drive the genre, I will focus here on *The Real Housewives of Orange County* (*RHOC*) season 10 finale and consider its explicit use of Christian rhetoric, particularly around martyrdom and the imitatio Christi, in the context of three types of saint vita: martyr, ascetic, and stigmatic. I argue that hagiographers and Housewives use similar narratives of suffering to center their subject—for hagiographers, the saint; for Housewives, themselves—and gain devotees. I also argue that Vicki Gunvalson's use of Christian rhetoric of suffering in this episode, as a craven and narcissistic refusal to accept responsibility for the pain she caused her friends, misses entirely suffering's purpose in medieval hagiography: to demonstrate selflessness and glorify God. Instead, Gunvalson centered herself as the victim of her friends' "attacks," asserting that their lack of support created a "passion" she had to endure.

In so doing, this essay demonstrates that medieval and modern texts can usefully inform each other, both in the classroom and in scholarship. I have found that references to rhetorical strategies that persist from saints' texts through to modern reality television can frequently engage students who might otherwise find those texts inaccessible. Similarly, the sprawling *Real Housewives* franchise, along with other aspirational reality programming, has demonstrated that the genre has broad appeal, with characters, narratives, and themes that engage viewers, especially women. Anecdotal evidence, and the popularity of the *Historians on Housewives* podcast and project, suggest that academics are especially drawn to these stories. Investigating how the stories we watch and the strategies these (partially) self-written characters employ to draw, engage, and keep an audience can provide a useful framework for approaching primary sources in our scholarly work.

Meet the Housewives

The *Real Housewives* docusoap franchise premiered on the cable network Bravo in March 2006 with *The Real Housewives of Orange County*. The show has run for fourteen seasons and spawned ten official U.S. franchises that consistently present moderately wealthy women leading lives they hope audiences perceive as aspirational. *The Real Housewives* franchise has been a massive success, demonstrated by its longevity; cultural impact in spawning podcasts, parodies, columns, and a BravoCon convention; and financial success, "with a rumored value in excess of half a billion dollars and a peak rating of 3.1 million viewers over *The Real Housewives of Atlanta* season five," with "most of them representatives of the target demographic of women in the eighteen to forty-nine age range."[1] That success has made Bravo a powerful player in the advertising market, which, as Cox and Proffitt argue, illustrate "from a feminist political economic perspective . . . that not only do *TRHW* bring in high ratings and revenues, but also that Bravo strategically garners those ratings from *female* audiences." The "significant buying power" of women who make up the Housewives audience means that the shows have both a powerful cultural and economic impact.[2]

Each season, Bravo follows *Real Housewives* cast members through a period of their lives, as the women gather in a variety of social formations for lunches, parties, cast trips, beauty treatments, exercise classes, fashion shows, and other activities. The women also record talking-head testimonials to offer commentary on their activities and reactions through the season. Many experienced Housewives have a plotline—that is, a specific journey they follow through the season, such as training for a marathon, opening a new business, or preparing for a significant personal milestone. The seasons have a finale episode that includes text overlay updates on the cast member's status on this journey, and then the Housewives gather for a reunion several months after the finale episode. The season narratives are opportunities for Housewife self-fashioning and self-promotion, and the Housewives emphasize aspects of their lives that they expect will garner them sympathy as well as attract a great deal of drama and attention. This is primarily achieved by focusing on female friendships and their breakdowns through factionalism, with "female competition as operationalized through fighting" being a signature feature of the franchise.[3] As Suzanne Leonard observes, "Reality wives understand that being expressive and even controversial constitutes part of the job," and "because wifely reality television has tended to promote a catfight mentality, wives face pressure to manufacture fights in order to legitimize their presence on their respective shows and meet network expectations."[4]

I have long joked that this conflict is my primary reason for watching *The Real Housewives,* since my book *Superior Women: Medieval Female Authority in Poitiers' Abbey of Sainte-Croix* traces conflict that plagued Sainte-Croix's abbesses for 900 years, and *The Real Housewives* brings that focus on conflict and dispute into the present. Housewives' drama might focus on banal and petty squabbles—like over a castmate's tardiness to coffee or taking another woman's seat—or on serious issues, such as parenting, finances, or drug use. Regardless, the fights and reconciliations that drive seasons of *Real Housewives* excite Bravo's target audience and hold their rapt attention. This format encourages the Housewives castmates to amplify contentious issues in ways that are both fabricated and over the top. As Emilie Brinkman observes in this volume, the Housewives "are constantly performing for their audience and their fellow castmates," which Noah Guynn argues is central to the Housewives franchise, whose "ironic goal is to refashion conventions of wifely self-effacement into innovative forms of female protagonism."[5] This chapter puts aside questions of how "real" the Housewives are, and focuses instead on the power of the narrative of suffering for the Housewives and their large audience, as well as on the resonances of suffering narratives in articulations of sanctity during the Middle Ages.[6]

Saints' vitae constitute a genre often accused of fabrication and notorious for recycling tropes, borrowing from other hagiographers, and fitting saints' deeds to audience expectations. The saints, too, were performing holiness through their deeds and in their texts. Vitae typically contain descriptions of miracles and should be considered literary more than nonfiction. Just like in *The Real Housewives,* saints' vitae tailored their subjects to draw an audience, win fans, and encourage devotion, often with theatrical drama. Saints, like the Housewives, were aware of the requirements of their position: just as Housewives use their glam squads to show their best faces to the camera, saints made sure someone recorded their holy deeds for posterity. *Real Housewives* producers and hagiographers alike know that featuring their subjects' private turmoil and pain produced the most compelling, can't-change-the-channel stories.

I do not mean to suggest that the *Real Housewives* cast members are saints—far from it. Yet narratives of sanctity, perfection, and martyrdom frequently used by the Housewives are powerfully displayed on *RHOC* season 10. The Housewives are mundane, if wealthy, women typically interested in demonstrating conspicuous consumption, sculpted bodies, and fabulous lifestyles, but they are not afraid of speaking their minds or airing their dirty laundry. The audience responds most actively to Housewives whose lives are upset by divorce, scandal, or misery—and those who are open to sharing these pains with the audience. As Emma Lieber notes, "Our voyeuristic pleasure explained solely by the element of *Schadenfreude* that creeps into our perception of the women's misfortunes, the satisfaction we get from the assurance that rich people suffer too."[7] Johnson and Trelease term this sense that viewers want to see women with aspirational lives suffer as "humilitainment," a fitting description of Housewives shows in which "a large part of the narrative of every individual program is the mismatch between the expectations the women have (of themselves and others) and the frustrations and embarrassments that befall them."[8] Further, the humilitainment has an ethical component. Viewers—myself included—want to watch these women grapple with their misdeeds and learn from them: "Underneath all of the recriminations and the heightened drama of the reunion shows seems to lie a demand for compulsory self-examination and self-doubt, with the question at issue not so much that of who did what to whom, as that of whether a cast member is capable of taking criticism, willing to admit her guilt, and trying somehow to change."[9] These are also the key features of Christian penitential justice, in which sinful deeds are confessed, repented, atoned for, and forgotten. Housewives most frequently demand that their castmates apologize, and once the misdeeds are confessed and regretted, the cast can "move forward" until the next offense. Often, however, the Housewives resist these moves, denying responsibility and instead depicting themselves as victims of others' misdeeds to position their castmates as the ones requiring self-reflection and penance. Some of the more frustrating seasons have included narratives in which Housewives refused to show humility or to apologize for their misdeeds, and *RHOC* Housewife Vicki Gunvalson, until her recent dismissal from the cast, embodied this problem.

Baptism by Fire

An excellent example of the suffering narrative strategy is the finale to season 10 of *RHOC*. Episode 19, "Baptism by Fire," focuses on the adult baptism of Housewife Tamra Judge, whose turn toward Christianity was an apology tour after her villain role in season 9. Tamra narrated her newfound spirituality as a balm for the wounds she suffered in a difficult custody battle with her ex-husband Simon Barney, as well as for her rocky relationship with her good friend Vicki Gunvalson.[10] Tamra offered this difficult time in her life as explanation for her season 9 behavior, and her turn toward religion was her attempt to demonstrate a more positive path forward.

Vicki Gunvalson is an original OC Housewife and a devoted mother to her two children, both of whom have been visibly uncomfortable with her attention and affection on camera. In season 10, she grieved the sudden death of her mother midseason, navigated her ongoing divorce from longtime husband Donn Gunvalson, and was frustrated by confusion around the health of her then boyfriend Brooks Ayers. Her castmates questioned Brooks's claims to be battling cancer, claims Vicki fiercely championed. Brooks has since admitted that he fabricated claims of receiving treatment at City of Hope for stage 3 non-Hodgkin's lymphoma, including falsifying documents he produced to the Housewives and media outlets. Brooks had already been a sore spot in Vicki's relationship with her daughter Brianna as well as in her friendship with Tamra, as both Brianna and Tamra vocally disapproved of Brooks when Vicki started dating him. The complications this caused in Vicki's relationship with her daughter intensely distressed her, but she was unwilling to prioritize Brianna over Brooks. During season 10, Vicki demanded her friends' unquestioning support for Brooks's cancer struggle. The level of Vicki's involvement in Brooks's alleged cancer scam remains unclear; Vicki has denied any involvement despite admitting to fabricating stories around his health. Rather than accept responsibility for being part of a scam about cancer—probably intended to win sympathy for Brooks—Vicki attacked castmates who offered anything other than blind loyalty. Even into the second hour of the season 10 reunion Vicki continued to protest that castmates should have brought her casseroles instead of questioning her.

One friend who supported Vicki through most of season 10 was Shannon Beador, who joined *RHOC* in season 9. This friendship fell apart at the end of season 10 when Shannon urged Vicki to show Brooks's medical records in order to settle questions about his health. Vicki saw that advice as an unacceptable betrayal, causing her to walk out of a lunch with Shannon, who then stopped returning Vicki's calls.

Shannon's season 10 narrative also focused on suffering. At the end of season 9, Shannon learned that her husband, David, had been having an affair. Rather than leave him, Shannon convinced David to join her in therapy. In the season 10 finale, Shannon claimed success in repairing this relationship, and the couple would go on to renew their vows in season 11.[11] This context drives Shannon's season 10 narrative, as well as part of the conflict between Shannon and Vicki in episode 19, as information about the affair had not yet been made public, and it embarrassed Shannon when Vicki revealed it.

Nailed to the Cross

"Baptism by Fire" interweaves the suffering narratives of Tamra Judge, Shannon Beador, and Vicki Gunvalson. While the focus of the episode is Tamra's baptism, and especially her release of guilt about past misdeeds and anger, the baptism's celebratory party became an opportunity for the women to confront Vicki about the questions they had regarding Brooks's health. In the process, Shannon learns that Vicki had shared private details about David's affair beyond their circle, and the two women's betrayal threatens to end their friendship.

Religious themes fill the episode, from the baptism to the metaphors Vicki uses to describe her anxiety about attending the party: "I don't know if these ladies are my enemies or if they're just confused. So I'm trying to right now stay a pillar of strength. Satan is the author of confusion so he wants them all to be confused. I know the truth. And I will pray for everyone that's confused."[12] In later episodes, Vicki persists in portraying the women's questions about Brooks's cancer diagnosis and treatment as demonic, even after the revelation that their questions had merit, and shows no humility or remorse about her behavior this season.

Through the second half of the episode, the women's skepticism about Brooks's cancer and Shannon's sensitivity about David's affair become intertwined. Vicki's friend Ronda chastises Shannon for not being more supportive of Vicki, because Shannon had encouraged Vicki to share Brooks's medical records and curtail debate about his health. Ronda retorts, "She didn't ask you to see the records when you thought that your husband was cheating on you but you want her to show you the papers when her boyfriend has cancer," revealing that Vicki had betrayed Shannon's confidence about David's affair.[13] This leads Shannon to accost Vicki, Vicki to flee the party, and Tamra to chase after Vicki. Outside the venue, Vicki delivers the key line of her season: "I've done nothing wrong! I've done nothing wrong here! I'm being nailed to the cross like Jesus was and he did nothing wrong! He's Jesus Christ and he did nothing wrong and he was nailed to the cross. That's how I feel." And then she thrusts her arms open wide in the shape of the cross.[14]

Vicki Gunvalson was referring to the Passion of Jesus Christ. "Passion" in Latin comes from the verb *patior*, "to suffer," and the events of the Passion—most significantly Jesus's arrest, flogging, carrying of the cross, and crucifixion, as described in the Gospels of the Christian New Testament—emphasize the pain he endured. Jesus was a Jewish preacher in first-century Galilee, a client-state of the Roman Empire that, at this time, controlled the province of Judea. Jesus's arrest initially caused a jurisdictional crisis, as temple guards appear to have arrested and taken him first to a Jewish court, the Sanhedrin, but he was then taken to the Roman provincial governor, Pontius Pilate, who sent him to the client-king of Galilee, Herod. Herod returned Jesus to Pilate, who eventually sentenced Jesus to a Roman death reserved for noncitizen troublemakers: crucifixion. This is a nasty death in which victims were attached to a large wooden cross, sometimes with rope and sometimes with seven-inch nails, which was then raised in a visible place—a hill such as Golgotha—to make an example of the executed. Death was a slow and painful process, as once the limbs were exhausted, the victim's full weight would hang on his chest, causing a struggle to breathe and then collapsing his lungs so that he eventually asphyxiated, a process that took one to three days. Adding the requirement to carry the cross—about 300 pounds for the full cross that Jesus carried rather than just the crossbar—to the execution site increased the victim's exhaustion and could hasten death; breaking his legs would similarly speed exhaustion, and using nails would exacerbate the pain through blood loss and injury.

During the Passion, according to the Gospels, Jesus received "five precious wounds" from the nails in his arms (depicted later as in his hands), the nail in his feet, the crown of thorns placed on his head by soldiers, and the lance that pierced his side. After his death, Jesus's body was removed from the cross, entombed, and mourned, and then—according to his followers—rose again to walk the earth for forty days before his ascension into heaven. Christians celebrate the Passion at Easter, and according to the writings of Paul, this was the key event that separated Christianity from Judaism: that Jesus's suffering and death offered to all followers, Jew or Gentile, the opportunity to be redeemed and have the hope of salvation. The cross and nails became crucial relics of Jesus's sacrifice once they were "discovered" in the fourth century by Helena, the mother of Constantine—the first Christian Roman emperor—and the cross and crucifix became crucial symbols of the Christian faith. Jesus's suffering inspired Christians to demonstrate their faith through sacrifice, physical pain, self-abnegation, and charity.

While Vicki's exclamation that she was "being nailed to the cross like Jesus was" encapsulates the narrative of suffering so many Housewives employ to garner sympathy, generate drama, win screen time, and maintain the spotlight on these programs, it is definitely not an imitatio Christi based in sacrifice, physical pain, charity, or denial of self. Vicki admitted in the second part of season 10's reunion that she had "fabricated" stories about Brooks's cancer and that in her "gut" she believed he did not have cancer, yet in the finale episode, filmed several months before the reunion, she persisted in presenting herself and her boyfriend as persecuted by her costars. Her defensiveness—"I've done nothing wrong!"—at the end of the party was foreshadowed at the episode's beginning when she proclaimed, "I've got nothing to hide, I've done nothing wrong."[15] Although Vicki was revealing Shannon's secrets, calling Shannon a bad friend for not returning her calls, referring to Shannon as "that's the devil out there," and participating in a deception about cancer, Vicki saw *herself* as the victim of her friends' persecution and took no responsibility for her own misdeeds.[16] Tamra, at her most sympathetic, observed in testimonial, "Well, you're not Jesus and you're not being nailed to any cross, but you could be going to hell if you're lying."[17]

Martyrdom

To understand the significance of Vicki's claim to OC martyrdom, it is necessary to examine what martyrdom entailed. Hagiographical texts have rich explorations of the themes of suffering, victimhood, and persecution. Vicki's comparison of herself to Jesus on the cross recalls the lives of the saints—especially the martyrs, whose ascetic practices included an imitatio Christi, and the saints who received the stigmata. The language of martyrdom is common in the modern day, and in the same episode Shannon even used it casually to refer to persecution *she* had felt from *Vicki*. In testimonial,

Shannon explains why she was not going over to Vicki at the party: "I'm angry at Vicki, so I'm not itching to walk up to her. I'm not going to throw myself into the lion's den, and potentially get my head ripped off. Again."[18] This is a reference to the deaths of martyrs, particularly Daniel 6:24, but also to Christians tossed to the lions in the Roman arena.

Martyrdom was a common phenomenon in the first few centuries of Christianity in the Roman Empire, which controlled most of the Mediterranean world. Before Constantine converted to Christianity and ended the period of persecution in 313, Roman authorities questioned, held in prison, and executed Christians denounced by neighbors. Their main crime was not Christianity, as Romans were fairly open-minded about religion and comfortably adopted new foreign gods into their pantheon, but treason: Christians refused to sacrifice to the emperor's genius, a Roman loyalty test. Jesus's followers were associated with anti-Roman strongholds such as Galilee, a famous gathering spot for Zealots, who advocated for Jewish rebellion against Rome. There were many inventive executions for Christians, but the most spectacular and vicious took place in the arena, where Romans forced them to fight armed and trained gladiators or wild animals such as lions, tigers, and, in the case of Saint Perpetua, a cow. Christians who went courageously to their deaths became known as martyrs, or witnesses for the faith. Their public examples proved effective recruiting tools for Christians, rather than the deterrents Romans anticipated. Christians could not *seek* martyrdom, as that resembled suicide, but they could face their deaths in the name of Christ courageously.

The Roman noblewoman Vibia Perpetua died in March 203, executed in the arena in Carthage, North Africa, along with a group of fellow Christians. A Latin Passion text, partially composed by Perpetua, recalls her days in prison awaiting execution, visions she and others experienced during this time, and the story of her death, added by another author. (A Passion text is a story of martyrdom and suffering experienced in the name of Christ and in imitation of his Passion, as described in the Gospels.)

Perpetua was arrested, along with four other Christians, as a married noblewoman with a newborn in her arms. Perpetua's father made frequent trips to the jail to convince her to renounce her faith, and he was willing to use violence when he heard her call herself a Christian, threatening to "pluck out" her eyes.[19] By embracing Christianity, Perpetua joined a new family, turning from her natal one, and suffered a violent execution for that choice.

The experience of the prison even before her martyrdom was difficult. Perpetua notes that it was hot and dark, the soldiers were cruel, and she struggled as a nursing mother to care for her son.[20] Tending to an infant in a hot prison without any light or water is challenging enough, but Perpetua's narrative emphasizes that the nursing gave her particular stress, both when they were together and after she passed him into the care of her family.[21]

Perpetua exchanged difficult care of an infant for the torment of a nursing mother being apart from her child. Beyond the emotional toll that absence can take on a new mother, an inability to express milk can lead to extraordinary pain, infection, and even death for a nursing woman.[22] Perpetua realized she needed to resume care of her baby and asked for him to be with her in prison again: "Immediately I recovered because I was relieved from the work and care for the baby."[23] Perpetua had received a miracle: "How God willed, neither the baby had any further desire for the breast, nor did I suffer any fever, nor did care of the infant or pain in my breasts trouble me."[24] Perpetua remained torn between her spiritual desire to shed her family responsibilities and her physical and emotional needs for her child.

In some ways, Vicki saw herself similarly as a woman pulled in one direction by her family and friends, and in another by the man she chose, essentially a prison of her own making. However, the other Housewives, in their critiques of Gunvalson, did not imprison her or cause her to endure any physical discomfort. Vicki desired space to pursue a romantic life with Brooks to the point that she pushed her daughter Brianna away when Brianna questioned the relationship. Gunvalson claimed her friends and family subjected her to a passion in an imitatio Christi for her faith in Brooks.

During one of his visits, Perpetua's brother suggested that she ask God for a vision. She received her vision and saw an enormous ladder with rungs made of weapons and a dragon guard at its base. Perpetua stepped on the dragon's head and began to climb, finding at the top a garden and an old shepherd who welcomed her. After Perpetua told her brother of her vision, "we understood that a Passion was our future and we began to have no hope in this world."[25] This image of life as suffering and the Christian faith as release, with hope focused on the eternal life after the suffering of the earthly one, is common in saints' narratives.

The night before their execution, the Christians had a last meal, after which they spoke to a mob, warning them "of God's judgment, testifying to the joy of their suffering."[26] The "joy" of the martyrs going to their death is repeated—walking joyfully, trembling "with joy rather than fear." When the crowd demanded that they be whipped by gladiators, the Christians "rejoiced . . . that they were united in the Lord's sufferings."[27] These martyrs reveled in the suffering because they knew of the rewards promised them in heaven.

In the arena, God answered the Christians' prayers by allowing them each the death they had wanted. Perpetua was attacked by a mad cow. Like a Housewife needing reunion mid-fight touch-ups from her glam squad to restore her modesty, Perpetua, after being gored by the cow, thought mostly of arranging her clothes and "asked for a pin to fasten her disheveled hair: for it was not right that a martyr should suffer with her hair streaming in all directions nor be seen lamenting in her glory."[28] Perpetua's concern for her modesty and her holy appearance in this moment is both a part of her self-fashioning as a saint, apparent throughout her narrative of her arrest and imprisonment, and a part of her understanding that, as Haley Schroer observes in this volume, clothing is "a means to project social, religious, and ethnic status."[29] After fighting the animals, the martyrs came together and exchanged the kiss of peace to seal their martyrdom.[30] There they were killed by the sword, and Perpetua guided "the uncertain right hand of the inexperienced gladiator to her throat herself."[31] With their deaths, the martyrs' passion was complete, and their narrative demonstrated the sanctity they earned through this physical pain, suffering, and sacrifice.

Housewives' physical bodies are also frequently depicted as a site of pain and suffering, whether undergoing cosmetic surgery treatments—even leeches for *Real Housewives of Orange County* star Heather Dubrow—or resolving medical issues, such as *Real Housewives of Beverly Hills* star Yolanda Hadid (then Foster) and her many treatments resulting from her battle with Lyme disease. Vicki is among the most frequent indulgers in plastic surgery.[32] As Lieber observes, "Doctors' offices are some of the most frequented interiors in the television series."[33] The women also reveal their mental and emotional struggles by bringing cameras into their therapy appointments, such as Bethenny Frankel's visits to Dr. Xavier Amador on *Bethenny Ever After* and *Real Housewives of New York*. The Housewives undergo these painful procedures—and televise them—in pursuit of perfect beauty. They portray the emotional suffering of their lives to a public audience in pursuit of glory—not the glory of the Christian martyrs but the glory of fame. The Housewives televise their pursuit of beauty as a public performance, just as the martyrs' presented their pursuit of salvation to the crowds to show the beauty of Christian perfection. The martyrs were ambassadors for their faith, while the Housewives accept payment to serve as beauty product ambassadors on Instagram.

The suffering and devotion of the martyrs was physical and extreme to provide a spiritual freedom. Christians believed the martyrs accessed heaven and spiritual reward for their service to the faith and their extraordinary devotion. Their physical imitation of Jesus's sufferings marked them as holy and worthy of emulation. They had, in Vicki's words, "done nothing wrong," but they exulted in their opportunity to be "nailed to the cross like Jesus was" through their own passion. But Vicki's martyr complex is not a martyrdom.

Asceticism

After the conversion of Constantine to Christianity, the era of martyrdom came to an end. Christianity became a path to preferment in Rome and, eventually, the only legal religion in the empire. The method for devout Christians to become witnesses for their faith shifted in response. With no martyrdoms available, pious men and women focused on ascetic practices that denied physical pleasure, such as celibacy, extreme diets, and self-mortification. In the fourth and fifth centuries, groups of Christians who had turned toward eremitical lives started joining together and living under a shared rule, or a set of guidelines governing their lives in monasteries. Monasticism became a popular institution in the fourth and especially fifth centuries, with monastics focused on their devotion to God. Some took on more extreme ascetic practices by wearing a hair shirt, practicing self-flagellation, or living on meager amounts of food.

In the sixth century, Saint Radegund founded a monastery, the Abbey of Sainte-Croix in Poitiers, France, and lived as a nun after rejecting her life as queen of the Franks, literally giving her royal clothes and jewels to the church. Radegund found her retreat into a monastery insufficient and created further challenges for herself. She entered a cell within the monastery, where she could communicate only through the window. One year she not only spent Lent denying herself food and wearing a hair shirt but also bound herself with iron bars for forty days, permitted her skin to grow over them, and then ripped the bars away, as a way to experience Christ's pain in a living martyrdom: "Thus a woman received freely all bitterness for the sweetness of Christ!"[34] Another year, Radegund had a brass plate made in the shape of Jesus's face, heated it, and then pressed the plate to her skin.[35] Radegund's holy biography depicted this imitatio Christi to present her as a candidate for sanctity, as another biographer put it, a living martyr with a "long, protracted martyrdom for the love of God."[36] Her biographers made clear that Radegund ate very simple food and little of it, and that she worked long hours in self-effacing ways, like washing shoes and sweeping the altar's dust. Many of these activities were performed in secret and were known only by her confessor, who, as her biographer, revealed them after her death.

While Radegund was not actively persecuted for her faith, she was able to create a narrative of martyrdom through her experience of self-abnegation and self-inflicted pain. She founded a monastery where she might retreat from the world, and later retreated farther still into her cell. Radegund was persecuted by her husband, Chlothar, king of the Franks, who had taken her as a prisoner of war when she was a child and pressed the marriage on her when she wanted to be a nun. According to one story, when Radegund fled from Clothar to join the church, he chased after her. She hid in a field of oats and prayed; God heard her prayer and made the oats grow tall to hide her.[37] Here, according to her biographers, God showed Radegund that her mission to found a monastery was a life change he approved of and would assist her ability to pursue it.

While Radegund's ascetic practices were private and hidden away, Saint Angela of Foligno engaged the public and performed her asceticism for all to see. Angela spent time in the public square washing the poor and the sick, giving special attention to people suffering from leprosy, a disease that disables its victims and affects their skin. According to one story, Angela washed a leprosy patient "whose hands were withered and decomposing." She then drank the wash water, which she found as sweet as a Communion wafer. "And when a scab from the . . . sores had become lodged in my throat, I tried to swallow it; and my conscience kept me from spitting it out—just as if I had received Holy Communion; and so I did dislodge it—not in order to spit it out, but so that it could go down my throat."[38] Angela embraced physical danger because it brought her closer to the suffering Jesus had endured.

For Radegund and Angela, suffering was a way of experiencing God and engaging with Jesus physically. Radegund tortured her body to feel the suffering Jesus experienced in the Passion. Angela's willingness to put her body in physical danger by not only washing the leprous body but also ingesting the wash water was an ascetic act; her delight in swallowing a scab and imagining it to be a Communion wafer—for her the literal body of Christ—was to take Jesus into her own body. These were ways of demonstrating sanctity after the age of martyrdom, or to create through physical torment a martyrdom without persecution.[39] Radegund and Angela metaphorically nailed themselves to the cross in devotion to God, although they had done nothing wrong, because the suffering they experienced brought them closer to him.

Stigmata

The most high-status imitatio Christi was to receive the stigmata, the wounds of Christ. For the crucifixion, nails went through Jesus's arms and legs to secure him to the cross. Some saints, such as St. Francis of Assisi (d. 1226) and St. Catherine of Siena (d. 1380), received physical memorials of these wounds as demonstrations of their devotion to God. Such a blessing indicated the saint's purity and special status as a holy vessel.

The word "stigmata" appears in the New Testament only in Paul's letter to the Galatians: "Ego enim stigmata Iesu in corpora meo porto" (For I carry on my body the marks of Jesus) (Gal. 6:17). Scholars agree that Paul was not suggesting that the stigmata were literal physical marks on his body or even necessarily a reference to the five wounds of Christ; Paul meant his stigmata as a metaphorical mark.[40] Some church fathers, such as Jerome, argued that the stigmata could also arise through self-mortification—that is, by whipping or harming themselves in imitation of Jesus's suffering. Others, such as Marius Victorinus, interpreted the stigmata in Galatians as metaphorical: "Paul said, *I bear the marks of the Lord Jesus Christ on my body*: that is, I have suffered, and when I serve Christ in the mystery, I endure Christ's mystery. . . . Paul will be with Christ as he suffers with Christ, and those things which Christ suffered, also he begins to suffer in his action of opposing adversaries."[41] This last interpretation is useful for understanding Vicki's exclamation, as she saw herself as the victim of her enemy castmates, creating adversity she likened to Jesus's Passion.

Vicki would not approve, however, of St. Augustine's (d. 430) interpretation, which suggests that the stigmata were "the signs of punishment slaves bear because they have done something wrong."[42] Vicki's complaint was that her punishments were unfair because *"I've done nothing wrong* here! I'm being nailed to the cross like Jesus was and *he did nothing wrong*! He's Jesus Christ and *he did nothing wrong* and he was nailed to the cross. That's how I feel" (emphasis added). According to Carolyn Muessig, medieval commentators understood Augustine to mean that Paul bore a tattoo (*stigma*) as a soldier of Christ, or as a result of persecution "like a misbehaving slave" for "a punishment he deserved."[43] For Augustine, the stigmata were penitential and allowed Paul to atone for his previous role in persecuting

Christians.⁴⁴ Vicki, however, resisted—and continues to resist—any notion of wrongdoing or a need to apologize for her misdeeds. She insisted that her "friends" had harmed *her* and thus crucified her.

Medieval monasticism provided an opportunity for devoted Christians to retreat from the world to focus on a life of prayer and holy work. As we have seen with Radegund, ascetics found opportunities for the imitatio Christi. Within monasticism, the meaning of the stigmata shifted from suffering, as with Paul, or penance, as with Augustine, toward a path of physical connection to Christ. Some authors, such as the theologian Peter Damian, saw that physical connection as a battle, with the monastic fighting as a soldier of Christ, while others saw the stigmata as a physical manifestation of divine connection.⁴⁵

The Dominican nun Catherine of Siena received the stigmata in 1375 in Pisa, as was observed by her confessor Raymond of Capua (d. 1399). According to Raymond, Catherine said that after receiving Communion from him, she had a vision of "the Lord fixed to the cross above me descending in a great light" that raised her body. "Then from the scars of his most sacred wounds I saw five bloody rays descending towards my hands, my feet, and my heart." Catherine asked God not to "let these scars show externally on my body." While she was saying this, "before the rays had reached me their color changed from blood red into brilliant light, and in the form of pure light the rays reached the five places of my body, namely my hands, feet, and heart."⁴⁶ Thus, God gifted her with wounds invisible to all except Catherine and Christ.

Catherine's modesty in wanting the stigmata to remain invisible was an important element of her saintly humility, in contrast to the visible demonstration of St. Francis's stigmata. Similarly, the beguine Mary of Oignies hid the fact that she had wounds on her body until they were discovered by those preparing her body after her death in 1213.⁴⁷ While holy women were appropriate vessels for the stigmata, their privacy during their lives was an important element of receiving such a blessing. The revelations were important demonstrations of their imitatio Christi.⁴⁸

Catherine's hagiographers, such as Raymond, were invested in advertising the stigmata, and painters involved in creating depictions of the saint that would promote her canonization made the "invisible" wounds apparent to viewers.⁴⁹ Images like these helped to shift association of the stigmata from men like Francis toward women, and there were more women among late medieval stigmatics than men.⁵⁰ Claiming the stigmata for the Dominicans out of competition with Francis may have even been Raymond's point. Raymond's discussion of Catherine's spiritual blessings portrays a connection with Christ that goes much further than the stigmata; as John Coakley observes, Christ "removes her heart and replaces it with his own, appears to her frequently during Communion, gives her sublime new visions, endows her with his own will in place of her own and then the stigmata (invisible to others, like her ring), and finally grants her request to feel the pain of his sufferings—thus causing her 'death,' in which she spends four hours with him in heaven before returning to life."[51]

Not only does Catherine imitate Christ's suffering, but she experiences it in a vision. She was not nailed to the cross but suffered the wounds as a reward for doing nothing wrong, to use Vicki's framing. Catherine's suffering is private, invisible, and passionately desired.

A Housewife would, like Catherine, beg God to help her not "let these scars show externally on my body," but not out of modesty, humility, or a desire to keep Christ's blessings private, as it was for Catherine and other early stigmatics. The Housewives are eager to demonstrate their financial access to procedures that will make their bodies perfect, not by showing wounds but by smoothing away age and seeking enhancements. After a characteristic plastic surgery—many of them filmed for the show—a Housewife might also beg God to hide the scars, but out of vanity rather than any attempt to hide their body's alterations. Vicki bore many of these scars, hidden from her procedures, but none of them was the stigmata.

Conclusion

Vicki Gunvalson made the rhetoric of suffering and martyrdom, so often used by Housewives, explicit in the *RHOC* season 10 finale. She exclaimed that she was being nailed to the cross, not out of her extraordinary faith, humility, devotion, or sacrifice but because of her castmates' failure to offer her unswerving loyalty or to believe that Brooks Ayers's cancer was real.[52] While she embraced the Christian language of this rhetoric, her repeated failure to take responsibility violates both its religious origins and the principles of the *Real Housewives* genre: that those who behave badly confess their mistakes, reckon with the consequences of their behavior, apologetically perform penance, and then agree to move on. Somehow, Tamra uses the spectacle of conversion to claim a moral space in which she attempts to gain the moral high ground, despite extensive mockery of the faith of another Housewife, Alexis Bellino, by calling her "Jesus Jugs." Vicki's conviction in her own martyrdom—in her supposedly Christlike blamelessness—permits her to believe that these women are her persecutors and she is the victim in the arena: the one suffering an enforced asceticism bereft of her friends' support, the one whose stigmata are marked out on her flesh but invisible to such nonbelievers.

And lest I suggest that Vicki is alone in using this imagery, Erika Girardi from *Real Housewives of Beverly Hills*, who uses the stage name Erika Jayne, has used similar references to the cross and martyrdom on two notable occasions. First, at the season 9 reunion, when costar Lisa Vanderpump sent a statement explaining she would not attend the reunion after what she saw as unfair treatment of her that season, Erika responded, "Get off the cross, we need the wood," dismissing Lisa's notion of her own martyrdom. Then, in May 2021, Erika reposted a cartoon drawn and shared by artist Ryan Casey (Instagram handle @drunkdrawn) that referenced legal trouble for Erika and her husband Tom Girardi, a class-action lawyer accused of, among other things, mishandling payments due his clients from lawsuits he won. In the cartoon, Erika hangs on a cross, clad only in a string-bikini bottom, shouting, "BALENCIAGA!" with drop earrings that read "orphans" and "widows," and flames eating the bottom of the cross. The cartoon is hardly flattering, as it references legal claims that Tom used funds he owed vulnerable clients to support Erika's extravagant lifestyle. Yet when she reposted the image, Erika added the caption "scapegoat." So while she suggested at the season 9 reunion that Lisa's martyrdom was illegitimate— "we need the wood"—she had no problem using the same imagery to claim her own martyrdom in her season 11 storyline.

Vicki's claims that she is "being nailed to the cross like Jesus was" and Erika's Instagram post are not spiritual devotions to help them find God but spectacles designed to win sympathy and screen time by advertising their own perceived suffering. Vicki especially is her own hagiographer. Unlike the holy vitae of the saints, however, the Housewives' propaganda was not intended to amplify the majesty and power of God but to deny responsibility for an alleged cancer scam or embezzlement and to attack the women who had dared to question them. Emma Lieber observes that the narrative of humility is a good fit for the Housewives franchise because its protagonists are female: "With female protagonists questions of moral improvement through self-abnegation are practically a given, as are plot lines that take the form of conversation tales—or at least stories in which transformation and self-improvement are prominently at stake."[53] But while Vicki Gunvalson is eager to claim status as a martyr, persecuted for her faith, she has notably displayed neither humility nor remorse for her admitted lies in pursuit of this status. Her costars Tamra Judge and Shannon Beador similarly argued that they had suffered unfairly—Tamra during her divorce and Shannon during her husband's affair and at Vicki's betrayal—in challenge to Vicki's assertions of martyrdom. Each also tried to use faith-based metaphors for their assertions. Vicki's, and now Erika's, depiction of herself as Jesus on the cross, however, is the ultimate in Housewife claims of suffering in pursuit of glory, status, and self-promotion. Ultimately, however, Catherine, Radegund, and Perpetua may be forgiven for telling the Housewives not to sit with them.

Notes

Many thanks to Jessica Millward, Kacey Calahane, and Max Speare for their kind patience and encouragement for this project. I appreciate also the Bravo fellowship and support of Elisa Miller, Brittany Fallon, Deirdre O'Leary, Evelyn Scaramella, Carissa Harris, Sally Livingston, and all the GMs and Alenes.

1. Udy, "Secrets, Lies and *The Real Housewives*," 97; Lieber, "Realism's Housewives," 114. For podcasts, see *Historians on Housewives*, *BitchSesh*, and *Watch What Crappens*. For parodies, see the Hotwives series, as well as various *Saturday Night Live* episodes. For one example of a column, see Brian Moylan's recaps at *Vulture*.
2. Cox and Proffitt, "Housewives' Guide to Better Living," 298.
3. Leonard, "From Basketball Wives to Extreme Cougar Wives," 133.
4. Leonard, "From Basketball Wives," 137–38.
5. See chaps. 3 and 4 in this volume.
6. While the Housewives are no saints, there has been a trend of creating prayer candles with Housewife faces on them, a product sought after by Bravo devotees.
7. Lieber, "Realism's Housewives," 121.
8. Johnson and Trelease, "Glocalization, Hard-Won Status, and Performative Femininity," 325.
9. Lieber, "Realism's Housewives," 121–22.
10. Tamra's daughter Sidney famously asked her mother to quit the show and stop including her in its production. Instead, Tamra remained on the show until her firing in 2020 and made her estrangement from her daughter a key storyline.
11. The couple is now divorced.
12. *RHOC*, season 10, episode 19, "Baptism by Fire," aired October 12, 2015, on Bravo.
13. I should note my skepticism and frustration with this recurring theme in *Real Housewives* episodes. The women frequently share information on camera with one person, and then feel betrayed and angry when their confidant tells someone else. Since the show broadcasts material to a national audience, outrage at betrayed confidences disclosed on camera is more overtly manufactured drama than the shows typically present. In Shannon's case, her reaction seems based on the fact that Ronda announced the infidelity at a party and embarrassed her in the moment and that

Vicki was setting certain standards for friendship while simultaneously betraying them.

14. *RHOC*, season 10, episode 19.
15. *RHOC*, season 10, episode 19.
16. *RHOC*, season 10, episode 19.
17. *RHOC*, season 10, episode 19.
18. *RHOC*, season 10, episode 19.
19. *Passio sanctarum Perpetuae et Felicitatis*, 3.
20. *Passio*, 3.
21. *Passio*, 3.
22. Mastitis-inflamed breast tissue can involve an infection that is fatal if not treated. It is incredibly painful. A less serious plugged duct that many nursing mothers experience when not adequately draining the breast is also painful and distressing.
23. *Passio*, 3. Many mothers with plugged ducts or similar lactation issues find that the baby's nursing suction is the best way to clear the problems and ease their pain.
24. *Passio*, 6.
25. *Passio*, 4.
26. *Passio*, 17.
27. *Passio*, 18.
28. *Passio*, 20. I am thinking here of *Real Housewives of Atlanta* star Kandi Burruss's tearful response to a tough reunion in season 9, when Andy told her squad to "touch it up," meaning to reapply makeup to her face.
29. See chap. 2 in this volume.
30. *Passio*, 21.
31. *Passio*, 21.
32. A former "house husband," as the Housewives' male partners are termed, Slade Smiley cruelly attacked Vicki's appearance in a series of comedy shows, likening her to Miss Piggy.
33. Lieber, "Realism's Housewives," 124.
34. Fortunatus, "De Vita Sanctae Radegundis, Liber I." For more on my reading of Radegund, see J. C. Edwards, *Superior Women*.
35. Fortunatus, "De Vita Sanctae Radegundis," 26.
36. Baudonivia, "De Vita Sanctae Radegundis Libri Duo," 21.
37. Baudonivia, "De Vita Sanctae Radegundis," 4.
38. Translated in Mazzoni, *Angela of Foligno's Memorial*, 53.
39. For more on medieval women's bodily experience of faith, see Bynum, *Holy Feast and Holy Fast*.
40. Davidson and Fritz-Morkin, "Miracles of Bodily Transformation," 456. While Francis of Assisi's stigmatization is the most famous example, historians Richard Trexler, Giles Constable, and Carolyn Muessig have demonstrated that the concept of stigmata predated Francis. Trexler, "Stigmatized Body of Francis of Assisi," 463–97; Constable, *Three Studies in Medieval Religious and Social Thought*; Muessig, "Signs of Salvation," 40–68.

41. Marius Victorinus (d. ca. 365), quoted in Muessig, "Signs of Salvation," 43.
42. Muessig, "Signs of Salvation," 44.
43. Muessig, "Signs of Salvation," 45.
44. Muessig, "Signs of Salvation," 46.
45. Muessig, "Signs of Salvation," 55.
46. Raymond of Capua, Vita S. Catharina Senensis, Acta Sanctorum, April 3, 30 (Antwerp, 1675) 2.7, col 901F, quoted in Muessig, "Stigmata Debate in Theology and Art," 487.
47. Constable, *Three Studies in Medieval Religious and Social Thought*, 216–17.
48. Muessig, "Signs of Salvation," 67.
49. Muessig, "Stigmata Debate in Theology and Art," 489n22.
50. Muessig notes that 87 percent of stigmatics after Francis were women. Muessig, "Signs of Salvation," 67n109.
51. Coakley, "Managing Holiness," 178.
52. Vicki might have more ably compared Tamra and Shannon to Judas for their supposed betrayals.
53. Lieber, "Realism's Housewives," 122.

2 From Sumptuary Laws to Glam Squads
Clothing and Identity in the Spanish Empire and *The Real Housewives of Beverly Hills*

HALEY SCHROER

In 1691, Fray Antonio de Ezcaray decried the "plague and contagion" of extravagant garments and accessories that had descended upon Spanish imperial society.[1] According to the friar, subjects throughout the Iberian Peninsula and the Americas had forsaken their Christian values in favor of excess and opulence. While men covered themselves in feminine ruffles, women donned skirts so full they "could dress four poor women."[2] More than 300 years later, Ezcaray's laments found an unlikely ally on reality television. In the spring of 2020, Kyle Richards, an affluent Beverly Hills resident and member of Bravo's *Real Housewives* franchise, condemned fellow castmate Dorit Kemsley for her vanity. When Kemsley arrived late to a cast wellness retreat, Richards took offense that Kemsley prioritized hours with her hair and makeup team over her friends, complaining, "I knew that Dorit was coming late, but clearly, she's been in glam for hours. I mean, is glam the reason that she had to come late today? Really?"[3] Notorious for her own extravagant style, Richards personified the very world shunned by Ezcaray. Yet both disapproved of their peers' excessive devotion to attire and appearance. In spite of such chronological, geographical, and philosophical differences, they found common ground in their judgments on the sartorial choices of others.

This chapter examines the comparable relationship between clothing and identity found in the early modern Spanish Empire and the contemporary reality television show *The Real Housewives of Beverly Hills* (*RHOBH*). An unlikely comparison, the two cases possess vast historical differences. However, individuals in these examples conceptualized the role of attire in a similar manner. In distinct yet parallel ways, Spanish subjects and *RHOBH* cast members approached garments as performative objects that allowed them to manipulate perceptions of their place in society. Evaluating this common thread highlights the continuous power of materiality across distinct historical contexts and creates a unique window into the enduring sociopolitical influence of garments in popular culture.

This chapter is divided into three parts, the first of which evaluates the climates surrounding both case studies. Although similar relationships developed, so too did distinct social, political, and economic values. It is necessary to recognize the disparities caused by chronological distance before offering further comparison. The remaining parts examine how both historical and contemporary actors conceptualized the role of clothing in public life. Throughout the sixteenth and seventeenth centuries, the Spanish Empire witnessed an increasingly apparent international decline, domestic mobility, and the consolidation of the American colonies. While legal restrictions attempted to define status through attire, subjects simultaneously manipulated the rules to improve their standing. Centuries later, cast members of *The Real Housewives of Beverly Hills* turned to fashion to express multiple identities, curry favor with viewers, and assert their belonging among the American elite. Ultimately, Spanish imperial subjects and the *Real Housewives* stars used clothing to enhance their social standing and project perceived belonging in the elite sphere.

Historical Differences: Early Modern Regulation and Contemporary Self-Expression

The sartorial parallels found between the Spanish Empire and *The Real Housewives of Beverly Hills* developed within unique political, economic, and social contexts. Given the considerable chronological gap, both examples existed within distinct governing systems, financial structures, and hierarchies. The former experienced profound changes throughout the seventeenth century that shifted the attention of officials and subjects alike toward controlling the material sphere. In contrast, the latter developed alongside the contemporary fashion industry—a socioeconomic behemoth in its own right. Surrounded by self-expression, *RHOBH* cast members drifted toward multiplicity and access. Different environments bred distinct conceptualizations of garments in daily life.

Within the everyday reality of the early modern period, established hierarchies defined the public sphere. By 1500, apparel across Europe had acquired increasingly complex social and political meanings. A century earlier, changes in style had shifted popular attire away from draped, unisex robes toward tailored masculine and feminine pieces.[4] This refashioning allowed clothing to interact more directly with the physical shape of the body to produce new silhouettes. Individuals wore increasingly structured clothes, creating a new concept that envisioned "the garment as making the body."[5] Furthermore, prevalent sixteenth-century thought asserted that society existed as a natural hierarchy and that everyone held a distinct place along the scale. Practical enforcement of this concept relied, in part, on using apparel as visual expressions of identity to create and maintain stratification in everyday life.[6] Developing simultaneously to each other, increased access to personalized items and popular political thought created increasingly complex connotations in daily life.

Like much of early modern Europe, the Spanish Empire depended on objects as status markers. However, political and economic problems at the turn of the seventeenth century increased anxieties over such possessions. By the seventeenth century, Spain's decline as an international power had become increasingly apparent to peninsular elites.[7] Hoping to reverse their weakening status, they began to associate the country's deterioration with a medley of monetary and ethical errors.[8] Critics blamed not only a failing economy but also relaxed values and behavioral codes as the cause of Spain's hardships. They saw increased luxury among nobles and commoners alike as threats of domestic preservation.

While the political and financial situations worsened, the Iberian Peninsula witnessed increased mobility among non-aristocratic groups. Between the sixteenth and eighteenth centuries, the rate of urbanization doubled, pushing large numbers of previously rural populations into metropolitan areas.[9] As cities increased in size, the anonymity of larger crowds made it easier for inhabitants to blur established social stratifications.[10] Although residents already associated identity with garments, they increasingly distrusted their power to deceive.

Across the Atlantic Ocean, Spanish colonial authorities experienced similar concerns over social control. The conquests of Mexico and Peru throughout the sixteenth century led to the decimation of Indigenous populations and the importation of African slaves. As Spaniards, surviving native communities, and enslaved and free Africans increasingly intermingled, numerous multiethnic groups developed. Officials created a caste system that legally organized colonial subjects along a sociracial hierarchy. Status considered not only one's lineage but also one's physical appearance, clothing, occupation, and behavioral characteristics. In addition to these groups, large numbers of Portuguese immigrants traveled to Mexico at the turn of the seventeenth century in exchange for considerable sums of money paid to the crown.[11] Suspicion from colonial subjects surrounding these new arrivals added to an already tense environment characterized by unprecedented diversity.

In response to such growing mobility and diversity, the crown instituted new sumptuary prohibitions—statutes that barred select groups from wearing certain dress or using particular items. Luxury restrictions had been present in the Iberian Peninsula since the twelfth century. However, the late sixteenth and early seventeenth centuries witnessed a surge of legislation as officials responded to internal anxieties surrounding economic problems and loss of international prestige. Laws decreed by Phillip II, Phillip III, and Phillip IV reached a level of specificity "unequalled elsewhere," evolving into a tool to assuage perceived cultural shortcomings.[12]

Thus, the material sphere developed within an atmosphere of control. On the peninsula, a deteriorating economy and increased urbanization helped blur previously established hierarchical distinctions. In the Americas, unprecedented levels of diversity left authorities anxious to define new hierarchies. For imperial officials, garments provided an opportunity to constrain an increasingly diverse population and restrict the sartorial freedoms that would become characteristic of modern fashion.

Unlike early modern antecedents, the contemporary clothing industry of the twenty-first century has faced minimal oversight from governing forces. Increased accessibility acts as one of the most apparent distinctions of modern fashion. Although scholars situate the birth of mass consumption within the mid-eighteenth century, fashion did not become widely available to all socioeconomic levels in the United States until the 1930s.[13] Since then, advertisements of trendy styles have offered the possibility to escape, transform, and or self-realize.[14] Following established styles demonstrates that "you matter" in mainstream society.[15] Companies target potential customers through television, internet, and social media campaigns, bombarding individuals with increasingly chaotic information overload.[16] Attire and appearance provide the outlet needed to form a cohesive identity within such polarizing forces.

Despite individuality, the desire to belong remains important. Consumers seek to satisfy a certain level of conformity to maintain acceptance within any given group.[17] Fashion acts as an immediate marker of inclusion or exclusion. Consumption thus reflects a relational transaction in which the wearer considers the judgment of others when purchasing and sporting specific items.[18] Individuals measure the correct ratio of blending in to standing out. Despite the lack of formal sumptuary legislation, social norms continue to dictate a level of compliance.

Scholars have long debated the relationship between garments and the body. Historian Fiona Anderson and sociologists Patrick Aspers and Frédéric Godart have highlighted the critical link between visual expression and personal identification. According to Anderson, public versions of oneself cannot be separated from fashionable clothing.[19] Although "defined by ephemerality," fashion acts as a grounding force for otherwise fragile understandings of self-identity.[20] Aspers and Godart agree, suggesting that appearance can be located at the very core of the relationship between group and individual identity.[21] As such, whether regulated or unrestrained, clothes provide the means to visually express ideas surrounding one's place in the world.

Within this visually charged climate, *RHOBH* reflects this relationship between materiality and belonging. The Bravo television network hinges on displays of overt luxury, and *The Real Housewives* franchise acts as only one series in a lineup of programs that depict the lavish lives of the wealthy. Cast members depend on ostentatious displays of wealth to signify their belonging on the network. While their homes and vacations reflect their opulent lifestyles, participants also depend on aspirational fashion to project more elite versions of themselves. At the same time, they regularly employ extravagant hair and makeup teams, wear the latest styles, and sport the trendiest accessories to stand out from their fellow castmates. Garments provide the opportunity to demonstrate their belonging among the rich and famous while also differentiating themselves from their on-screen competition.

The bustling fashion industry that surrounds *The Real Housewives* franchise differs socially, politically, and economically from the regulated production in the Spanish Empire. Individuals in the early modern period conceptualized clothing to visually express one's place in society. Authorities, however, viewed possessions as indicators of socioracial standing and sought to regulate the use of attire by instituting sumptuary regulations to stymie their efforts. In contrast, contemporary consumers like Bravo cast members use attire to reflect a multitude of emotions, characteristics, and personas, highlighting the creativity that characterizes the sartorial world of today against the control that characterized that of the early modern period.

Clothing and Identity in the Spanish Empire

Within the colonial Spanish world, both authorities and subjects relied on attire. On the one hand, the crown implemented sumptuary laws that sought to stabilize increasingly complex hierarchies. On the other, inhabitants simultaneously manipulated regulations for personal benefit. Restrictions focused on reasserting traditional social and religious identities. In doing so, authorities aimed to use clothing to restore a perceived sense of structure within a period of international decline.

Prohibitions focused on restoring social order across the empire. On the peninsula, they sought to reestablish archetypal identities. Popular jurists like Antonio de Ezcaray asserted that "different classes correspond to different garments . . . so that everyone may be distinguished from each other."[22] Decrees sought to limit access to specific fabrics for various socioeconomic groups, creating de facto "uniforms" through detailed regulation and exemption. One 1623 law prohibited everyone but the royal family from sporting brocade, gold cloth, or gold thread, reasserting the subservience of even the most privileged nobility.[23] Another clause addressed laborers, differentiating between manual and agricultural workers through their strategic access to silk. For textile workers, the mandate permitted free reign for approved embellishments, but it explicitly prohibited "those that ordinarily worked plots of land with their hands" from backstitching or embroidering their silk ribbons.[24] Even within the same socioeconomic stratification, authorities sought to reinstate status inequalities.

By assigning different restrictions based on occupation, the crown reasserted laborers' unequal positions on the social hierarchy, even among their peers. Carpenters and blacksmiths faced stricter stipulations than shop owners and street vendors.[25] The crown's distinct rhetoric, referring to the "most lowly" professions, emphasized the laboring class's subordination during a period of obvious economic decline and reinforced Spain's hegemony over its own subjects.

While authorities attempted to distinguish between socioeconomic groups, they also worked to prop up traditional masculine ideals. Seventeenth-century definitions of manhood centered on performative masculinity. Men proved their virility through external markers, like behavior and appearance.[26] In particular, demonstrating substantial martial skill acted as one of the key tenets to becoming a man.[27] Harking back to the glorified era of medieval knights provided the opportunity to rejuvenate the ideal of armed forces.[28] Reestablishing male honor through militaristic concepts sought both to reform lax definitions of masculinity and to reassert Spain's international honor.

The crown conceded privileges to military orders that significantly increased their ability to wear gold and silver. During wartime, the cavalry received the authority to wear brocade, gold cloth, and "whatever other things they want[ed]."[29] Exemptions also permitted soldiers to decorate sword sheaths and warhorse saddles with gold and silver thread and hammered silver.[30] Ordinarily, the crown strictly regulated the use of precious metals. Permission to sport such materials underscored attempts to revamp masculine ideals by promoting glamorous perceptions of soldiers. Infantrymen stationed throughout the realm also received some concessions. Laws allowed soldiers to wear ruffled collars of gold and silk, as well as otherwise prohibited gold cloth embellishments.[31] Permitting extravagance among the military classes highlighted their honored status while promoting an image of Spanish prosperity and power.

Similar concerns over extravagant garments surfaced in the Americas. In Mexico, authorities and travelers commented on the opulence with which every individual seemed to dress. A 1648 travelogue published by Englishman Thomas Gage depicted scenes in which males and females adorned themselves in silk, jewels, and precious metals.[32] Similarly, the archbishop of Michoacán complained to the king in 1679 that "nobles as well as commoners dress in silks and fine cloths and wear pearls and gold jewels."[33] The letter blamed the viceregal court in Mexico City as the source of moral decay. Much like peninsular Spain, fear spread that attire possessed the power to equalize social distinctions.

At the same time, Spanish American regulations incorporated efforts to maintain strict ethnic differences. Colonial society consisted of a socioracial hierarchy that prioritized European lineages. As described earlier, one's ethnic categorization acted as a fluid, and often oscillating, state. Socioracial designations embodied this changeability by considering factors like appearance, behavior, speech, reputation, and residence.[34] As the Americas became increasingly diverse throughout the sixteenth and seventeenth centuries, authorities feared the fluidity of identity and the possibility of manipulation through garments.[35] Clothing thus became a means through which officials sought to separate Spaniards, Indigenous communities, Africans, and multiethnic populations in public life.

It is impossible to discuss sixteenth- and seventeenth-century legislation without addressing its socioeconomic implications. Garments and accessories acquired sociopolitical meanings in which fashion determined the empire's international status and blurred social stratification. Thus, for individuals who aspired to wear luxury items, such coveted objects exemplified their struggle to climb the social ladder. For authorities, the same clothing functioned as a means to reestablish control through clothing regulations.

Anxieties in the social sphere bled into the religious sector. While belief-based segregation had existed in the Spanish Empire since the medieval era, renewed efforts throughout the sixteenth and seventeenth centuries focused on defining communities through their sartorial choices.[36] Laws against minorities like converted Jews and Moors limited access to cultural styles. Similarly, secular and ecclesiastical publications aimed to guilt Catholic subjects into returning to their "Christian values" through the renunciation of material excess. Such efforts sought to soothe growing anxieties surrounding the fluidity of identity and the perceived crisis of morality in the empire.[37] By using such tactics, authorities simultaneously restricted the newly converted and shamed Old Christians into appropriate behavior.

Laws against Jews had existed in the Spanish Empire since the thirteenth century. However, by the sixteenth century, royal decrees had presumably exiled non-Christians from all Spanish lands. Those that remained had endured forced conversions to Catholicism. Dubious of the legitimacy of these New Christians, Spanish authorities used garments to root out potential heretics. For example, on the peninsula, residents in Seville identified potential heretics by their weekend garb.[38] According to the Jewish faith, Saturday marked the holy day of rest and ritual in which believers wore their finest clothes. Catching one's neighbor in their best dress on that day frequently resulted in accusations of heresy to the Inquisition in Seville.[39] On the other side of the Atlantic, convicted Jews faced trial for disobeying sumptuary laws. Residents reported instances in which known heretics appeared to sport extravagant or prohibited items.[40] Both peninsular and colonial authorities declared the individuals in question guilty and deserving of punishment. Clothing, in part, acted as a form of surveillance.

As personal styling increasingly functioned to identify secret Jews, locals monitored their peers at all times. Those already convicted of heresy faced regulations that limited their ability to blend into affluent society. Without access to fabrics like silk, taffeta, and velvet, religious convicts could only wear rougher fabrics indicative of poverty and low status.[41] Witnesses reported individuals who bypassed the prohibitions, demonstrating the importance of containment in everyday life. For example, convicted heretic Simón Díaz faced arrest and punishment after three of his neighbors reported seeing him in fine silks and decorative swords.[42] Garments both defined and confined non-Christian groups.

Evaluation of Spanish imperial sumptuary laws demonstrates the extent to which ideas surrounding appearance and identity pervaded the Iberian Peninsula and its colonies. Not only did the crown create socioeconomic regulations for peninsular life, but authorities instituted unique socioracial statutes for the Americas. Likewise, restrictions permeated the ecclesiastical sphere and attempted to further define new converts and secret Jews. In contrast, legal cases and bureaucratic complaints demonstrated that inhabitants challenged these regulations as they fought to gain access to restricted items. In each scenario, fashion meant different things according to different contexts. Yet both officials and residents conceptualized clothing as a means to project social, religious, and ethnic status. It is this same transformative capability that grounds the sartorial choices portrayed on contemporary reality television.

Strategic Excess: Sartorial Choices on *The Real Housewives of Beverly Hills*

The crown jewel of the Bravo network, *The Real Housewives* franchise depends on opulence. While filming locations prioritize extravagance, the Beverly Hills cast has depended on personal style to solidify storylines and curry favor with viewers. The ladies use garments to express different personas, alter public perceptions, and assert belonging. Thus, much like their early modern counterparts, these reality stars approach attire as a conduit for personal identification. Fashion acts to express accepted social norms.[43] Although the series has featured overt glamour from its debut in 2010, the use of clothing and accessories to shape identity has reached its peak in the last five years. In particular, the additions of Lisa Rinna, Erika Girardi, and Dorit Kemsley pushed styling on the show to evolve from obvious excess to strategic self-expression.

Debuting on the show in 2014, Lisa Rinna arrived with a trademark hairstyle and no hesitation. While her erratic behavior elevated the on-screen drama, her never-changing locks garnered recognizability with viewers. Even her fellow cast members acknowledged the identifying power of her hair. At the 2015 season 5 reunion, Brandi Glanville snapped at Rinna, shouting, "You've had the same hairdo for twenty years!"[44] Attacking her hair acted as a substitute for denigrating Rinna as an individual.

In the seasons that followed, the veteran housewife noticeably rejected her signature hair in favor of revolving wig identities. She introduced several "characters," defined by their removable hairpieces, and depended on these personas to justify unexpected behavior. In a 2022 interview with *People* magazine, Rinna admitted that Glanville's comment inspired her to start experimenting with her locks while also praising the wigs as a key prop during filming.[45] "Let's say there's a scene I'm doing and I'm feeling like 'Oh God, I'm dreading going," she stated, "I throw a wig on and honey, I just walk through that door with confidence. . . . They've been such a great form of expression for me." Changing her hair allowed Rinna to reframe her personality.

Most notably, she arrived at the season 9 Halloween party dressed as fellow Housewife Erika Girardi's pop star alter ego, Erika Jayne. Rinna embraced the costume to the extent that she also altered her demeanor. She became an aggressive instigator, shouting expletives at other cast members and initiating conflict with the host's sister, Kim Richards.[46] In her confessional interview, Rinna proclaimed that she often adjusted her behavior based on the way in which she styled herself.[47] This philosophy continued off-camera as well. Her personal Instagram account highlighted several instances in which the former actress debuted a series of characters defined by distinct wigs and accessories. Between March 1 and June 1, 2020, Lisa introduced her followers to Sasha, Patricia, Charlene, Heidi, Roxanne, Kiki, and Stevie.[48] In each case, Rinna used her hair to embody alternative identities and embrace distinct personality traits. Using such personal styling, she created outlets through which she expressed actions and ideas deemed unacceptable for "Lisa Rinna" yet wholly on par with other sartorial characters. Thus, for Rinna, fashion acquired a transformative and liberating meaning, allowing her to behave differently without taking accountability for her actions.

Just as Rinna used interchangeable hair, Erika Girardi depended on clothing to create her own coterie of characters. Girardi's first season on the show centered around this very premise. By day, Girardi appeared as the well-groomed wife of now-disgraced attorney Tom Girardi. By night, she performed as club music star Erika Jayne, clad in highly sexualized bodysuits with tall heels and wild hair. The personality differences between the two further reflected this bifurcation of identity. While Girardi appeared reserved during her first season, Jayne expressed a dominant personality with a daring attitude.[49] When Girardi invited the cast to a show, castmates Eileen Davidson and Kyle Richards referenced the material and behavioral attributes of Erika Jayne. The former squealed, "I'm so excited! What are you going to *wear*?" while the latter proclaimed, "I'm gonna release my own Erika Jayne" on the dance floor.[50] Girardi's entire introduction to the series depended on the relationship between garments and identity.

After her first season, Girardi increasingly depended on sartorial decisions to craft unique personalities. Her participation in various *Real Housewives* events reflected a calculated connection between appearance and behavior. First, consider the 2018 cast vacation in Berlin. Girardi arrived at dinner wearing a red latex bodysuit, a sharp black leather pencil skirt, blunt bangs, and a severe ponytail.[51] Portraying a dominant, aggressive persona, Erika's behavior changed to fit the character. Upon her arrival, she almost collided with a passing bicyclist yet displayed no reaction to the near accident. Rather, she remained sullen and straight-faced. In the middle of the otherwise tranquil dinner, Erika became aggressive and confronted fellow cast member Teddi Mellencamp on comments she made about Girardi several weeks prior.[52] Second, during a trip to France in 2019, Erika expressed a muted aesthetic.[53] She wore sensible garments and little makeup. Traveling without her entourage, she appeared reserved, stoic, and much less assertive than on the previous vacation. Instead, she often avoided conflict or attempted to de-escalate pointed attacks. In contrast to the harsh Berlin encounter, this version of Erika appeared more tranquil. In both cases, Girardi matched her behavior to her appearance.

Away from her castmates, Girardi's confessional looks also evolved from fashionable clothes to full-blown storylines of their own. For example, in season 9, Erika appeared in a leopard dress with a short teased blond wig and a glass of champagne.[54] Nodding to the excess of the 1980s, this character projected an over-the-top and blasé attitude focused on enjoying life's material pleasures. The commentary provided in this ensemble mimicked such nonchalance. However, season 10's debut in 2020 introduced a more conservative aesthetic. Although Girardi still flaunted a low-cut sequined blazer, she sported only a thin diamond necklace and diamond hoops, paired with a simple hairstyle and natural makeup.[55] In these interviews, she acted as the voice of reason and calmly described the boisterous antics of her peers. On camera, Girardi used clothing to reflect different facets of her personality.

The season 10 reunion further underscored Girardi's strategic fashion choices. When asked by Lisa Rinna who inspired her look, Girardi responded, "I don't know, someone fierce."[56] Andy Cohen chimed in by speculating that her stylists must create full-blown storyboards. She confirmed that her team created a series of cards that described various identities and styles.[57] In this case, the Housewife directly confirmed her use of fashion to portray various identities. By choosing unique styles, Girardi alerted viewers to different facets of her personality.

While Rinna and Girardi relied on appearance and attire to craft multiple personas, newcomer Dorit Kemsley clung to clothing in order to establish her character as a rightful member of the most affluent echelon of Beverly Hills. Dorit debuted on the show in 2016 and immediately ruffled feathers by judging the wardrobes of her new castmates. In particular, Kemsley and Girardi feuded over the question of appropriate undergarments. One night, Girardi arrived at a gathering wearing a formfitting white dress. After sitting across from Kemsley's husband, it became apparent that Girardi wore nothing underneath her frock. For Dorit, the question of no underwear became a judgment of Girardi's personal morals.[58] She engaged in debates with Lisa Rinna and cast member Eileen Davidson to dissect whether the unintentional flashing involved ulterior motives.[59] Kemsley complained, "It's one thing when you're with a group of girls, but when you're sitting across from someone's husband . . ."[60] While Girardi consistently insisted that she did so to prevent creases in the dress fabric, Kemsley believed Erika's decision to be primarily promiscuous in nature. To publicly shame her for the gaffe, Dorit gifted Erika new underwear during an on-camera group outing.[61] This exchange nonverbally communicated Kemsley's judgment of Girardi's fashion misstep. In using attire as a gift, Dorit juxtaposed herself as the refined wife against what she perceived as Erika's morally loose styling.

Four years later, Dorit's own fashion became a fully developed storyline as cast members increasingly criticized the amount of time she spent with her glam squad. In particular, season 10 witnessed a drawn-out conflict in which Kyle Richards took personal offense to the tardiness with which Kemsley arrived at a group wellness event. Rather than participate in a boxing class, she appeared to spend hours with a hair and makeup team crafting a meticulous sportswear ensemble (see fig. 2.1).[62] After the fact, Richards complained, "You had a full photo shoot with glam posing in your living room for I don't know how many hours. I mean, hello, I have a life." Richards then continued to malign Kemsley to the other women, citing a series of Instagram posts that suggested the Housewife had prioritized her outfit over the event in question.

Shortly thereafter, Richards instigated another argument about Kemsley's appearance at a family barbecue. Calling her aesthetic "disingenuous," Richards attacked her friend's character through her fashion choices.[63] In a heated argument, Richards confessed, "Do I think it's [expletive] weird that

FIGURE 2.1 Dorit Kemsley, "Comment if you wear workout clothes when you're not working out #beverlybeachbydorit," Instagram, May 4, 2020, https://www.instagram.com/doritkemsley/p/B_xSbTanoKd.

you have [expletive] glam to meet friends for a workout? Yeah, I think it's [expletive] weird!"[64] Although the conflict originated from a single event, it became a key arc in the storyline.

Much of the squabble highlighted the immature fodder characteristic of reality television. However, the underlying crux of the matter centered around Dorit's devotion to crafting her public persona through clothes, makeup, and accessories. Prioritizing how she looked over quality time with her friends suggested that her appearance ranked higher than her character. Richards viewed Kemsley's level of "glam" as a measure of the sincerity, or lack thereof, she possessed as a person. External appearance became code for inner values. Much in the same way that Dorit judged Erika's moral values based on her fashion choices, so too did Kyle use Dorit's glam squad to question her priorities.

In addition to influencing perceptions of her character, Kemsley has recently relied on using clothing to combat rumors surrounding her financial stability. Throughout the last two years, she and her husband have faced a growing number of lawsuits and bankruptcy allegations. Season 9 witnessed the saga of two separate accusations against Dorit's husband, PK.[65] Housewives like Camille Grammer took the opportunity to openly question Kemsley's financial standing on camera. "You know, I see Dorit running around in very expensive clothes," Grammer stated in a 2019 Bravo TV interview, "Some of her tops could be two to three thousand and the pants two to three thousand . . . I question that. I question, like, how can you afford that?"[66] Grammer even directly confronted Kemsley on her supposed destitution at a cast dinner. In addition to asking Kemsley where her wealth came from, Grammer also asserted that PK owed money to several of her friends.[67] Such attacks threatened Dorit's carefully crafted image of luxe opulence.

Season 10 similarly showcased Dorit's financial struggles. In one confessional, Dorit happily stated that her lawsuit with a former business partner of Dorit's swimwear line, Beverly Beach, had finally been settled.[68] In addition, she debuted her new 8,679-square-foot home in Encino, California. While subsequent episodes appeared to show the Kemsleys bounce back from rumored financial ruin, tabloids revived their speculations when the pair put the aforementioned "dream home" on the market in September 2020.[69] Throughout the last two years, Dorit's wealth was repeatedly put into question both on- and off-camera.

The more legal troubles Dorit has experienced, the more her wardrobe has become increasingly excessive and over the top. Historian Claire Crowston has demonstrated that economic credit cannot be separated from the social, cultural, and political spheres.[70] Although monetary capital represents an important factor, more fluid resources like reputation, status, and appearance also play a critical role.[71] As Dorit's financial struggles played out on national television, she turned toward material opulence to recoup some of her damaged reputation. For example, at the very dinner in which Grammer confronted Kemsley, the latter wore a diamond-encrusted hairpin that said "Drippin'."[72] At the season 9 reunion, Dorit sported a helmet of bejeweled hair clips with words like "glam," "icon," and "boss."[73]

Amid a swirl of rumors surrounding her husband's money problems, Dorit used fashion to represent herself as the literal embodiment of wealth.

The season 10 storyline surrounding Dorit's extreme personal styling and over-the-top glam squad thus acquired an additional perspective. By focusing on dramatic fashion and time-consuming hair and makeup, Kemsley performs scenes of luxury and opulence. To her, fashion helped reject any notions of questionable financial standing. Arriving to dinner in a head-to-toe Chanel logo ensemble, for example, visually challenged rumors of ruin in a very public way. Material extravagance worked as cultural credit to verify her elite status when her financial standing was in question. Playing the part of a glamour-obsessed diva thus demonstrated to the *Real Housewives* audience that she still belonged to the upper echelon of society.

Among the women of *RHOBH*, clothing became a tool to visually transform the ladies and portray internal values. On a television show in which extravagance reigned supreme, cast members used fashion to stabilize their positions on the series. Whereas Lisa Rinna initially depended on an iconic hairstyle to maintain recognizability, her later foray into wigged personalities allowed her to explore different aspects of herself through visual transformation. Similarly, Erika Girardi depended on materiality to separate herself from her performing alter ego, Erika Jayne, throughout her earlier seasons. As she became more comfortable on the show, she increasingly manipulated her appearance to reflect different versions of herself. Dorit Kemsley also used personal styling to shape identity, yet she sought out stability over versatility. While previous seasons only documented her consistent style, episodes aired in 2020 created an independent storyline around her desire for glamour. Facing constant interpersonal conflict as well as rumored economic hardships, Kemsley clung to opulent attire to assert her belonging among the ultra-rich inhabitants of Beverly Hills. These three women represented only a small sampling of the larger sartorial strategies used by franchise cast members. Just as imperial subjects sought to manipulate and solidify public perception through clothing, so too did the Bravo housewives turn to attire to reflect a constructed identity to viewers.

Conclusion: Clothing and Perception

Cast members of *The Real Housewives* and inhabitants of the Spanish Empire make an unlikely pair. Obvious differences exist between the early modern and contemporary eras. The Spanish crown existed as an early modern monarchy with imperial holdings across the Americas. While military losses on the international stage and poor financial management had caused a perceived decline, increasing social mobility due to growing urban centers further agitated authorities. Clothing acquired definitive connotations throughout the early modern period, and imperial officials further solidified these implications by imposing sumptuary laws. Garments became a field of conflict in which legislation sought to pin down various socioeconomic groups.

In contrast, *The Real Housewives of Beverly Hills* exists within a contemporary society defined by American capitalism. The fashion industry that surrounds the women represents a multibillion-dollar business. Myriad labels and brands offer endless options at various price points for every consumer to access. Although shoppers do not face sumptuary restrictions, they do face nonstop marketing that promotes distinct lifestyles through clothing. Affordable retailers mimic high-end designer patterns, producing almost identical products for a fraction of the price.[74] Fashion no longer exists just for the elite. This climate has allowed *RHOBH* cast members to access unique personas through personal styling. Thus, while attire is still engaged with socioeconomic standing, modern expressions as seen on reality TV have been grounded in creativity rather than confinement.

Despite such distinct environments, both case studies approach garments in a similar fashion. In each situation, individuals view clothing to alter or solidify public identity. Spanish imperial authorities interpreted this principle through the lens of managing an increasingly diverse population. Through sumptuary laws, officials hoped to restrict various pieces to specific socioeconomic and socioracial groups to make identification easier. In turn, subjects understood the same principle and sought to improve their situation by manipulating their standing through their appearance. So too do Bravo reality stars espouse the transformative qualities of fashion. Although the Housewives already belong to the wealthy elite, they use personal possessions to visually assert their belonging. In addition, they create distinct characters that connect with viewers and solidify their positions on the show. It is this strategic planning that links this otherwise disparate group to the material world of the Spanish Empire. Attire possesses concrete performative qualities. It does not just act as a frivolous expense to demonstrate wealth but acts as a conduit to express personal values and emotions.

Yet at the same time, it is important to consider how the meaning of luxurious garments and accessories shift according to the wearer. To early modern subjects of the Spanish Empire, such items acquired connotations of nobility, elite socioeconomic standing, and privilege. Yet to some authorities, the very same objects reflected the downfall of Christian society. In Beverly Hills, fashion still possesses status implications, but it has also acquired a transformative quality. Viewers of *RHOBH* scrutinize the behavior of their favorite cast members. Garments, handbags, hairstyles, and jewelry function as gateways to different characters.

The Bravo Network and *RHOBH* provide an unexpected opportunity to consider the continuities between past and present. Although much has changed between the seventeenth and twenty-first centuries, garments continue to act as points of access to different sociopolitical circles. Using reality television to interface with scholarly trends like early modern material studies forces historians to consider how the contemporary fashion industry has both outgrown and continued the legacy of early modern predecessors. Despite the lack of formal sumptuary legislation in the United States, individuals still depend on personal adornment to self-fashion new identities in public life. Weaving together unlikely threads pushes academics to evaluate further the critical societal undercurrents within popular culture. Ultimately, sartorial perspectives ranging from Antonio de Ezcaray to Erika Girardi serve as valuable resources that reflect and shape social, political, and economic values across time and space.

Notes

1. Ezcaray, *Vozes del dolor*, 59.
2. Ezcaray, *Vozes del dolor*, 19.
3. *RHOBH*, season 10, episode 4, "All's Fair in Glam and War, aired May 6, 2020, on Bravo.
4. Welch, introduction, 6.
5. Bruna, "Puffed-Out Chests and Paunched Bellies," 32.
6. Hayward, *Rich Apparel*, 43.
7. Lehfeldt, "Ideal Men," 465.
8. Vilches, *New World Gold*, 9.
9. Álvarez-Nogal and Prados de la Escosura, "Decline of Spain," 321.
10. Bass and Wunder, "Veiled Ladies of the Early Modern Spanish World," 101.
11. Liebman, *Jews in New Spain*, 188.
12. Hume, *Year after the Armada*, 210.
13. Anderson, "Fashion," 69.
14. Anderson, "Fashion," 77.
15. Anderson, "Fashion," 77.
16. E. Wilson, "Fashion and the Postmodern Body," 6.
17. Anderson, "Fashion," 72.
18. Aspers and Godart, "Sociology of Fashion," 183.

19. Anderson, "Fashion," 70.
20. Anderson, "Fashion," 81.
21. Aspers and Godart, "Sociology of Fashion," 172.
22. Ezcaray, *Vozes del dolor*, 90.
23. *Nueva Recopilación de las Leyes de Castilla*, Tomo 3, Libro VI, Titulo XIII, *Ley I*.
24. NR, T. 3, Lib. VI, Tit. XIII, *Ley I*. Original text: "y de otros qualesquier oficios semejantes á estos mas baxo" and "los que ordinariamente labran las heredades por sus manos."
25. NR, T. 3, Lib. VI, Tit. XIII, *Ley I*.
26. Lehfeldt, "Ideal Men," 464.
27. Lehfeldt, "Ideal Men," 470.
28. Lehfeldt, "Ideal Men," 475.
29. NR, T. 3, Lib. VI, Tit. XIII, *Ley I*. Original text: "qualesquier otras cosas que quisieren."
30. NR, T. 3, Lib. VI, Tit. XIII, *Ley I*.
31. NR, T. 3, Lib. VI, Tit. XIII, *Ley I*.
32. Gage, *Travels in the New World*, 180–88.
33. Archivo General de Indias, México, Legajo 374, Folio 646R-647V.
34. For resources on the fluidity of ethnicity in colonial Spanish America, see Schwaller, *Géneros de Gente in Early Colonial Mexico*; Van Deusen, *Global Indios*; Fisher and O'Hara, *Imperial Subjects*; Carrera, *Imagining Identity in New Spain*; Twinam, *Purchasing Whiteness*.
35. For example, see Schwaller, *Géneros de Gente in Early Colonial Mexico*; Carrera, *Imagining Identity in New Spain*; Twinam, *Purchasing Whiteness*.
36. Hume, *Year after the Armada*, 211.
37. For example, see Ramón, *Nueva prágmatica de reformación*; Carranza, *Discurso contra malos trajes*; Marqués de Careaga, *Invectiva en discursos apologeticos contra el abuso público de las guedejas*; Jimenez Patón, *Reforma de trajes*.
38. Schroer, "Sartorial Subversions," 80–121.
39. Archivo Histórico Nacional, Inquisición, legajo 2075.
40. Archivo General de la Nación, Ramo de Inquisición.
41. AGN, Ramo de Inquisición.
42. AGN, Ramo de Inquisición, vol. 298, expediente 6.
43. Anderson, "Fashion," 83.
44. *RHOBH*, season 5, episode 21.
45. Dave Quinn, "Lisa Rinna Opens Up about Her Love of Wigs and How Brandi Glanville Inspired Her Hair Changes," *People*, March 24, 2022.
46. *RHOBH*, season 9, episode 16, "Meet Rinna Jayne," aired May 28, 2019.
47. *RHOBH*, season 9, episode 16.
48. Rinna, "Meet Sasha"; Rinna, "Say Hi to Patricia. She's bored and ready for a cocktail"; Rinna, "The Category is WIGS. Her name is Charlene"; Rinna, "We Miss Heidi"; Rinna, "Roxanne is So Ready for #RHOBH TONIGHT"; Rinna, "Let's Have a Kiki"; Rinna, "We Call her Stevie. She gives good side eye."
49. *RHOBH*, season 6.

50. *RHOBH*, season 6, episode 11, "Please Welcome Erika Jayne!," aired February 9, 2016, on Bravo.

51. *RHOBH*, season 8, episode 17.

52. *RHOBH*, season 8, episode 17.

53. *RHOBH*, season 9, episodes 18, 19, 20.

54. *RHOBH*, season 9.

55. *RHOBH*, season 10.

56. *RHOBH*, season 10, episode 19, reunion, pt. 3, aired September 16, 2020, on Bravo.

57. *RHOBH*, season 10, episode 19.

58. *RHOBH*, season 7, episode 3, Going Commando," aired December 20, 2016, on Bravo.

59. *RHOBH*, season 7, episode 4, "Pantygate," aired December 27, 2016, on Bravo.

60. *RHOBH*, season 7, episode 4.

61. *RHOBH*, season 7, episode 4.

62. *RHOBH*, season 10, episode 4, "All's Fair in Glam and War," aired May 6, 2020, on Bravo.

63. *RHOBH*, season 10, episode 5, "Let the Mouse Go!," aired May 13, 2020, on Bravo.

64. *RHOBH*, season 10, episode 5.

65. Laura Rosenfeld, "Dorit Kemsley and Husband PK 'Look Forward to the Next Chapter' After Settling 2 Lawsuits," The Daily Dish, Bravo, October 17, 2019.

66. Bravo, "Dorit Kemsley Addresses Camille Grammer's Accusations about PK: *RHOBH After Show*."

67. *RHOBH*, season 9, episode 20.

68. *RHOBH*, season 10, episode 1; Laura Rosenfeld, "Dorit Kemsley Confirms Beverly Beach Lawsuit 'Finally Came to a Resolution,'" The Daily Dish, Bravo, April 15, 2020.

69. Ryan Naumann, "'RHOBH' Star Dorit Kemsley Struggles to Sell $7.5 Million Beverly Hills Mansion," Blast, April 16, 2020.

70. Crowston, *Credit, Fashion, Sex*, 21.

71. Crowston, *Credit, Fashion, Sex*, 21.

72. *RHOBH*, season 9, episode 20.

73. *RHOBH*, season 9, episodes 22, 23, 24.

74. Brucculieri, "How Fast Fashion Brands Get Away with Copying Designers."

3 Drama Queens

The Politics of Performance in the Early Modern Royal Court and the Housewives Franchise

EMILIE M. BRINKMAN

Being a woman in the royal court of early modern Europe was very much like being on modern reality television, especially *The Real Housewives* franchise. Indeed, female courtiers share many striking similarities beyond their opulent lifestyles with Housewives: They wore luxurious clothing and rode in expensive conveyances. They were involved in dramatic altercations fueled by games and alcohol. They dressed up for costume parties. They were married to royals, nobles, and rich men or came from illustrious families with name recognition. They consulted fortune tellers and indulged in (often bizarre) antiaging cosmetic regimens. They supported charities and inserted themselves in political debates. They used their connections for their own individual success or for that of their family. But most importantly, they performed every day within a highly visible space wherein every comment, gesture, facial expression, and garment was scrutinized by all-to-eager observers.[1]

This chapter explores the connections between the early modern royal courts of Europe, specifically those of the seventeenth century, and Bravo's *Real Housewives* franchise, revealing how royal women and Housewives have similarly used performance as a means of agency in highly public and visual spaces. I argue that, in the context of both modern reality television and the early modern royal court, performance was a form of self-fashioning and representation. Even in seemingly "real" unscripted television series like *The Real Housewives*, the stars are constantly performing for their audience and their fellow castmates. Many Housewives themselves have even acknowledged that they are always "on" when the cameras are rolling. So too was it for the women who used the court as their stage in early modern Europe. This chapter examines how royal women and Housewives used their personal appearance and possessions—including dress, accessories, and apartments—to communicate carefully constructed images to audiences.

I analyze how such messages have been transmitted and interpreted within Bravo storylines as well as historical episodes, such as the "Pantygate" of the English royal court in 1662. Ultimately, this chapter demonstrates how self-fashioning and representation continue to function as a means of cultural, social, and political agency for women—and men, for that matter—throughout our modern world.

Throughout history, physical appearance and material possessions have served as a form of self-expression as well as an emblem of power. In fact, the first social hierarchies were determined by material wealth—that is, the accumulation of "stuff"—beginning 8,000 years ago during the Neolithic period. Indeed, the control of resources translated to power. Initially these resources were crops, livestock, and other tangible items, but with the rise of metalworking, the resource pool soon grew to include objects of increasing material value, particularly those forged of copper, gold, silver, bronze, and iron. Beginning in 1200 BCE, warriors, armed with the finest iron weaponry and commanding large armies, had grown in influence and power to create kingdoms and monarchies. These royals, the first kings and queens of Europe, centralized their power into clearly defined territories and kingdoms, with formal royal courts to follow over the coming centuries.[2] By the early Middle Ages, monarchs and other rulers began to establish residences and gather around them an entourage of officials, administrators, courtiers, and servants. These early courts were often small and itinerant, moving from one place to another as the monarch traveled "on progress" throughout their realm. Over time, however, royal courts became more permanent and elaborate, with the creation of formal court offices and household departments.

There was not any single universal model of a royal court; the structure, operation, and purpose of the court differed across time and space, being shaped by regional differences as well as the specific historical circumstances of each era. Yet courts were rather multifaceted during the early modern era; they could be royal, princely, ducal, or viceregal.[3] The royal court was a particularly nuanced entity, being both a political institution and a semipublic physical space.[4] Mia Rodríguez-Salgado proposes that three essential features characterized the court: sovereign power, organs of a central government, and a household structure.[5] In this sense, the court was where the monarch governed and resided. It was a part of the state apparatus, a social milieu, and a cultural center with its own unique way of life. Since the emergence of court studies more than fifty years ago, cultural historians have extensively examined the majesty of the court, thereby producing architectural biographies and dazzling portraits of its pomp and circumstance. The court—often portrayed as a gilded nexus of corruption, conspicuous display, favoritism, and sycophancy—was understood to be merely a space where the royal family and their friends lived and partied. This view has been redressed over the last several decades as historians have looked beyond the court's glamorous veil and identified its primary function as a political, social, and cultural institution. The royal court was not simply a center of conspicuous display and ceremony but an arena wherein important matters of state were conducted, patronage was granted, and alliances were forged.

That's not to say that royal courts were not filled with scandal and drama, as their inherent political nature certainly contributed to a great deal of spectacle, intrigue, and conspiracy. Some early modern royal courts were more dramatic than others, especially when enigmatic kings with large (sexual) appetites sat on the throne. In such cases, the atmosphere of the royal court could be compared to another reality show, *The Bachelor*. In *The Bachelor* (and its female-centered counterpart *The Bachelorette*), contestants vie for the attention of the eligible bachelor (or bachelorette) and compete in elaborate games and challenges each week to earn a prized rose—and hopefully, by the end of show, an engagement ring. At the outset, the goal is to stand out from the competition while working to secure the affections of the bachelor. The environment was similar in the royal court of King Louis XIV of France, "the Sun King" (r. 1643–1715), and that of his paternal cousin King Charles II of England (r. 1660–85). Louis's father, King Louis XIII (r. 1610–43), was the brother of Charles II's mother, Henrietta Maria, who had married Charles I of England (r. 1625–49). The two kings had much in common beyond their familial connection, including similar ruling styles and exquisite cultural tastes. While a parliamentarian regime ruled after his father's execution in 1649, Charles II spent time at Louis's court, where he developed an affinity for French court culture, which was particularly rich and highly orchestrated.

Louis was the sun in the universe of the royal court, and all others circulated around him, including a constellation of beautiful women. While male courtiers also sought Louis's favor for political or personal gain, ladies contended for the king's love and the rewards that such romantic interest would reap upon them and their families. Since Louis was already married to the Spanish princess Maria Theresa, marriage was not necessarily the desired outcome of such pursuits (as in *The Bachelor*) but rather prestige and elevation as well as material wealth, all of which would solidify one's power in the court and, by extension, the country. During his long reign (the longest in history), King Louis engaged in numerous affairs with an assortment of paramours and mistresses.

When the English monarchy was finally restored in 1660 after a decade of staunch parliamentary rule, Charles returned from the Continent and began his reign at the age of thirty with considerable pomp and ceremony, reminiscent of his cousin's opulent court. Often referred to colloquially as "the Merry Monarch," Charles II has been noted, in a historiographical sense, for his grand parties and stylish attire as well as for his own impressive array of mistresses. Charles II's court presents an interesting case study for a comparative analysis between the royal court and the Housewives franchise. Not only did Charles delight in the company of many beautiful women and institute a rich court culture modeled, in part, after Louis XIV's, but during his twenty-five-year reign, England experienced substantial luxury consumption and cultural borrowing, particularly from the Continent as well as from the East and the Americas. It was during this time that England's global commercial empire truly began, due in great part to the acquisition of trading rights with Brazil as well as the colonies of Bombay and Tangier upon Charles's marriage to the Portuguese princess Catherine of Braganza in 1662. More goods were entering London than ever before, and these luxury items maintained an ever increasing significance among the English elite as symbols of power and prestige. In such a highly visible space as the Restoration court, material wealth took on new meaning, especially for elite women, who used these items as vehicles for self-fashioning and personal agency, much in the same manner as the Housewives use material items and conspicuous displays on their show.

During the early modern period, a woman's clothing and other items were symbolic of her station. Elite women used their material wealth— including gowns, jewels, and apartments—to establish a dominant position within the court. In addition, their display of dress and objects—such as furniture, curiosities, and even carriages—allowed these women to communicate political and confessional loyalties within the space of the royal court and thus engage in the dynamic world of court politics despite their exclusion from official governmental positions. And notwithstanding their exclusion, female courtiers consistently acted to promote their own personal or familial interests by establishing factional alliances within the court, granting patronage, and attempting to gain the monarch's favor.

Clothing and dress have long been used as a medium for expression, and there is no doubt that fashion was, and still is, a key aspect of identity.

Susan Vincent explains that the significance of dress lies in its fundamental relationship with the self and its subsequent contribution to the formation of one's identity; the "vestimentary" fashioning of the human body helps shape cultural norms as well as individual personality. Additionally, Vincent argues that fashion is not simply a consequence of choice but a kind of causal agent: "Clothes, in a very real sense, do 'make' the man and woman."[6] In other words, a person does not determine one's dress; dress determines the person. Although Vincent emphasizes the importance of a garment's physical properties within the politics of display, she states that equally significant was "the manner in which these garments were borne, displayed and manipulated" by royal women and female courtiers.[7] An excellent example of such agency can be observed in May 1662, when the English royal court experienced its own "Pantygate."

"Pantygate," of course, refers to the explosive storyline in season 7 of *The Real Housewives of Beverly Hills* (*RHOBH*), when Erika Girardi acknowledged to a group of fellow Housewives, including Kyle Richards, Lisa Vanderpump, and Dorit Kemsley, and their husbands, Ken Todd and Paul "PK" Kemsley, that she was not wearing any underwear during a pre-white party cocktail hour. When Lisa jokingly asked if Erika had a spare set of underwear to give to Kyle, Erika responded, "I don't have any," claiming that a panty line would ruin the silhouette of her white Mugler dress.[8] Such an admission, clearly stated for shock value to the group and viewers, certainly corresponds to Erika's alter ego, Erika Jayne. The absence of Erika's underwear, and the pointed acknowledgment thereof, caused such an uproar among both castmates and viewers that it dominated the entire seventh season (including the reunions) of *RHOBH*. However, in Restoration England, it was the very public presence and display of royal mistress Barbara Palmer's undergarments in the palace gardens that caused the scandal.

On May 21, 1662, Charles II and the Portuguese princess Catherine of Braganza were officially wed in Portsmouth. The royal couple was married publicly in the Church of England, as well as in a secret Roman Catholic service. While the king, his new bride, and their intimate wedding party celebrated the nuptials, Barbara Palmer (née Villiers) — Charles II's principal mistress — conducted her own ceremony of sorts back in London. Born into the powerful Royalist Villiers family, beautiful Barbara married Roger Palmer, a lawyer, in April 1659, before she met Charles. The precise circumstances of their first meeting remain unclear, yet the royal affair certainly began shortly after Charles's ascension to the throne, since he publicly acknowledged her first daughter, Anne, who was born in February 1661.

Barbara's husband was bestowed the title of Baron Limerick and first Earl of Castlemaine, thereby ennobling Barbara to Countess of Castlemaine. She would be elevated even higher to Duchess of Cleveland in 1670. By 1662, Barbara reigned in the English court as Charles's most beloved mistress and would later be referred to informally as the "uncrowned queen" due to the power and influence she wielded in the court. At the time of the royal wedding in 1662, Barbara, who was pregnant with her first son by Charles, resided on King Street, which was located directly across from the Privy Garden at the Palace of Whitehall.

The courtier Samuel Pepys, renowned for his detailed diaries of life at the Restoration court, observed that Charles II dined at Barbara's house every day the week before he traveled south to meet his bride. He further noted that "the night that the bonfires were made for joy of the Queenes arrivall, the King was there; but there was no fire at her door, though at all the rest of the doors almost in the street; which was much observed." Barbara did not light the customary bonfire outside her home in honor of Catherine's arrival, a move that Pepys and others were quick to observe. Apparently, Barbara refused to celebrate the royal nuptials and remained, according to Pepys, "a most disconsolate creature, and comes not out of doors—since the King's going." Instead of honoring the arrival of the new queen, she conducted a sartorial power play. On the day of the royal wedding, Pepys recorded how he enjoyed a leisurely stroll through the Privy Garden, wherein he observed "the finest smocks and linnen petticoats of my Lady Castlemaynes, laced with rich lace at the bottom, that ever I saw; and did me good to look upon them."[9]

Barbara had evidently ordered her freshly laundered undergarments to be hung in the royal gardens for every courtier of note to witness. She used her clothing to convey a very deliberate and meaningful message: that her relationship with the king and her position at court would not be diminished despite Charles's marriage to the foreign princess. Barbara was literally "marking her territory" with a woman's most intimate garment, thereby claiming ownership of the king himself and, by extension, the space of the royal court. In this sense, the spectacle of the undergarments in the palace garden was a calculated display of power, a performative act to promote herself and her position within the court. For Erika Girardi, her panty remark can be interpreted as a means of promoting herself and her Erika Jayne brand, a unique performance persona built on unapologetic female sexualization and overly conspicuous displays of disposable wealth.

Conspicuous consumption lies at the heart of both the royal court and *The Real Housewives* franchise. The royal court was certainly a space that emphasized the visual and the material. For monarchs, the physical space of the court, including its inhabitants, was perceived as an extension of their royal rule, and it needed to reflect such majesty. In a similar sense, the basis of *The Real Housewives*, at least initially, was to provide an intimate glimpse into the fabulously glamorous (and dramatic) lives of wealthy women in select cities. While the drama keeps viewers watching week after week, the luxurious lifestyles are, undeniably, another primary motivation for tuning in. Viewers want to watch as Housewives purchase expensive jewelry, clothes, cars, and homes; eat caviar; sip the finest champagne, rosé, and tequila; and go on luxury international holidays, all of which is purposefully depicted on camera. Like the royal court, opulent displays of wealth on *The Real Housewives* serves a purpose: to indicate one's power, prestige, influence, or status within highly visible spaces.

Perhaps the most obvious representation of conspicuous consumption in *The Real Housewives* is Erika Girardi, aka Erika Jayne. Drawing inspiration for her sobriquet from the iconic soap opera character Erica Kane from *All My Children*, Erika began her singing career in the early 2000s, after moving to Los Angeles and marrying Tom Girardi, a now disgraced attorney renowned for his work on the Erin Brockovich case against Pacific Gas & Electric. As Andy Cohen commented during the season 11 reunion, "The Erika Jayne character is built on consumption."[10] When Erika first joined the cast in season 6, her over-the-top lifestyle was vividly captured on camera: closets full of luxury clothing and accessories, expensive cars, a multimillion-dollar mansion in Pasadena, and private planes. Indeed, Erika stated that with her husband, the couple maintains not one but two private planes—one for short domestic travel and another for cross-country and international trips.[11] Even Erika Jayne's 2017 single "XXpen$ive" contains the telling refrain: "It's expensive to be me . . . Looking this good don't come for free." These lines are a clear reference to Girardi's extravagant lifestyle and her notorious monthly "glam budget." During a 2018 appearance on *The Wendy Williams Show*, Girardi confirmed that it costs at least $40,000 a month to maintain her glamorous physical appearance: "If you want to look good it's hair, it's makeup, it's wardrobe, and then those people that help facilitate that. They're not cheap."[12] Her open displays of wealth on television have even been the subject of legal scrutiny, as her husband faces both federal and civil suits against him for fraud and misappropriation of clients' funds.

On *The Real Housewives*, the superfluous nature of the items featured serve a purpose beyond mere entertainment—they serve as tangible symbols of one's disposable wealth. Beverly Hills "friend" Dana Wilkey provided one of the most memorable examples of such display when she pointedly remarked in a now iconic scene from season 2 that her diamond and gold Luxuriator sunglasses were valued at $25,000: "Did you know? $25,000!" Dana repeatedly bragged on-screen to Kyle Richards, Taylor Armstrong, and Camille Grammer.[13] She later stated that these sunglasses were a gift from her then fiancé John Flynn.[14] In a later episode during a trip to Las Vegas, Dana wore a $1 million lollipop holder necklace, a fashion statement that shocked viewers as well as her castmates. The necklace, known as a Couture Pop, contains 125 carats of white diamonds and 200 grams of 18 karat white gold. Yet when Dana was later criticized for this ostentatious bauble, she clarified in her Bravo blog that it was lent to her by the Sugar Factory, which is well-known for their celebrity endorsements, including those from Kylie Jenner, Kendall Jenner, Britney Spears, and Kim Kardashian West.[15]

Similar conspicuous displays can be observed in the royal court, as expensive gowns, jewels, and other goods were constantly and publicly displayed to showcase one's wealth and position. And like in *The Real Housewives*, ostentatious nonessential items held a special privileged status all their own. For example, elite women of the royal court dressed their pets in custom luxury garments, much in the way Lisa Vanderpump (Beverly Hills cast) did with her pomeranian Giggy, and Tinsley Mortimer (New York City cast) did with her chihuahua Bambi and her poodles Strawberry and Shortcake. During the medieval and early modern eras, pets themselves were luxuries, as the mere act of keeping, feeding, housing, and caring for these animals signaled that the owner had substantial monetary resources. Accessories such as ornate bed coverings and cushions, jeweled pet collars and gilt chains and harnesses, embroidered muzzles, birdcages and cage coverings, and fur-lined capelets and coats emphasized owners elevated social positions. As John Friedman has demonstrated, the significance of pet fashions was not simply their material value but their role in the self-construction of noble identity, as many of the styles included heraldic symbols or familial colors.[16]

In both the early modern period and today, pet accessories serve as status symbols, but even more so do accessories for the humans themselves. In *The Real Housewives* franchise, handbags—especially the Hermès Birkin handbag—are particularly high indicators of one's social and material currency. Purses, as we now know them, did not emerge as a woman's accessory until much later in the modern period. However, heavily embellished bags were frequently used by elite women to store precious objects, such as gems or prayer books, or as sachets to sweeten the smell of clothing. While these were certainly prized possessions, they were not considered the greatest. Rather, gems and jewels held the greatest material and symbolic value for early modern women. Indeed, as French scholar Patricia Cholakian notes, jewels were "traditionally a woman's most sacrosanct property."[17] The Housewives also certainly appreciate and value jewelry, especially pieces with a high price tag. But for many Housewives, there is also a need to not simply display or wear their jewelry but also acknowledge (on camera) its monetary value. When Lisa Barlow from *The Real Housewives of Salt Lake City* lost her beloved emerald-cut diamond ring in an airport bathroom on a cast trip, she could not help but continually comment on the fact that it was worth $60,000 (later clarified to be worth $58,000).[18] Especially among the Beverly Hills cast, no season can be considered complete without a trip to a high-end jeweler, where the women shop for jewelry, often trying on pieces worth hundreds of thousands and even millions of dollars, and occasionally buying other items at a lesser price. For example, in season 13, Sutton Stracke visits Martin Katz with her daughter Porter to purchase a piece of jewelry; Sutton tries on a $455,000 diamond tennis bracelet and a $9,000,000 blue diamond ring before purchasing a pair of $68,000 sapphire earrings.[19] In such instances, the act of shopping itself is a performative act meant to convey one's wealth and elevated status, being that they would even be able to afford such costly gems.

These fashion statements demonstrate how royal women and Housewives have made power plays through displays of wealth. Yet it is not simply the expense of the jewels and clothes themselves that dictate one's status but the extensive nature of one's wardrobe—that is, quantity as well as quality. For a Housewife, it is critical to never be seen in the same outfit twice, even within the same season. As Brian Moylan notes, a single season on the Housewives demands as many as 100 different outfits, including dozens for everyday filming, several different confessional shoots, and one dynamic look for reunion episode(s).[20] However, this number pales by comparison to Queen Elizabeth I of England (r. 1558–1603), who owned over 600 pieces of jewelry and over 2,000 dresses during her reign.[21] As a female monarch ruling in her own right without a male partner or husband, Elizabeth certainly understood the importance of conveying a majestic physical appearance, and she used her extensive and opulent wardrobe to fashion a unique image that emulated wealth, authority, and power.

Inherently, there is also a competitive aspect to displays of wealth and status in the royal court and on *The Real Housewives*, and fashion plays a central role. Labels are very important within a Housewife's wardrobe, with many Housewives proudly donning clothing and accessories from Chanel, Gucci, Dolce & Gabbana, Fendi, Louis Vuitton, Christian Louboutin, Prada, Versace, Tom Ford, Balenciaga, Fenty, Yves Saint Laurent, Cartier, Givenchy, Hermès, and more. Most recently, Housewives (most notably Dorit Kemsley) have selected to wear luxury clothes with blatant branding on-screen, a move to definitively indicate which fashion house they patronize. So important are luxury labels to a Housewife's appearance that some are often criticized for their lack of style or even accused of wearing counterfeit clothing. For example, Karen Huger from *The Real Housewives of Potomac* received considerable criticism from fellow Housewife Gizelle Bryant, and fans on social media, for allegedly wearing a knockoff Fendi dress during season 5. At Ashley Darby's "sip and see" party, Karen's off-the-shoulder Fendi dress was visibly missing an "F" in the back, clearly spelling "Endi."[22] But at the season's reunion, Huger clarified that this was due to alterations.[23]

But the competition regarding fashion is even more complex, as there was an underlying but still palatable tension between Sutton Stracke and several of her castmates—including Erika Girardi—during Stracke's first season on *RHOBH* over the issue of couture. (Haute couture refers to very high-end attire that is custom-made for an individual and tailored specifically to the wearer's tastes and body. Even in today's age of mass production, such garments are typically created by hand, from design to stitching to tailoring. In contrast, ready-to-wear clothing, or prêt-à-porter, is produced on a mass scale and in a range of standardized sizes to appeal widely to customers; such clothes and accessories can, therefore, be purchased "off the rack." Couture is almost always more expensive than ready-to-wear due to its exclusivity and one-of-a-kind nature, its high-quality materials, and the labor needed to fashion such unique garments.) Most luxury fashion houses today create both ready-to-wear and couture, and Stracke was always quick to assert that her clothing was haute couture. Such pointed comments appeared to annoy Girardi, who remarked on one occasion: "I don't think we need to announce that we are wearing couture. You know, it's kind of elitist. Like, 'This is couture, and yours isn't.'"[24]

Similar competition between royal women was also prevalent throughout the Restoration court, and frequently remarked upon by observant courtiers. Like Pepys, John Evelyn—a courtier who held a minor governmental position in Charles II's administration—recorded his observations of the Restoration court in vividly detailed diaries. On September 10, 1675, Evelyn remarked: "I was Casualy shewed the Dutchesse of Portsmouths splendid Appartment at Whitehall, luxuriously furnished, and with ten times the richnesse and glory beyond the Queenes, such massy pieces of Plate, whole Tables, Stands etc: of incredible value."[25] The spectacle of fine things within the court was not simply a demonstration of who owned more extravagant garments but an expression of personal power. Sonya Wynne describes how the English royal court measured a mistress's personal and political influence by the opulence of the gifts given to her by Charles II. She notes, "When challenged by courtiers, the mistresses' best answer was to draw attention to Charles's esteem for them."[26] Such a visual display of good favor often included gem-encrusted gowns, luxurious apartments, and modish equipages. Barbara Palmer and another of Charles II's favorite mistresses, the Frenchwoman Louise de Kérouaille, were noble by birth and received considerable annuities from the crown. They made sure to broadcast their influence over the king through their extravagant clothes and possessions. Louise and yet another mistress, Nell Gwyn—a lowborn former actress—had a particularly notorious rivalry for many years. Their feud escalated when Nell slipped Louise a laxative during her date night with the king, to which Louise responded by continually riding past Nell's comparatively humble abode in her ostentatious coach. Such a performative act of superiority, in both title and wealth, served as a very visual reminder of how much better the king kept his noble mistresses.

Noble titles are integral to court societies in general but even more so within the royal court, an institution that is inherently hierarchical. Expressions of rank, even in seemingly inconspicuous forms such as clothing and gestures, were also expressions of power within court societies, where everyone understood and conformed to shared codes of conduct. Similar conflicts regarding titles and social status can be observed in *The Real Housewives* franchise, which boasts some "royals" of its own, most notably Luann de Lesseps (1965–) and Carole Radziwill (1963–) both from *The Real Housewives of New York City* (*RHONY*). Luann (née Nadeau), an original New York City castmate, was married to Count Alexandre de Lesseps (1949–) for sixteen years before their divorce in 2009. Alexandre de Lesseps, an entrepreneur and financier, is a descendant of Ferdinand de Lesseps (1805–94), a French diplomat who built the Suez Canal and began construction on the Panama Canal.[27] Emperor Napoleon I ennobled Ferdinand's father, Mathieu de Lesseps (1771–1832), conferring upon him the title of *comte*, or count.[28]

Journalist and author Carole Radziwill (née DiFalco) joined the New York City cast in 2011, and tension immediately emerged within the group as several of her fellow Housewives delighted in emphasizing Carole's "princess" status in contrast to Luann's "countess" status. Carole's husband was Anthony Radziwill (1959–99), the son of Prince Stanislaw Albrecht Radziwill (1914–76) and his third wife Lee Bouvier (1933–2019), the younger sister of former U.S. First Lady Jacqueline Kennedy (1929–94). Originally from Poland, the Radziwills were a powerful noble dynasty and were entangled within much of modern European politics. In 1547, Charles V, Holy Roman emperor, bestowed the hereditary title of imperial prince on cousins Mikołaj "the Black" and Mikołaj "the Red" Radziwill. The title was confirmed years later by Sigismund II Augustus (1520–72), king of Poland and grand duke of Lithuania, after he married his mistress, Barbara Radziwill.[29] The title was an honorary one, as the Radziwills did not possess an imperial fief, nor did they hold a vote in the Imperial Diet. They were, in fact, foreigners, however distinguished, within the Holy Roman Empire. Yet it is critical to note that this imperial title did not signify royal blood or status.[30] Consequently, despite the titles of "prince" or "princess," the Radziwills were not, technically, royals. That being said, the Radziwill family frequently married into royalty, with occasional issue. Barbara Radziwill briefly served as queen consort to Sigismund II Augustus before her death in 1551. Ludwika Karolina Radziwill was married to the future Charles III Philip, elector palatine, the brother-in-law of Leopold I, Holy Roman emperor. Such powerful marital alliances helped secure the Radziwills' status as a powerful magnate family well into the modern era.

While Carole frequently downplayed her title on the show, Luann capitalized on hers. Even after her marriage to de Lesseps ended, and she subsequently married and divorced Tom D'Agostino Jr., Luann continued to use the "Countess" title in her growing cabaret career. Indeed, Luann has justified the continued use of her title for her performance persona, citing Lady Gaga and Queen Latifah as examples of individuals with stage names not based on actual titles or bloodlines. It is certainly an integral aspect of her on- and off-screen identity, and a source of many arguments and ridicule from her fellow New York castmates.

Similar tension over social status can be observed with New York City castmate Sonja Morgan (née Tremont). Sonja so habitually referred to her past eight-year marriage to a Morgan that, like Luann, the status it granted became a significant component of not just the show's storylines but also her on-screen persona. Sonja's ex-husband, John Adams Morgan (1930–), boasts a storied lineage as a descendant of two prominent American dynasties. His mother was Catherine Frances Lovering Adams (1902–88), a direct descendant of two American presidents: John Adams and his son, John Quincy Adams. His father was Henry Sturgis Morgan (1900–82), the cofounder of Morgan Stanley, and his great-grandfather was the banking colossus J. P. Morgan (1837–1913). Since joining the New York cast, Sonja continued to reminisce on-screen about her life when she was "Mrs. Morgan," making frequent reference to the fact that the couple owned multiple homes in the United States and a chateau in France, as well as a yacht on which she reportedly partied with A-list celebrities. While her nineteenth-century town house, which she received in her divorce settlement, stands as a particularly poignant symbol of her former life, her clothes are also representative.

During a spa trip to Connecticut in season 10 of *RHONY*, Sonja shared with the group a piece from her collection with shoe retailer French Sole. Sonja modeled a pair of flat loafers in black, embellished with an embroidered red stag, and commented that "the deer's from my family crest."[31] Sonja was, of course, referring to the Morgan crest, which is described as "on a wreath a stag's head couped or, attired gules [heraldic red]" in the family's heraldic history.[32] When questioned by Dorinda Medley, Sonja then revealed a gold signet ring, presumably bearing the Morgan emblem, on her right pinky finger and explained, "I wear this every day. This is from my ex-husband." Sonja later stated in her confessional: "I feel very comfortable wearing the Morgan insignia. I'm still very much a part of the family and the history. And I have a huge responsibility and I'm not letting this family down."[33] On the next episode, the issue reemerged during a group dinner and erupted in an argument, with Sonja passionately yelling, "That's my family!"[34]

Sonja's sartorial use of the Morgan emblem follows a popular trend within Western history. The use of heraldic symbols and dynastic insignia on clothing was particularly prominent in medieval and early modern Europe and continued well into the modern period. Susan Crane has described how fourteenth-century European noblemen intentionally communicated dynastic and political allegiance through the "talking garments" of their livery, crests, banners, badges, and armor during the Hundred Years' War. Such vestments were thus an integral, material part of what Crane terms "self-performances," or deliberately communicative behaviors and public displays that drew on both visual and rhetorical devices.[35] Perhaps the most iconic example of such displays during the early modern period is Anne

Boleyn's now famous portrait, wherein the future queen consort to King Henry VIII (r. 1509–47) dons a pearl necklace with a gold "B" monogram. Such a display served to reinforce her identity as a Boleyn and thus her dynastic connections to the powerful Howard family within the Tudor royal court.

Patronage, both formal and informal, also served as a means of cultural and political agency within the royal court. In the early modern court, this usually took the form of artistic patronage. For consorts, it served as an optimal opportunity to shape the cultural milieu at court. During her tenure as queen, Henrietta Maria, Charles II's mother, served as a patron for many acclaimed European playwrights, musicians, and artists, including Orazio Gentileschi, the Italian painter who previously served her mother at the French court.[36] Charles's queen, Catherine of Braganza, used the act of patronage to shape a new identity for herself at the royal court. During the 1660s, Sir Peter Lely, a Protestant, was the sole artist to paint the queen, but Catherine soon gave her patronage to the Catholic artist Jacob Huysmans, who "succeeded in giving her a magnificent new image" in portraiture.[37] Catherine's transformation was evident not only within the paintings she posed for but in her patronage of Continental artists as well. Catherine became *the* patron of Italian culture at the court, fashioned in direct opposition to the French culture promoted by the French faction, which included Charles's French mistress Louise de Kérouaille. Catherine commissioned the baroque artist Benedetto Gennari to paint numerous devotional works and court portraits, and also appointed Italian composer Giovanni Sebenico to the position of master of Italian music at her own personal chapel. So absolute was Catherine's musical influence that, by the 1670s, the prevailing taste for music at the royal court had shifted from French to Italian.[38]

Housewives also serve as patrons of art, evidenced most notably in season 11 of *RHONY*. Sonja Morgan brought Bethenny Frankel to the Brooklyn studio of her friend Hunt Slonem (1951–), whose paintings she had collected for many years.[39] During their Miami trip later that season, the group (except Ramona Singer) visited Wynwood Walls, an urban artistic center renowned for its outdoor graffiti. There, viewers observed Bethenny's patronage of Brazilian-born pop artist Romero Britto (1963–) and Luann's patronage of Peter Tunney (1961–).[40] Tunney distributed thousands of dollars of artwork to all the ladies except Bethenny, who instead purchased a piece; he gave Tinsley a Campbell's soup can piece, encouraging her to use it as a clutch for Art Basel, which would occur later that week. In this sense, the wearing and displaying of items that have been gifted to them also served as a form of patronage, as the purpose is to be seen and promote the artist and, by extension, the Housewife herself.

Similarly, Housewives are also known for bestowing patronage on specific fashion designers. Sutton Stracke has prominently flaunted her connections to the luxury fashion house Dolce & Gabbana over the years, repeatedly mentioning how she is gifted elaborate gold crowns every year for her birthday as well as her inclusion in the *Queens: Alta Moda di Dolce & Gabbana* coffee-table book. In the season 10 premiere, Sutton is first introduced to viewers when she invites Lisa Rinna to accompany her to a private fitting at the New York apartment of Domenico Dolce, who founded the luxury Italian fashion house with partner Stefano Gabbana in 1985.[41] Later that season, Sutton again welcomes fellow castmates Kyle Richards and Dorit Kemsley (and the cameras) to a Dolce & Gabbana store in Rome for an exclusive shopping experience, stating that she was personally invited by Dolce and noting, "I didn't ask. I don't have to ask."[42] In New York City, Dorinda Medley broadcast her patronage of Jovani, a formal-wear brand founded by Jacob Maslavi and his sons, Abraham and Saul, when she invited Luann de Lesseps to the storefront to select dresses for her inaugural cabaret show in season 10.[43] By the next season, de Lesseps's patronage of Jovani had become an integral component of her Housewife identity as well as her new cabaret persona. Indeed, her on- and off-screen tensions with Dorinda over the wearing of Jovani dresses continued for three seasons and served as the inspiration for her 2019 single, "Feelin' Jovani."

Conclusion

The royal court and reality television both operate as performative platforms, as arenas for self-fashioning and promotion. The women of the early modern royal court and *The Real Housewives* franchise have used many similar facets of identity to develop personal agency in very visual spaces. In these instances, representation and display function as performative acts to communicate specific images, meanings, or messages. Over the last decade, audiences have become increasingly cognizant of the performative aspect of reality television, despite the insistent assertion from producers and stars that these shows are firmly grounded in authenticity. It has even been acknowledged on *The Traitors*, a competition show featuring contestants across multiple reality franchises (including *The Real Housewives*), that the women of Bravo are not wholly authentic on camera. When speaking of her Housewives castmates Larsa Pippen, Tamra Judge, Phaedra Parks, and Shereé Whitfield, fellow reality TV personality Parvati Shallow from *Survivor* stated, "They perform every day on Housewives." Pippen later retorted, "We don't act, my friend. We live our life. We live our life," which prompted Shallow to respond, "It's performance as well."[44] Several Housewives have been known to react negatively to any insinuation or direct accusation that they are performing for the cameras, perhaps because acknowledging such performance would mean they are fake and thus shatter the illusion that their lives are exactly as they appear on camera. Yet performance in this sense, and in the case of the early modern royal court, does not necessarily mean playacting or inauthenticity; here, it translates as agency over the fashioning and display of specific images. At a time when women were expected to be seen and not heard, especially in a political sense, the women of the seventeenth-century royal courts successfully used dress and material objects as a form of self-expression. The Housewives' similarly successful use of their personal appearances reveals the power of material culture as universal tools of self-representation and identity that transcend time and space.

Notes

1. Much gratitude to Missy Mando and Molly Mando.
2. Gyucha and Parkinson, *First Kings of Europe*.
3. See Asch and Birke, *Princes, Patronage, and the Nobility*.
4. Orr, *Queenship in Britain*, 24.
5. Rodríguez-Salgado, "Court of Philip II of Spain," 205–44.
6. Vincent, *Dressing the Elite*, 4–5.
7. Vincent, *Dressing the Elite*, 9.
8. *RHOBH*, season 7, episode 3, "Going Commando," aired December 20, 2016, on Bravo.
9. Pepys, *Diary of Samuel Pepys*, 3:87.
10. *RHOBH*, season 11, episode 23, "Part 3," aired October 27, 2021, on Bravo.
11. *RHOBH*, season 6, episode 3, "Horsing Around," aired December 15, 2015, on Bravo.
12. Lex Briscuso, "*RHOBH* Star Erika Jayne Has Changed a Lot over the Years—but Has She Gotten Plastic Surgery?," *Life and Style*, June 1, 2023, https://www.lifeandstylemag.com/posts/has-erika-jayne-gotten-plastic-surgery-before-after-photos.
13. *RHOBH*, season 2, episode 5, "$25,000 Sunglasses?!," aired October 3, 2011, on Bravo.
14. Lauren Metz, "Dana Wilkey Explains Those $25,000 Shades," accessed October 1, 2020, https://www.bravotv.com/the-daily-dish/dana-wilkey-explains-those-25000-shades.

15. Dana Wilkey, "The Lollipop Guild," December 13, 2011, https://www.bravotv.com/the-real-housewives-of-beverly-hills/season-2/blogs/dana-wilkey/the-lollipop-guild.

16. Friedman, "Coats, Collars, and Capes," 61–94.

17. Cholakian, *Women and the Politics of Self-Representation*, 95.

18. *RHOSLC*, season 4, episode 2, "Vacation Crashers," aired September 12, 2023, on Bravo.

19. *RHOBH*, season 13, episode 17, "Soirees and Separations," aired February 21, 2024, on Bravo.

20. Brian Moylan, "What the Real Housewives Really Spend on Fashion," August 18, 202, https://www.townandcountrymag.com/style/fashion-trends/a40745475/real-housewives-fashion-cost.

21. See Arnold, *Queen Elizabeth's Wardrobe Unlock'd*.

22. *RHOP*, season 5, episode 20, "Sip and See You Later," aired August 16, 2020, on Bravo.

23. *RHOP*, season 5, episode 20, "Reunion Part 1," aired December 13, 2020, on Bravo.

24. *RHOBH*, season 10, episode 2, "To Live and Text in Beverly Hills," aired April 22, 2020, on Bravo.

25. Evelyn, *Diary of John Evelyn*, 3:258.

26. Wynne, "Mistresses of Charles II and Restoration Court Politics," 173; Corp, "Catherine of Braganza and Cultural Politics," 56–60.

27. Ferdinand de Lesseps was at the center of the Panama Affair of 1892, a corruption scandal in which he was accused and convicted of bribing French officials.

28. Lesseps, *Class with the Countess*, 10.

29. Barbara Radziwiłł's brother was Mikołaj "the Red" Radziwill, while her cousin was Mikołaj "the Black" Radziwill. Both were integral political players in sixteenth-century Poland and worked to have her marriage formally recognized so that she could be crowned queen of Poland. See Kosior, *Becoming a Queen in Early Modern Europe*.

30. Imperial nobles used a number of different titles, including archdukes, dukes, counts, and princes, for various historical reasons.

31. See *RHONY*, season 10, episode 12, "Every Mayflower Has Its Thorn," aired June 20, 2018, on Bravo.

32. The heraldic crest is a component of a family's coat of arms. Morgan, *History of the Family of Morgan*, 9.

33. *RHONY*, season 10, episode 12.

34. See *RHONY*, season 10, episode 13, "Arrest and Relaxation," aired June 27, 2018, on Bravo.

35. Crane, *Performance of Self*, 3.

36. Griffey, introduction, 2. See also Griffey, *On Display*.

37. Corp, "Catherine of Braganza and Cultural Politics," 60.

38. Corp, "Catherine of Braganza and Cultural Politics," 56, 59.

39. *RHONY*, season 11, episode 18, "Birds, Broads and Breakups," aired April 24, 2019, on Bravo.

40. *RHONY*, season 11, episode 14, "Caught between an Ex and a Hard Place," aired June 5, 2019, on Bravo.

41. *RHOBH*, season 10, episode 1, "The Crown Isn't So Heavy," aired April 15, 2020, on Bravo.

42. *RHOBH*, season 10, episode 13, "There's No Place Like Rome," aired August 5, 2020, on Bravo.

43. *RHONY*, season 10, episode 14, "Dating Wishes and Cabaret Dreams," aired July 11, 2018, on Bravo.

44. *The Traitors*, season 2, episode 4, "The Funeral," aired January 17, 2024.

4 The Real Housewives of Medieval France

Feminism, Domestic Drama, and the
History of the Household

· ·

NOAH D. GUYNN

Bravo TV's *Real Housewives* franchise doesn't always get good press from feminists. Gloria Steinem famously despises the shows and offers compelling reasons why: they present women's bodies in absurdly stylized ways, "all dressed up and inflated and plastic surgeried and false bosomed"; they glamorize domestic leisure, depicting women as "rich, pampered, dependent"; and they stage "manufactured" conflicts in which women are "made to fight with each other," even as they profess sisterhood.[1] In short, "it's a minstrel show for women," purveying sexist stereotypes just as minstrelsy purveyed racist ones.

While there are unmistakable signs of sexism—and racism, too—in Bravo's casting choices, story designs, and promotional strategies, I posit that there is also something transformative in *The Real Housewives* phenomenon, and that the household—and the social identities and cultural fictions associated with it—affords women unsuspected opportunities for agency. I stake this claim by resituating the franchise within a long history of marriage and family, extending from the Middle Ages to the present. My focus is the household model that was predominant among common folk in northwestern Europe by 1500, characterized by late marriages; nuclear families; and highly flexible, loosely defined, and extensively overlapping gender roles—clearly the precursor of mainstream American domesticity. As a scholar of early vernacular drama, I am also interested in theatrical depictions of the household from the period when this model took hold, specifically the medieval French genre of farce, which targets mass audiences, thematizes familial relations, and is often decried as sexist. Considered alongside *The Real Housewives*, farce shows us how much continuity exists between medieval and modern mass media and how much we can learn about the gender politics of household fictions by interrogating their history. It also reminds us that mass genres are conditioned both by the culture industry, which uses predictable formulas to create docile consumers, and by popular modes of reception, which use the everyday tactics of subordinate groups to push back against normative limits and restrictive identities. Reading farce and *The Real Housewives* as mass culture allows us to see them as sites of contradiction—as sexist minstrel shows that use hackneyed stereotypes to reinforce patriarchal rule but also as cultural vehicles for women to imagine and enact resistance.

Before launching into my reading, I should say a few words about the particular series I have chosen, *The Real Housewives of Atlanta* (*RHOA*), which features a Black cast. On its face, the choice may seem ill-considered, as it requires me to make a leap from European common households, which are linked to the rise of Western hegemony and global capitalism, to minority African American ones, which have both African and European influences and are marked by the traumatic legacy of racial capitalism. I will address these differences, but for now, let me identify the common ground I see among the disparate elements of this project. To begin with, the histories of the family I draw on share a notion of the household as a political rather than a private space, as a place of work rather than a refuge from economic forces, and as a mixed-gender sphere in which female agency and labor are social and economic necessities and in which patriarchal rule is negotiated rather than absolute. For Thavolia Glymph, even the plantation household, with its myth of white female leisure, was a workplace, one in which mistresses were responsible for managing the labor of enslaved women and did so using sadistic violence and racial terror.[2] Despite conditions of unfree labor, however, household rule was negotiated: Black women didn't simply acquiesce to white women's authority but pursued agency using artful tactics of evasion (like foot-dragging and pilfering) and discursive forms of resistance (like calculated ambiguity, rumormongering, and dissimulation). This was the standard repertoire for European common folk and for the tricksters who are ubiquitous in farce. It is also redolent of African American "signifying," which originated in slavery and uses artful troping and encoded intentions to achieve advantage, deflect blame, and affirm identity in the face of antagonism or oppression. The fact that *RHOA* and farce both make use of tricks and tactics like these suggests that they arise from social and cultural settings in which conformity to a dominant ideology is required but does not preclude veiled or latent dissent.

Ultimately, then, Steinem's analogy to minstrelsy may not be entirely misplaced, as minstrel shows entertained white audiences with crude expressions of ideological racism. The analogy needs to be carefully qualified, however, as minstrelsy, like farce, also allowed for the covert expression of counterideological resistance. According to Karen Sotiropoulos, Black minstrel theater not only sought to please white audiences by purveying racist imagery to them but also afforded Black performers opportunities to gain access to commercial culture, pursue fame and fortune, and use stage masks to conceal—and discreetly promote—Black cultural and political power.[3] Similarly, *RHOA* plays on sexist fantasies of female domesticity and racist stereotypes of angry, uncouth Black women even as it grants visibility and influence to a population that rarely benefits from them: middle-aged women of color.

Women on Top

An obvious analogy between *The Real Housewives* and farce is that both are driven by recursive conflict and take pleasure in the ingenuity and obstreperousness of female characters. For Christopher Lucken, the farce heroine not only "rules the stage" with her "chattering," "quarrelsome" nature; she also imposes herself as "the foundation and the emblem of the genre," which is characterized by a boisterous, topsy-turvy poetics.[4] In settings ruled by men, she uses verbal dexterity, theatrical make-believe, and physical violence to pull focus from male characters. She thereby transforms the sexist cliché of the crafty, unruly, garrulous woman into the raison d'être for performance: "Without her," says Lucken, "there would be no play."[5] Thus, the tropes used to disparage her ensure her relevance.

Something similar can be said of the Housewives, who use the sexist lie of the franchise's title as a platform for self-invention and self-display. Nearly all work outside the home, some are not married at all, and none are willing to allow a male partner to pull focus for long. In truth, they wouldn't belong on the show if they did, for the series' ironic goal is to refashion conventions of wifely self-effacement into innovative forms of female protagonism. Obviously, there are stark differences between Bravo stars and farce heroines, the most obvious being that the latter are typically neither rich nor pampered but working class or poor. Yet they otherwise closely match Steinem's description of the Housewives. Farce heroines are certainly inflated and false bosomed, as females were largely excluded from the stage, meaning their roles went to male actors. Farce heroines also personify the crudest of sexist stereotypes: woman as shrew or scold, cheat or slut, ditz or dupe, temptress or femme fatale.

Indeed, theater historians have often argued that sexism is both medium and message in farce. For Konrad Schoell, the genre uses cross-dressed theater to disparage women, urge men to silence their wives, and ensure that those wives will have few chances for retort.[6] The exclusion of women from the stage was said to protect their virtue and reputation, yet it denied them cultural expression and political voice and reminded them of their proper place: the home. As Schoell maintains, women's lived reality of domestic service belies the farce heroine's demand for sovereignty and voice, which is therefore a counterfactual scenario designed to reinforce subservience. This reading owes a debt to functionalist anthropology, which holds that rituals of inversion normalize the status quo by casting deviations as liminal fictions, bounded and temporary. Reading farce through functionalism, Charles Mazouer instructs us not to "overestimate the scope of [its] free laughter," least of all the noisy disruptions of farce wives, for festive license is "confined to the imaginary world of the theatrical fiction," and dissent gets purged by "comic catharsis."[7]

Yet this reading fails to take seriously a pioneering feminist critique of functionalism, Natalie Zemon Davis's "Women on Top."[8] Davis's subject is the defiant female characters who pervade medieval and early modern festive culture, who often breach the boundaries of fictional enclosure, and who suggest the capacity of real women for meaningful social action. The role of the woman on top was to invert gender hierarchies, sow chaos and violence, and take a position atop a man, sometimes literally subduing him like a beast (see figs. 4.1 and 4.2).[9] This isn't to say depictions of unruly femininity were necessarily empowering; rather, they were used to justify the use of cucking stools, scold's bridles, and other humiliation and torture devices (see figs. 4.3 and 4.4).[10] Moreover, the woman on top doesn't seem to have inspired feminists of the era to challenge the family order. Hardly anyone considered that the patriarchal household might have "a 'history'"; instead, they traced it "back either to the Garden of Eden . . . or to the first moment in human history" and viewed the subjection of women as natural, necessary, and permanent.[11]

Even so, the woman on top played subversive roles. For Davis, she "kept open an alternate way of conceiving family structure," offered "a resource for feminist reflection on women's capacities," "enriched the fantasy of a few real women," and enabled some to translate fantasy into reality.[12] In "exceptional" cases (like Joan of Arc), women were able "to hint at the possibility of a wider role of citizenship for [their sex]" by emulating cross-dressed saints.[13] In "unexceptional" (but mostly invisible) cases, married

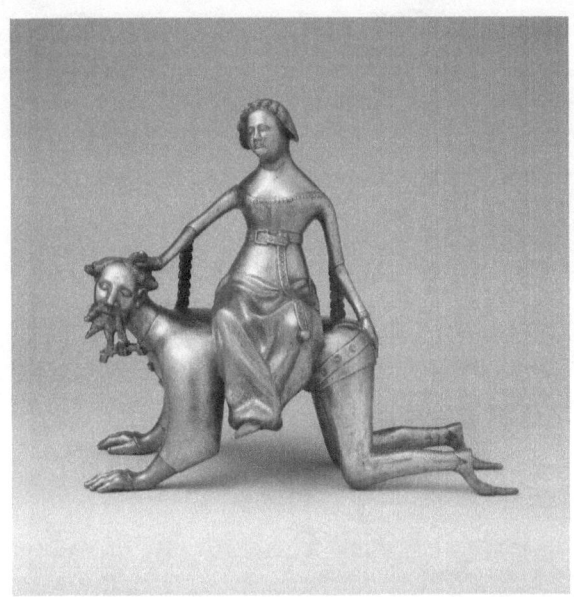

FIGURE 4.1 Aquamanile featuring Aristotle and Phyllis, Netherlandish, late fourteenth or early fifteenth century. Metropolitan Museum of Art. In this widespread tale, Aristotle chastises his pupil, Alexander the Great, for his excessive devotion to his Indian lover, Phyllis, whose country has been conquered by the Greeks. Phyllis gets revenge by persuading the philosopher to allow her to saddle and ride him as Alexander looks on aghast.

FIGURE 4.2 Casket with scenes from romances, French, ca. 1310–30. Metropolitan Museum of Art. On the left, Aristotle teaches Alexander, illustrating the superiority of intellectual achievement over knightly valor. On the right, Phyllis wears a crown as a symbol of her victory over Aristotle, whom she controls with bridle and whip; above, Alexander gestures emphatically but impotently to his master and mistress, presumably in an attempt to restore masculine dignity.

FIGURE 4.3 *Cucking Stool*, sixteenth-century English woodcut from *A Strange and Wonderful Relation of the Old Woman Who Was Drowned at Ratcliff Highway* (London: n.p., n.d.), printed in Townsend, *Town and Borough of Leominster,* 317. The cucking stool was a seesaw contraption used to dunk men or (more often) women in a pond or river as punishment for violations of communal norms, including scolding. See Underdown, "The Taming of the Scold," 123–25.

FIGURE 4.4 *Scold's Bridle or Branks*. Ralph Gardiner, *Englands Grievance Discovered in Relation to the Coal-Trade* (London: R. Ibbitson and P. Stent, 1655), 110. British Library, Public Domain. This image accompanies an account of a historical episode in which Ann Bidlestone was "drove through the streets by an Officer . . . holding a rope in his hand, the other end fastened to an Engine called the Branks, which is like a Crown, it being of Iron, which was musled over the head and face, with a great gap or tongue of Iron forced into her mouth, which forced the blood out. And that is the punishment which the Magistrates do inflict upon chiding, and scoulding women, and that he hath often seen the like done to others" (110–11).

women thwarted male rule through "sneaky manipulations" or rebelled against it by cursing or beating husbands in imitation of fictional viragos.[14] Finally, there are the cases of women who were "disorderly in public," rioting against official male authority. Sheltered by laws that punished "the *sexus imbecillus* [weak sex] . . . less severely," they "turn up telling off priests and pastors, being central actors in grain and bread riots in town and country, and participating in tax revolts and other rural disturbances."[15] Paradoxically, the stereotype of women's weakness was here their greatest strength, as jurists couldn't imagine how to punish female rebellion without conceding female self-rule. The ubiquity of the woman on top suggests a similar paradox: by their recurrence, these sexist fictions not only justified cucking shrews and bridling scolds but also attested to the resilience of oppositional femininities in everyday life.

Topping from the Bottom in Farce

If we turn to French farce with Davis's claims in mind, we can see that feminist fantasies often reside within sexist genres and that prevailing social patterns often yield unintended or unrecognized consequences. The play I use to illustrate this claim—*Le galant qui a fait le coup* (The cad who pulled a fast one), an anonymous work dated before 1535 and based on a tale from Boccaccio's *Decameron*—is an unlikely choice in that it doesn't feature a woman on top at all, rather a naive, loving wife who is cruelly betrayed by her roguish husband.[16] Moreover, the "coup" of the title, which implies sexual exploits and armed conflict as well as skullduggery, signals the victory of men in the battle of the sexes. That said, the husband in this play must pretend to be pregnant to escape the consequences of an affair with his maid, thus illustrating how sexist tricks can turn against the men who play them by tasking them with reproductive labor. Moreover, because those tricks work to achieve social elevation for both wife and maid, they suggest to the audience (especially its female members) that women are able to control the household by strategically submitting to the subordinate roles they are assigned within it.

On its face, there is no disguising the misogyny of *Le galant*, which stages the vulnerability of women to men's verbal and sexual aggression. In the opening scene, the titular cad, Oudin, sets out to seduce his sexually curious but inexperienced maid, Malaperte, while his pious wife, Crespinete, is away on pilgrimage. The maid worries she will lose her reputation along with her virginity, but Oudin orders her to shut up and put out, promising to ensure her honor through cunning. Once the deed is done, however, Malaperte reminds Oudin of his own vulnerability, in that his "faictz vertueulx" (83; "vigorous actions/manly thrusts") may have left her with "un enfant au ventre" (84; "a child in the womb/belly") and a stain on her (and thus also his) reputation. As Crespinete nears home, Oudin, for whom the pregnancy is no longer notional but real, runs to the physician to seek counsel. Although the physician denounces Oudin's betrayal of his marriage, he soon hatches a plan to rescue his patient. When Oudin sees his wife, he must greet her with an embrace, then cry out in pain, pointing to his breast and belly. The devoted Crespinete, fearing for her husband's life, will ask for a urine sample to carry to the physician. The physician will then offer a diagnosis that will save Oudin from scandal and enable him to do as he pleases henceforth. When Oudin returns home and boasts to Malaperte that he has devised a trick to save them both from dishonor, the maid praises him for his cleverness, only to be demeaned as a "vielle lisse" (268; "old bitch/slut") and ordered once again to shut up.

The trick doesn't belong to Oudin, however, and soon works to undercut his sexist bravado. Additionally, since the trick is the farce's central coup, we can reasonably ask whether the play aims to solidify male power or subvert it. After examining the urine sample, the physician reveals to Crespinete that her husband is pregnant, that it is she who has begotten the child by embracing him, and that the only way she can redeem her sin and preserve her "honneur" (303) is by convincing Oudin to sleep with the maid and thus transfer the child from his body to hers. If Malaperte is unwilling, she must be given a rich reward. Returning home, Crespinete finds Oudin doubled over in agony and shrieking that the Antichrist has implanted itself in his "ventre bendé" (317), an unintended pun signifying both "swollen belly" and "erect womb" (from *bander*, "to have an erection"). Crespinete takes Malaperte aside and promises the maid all her worldly goods if she will sleep with Oudin. The shrewd Malaperte again evokes the specter of pregnancy, but Crespinete promises to rescue her reputation by finding a suitor willing to raise another man's child. Crespinete then tells Oudin about the physician's cure, though without revealing his diagnosis, which he never learns. As Crespinete leaves the stage so that husband and servant can betray her at her own request, she promises to pray for them. Oudin then turns to the audience and offers a closing monologue dripping with unintentional irony. First, he boasts of his acting skills, the "grace et maintien" (377; "grace and bearing") that enabled him to deceive his wife while keeping a straight face. Then he prays for Jesus, "de sa grace" (379;

"in his grace"), to help us all deceive the Devil, "l'anemy / Qui est sy remply de falace" (380–81; "the enemy who is so filled with lies").

Outwardly, this denouement illustrates the triumph of masculine intellect, morality, and will over feminine credulity and weakness. If Crespinete falls into the physician's snare, sets the stage for her own betrayal, and shoulders the burden for crimes committed against her, perhaps women deserve the label *sexus imbecillus*. Likewise, if Malaperte fails to protect her virginity, betrays the family that employs her, and saddles her future husband with a bastard, perhaps it's fair to conclude that women can't be trusted with self-rule and should be brought to heel. Appalling as these readings are, the play's sexism gets starker when we compare it to its source, *Decameron* 9.3. In Boccaccio's tale, the dolt Calandrino is tricked by his friends and physician into believing that his wife, Tessa, has impregnated him by taking the prohibited position on top during intercourse. The physician gives him a potion to abort the child but warns he must never again commit such indiscretions, which are associated with female pleasure and usurpation. The tale then ends with Tessa, who wasn't deceived by the ruse, muttering against her husband, presumably embittered by the loss of a preferred sexual position. Yet if the woman on top is literally unseated by male authority here and can do no more than grumble about it under her breath, Boccaccio makes clear that imbecility knows no sex: Tessa retains intellectual superiority, which she shares with the men who have tricked her husband.

By contrast, the farce consistently associates cunning and autonomy with men, ignorance and infirmity with women. Like Calandrino, Crespinete is a dolt who fails to grasp the realities of sexual difference and procreation and is outwitted by everyone. Not only does she lose the expectation of faithfulness from spouse, servant, and physician, but she also relinquishes her wealth to convince her maid to betray her. Yet Malaperte hardly emerges unscathed; rather, she is repeatedly targeted by sexist slurs and double standards. Oudin silences her to privilege his ingenuity and desire, he demeans her as a slut after she submits to his lust, and everyone (Crespinete included) treats her body as a commodity. By comparison, the male characters assert intellectual and moral distinction, despite their hypocrisy. The physician uses medical authority to ensure that Oudin's adultery will go unpunished yet preserves a claim on rectitude by defending the sanctity of marriage. Similarly, Oudin uses his monologue to deflect attention away from his infidelity and to claim that he duped his wife with "grace," just as he hopes to deceive the Devil with help from Jesus. Although Oudin conflates pieties with misdeeds and truth with falsehood, many male spectators likely chose to overlook his sophistry so they could align themselves with him, his physician, and his male God against the play's female characters. Certainly the cards are stacked against Malaperte, whose name (from *mal*, "wicked," and *aperte*, "open") suggests the evil women do when they open their mouths and legs to married men. Read this way, the farce celebrates Oudin's coup as a moral victory, rescuing men from female speech and allure and from the claims women make on male freedom and sovereignty.

Yet it is equally reasonable to conclude that the play's female characters achieve victory in their surrender to sexist stereotypes and that they recover the position on top Tessa lost. While laughing at Crespinete's faith in her husband and physician, we shouldn't neglect what her acceptance of Oudin's diagnosis reveals about her fantasy life and domestic situation. If she accepts the delusion of male pregnancy, she presumably already holds deviant beliefs about women's phallic, inseminating power and men's passive uterine receptivity. Indeed, those beliefs are reflected in the distribution of roles in her household. It is she who moves freely, traveling to pilgrimage sites without escort, whereas Oudin remains bound to the home—precisely the sort of spatial confinement associated with women and indicative of their subordination. If Oudin's coup is meant to redress this imbalance by freeing him from the tyranny of marriage, it fails badly. For Crespinete's embrace leaves her husband with tender breasts and a swollen womb; and while his diagnosis allows him to enjoy "faictz vertueulx" with impunity, his body is no longer a site of turgid, thrusting manhood but of androgyny: an erect penis as gravid uterus. Even his attempt to have the last word in the play, and to seize the high ground with help from Jesus, backfires, for his twisted rhetoric makes it impossible to distinguish his lies from the Devil's "falace" and reminds us that he carries the Antichrist in his womb and is therefore the mother of all evil. By contrast, Crespinete is a model of domestic piety. No doubt she, too, is a hypocrite, as she condones adultery to cover up what she takes as her sin. Yet she does so to restore her husband's health and secure her family's honor. Her commitment to bourgeois respectability—to the "honneur" required for economic and social privilege—suggests it is she, not Oudin, who is the responsible head of household. Crespinete thus assumes the role of woman on top even as she acquiesces, dutifully and meekly, to patriarchal rule.

If anything, though, it is Malaperte who achieves the greatest victory in the play. In part, that victory is a sexual one, as she defends female desire in the face of male aggression. In the first scene, she sings as she works, voicing the fantasies of a virgin who is seduced by a lecher and brought to a "fin . . . friant" (10; "delicious climax"). Overhearing Malaperte, Oudin invites her to serve her master and his "membre qui frissonne" (21; "quivering member"). She is no fool, however, and in yielding to seduction, she turns it to her advantage. Again she sings a song, this time using the lyric pose to demote Oudin from master to lover and to address him with "tu," as he does with her, to mark inferior status: "Prens en moy ton esjoyssance," she purrs, "Ainsy c'un amoureulx doibt avoir" (25–26; "Take your pleasure with me, as a lover should"). Malaperte's situation changes radically after sex, when she realizes—or pretends to realize—that Oudin has seized one of the few assets a servant girl can possess. Her lament is obviously calculated, however, and swiftly turns calamity to her advantage, instilling the possibility of pregnancy as a reality in Oudin's mind, setting in motion the machinations of physician and wife, and enabling her ascent from menial domestic to affluent bourgeoise.[17] Soon Malaperte will have her own household, her own maid, and a husband she can control. For if the witless Crespinete can trick or persuade a suitor into raising another man's child, presumably the wily Malaperte will be able to govern him as she pleases. By allowing herself to be persuaded into sexual service she finds "delicious" and by commodifying herself on the marriage market, she comes out on top and regains the position Tessa lost. Put simply (if paradoxically), Malaperte shows us how subordinate women could achieve social mobility and self-rule, if not true emancipation, by tactically submitting to patriarchal norms. She also demonstrates that the tricks that are the very essence of farce don't belong to men alone but can be reclaimed.

Housewives, Households, and the Western Family Pattern

In my view, *The Real Housewives* features characters much like Malaperte and Crespinete: women (some wily, others witless) who simultaneously comply with and deviate from a ruling ideology and who disrupt, without displacing, normative constraints. Before I explore this paradox, however, let me first sketch a history of the household model that, I hold, serves as the backdrop for both medieval farce and Bravo. I am guided here by Mary Hartman, whose "subversive view of the Western past" rests on the claim that common households were not "reactors to outside developments" but "places from which far-reaching transformation might emanate," not "permanent sites of women's oppression" but "places where women could be imagined as significant social actors."[18] Even if medieval and early modern people were unable or unwilling to imagine that the family had a history, the reality is that the household was—and is—a powerful matrix for social change, one in which expectations of female obedience and submission were met with enhanced forms of female responsibility and independence.

The origins of the so-called Western family pattern are elusive, though Hartman traces them to the decline of the Roman Empire, when landlords ensured labor needs by offering incentives to peasants, including guarantees that the most industrious could acquire title to the lands they farmed. To ensure their advancement, peasants put their entire families to work and postponed marriage for both sexes. As the population grew, life-cycle service was introduced, with adolescent women seeking domestic employment and marrying only when they had the resources needed to form households. Because these women left home before marriage, they chose their own husbands, were responsible for contributing to and managing household capital, and were granted extensive property rights as widows. Most crucially, because late-marriage households were nuclear and too small to uphold a division of labor, women did men's work in their husbands' absence. These conditions spawned novel identities and behaviors, including modes of socialization that strained the gender binary considerably. As Hartman observes, "Whatever notions children in these households absorb[ed] about an official division of roles by sex, they [were] destined to observe more day-to-day boundary crossing."[19] Men were dependent on wives as "deputy husbands," even as women were called on to handle household affairs with "assertiveness and even aggressiveness."[20]

Hartman doesn't present this as a progressivist history in which demographic and economic pressures led inexorably toward greater equality. On the contrary, she concedes Martha Howell's claim that inequality worsened as medieval customary systems (in which women were viewed as reliable "creators of property") gave way to early modern contractual ones (in which women were treated as unreliable "carriers of property").[21] Hartman explains escalating antifeminism differently, however, viewing it as evidence of the contradictions at the heart of "the Western gender story."[22] On the one hand, new domestic arrangements obliged men to grant power and deference to women, whose work was invaluable to them. On the other hand, the late-marriage household introduced so much precarity into the sex-gender system that it spawned compensatory forms of repression, including the sharpening of discourses of female submission, which eased men's "uncomfortable awareness of their new dependence upon wives."[23] Under such conditions, women were obliged to negotiate as skillfully as possible the contradictory postures of the deputy husband: meek and confident, submissive and enterprising. Despite this predicament, many turned late-marriage norms to their advantage, claiming greater agency and livability despite double binds. The woman on top reflects these contradictions, as her disorderliness serves, for Davis, both "to clarify [hierarchy] by . . . reversing it" and "to widen behavioral options for women within and even outside marriage."[24] Extending Davis's argument, Hartman argues that the woman on top was not only phantasmal but also mimetic, meaning that even as she enriched real women's fantasies and encouraged their self-assertion, she also reflected their lived experience under a household regime that obliged them to "become more assertive marriage partners."[25] Subjection to that obligation enabled women to thwart subjection itself and to use subordinate roles to experiment with emancipation.

Fictional as they may be, the characters in *Le galant* reflect the contradictions and opportunities of the Western family pattern, as they simultaneously uphold, defy, and transform the roles assigned to them. Oudin is the reigning patriarch responsible for ensuring domestic order and moral instruction, yet he is also emasculated by the trick meant to liberate him, a trick that deprives him of knowledge and mastery, makes him the butt of a humiliating joke, and compels him to embody a critique of bourgeois masculinity as swollen, diabolical "falace." As for Crespinete, she is the image of wifely obedience and imbecility, willing to sacrifice herself without hesitation for husband, household, and honor. Yet she is also a sly, willful, wandering woman who keeps compromising secrets, usurps the role of householder, and reinvents bourgeois femininity as phallic, inseminating power. Finally, we have Malaperte, who serves her masters by acceding to their sexist demands but also chooses her pleasures and authors her destiny at the expense of those who take her for a pawn. In the end, she pulls her own fast one, translating her body's vulnerability to shameful defilement and unplanned pregnancy into a chance to dispossess her betters and achieve social advancement.

If this stagey trick falsifies her body to alter her circumstances, it also reflects the practices of a cross-dressed theater, which mimics the social reality of gender even as it shows how falsifiable that reality is. This doesn't mean transvestism was inherently subversive, and Schoell is right that it worked to exclude women from social visibility and cultural expression. Yet this is only part of the story, for *Le galant qui a fait le coup* also asks its audience to imagine perverse counternarratives: biology is not destiny, male bodies can be tasked with reproductive labor, and bourgeois wives and servant girls can claim a position on top by reclaiming the role of bottom. Put another way, just as "the Western gender story" involves meaningful advances for women and repressive actions against them, so, too, does medieval mass culture deploy misogynistic tropes even as it enables opposition.

The Gender Politics of *RHOA*

The question that remains is whether a similar claim can be made of the Housewives franchise. Does a modern mass media genre that celebrates women for embracing a self-effacing role lend itself to oppositional readings? Is it possible that Bravo's heroines not only submit to oppressive, manufactured identities and norms but also expose the mutability of those identities and norms and the strategic possibilities for women that lie within the household? To answer these questions, I turn to an iconic scene from *RHOA* in which the Housewives achieve spectacular advantage over their male costars using theatrical conceits that recall women on top and farce heroines. To do justice to *RHOA*'s cultural specificity, however, I first consider the differences between European American and African American households and reflect on how Black female signifying practices have been shaped by sexism and racism.

The first thing to acknowledge is that the household model Hartman views as typical of the West and as a mixed site of female subordination and emancipation applies principally to white women for most of American history. Enslaved women could hardly have imagined a story like Malaperte's: they weren't seduced by their masters but raped by them; they didn't negotiate with their mistresses but labored for them as property; and whatever hopes they had of security in marriage and children, those were often dashed by family separation. This isn't to say that African Americans lacked stable household patterns or that those patterns differed wildly from mainstream ones. Donna Franklin cites evidence that enslaved people achieved domestic stability despite precarious circumstances and formed companionate marriages and nuclear households whenever possible.[26] Moreover, slave marriages were characterized by mutual dependence, as women and men "were rendered equally powerless during slavery."[27] Emancipation introduced new forms of patriarchal repression, however, notably under the influence of federal agencies, which sought to bring Black families into conformity with white norms. Government intrusion proved especially pernicious when African Americans migrated to Northern cities. Women were obliged to work in domestic settings that paid poorly and perpetuated racist labor models, men struggled with unemployment and hostile law enforcement, and welfare agencies used "unsuitable home" policies to deny benefits to already disadvantaged households.[28] The Moynihan Report of 1965 blamed Black families for their own poverty, urged Black men to impose patriarchal authority on their wives, and contributed to "historic tension between black men and women in the public sphere."[29] With the rise of the New Right and Clintonian centrism, Black women were targeted by sexist and racist initiatives labeled "welfare reform" or "family values" and were deprived of entitlements and opportunities. Even in Atlanta, which "has been viewed as a mecca of economic empowerment, . . . blacks residing in ghetto neighborhoods were shut out of the emerging job markets" thanks to inadequate government support.[30]

While the Housewives belong to the city's elite, this history is unquestionably part of their lived experience; for the show (like the franchise) is less about inherited privilege than aspirational claims and self-fashioning. For *RHOA* cast members, this includes reappropriating the role of housewife, which Black women have long been denied, as well as myths of Southern gentility, which are historically inseparable from racist oppression. Reappropriation is not simply a question of imitation, however, but of the parodic forms of repetition that Robin Boylorn calls "ratchet respectability": a fusion of "upper-class white stereotypes" (affluence, privilege, luxury consumption) and "working-class black [ones]" (coarse language, lewd behavior, verbal and physical aggression).[31] For Boylorn, the politics of this fusion are a mixed bag. On the one hand, "ratchet behavior is linked to the ghettoization of black womanhood," which is shown to be "uncouth, classless, hypersexualized, and ill-mannered"; on the other, it enables women "to push back against rigid expectations of acceptable womanhood," to seize the trappings of respectability from white elites, and to reveal how "negotiable, flexible, and complicated" identity can be.[32] Ratchet respectability also offers reminders of the contradictions of Southern white femininity, which conceals sadistic brutality beneath demure appearances. With their distinctive brand of femininity, the *RHOA* stars not only stake a claim on elite status (by showing that Black women, too, can be housewives) but also show how elite status can be dismantled (by merging it with ratchetness); at the same time, they indirectly expose the violence of their history, the monstrosity of the Southern belle, and the ways in which her veiled aggression can be turned against structural oppression. True, the Atlanta Housewives don't turn their aggression against real historical adversaries but against one another in the "manufactured" conflicts

Steinem decries. Yet these conflicts have much in common with the "schooling" that, for Henry Louis Gates Jr., is foundational to African American signifying culture: practices of vernacular troping, verbal dueling, and ritual insult that not only help affirm identity and community but also prepare individuals to negotiate a racist, sexist world.[33]

In the *RHOA* scene I have chosen, the opponent is a swaggering patriarch whose arrogance provokes a range of defiant signifying responses. The scene appears at the culmination of an episode in which husbands and wives, on vacation in Mexico, find themselves debating the place of female aggression in public life and the role of men in conflicts between women.[34] When the men are alone, NeNe's husband, Gregg, confronts Cynthia's husband, Peter, for having reprimanded NeNe for uncouth behavior at a charity function. Inappropriate as such disputes may be by Peter's standards, they are precisely what generates audience interest in *RHOA*, which is therefore as much about testing norms as enforcing them. The show is also about who is able to use disagreements about norms to enhance interpersonal drama and grab audience attention. In this episode, Gregg claims that role for himself. He threatens a "showdown" if Peter should correct NeNe again rather than speaking to Gregg himself. Then, in a self-serving display of chivalry, Gregg proclaims that an injury to NeNe is also an injury to him: "Not only did you disrespect my wife, you disrespected me." Breaching his own standards of decorum, Peter responds by thumping his chest, uttering profanities, and proclaiming his right to speak to NeNe as he wishes. At this point, the women burst into the room, and NeNe demands to know what the men are arguing about. When she receives her answer, she launches her own war of words with Peter as Gregg tries, repeatedly but ineffectually, to intervene. While NeNe's intention is ostensibly to defend her husband, she also clearly wishes to deny him the right to defend her, to take back the spotlight for herself, and to assert female homosociality as the real focus of *The Real Housewives*.

She is hardly alone. Throughout the episode, the Housewives complain about the husbands' unwanted interference, specifically objecting to the patronizing tone they take in dictating norms. For the most part, the Housewives adopt the practices of verbal indirection that are typical of signifying. Like NeNe, Kenya also has grievances with Peter, who has expressed strong opinions about how she should handle friction with her friend Phaedra. Kenya doesn't air those grievances publicly, however, but saves them for a confessional, in which she simultaneously speaks down to Peter and says nothing to him at all: "Peter, if you're gonna stick your nose in our business, you need to have a pair of breasts. And since you don't, you need to stay out of our business." NeNe likewise objects when Kandi's husband, Todd, intrudes on an argument and asks NeNe to choose her words more carefully. In her own confessional, NeNe makes clear she has no intention of meeting Todd's standards of deportment, as he isn't a real protagonist: "I don't have to sweeten my delivery to make it work for Todd. I mean, who is Todd?" NeNe is especially enraged by Peter, however, as he repeatedly asserts himself as an arbiter of decorum, chiding the women to "watch what you say and how you say it" and to not "get into it." NeNe responds with a confessional in which she discredits Peter by casting doubt on his masculinity: "[He] is always in the women business," she grumbles, adding in a prim tone, "Are you Peter, or are you Patricia? Because we need to figure this out."

Obviously, this "need" carries normative force, and the claim that men should be ashamed of being seen as feminine is both sexist and homophobic. Yet NeNe's comments are more complicated than they appear. She doesn't simply humiliate Peter for crossing gender boundaries; she also stakes a claim on forms of media exposure and discursive power that rarely accrue to middle-aged women—least of all women of color—and that can only be earned on Bravo through the artful manipulation of female homosociality. Indeed, NeNe deftly expands what femininity means here, using paradoxical maneuvers that place norms of womanly submission in tension with her own unshakable ambition. To prove her value as helpmate, she rushes to her husband's side, only to push him away so she can fight for herself and seize camera time. To signal feminine propriety, she uses the confessional to avoid confrontation with Todd and Peter, even as she emasculates them and denies them the right to respond. Finally, she aligns femininity with abjection to show what men risk losing by being overly involved with women, yet she also reminds us that the only way to acquire status on *RHOA* is by manipulating the show's female-centered conventions and that men therefore have little status to speak of. Obviously, *RHOA* doesn't present us with feminism in Steinem's understanding of coalitional consciousness or collective action; rather, we see an individuated, situational response to the gendering of power. Yet there is something disruptive about NeNe's efforts to translate the norms used to subordinate her into opportunities for competitive, theatrical self-display. She also uses mediatization to expose the fragility of male power and to profit from homosocial rivalry in ways normally reserved for men. In short, she shows that the proper place for female aggression is in the public eye and that the proper role for men in conflicts between women is to stay quiet or risk alienating masculinity itself.

Unfortunately for Peter, he doesn't understand the tenuousness of his position and continues to fight with Gregg about his right to reprimand NeNe. Presumably offended at being discussed rather than addressed, NeNe leaps into action. She silences Gregg with a menacing manicured finger, then turns to Peter and warns him to correct his behavior or else: "You know I'm not gonna be disrespected. . . . Let me just say this. This what you need to do. You need to stay out of women business. You're causing fucking problems. You're the only husband, boyfriend, fiancé that gets involved in women business. . . . What we do as women is between us. You need to roll with these fellas and not try to roll with these women." When Peter attempts a lame retort, NeNe delivers a devastating final blow, which (thanks to sound effects) literally lands with a thud: "You stop trying to be a damn bitch!" Mortified, Peter sputters at the "inappropriate" comment, yet it is clear to everyone the fight is over. NeNe has won.

I don't mean to imply that NeNe's friends approve of her tactics; on the contrary, it is clear she has gone too far. Not only has she violated norms of what women are allowed to say to men, but she has also presumably triggered deep-seated cultural anxieties about the feminization of African American men, who were perceived as genderless chattel under slavery and were deemed failed patriarchs by a paternalistic federal government. Yet NeNe's victory is never in doubt, and she stubbornly refuses to back down. In the following episode, Cynthia (at Peter's cowardly behest) tries to convince NeNe to apologize, but when she does, she merely compounds the injury by repeating it: "I didn't purposely try to disrespect Peter. I just called a spade a spade. . . . I apologized because I didn't even realize that I called you a bitch. I really was trying to say you were *acting* like a bitch. I can't apologize for that."[35] NeNe's verbal dueling is so skillful it is nearly impossible to determine her meaning. Yet no matter how we parse her words, they work to empower women. If "bitch" refers to women like NeNe, who refuse norms of biddability, the implication is that men can't compete in their world despite the advantages afforded their sex. Rather than give orders, Peter is meant to take them; and paradoxically, the order NeNe gives him—to become a "fella" again and stop "trying to be a . . . bitch"—suggests that it is men who are biddable, not women. On *The Real Housewives*, husbands can't become protagonists in their own right, even as they are obliged to sustain illusions of domesticity by playing the paterfamilias. That role binds them to the households that launch their wives to stardom, and the household reveals itself to be the place of transformation Hartman describes. In Hartman's words, the household may be the "most important institution for realizing whatever measure of equality women . . . have come to possess," this despite the fact that for most of Western history, "neither women nor men consciously promoted a formal agenda of equality between the sexes."[36] It may also be a singularly vital institution for enabling Black women to seize power, despite the fact that formal governmental agendas that claim to rescue families and stabilize households have typically—and systematically—worked to disadvantage those women.

Conclusion

Of course, there isn't a formal agenda of equality on *The Real Housewives* either, and Steinem isn't the only feminist to critique the franchise's gender politics. For Jennifer Pozner, *RHOA* portrays African American women as "verbally and physically violent," degrades them "for their 'low-class,' 'ghetto' behavior," and then blames that behavior on race: "The old minstrel 'dandy' in a new gendered context, *RHOA* [implies] that all the money in the world couldn't make rich Black women civilized."[37] This reading is tendentious, however, in that it assumes a shared notion of what "civilized" means, of the role women play in the civilizing process, and of how antithetical female aggression and "ghetto" behavior are to that process. Does the arc of history bend away from the ghetto, the lower-class household, and its fluctuating, disruptive norms? Or is it instead rooted in those households, which are the real locus of change?

Adopting a long-term perspective, Davis and Hartman stake a version of this latter claim, asserting that common women have often made history by reclaiming the abject roles assigned to them, by turning the disorder associated with their sex against male domination, and by transforming domestic obligations into opportunities for self-fashioning and self-assertion. Is it possible the *RHOA* cast belongs to this centuries-old tradition? Not unlike their forerunners in northwestern Europe, the Housewives occupy the household to which they have been confined and reappropriate the normative roles they have been given. Similarly, they force mainstream culture to acknowledge and integrate without neutralizing ratchet behavior. Finally, they ask viewers to grant the same legitimacy to women's homosocial aggression that we unquestioningly grant to men's, even as we turn a blind eye to the harm associated with jock culture and warrior masculinity. Rather than dismiss *RHOA* as racist and sexist, then, we might see it as a mass cultural phenomenon that is centered on the protagonism of women of color, signals the reterritorialization of the household, and enriches the fantasy life of real women. This is how Boylorn interprets the series, arguing that "respectability politics" enables the Atlanta Housewives to lay claim to "hegemonic notions of femininity and southern sensibilities related to gender," even as they use ratchet signifying to defend their right to own—and mediatize—their lives.[38]

To be clear, I am not claiming *RHOA* is free from the racial and gendered stereotypes that proliferate in mass media and that generate stardom, nor would it be accurate to say that the Atlanta Housewives are somehow exempt from the demands the culture industry places on them, exploiting their labor to acquire audience share and advance profit motives. It is equally wrong, however, to view them as minstrels of patriarchy, shoehorned into typecast roles and manufactured scenarios whose sole function is to legitimize ruling ideologies. It is worth recalling here Sotiropoulos's claim that minstrel shows were themselves not a uniformly racist genre. Black minstrels didn't solely play "to the white desire for racist stereotypes"; rather, they "manipulated the stage mask in innovative ways that helped them forge a space for dialogue with their black audiences—dialogue that included both assertions of black nationhood and critique of the racism that perpetuated stereotyped imagery."[39] Like minstrels, the Atlanta Housewives are skilled performers, adept at deploying fantasies of bosomy, combative, ferocious femininity. The pleasure of the series is in seeing how deftly its stars use both reality and fantasy to draw attention to themselves as performers, engineer their circumstances, and organize a mass cultural phenomenon around a population the dominant culture routinely dismisses or overlooks. This isn't to say that feminists should embrace strategic cooptation, but rather that historical change has often resulted from it, especially in situations of ideological constraint. With due respect to Steinem and Pozner, my conclusion is that the Housewives—and before them, farce heroines like Crespinete and Malaperte—show us that women bound to, or defined by, the household and its norms nonetheless contribute meaningfully to the shaping of history, and that the pairings of submission and defiance, respectability and ratchetness, can be potent strategies for acquiring historical agency.

Notes

1. Gloria Steinem, interview by Andy Cohen, *Watch What Happens Live*, season 12, episode 195. Bravo TV, December 2, 2015.
2. Glymph, *Out of the House of Bondage*.
3. Sotiropoulos, *Staging Race*.

4. Lucken, "Woman's Cry," 152.
5. Lucken, "Woman's Cry," 162.
6. Schoell, *La farce du quinzième siècle*, 82–93.
7. Mazouer, *Le théâtre du Moyen Âge*, 358.
8. Davis, "Women on Top," 124–51.
9. Davis, "Women on Top," 135–36.
10. Davis, "Women on Top," 140.
11. Davis, "Women on Top," 143.
12. Davis, "Women on Top," 143, 144.
13. Davis, "Women on Top," 144–45.
14. Davis, "Women on Top," 145.
15. Davis, "Women on Top," 145, 146.
16. Upcoming parenthetical citations refer to line numbers in *Le galant qui a fait le coup*, 309–66. Translations are mine. While it may seem odd to refer to a sixteenth-century work as medieval, it is common to do so, as the genre was deeply rooted in medieval culture and was repudiated by Renaissance humanists.
17. Members of the lower classes often entered into domestic service as a means of social advancement, notably through ambitious marriages. See Fairchilds, *Domestic Enemies*, 58–61, 79–80, 85, 92, 98–99.
18. Hartman, *Household and the Making of History*, 31, 11.
19. Hartman, *Household and the Making of History*, 48.
20. Hartman, *Household and the Making of History*, 130, 131.
21. Howell, *Marriage Exchange*, 233.
22. Hartman, *Household and the Making of History*, 101.
23. Hartman, *Household and the Making of History*, 131.
24. Davis, "Women on Top," 131.
25. Hartman, *Household and the Making of History*, 206.
26. Franklin, *Ensuring Inequality*, 10–12.
27. Franklin, *Ensuring Inequality*, 31.
28. Franklin, *Ensuring Inequality*, 65.
29. Franklin, *Ensuring Inequality*, 174.
30. Franklin, *Ensuring Inequality*, 239.
31. Boylorn, "'Brains, Booty, and All Bizness,'" 28, 30.
32. Boylorn, "'Brains, Booty, and All Bizness,'" 35, 36.
33. Gates Jr., *Signifying Monkey*, 92.
34. *RHOA*, season 6, episode 19, "Mexi-Loco," aired March 23, 2014, on Bravo.
35. *RHOA*, season 6, episode 20, "With Friends Like These," aired March 30, 2014, on Bravo.
36. Hartman, *Household and the Making of History*, 273.
37. Pozner, *Reality Bites Back*, 186.
38. Boylorn, "'Brains, Booty, and All Bizness,'" 36.
39. Sotiropoulos, *Staging Race*, 2.

Part II   **Consuming Bravo**
....

Whereas part 1 considered the ways that individuals perform their identities through fashion and drama, part 2 shifts to consider the things that Bravo does as a brand to solidify its following. Viewers consume executive producer and face of the network Andy Cohen as avidly as they do the shows, creating a dynamic synergy between viewers, Bravolebrities, and production that influences story arcs and the intensity of the fandom. Bravo and *The Real Housewives* (*TRH*) phenomenon marks an evolution in television as Bravolebrities turn to entrepreneurial projects to transcend their on-screen characters, creating an intimacy between *TRH* and fans through consumption and branding. In turn, this creates an environment of viewers hyper-consuming both Bravo shows and Bravolebrity products. Yet none of this is without criticism, as viewers want to see both Bravolebrities and Andy Cohen hold each other accountable within their personal and public lives. And with this viewer pushback come conversations and editorial decisions about how to address, depict, and respond to criticism. In this part, scholars consider the ways Bravo has navigated the passionate culture of its viewership, shaped the public's consumption of its products, and responded in particular with forms of intimate partner violence (IPV) and Bravolebrities' political ideologies and activism in the aftermath of the 2016 presidential election.

Martina Baldwin charts the success of Andy Cohen and Bravo as a brand. Bravo brokers a unique relationship among the network via Andy Cohen, cast talent through Bravolebrities, and viewers (or Bravoholics) to create immersive consumer experiences that are not bound to the shows themselves. The casual intimacy that binds these pillars of Bravo branding makes Bravo more than a television channel; rather, *TRH* and other Bravo programming stake out important spaces in television history and popular culture.

Serenity Southerland and Jennifer Fogel examine how media shapes the housewife ideal and housewifery as a consumer good from early America to *TRH*. The concept of the housewife functions as a form of gendered and cultural mythmaking to sanction certain kinds of domesticity. *TRH* excels in engineering new expertise in selling domesticity, forging a relationship between fans who look to Bravolebrities as entrepreneurial leaders commercializing housewifery. Southerland and Fogel argue that *TRH* transformed the public housewife from a figure of instructional import to a commodity itself.

As Bravo, Bravolebrities, and viewers navigate the realities of daily life, Rosemarie Jones seeks to empower survivors by deconstructing the myths surrounding IPV through network and fan reactions. Bravo programming offers unique access to the public–private divide, allowing for an intersectional discussion of IPV through feminist readings of the shows. Jones's method echoes Southerland and Fogel's discussion of the private–public dynamics of the housewife portrayal in the media while offering examples of the ways that the shows exist beyond the screen through the relationships between Andy Cohen, Bravolebrities, and viewers. Jones argues that Bravo is an essential institutional site for tackling IPV as a systemic social problem, which can result in creating new policies, funding, and awareness to support survivors.

Connecting themes from the three preceding pieces, Nicole L. Anslover looks to *TRH* as a site of contestation, battling over the line between reality and reality TV, as these categories seemingly collapsed on each other during and after the 2016 presidential election. Anslover contends that *TRH* holds political relevance, as the characters and story arcs reflect the political pulse of the nation from this period. In the multilayered viewing and viewer experiences that Bravo provides, *TRH* becomes a lens through which to analyze the emotions, political ideologies, and political participation surrounding the Trump era. As the line between reality and reality TV collapsed, tracing Bravolebrities' connections to Trump, personal and political tensions within casts, and viewer desire to know individual Housewives' stances on candidates, Supreme Court nominations, police brutality, and Black Lives Matter became an increasing matter of importance. In turn, this drove insightful cultural conversations among Andy Cohen, fans, and cast members.

5 The Bravo Brand

Andy Cohen, Bravolebrities, and the Bravoverse

MARTINA BALDWIN

In March 2023, #Scandoval dominated mainstream news media and popular press. The trending topic erupted when it was exposed that Tom Sandoval of Bravo's *Vanderpump Rules* was having an affair behind the back of his partner of nine years, Ariana Madix, with close friend and fellow castmate Rachel Leviss.[1] News of the affair and subsequent breakup of Tom and Ariana became national news, covered by NPR, CNN, and everything in between. Because this secret was uncovered *while* the tenth season of the show was airing, ratings reflected the widespread obsession with the show and its cast members. Not only did season 10 of *Vanderpump Rules* reach 11.4 million average viewers, but the first episode of its three-part reunion drew 4.6 million viewers, making it the most watched Bravo episode of any series in nearly a decade.[2] Despite #Scandoval creating such a sensation that the channel and the show became watercooler fodder in a time when mass culture struggles to exist, Bravo didn't *need* #Scandoval. After reaching stable popularity in the early aughts and maintaining steady success since, Bravo has proven itself an exemplar of branded entertainment in contemporary television.

This chapter situates Bravo, a niche reality television–based product of the cable boom in the early 1980s, as a uniquely successful contemporary channel, which has proven to hold the attention of its devoted viewers. While the channel employs a myriad of strategies that contribute to its success in a competitive, changing television landscape, this chapter focuses on what I view as the nucleus of Bravo's branded identity: Andy Cohen and his show *Watch What Happens Live*, and the Bravolebrities' social media and entrepreneurial undertakings.[3] Together, the role of Cohen as the face of Bravo and the outside-the-show labor of the (mostly) women cast members that make up Bravo's programming create the content—on television and online—for the channel's insatiable viewers. Indeed, Bravo has nurtured a viewership whose devotion warrants a weekend-long convention aptly titled BravoCon, which has been held three times over the last five years, most recently in Las Vegas, Nevada, in November 2023.[4] And although an enthusiastic fan base does not alone equate to financial success in the television industry, Bravo is an outlier within the contemporary cable landscape and a proven pop culture phenomenon with staying power. In a moment when the subscription video on demand (SVOD) takeover, the demise of traditional cable bundles, and too much "good" television are at the forefront of conversation, Bravo has harnessed reality television to reinvigorate a relationship among content, social media, and fandom.

Television Today

As media have converged and platforms have expanded their offerings, it has become increasingly difficult to define television. For our purposes, television is composed of the traditional model plus series (as opposed to movies) found on SVOD offerings. The traditional television model, through which Bravo found its beginnings and sustains its primary presence, includes broadcast, cable, and even premium channels (HBO, Showtime, Starz). SVOD offerings include any streaming service, application, or website that allows for on-demand viewing, including Hulu, Netflix, Amazon Prime, Discovery+, Peacock, and Paramount+. Although Bravo has found its footing on traditional cable television, the launching of Peacock by its parent company, NBCUniversal, has given the channel the opportunity to expand its presence by offering exclusive seasons, series, and bonus episodes on the platform. With the seemingly never-ending stream of content available wherever you choose to consume it, Bravo's steady growth is unusual.

In a speech to the Television Critics Association (TCA) in August 2015, John Landgraf, CEO of FX Networks and FX Entertainment, labeled our contemporary televisual era "peak TV," wherein "good" television in America has become so widely available on traditional and SVOD platforms that it is difficult not only to create compelling original content but also to ignite any sort of excitement around programming.[5] He argued that the current rate and quality of production was not sustainable and that, as a result, original television content would begin to decline in 2016. More than a half decade later, we know that Landgraf was only half wrong. As recently as the end of 2021, new series were still increasing year after year; in 2022, new series fell by 2 percent, for a total of 248 new series produced over the year.[6] However, it *has* become harder for networks and channels to stand out and compete with their most formidable opponent to date, SVOD platforms. For the first time ever, in July 2022 SVODs captured more viewers than both cable and broadcast TV.[7] While SVODs have outperformed broadcast before, claiming higher numbers than broadcast *and* cable in the same month was a new feat. Shortly after this milestone, Landgraf addressed the TCA in January 2023 and, while admitting he'd been wrong in the past, declared 2022 as the new "peak," marking a downhill slide in the amount of original content produced, asserting, "We see a strong indication that we'll see decline in 2023."[8]

Furthering the negative outlook for traditional television, the death of "the TV hit" and a resulting lack of a common culture has been declared. As defined by Steven Zeitchik, the TV hit is "a universally recognized show that gathers a large, verifiable audience and becomes unavoidable in all the places people talk about television and endures well beyond its run."[9] Zeitchik argues that our niche television culture, in which only relatively small numbers watch even the most successful (as decided by ratings) shows, makes it difficult to have any type of common culture—that is, for viewers to unite based on common interest. For Zeitchik, ratings (including some delayed viewing via SVOD) equate to a reliable audience that is, in theory, talking about a particular show. The oversight embedded in this formula is that it doesn't account for the audiences that are watching and engaged enough to comment/share/like social media posts, listen to recap podcasts, and create fan accounts—all efforts that gain the cast members and the shows traction in the mainstream popular and trade press. What the equation of ratings equals success misses is that in our contemporary digital moment, there is more than one way to create a common culture and become a "hit."

Between declaring the second beginning of peak TV and arguing that television has gone beyond its ability to create common culture, the future of traditional television is intimidating. Landgraf's shifting of the goalposts reflects the perpetual worry broadcast and cable models have around the SVOD takeover, but it also demonstrates the resilience of the television landscape; eight years later we're *still* at the beginning of the end. For a traditional cable channel model, one that FX and other competitive cable channels like Bravo abide by, the paranoia makes sense. A downturn in original programming leads to fewer opportunities for ratings success, a lack of advertising revenue and interest, and ultimately a dip in revenue for the channel and its parent conglomerate—it's bad news. Contrary to Landgraf's claim, however, Bravo has continued to reliably produce original brand-building content to air on traditional cable and through NBCUniversal's (its parent company) streaming compliment, Peacock. The continual predicted demise, coupled with the increasingly competitive and crowded televisual environment, makes the success of a niche cable channel like Bravo even more curious. Very rarely does a Bravo airing reach even 1 million live viewers. Still, the channel has built a loyal fan base, continually provides fodder to the popular press, and maintains online attention that feeds growing numbers of fan-created social media accounts and recap podcasts.

If television in the third decade of the twenty-first century is defined by a lack of original programming, the death of "hits" that provide shared experience and culture, and a continued preference for on-demand over live, linear viewing, Bravo is an overlooked standout. Because both Bravo and its content are often written off as lowbrow, formulaic, non-complex, feminine, and queer, the channel and its brand are continually left out of the conversation around influential players in today's televisual landscape. By traditional Nielsen standards, Bravo performs respectably and was ranked twenty-third (out of a possible 159) among the most watched networks of 2022, and eleventh among the fifty top-rated networks of 2022 (according to adults 18–49).[10] By less traditional standards, Bravo has created a uniquely lucrative niche brand that is affectionately referred to as the "Bravoverse," led by executive/host/celebrity Andy Cohen, made up of original content featuring "Bravolebrities," and supported by "Bravoholics" (viewers) who are so engaged, that the channel is able to host a three-day audience-focused convention featuring the breadth of its programming and talent.

Andy Cohen and *Watch What Happens Live*

While some aspects of the channel's success are comparable to those of other cable channels, Andy Cohen—a former channel executive turned brand icon and late-night talk-show host—is distinctive to Bravo. No other network executive has ever cultivated the popular on-air presence that Cohen performs for fans of the channel. No other cable, broadcast, or premium channel today has an "Andy Cohen," and he is assuredly one of the most integral facets of Bravo's brand. As an openly gay man, Cohen teases that part of his popularity on Bravo comes from playing the part of a stereotypical gay man: "Every woman needs a gay best friend to hang out with. I play that role."[11]

Cohen's identity as the only openly gay late-night talk-show host in America seemingly provides him with a cover to make and ask otherwise inappropriate, forward, and even offensive comments and questions. Presumably viewed as less threatening because he is not sexually or romantically interested in the women he interviews, Cohen leverages his identity to encourage cast members to speak to him as if he were one of the girls. For example, Cohen consistently comments on cast members' appearances—from complimenting their breasts to asking if they've recently lost weight or had plastic surgery—and is almost never met with resistance. I highlight this type of interaction because it reflects another way in which Cohen is unlike any other host on television. It is hard to imagine other late-night hosts, such as Jimmy Kimmel, Jimmy Fallon, or Seth Myers, complimenting a guest's breasts or inquiring about plastic surgery procedures. Social mores, especially in an environment that is increasingly aware of the ways men use power over women to fulfill sexual desires, dictate that self-identified heterosexual men asking those types of questions are actively engaging in sexism and harassment. In many ways, Cohen's identity as a gay man brings a level of privilege and intimacy to the revealing conversations he has with female cast members.

Outside Bravo, Cohen has appeared as himself on various television comedies (HBO's *The Comeback*, Hulu's *Difficult People*), been impersonated on *Saturday Night Live* (1975–present), donned the cover of numerous magazines, been a guest editor for *Entertainment Weekly*, published four bestselling memoirs, and created his own Sirius XM radio channel, which debuted in fall 2015.[12] Although Cohen stepped down from his position as head of development for Bravo in 2013, he maintains his presence on the network as an executive producer and host of *Watch What Happens Live* (*WWHL*), host of all series' reunion episodes, and executive producer for all iterations of *The Real Housewives* franchise.

WWHL is the only live late-night talk show of its kind, allowing interaction with viewers over social media and by video call. Modeled after Cohen's own apartment den, *WWHL* is made up of kitschy games Cohen and his staff design, segments that dissect popular culture, some of the most casual and unique celebrity interviews on television, and a nightly drinking game guided by a secret word only the audience knows. Indeed, the collective vibe of *WWHL* is campy, as is Cohen's persona as he interacts with and mediates the channel's programming. "Camp," as Susan Sontag defines it, is an aesthetic that creates "a vision of the world in terms of style—but a particular kind of style. It is the love of the exaggerated, the 'off,' of things-being-what-they-are-not."[13] Even *The Real Housewives*, with its over-the-top personalities and editorial techniques that let viewers in on the joke, portrays a certain camp aesthetic, which is then emphasized via Cohen and

WWHL. Guests of the show include Bravolebrities from almost every program the channel produces, as well as contemporary celebrities ranging from *Saturday Night Live* cast members to A-listers like Sarah Jessica Parker and Jerry Seinfeld. Starting out as a once-a-week program, then moving to two nights a week, and ultimately achieving five nights a week in its fifth season (January 2012), the show was awarded the ranking of highest-rated late-night ad-supported cable talk show in 2019 among women between the ages of eighteen and forty-nine.[14]

Produced live from a SoHo studio in Manhattan and dubbed by Cohen as the "Bravo Clubhouse," *WWHL* interacts with its viewers (in Eastern and Central time zones) via video calls and social media, something none of the prerecorded late-night shows have the ability to do. Since it is only a half-hour program, *WWHL* does not feature the typical opening monologue, but it does provide all its viewers with more reality television cast members than any of its competitors. Further contributing to its uniqueness, *WWHL* features an on-set bar that serves guests, audience members, and Cohen during the show. Beginning in the 2014 season, a live-streaming *WWHL* After Show became available through Twitter, as well as next day via YouTube and the *WWHL* companion site.[15] Although the After Show is short (typically 4–10 minutes), viewer questions and a casual interview format extend the show without the commitment of filling a longer time slot.

One of *WWHL*'s most important roles is to provide updates to the current rotation of programs, which are usually filmed six months to a year prior to being aired. As an example, if *WWHL* follows a new episode of *The Real Housewives of Beverly Hills*, at least one of the guests will be from the cast. If the episode that just aired featured a storyline in which the cast member who is on *WWHL* was arguing with another castmate, the state of their collective relationship will be a topic of discussion. The cast member in the hot seat will then let Cohen and the audience know whether the two have made up or are still on the outs, or if viewers will just have to "watch what happens"—the most popular and coyest way to answer the question without revealing information that may ruin upcoming storylines. This aspect of the show allows Bravo to offer yet another way, in addition to its social media presence and those of its cast members, for fans to stay up to date with every detail of cast members' lives, with Cohen at the core.

WWHL not only exists to promote the channel and its programming but also works to establish Cohen as a star. Cohen serves as the gatekeeper on the show by appearing to filter audience questions (which are vetted by producers) and pose them to his guests on the spot. Furthermore, as he mentions often on the show, viewers expect Cohen to ask the questions audience members want to know the answers to; he is their mouthpiece, the *show* is their mouthpiece. Part of what makes Cohen likable, at least enough to watch regularly, is that he appears to be just as genuinely invested in each guest—and each detail of each series—as the viewers are. He not only shares in the enthusiasm of pop culture with the viewers, but is in the unique position to *do something* about it—to ask the questions every audience member wishes they could. Cohen acts as a surrogate for the viewers, making his guests accessible to the audience through nontraditional interviews and games. His fanboy enthusiasm and the show's open bar help to put guests at ease and keep the conversation flowing, creating an environment unlike that of any other talk show. While other networks and channels have aired recap shows (e.g., *The Talking Dead*) and reunion episodes for their most popular series (e.g., *Sister Wives Tell All*), none of these programs are hosted by someone who once served as a network executive or is a current executive producer. Cohen's tenure at the channel, his hand in creating *The Real Housewives* franchise, and his placement by the channel as the face of Bravo have cemented him as an interlocutor unlike any other and a Bravolebrity in his own right.

Cohen is also highly accessible to Bravo fans via a strong social media presence on X (formerly Twitter) and Instagram. Seeming to operate his accounts at least part of the time—a responsibility usually fully reserved for staff—Cohen interacts directly with fans and content, allowing him to always have a finger on the pulse of what viewers like, don't like, react to, and seem to ignore. Surely, he has help in this department; his assistants and employees of the production company and channel no doubt gather data and questions for him to ask during the show, of which he makes no secret. Still, Cohen comes across as having firsthand knowledge of general viewer consensus regarding everything from casting choices to storylines. In the same way the cast members of Bravo's most popular shows share their personal lives, showcase their latest entrepreneurial endeavor, and promote the show they're on, Cohen uses social media to build his own brand. He has shared the birth of his two children via surrogate, as well as conversations he's had with his toddler son, while also promoting the memoirs he's written and sharing behind-the-scenes footage of reunion or *WWHL* tapings. In doing so, Cohen and the other Bravolebrities find some autonomy outside television, but never outside Bravo.

Branded Bravolebrities

Many attribute the first "reality" series to PBS's 1971 twelve-episode documentary *An American Family*, but non-narrative television has been a part of television scheduling for as long as have scripted programs.[16] In conjunction with the widespread adoption of television during the 1950s, game shows like the popular *$64,000 Question* (1955–58) and talk shows like *The Tonight Show* (1954–present) represented nonfictional, non-narrative programming.[17] Although a popular definition of what constitutes reality programming—non-actors without scripts and no sets—does not completely match the game shows, talk shows, and soap operas that came before, these early televisual ancestors paved the way for what we know today as contemporary reality programming.

Of the genres that preceded it, perhaps none is more significant to contemporary reality fare as the talk shows of the 1980s and 1990s. In 2002, Laura Grindstaff published *The Money Shot*, wherein she discusses the emotional exploitation necessary to encourage real people (non-actors) to "perform" as guests on popular daytime talk shows. She observes, "Ordinary people are expected not just to discuss personal matters but to do so in a particular way. They're expected to deliver what I call, borrowing from film pornography, the 'money shot' of the talk-show text: joy, sorrow, rage, or remorse expressed in visible, bodily terms."[18] Similarly, most episodes of *The Real Housewives* focus on cast members' emotional conflicts, which consistently drive the narrative as well as social media buzz around the series. Different from talk shows in which each episode is self-contained, reality programming has the ability to frame and showcase the "money shot" easily for audiences through compacted storylines and strategic editing techniques constructed over a season of programming. In the case of Bravo, the buzzy storylines and emotional performances of its programs are not over at the end of an episode. Instead, social media has become an integral part of the brand building that cast members must participate in, where storylines are furthered, reputations are defended, and brand identities of both the participants and the channel are reinforced.

While many argue that the overproduced, hyper-edited narratives of the Housewives franchise exploit the women, which is absolutely true, a hallmark of Bravo is its cast members' ability to leverage social media as a tool to reclaim their narrative, create their own brand, and, in doing so, build Bravo's brand and presence within pop culture. The more active cast members are on social media and the more viral their content becomes, the larger their individual fan bases grow and the more Bravo circulates in the popular press and across trending topics. The fact that cast members harness social media for their own gain is not surprising or unique. What makes it stand out is that while they are reclaiming their narrative, they are continually adding fodder to the Bravoverse flame, creating content for social media fan accounts, podcasters, and the popular press alike. To be clear, nearly all Bravo cast members participate in the ownership of their edit through social media, which that ultimately furthers Bravo's brand, but the focus here is *The Real Housewives* franchise.

Beginning in 2006 with *The Real Housewives of Orange County*, the Housewives franchise now features nine active iterations of all-women cast members, including many women of color.[19] Participants and viewers alike are aware that reality television requires surveillance, and that no matter how carefully staged or humbly "authentic" a cast member presents themselves during filming, how their constructed televisual persona is ultimately represented is completely outside their control. Producers during filming and editors in postproduction make strategic decisions to craft storylines; highlight conflict, competition, and hypocrisy; manufacture heroes and villains; and so on. The editing process dissolves these women's representational sovereignty, placing them on the wrong end of an obvious power imbalance while making them beholden to the network, the production company, and even the audience. It is a purposeful strategy the industrial apparatus of reality television uses to reduce each cast member to their role within strategically manipulated narrative that will be packaged to attract a particular audience demographic (and, by extension, an advertiser), which can then be sold to benefit the network.

Reality television is viewed primarily as entertainment, and the degree to which it perpetuates and disguises surveillance is often overlooked.[20] Furthermore, viewers of reality television are required to partake in said surveillance, passing judgment on real people who have chosen to have their extraordinary lives filmed and packaged for mediated consumption. As Sears and Godderis contend, "The very nature of reality TV programming presents the audience with the opportunity to judge the actions of those who are being watched and encourages these audience members to take up the position of surveillant."[21] Surveillants of reality television, then, are those who take pleasure in watching the surveilled subject who knows they are being surveilled.

Foucault's seminal theorization of the panopticon reminds us that surveillance is always strategic and rooted in power. For Foucault, surveillance that encouraged good behavior based on the belief of always being watched and the ever-present fear of being disciplined for misbehaving was a tool of social regulation.[22] On *The Real Housewives*, cast members are cognizant that they are always being watched, on air and online, and are acutely aware that their "good" behavior is rewarded through contract renewal and increased popularity among viewers, and are undoubtedly fearful of discipline—being fired from the franchise or being rejected by the audience. Indeed, the power dynamics at work within the franchise are obvious. The women of *The Real Housewives* are cast for more than the purpose of acting out their extraordinary lives in front of cameras; they are ideologically meant to be objects of each other's gaze, as well as objects of the gaze of the producers and audience, and are acutely aware of the power of the surveillance they have agreed to and benefit from.

In reality television, cast members' knowledge that their behavior is continually surveilled encourages them to behave in ways they feel will maintain their importance within the series, both with production and viewers. Cast members' behavior is rewarded by becoming part of recurring storylines, which, in turn, preserves their relevance and allows them to reclaim part of the power they may have lost by way of entrepreneurial endeavors. What's unique to Bravo, however, is the way that motivation to build one's brand actually builds that of the channel. The emotional labor performed by cast members and surveilled by the network, production, and audiences alike pays literal dividends in terms of their ability not only to up their own fame quotients but also to publicize and sell the myriad product lines they have created, including clothing, makeup, shoes, handbags, perfumes, beauty products, bedding, advice books (particularly in the realm of diet and exercise), memoirs, cookbooks, wines and spirits, food, and workout accessories.

To create a commodified image for themselves, the women must strategically work to create a brand that is both attractive to audiences and maintainable in the long term. This notion is supported in Alison Hearn's work on the branded self when she argues, "The personae developed on reality television are often strategic choices made by the contestants, intended to persuade the camera, the producers, and the audience of the personal brand's viability."[23] Although the women don't have control over the way they're ultimately represented on-screen, watching even one season of the series reveals the obvious way many of the women who are returning cast members play *into* the representations they have been given by the editors. In purposefully playing the role production has created for them, the women solidify their job security and thus the cultivation of a brand that can ultimately result in capital, a reclamation of identity, and at least some power. Moreover, social media has become a lucrative platform the women can harness, a place where the strategic choices they make help to publicize their brand and persuade the audience to literally buy into it. As Hearn also notes, "Branding is a distinct form of marketing practice, intended to link products and services with resonant cultural meanings through the use of narratives and images."[24] Through a thoughtful curation of images, short videos, tweets, and more, the women are able to showcase their branded products and build their personal brand. In other words, they are able to embrace the identity and narrative Bravo has created on their behalf, use it to generate profit, and gain at least some control over the commodification of their person. What goes less noticed is that the branded identity created is intertwined so inextricably with Bravo that both the cast member and the channel win when the women are successful.

As an example, on *The Real Housewives of Beverly Hills*, actress and television personality Lisa Rinna was labeled and portrayed as a "pot stirrer" from the start of her time on show. Despite having hundreds of hours of footage to choose from each season, including scenes focused on her daughter, marriage, professional endeavors, and acting jobs, editors consistently chose to edit in a way that would ultimately depict Rinna as a big mouth who confronted others easily, couldn't keep secrets, and said exactly what she was thinking. Throughout her tenure on the show, Rinna questioned a fellow Housewife's sobriety, gossiped about her off-screen arrest, and confronted family members about enabling her destructive behaviors; accused another cast member of faking a chronic illness as a form of Munchausen syndrome; and insinuated that another cast member engaged in recreational cocaine use. Rinna continued to act as a pot stirrer throughout the eight seasons she appeared on the show, embracing her edit and providing production with the footage they needed to continue to present her that way, ultimately cementing her spot on the show.

Famous—or infamous—for her catchphrase "Own it, baby!" Rinna very obviously pandered to production by acting as a very reliable source of drama and conflict. Rinna is also known for her large, cosmetically altered lips. Parlaying her reputation as someone whose big mouth has gotten her into trouble time and time again into a company, she launched Rinna Beauty in 2020, a luxury makeup brand with only one product: lip kits. In the "About Us" section of the company's site, a letter from Lisa provides a rationale for the brand, opening with the line: "Rinna Beauty is not just a brand. It's me."

Embracing her edit and reclaiming some power over her reputation and persona through the acquisition of capital via her branded identity, Rinna harnessed her mediated identity to transform her fans into customers.

In addition to press coverage and social media publicity, the women have also learned to leverage their own screen time to their advantage. Within each season, many storylines revolve around cast members' businesses, products, or fundraising efforts. In fact, despite the entire most recent season of *The Real Housewives of Beverly Hills* revolving around the legal drama of one cast member, Rinna found a way to work in a launch party for Rinna Beauty that did make it to air. Indeed, no Housewife has ever launched a company or product outside of filming, and if they do, a large portion of their storyline includes the preparation for a launch or its direct aftermath: creating and attending photo shoots, conducting interviews with press outlets, or celebrating an anniversary or achievement like making the *New York Times* best-seller list. Filming these events becomes a mutually beneficial strategy that provides free advertising for the women while simultaneously giving production something to film and a venue for drama to unfold as part of a seemingly organic storyline, further meshing their branded identities and companies with the Bravoverse.

The women of *The Real Housewives* franchise—solely because of the way they are portrayed on reality television—have been ridiculed, mocked, blamed for the downfall of feminism, and attacked for their materialism and penchant for cosmetic surgery. Countless advertisers, Bravo, and its parent company NBCUniversal have commodified the women's identities and spun them into a lucrative worldwide television franchise. While their online personas and entrepreneurial ventures do not *change* the position they hold as powerless to their own commodification, the transformation of their commodified identities into for-profit self-brands that can exist outside the franchise complicate the dynamics of an otherwise straightforward imbalance. The effort to move beyond the precarious labor conditions of reality show participation, which provides the platform for notoriety in the first place, is a transformation that has the potential to create empowerment. That empowerment, however, is forever embedded within the Bravo brand.

Conclusion

As a genre-specific, multidimensional, social media savvy cable channel spearheaded by Andy Cohen, Bravo has created a functionally successful ecosystem of branded entertainment, celebrities, and viewers that has penetrated popular culture more than any of the lifestyle channels it's been grouped with, such as HGTV and Food Network, or its reality-heavy peers, including E!, VH1, MTV, and Discovery+. Even more impressive is that the channel exists and thrives within an increasingly competitive media environment, where every aspect of its success has been said to be difficult or impossible by critics and executives alike. As Marc Berman notes in his assessment of Bravo's 2022 New York convention: "One full weekend. Nothing but Bravo, Bravo. Bravo. In this immersive fan experience, where more than 30,000 people attended BravoCon (from October 14 to 16) for panels featuring the franchises' stars and photo opportunities with them, NBCUniversal has found a way for Bravo to stand out in the crowd. In today's era of 'Peak TV,' where finding an audience is a growing challenge, this is certainly no easy feat."[25]

BravoCon alone does not prove that Bravo has the most viewers, or that it's even the most successful niche cable channel. What it *does* undoubtedly demonstrate, however, is that at a time when television consumption is classified by fractured, on-the-go à la carte viewing habits, its viewers are watching or are familiar with close to everything the channel offers. Many long-running franchises, like *The Bachelor* and *90 Day Fiancé*, have dedicated viewerships, but very few would self-identify as an ABC or a TLC enthusiast. BravoCon makes it clear that tens of thousands of attendees are fans of *Bravo*. The November 2023 convention alone held in Las Vegas boasted more than 25,000 attendees, generated more than $13 million in ticket sales, and resulted in 56 million social media engagements.[26]

To attend BravoCon is to attend a full-on fan convention, with attendees dressed head to toe in intertext only devoted watchers can decode.[27] From immersive brand experiences to photo opportunities with cast members to panels featuring superstars from different series to an entire hall dedicated to Bravolebrities selling their wares, BravoCon is branded entertainment on steroids. Every wall of the Caesars Forum Conference Center was covered in quotes, pictures, and memorabilia from all the channel's most popular series, including *The Real Housewives, Below Deck, Summer House, Vanderpump Rules, Southern Charm*, and *WWHL*. In addition to the channel's branded content dressing every square inch of real estate, BravoCon was heavily sponsored with more than 160 brand participants, including DoorDash, Wendy's, Wayfair, Ulta Beauty and Clorox.[28] Beyond the typical signage and promotional coupons/pamphlets, the brand sponsorships at BravoCon were purposefully integrated into the Bravoverse through the adoption of the channel's intertext in the form of pop-up experiences. For

The Bravo Brand   119

example: "Clorox leaned into the idea that 'Housewives' stars 'have their messiest moments and take selfies.' And so the cleaning brand built its sponsorship in the venue's bathrooms. The activation included housewives trivia on the stalls, content via QR codes, shopping offers and giving out thousands of samples of Clorox disinfecting wipes; outside the bathrooms, Clorox also sponsored panels and worked with talent on social media campaigns."[29]

One of the most unique things about BravoCon was the sheer joy attendees were visibly experiencing as a result of participating in this shared culture. As Jamie Cutburth, executive vice president of Creative Partnerships at NBCUniversal, observes, "I think this is the best place in the world for these fans to be. This is what's bringing them together. This is their most amazing, happy place."[30] As a reminder, Steven Zeitchik argues that our niche television culture is devoid of "hits," and that since small numbers of people watch even the most successful shows, any type of common culture for viewers to unite around is a rarity. With even a relatively small chunk of the television audience, Bravo has created an ecosystem of branded entertainment to which its viewers are loyally devoted.

At a time when on-demand streaming services are taking viewers' attention away from their traditional cable subscriptions and fictional original programming is at an all-time competitive high, Bravo's success is worthy of attention. Fully reliant on unscripted reality fare, the channel continues to find success when many critics predict the end of reality programming *and* traditional cable. Because television plays such a significant role in our culture and economy, studying its success stories is imperative to understanding the industry's modern function. By establishing Andy Cohen as the face of the channel and a Bravolebrity, and through leveraging the online activity and entrepreneurial undertakings of its cast members to continually expand its own brand, Bravo is in a branded Bravoverse of its own.

Notes

1. *Vanderpump Rules* (2013–present) is a spin-off of *The Real Housewives of Beverly Hills* (2010–present).

2. Selome Hailu, "Thanks to #Scandoval, *Vanderpump Rules* Season 10 Hits 11.4 Million Viewers," June 16, 2023, https://variety.com/2023/tv/news/vanderpump-ratings-scandoval-season-10-viewers-1235646782.

3. Although the term "Bravolebrity" refers to all cast members across all programming on Bravo, this chapter focuses on the cast members of *The Real Housewives* franchise.

4. The first BravoCon was held in the fall of 2019, and the second in the fall of 2022. The proposed annual convention timeline was interrupted by the COVID-19 global pandemic. Tickets to BravoCon 2019 sold out in less than sixty seconds.

5. Tim Goodman, "TCA Journal No. 6: Welcome to the Platinum Age of Television—and Good Luck with That," August 9, 2015, http://www.hollywood reporter.com/bastard-machine/golden- age-tv-best-tv-814146.

6. Peter White, "Peak TV: 599 Original Series in 2022 but FX's John Landgraf Predicts Decline," January 12, 2023, https://deadline.com/2023/01/peak-tv-599 -original-series-in-2022-but-fxs-john-landgraf-predicts-decline-1235220147.

7. Wynne, Davis, "Streaming Outperforms Both Cable and Broadcast TV for the First Time Ever," August 18, 2022, https://www.npr.org/2022/08/18/1118203023 /streaming-cable-broadcast-tv.

8. White, "Peak TV: 599 Original Series in 2022 but FX's John Landgraf Predicts Decline," January 12, 2023.

9. Steven Zeitchik, "The TV Hit Isn't Just Dying—It May Already Be Dead," June 22, 2021, https://www.washingtonpost.com/business/2021/06/22/tv-hit-isnt -just-dying-its-already-dead.

10. Michael Schneider, "Most-Watched Television Networks: Ranking 2022's Winners and Losers," December 29, 2022, https://variety.com/2022/tv/news/most -watched-channels-2022-tv-network-ratings-1235475170.

11. Ronald Grover, "It's Andy Cohen's Reality at Bravo," April 7, 2011, http://www .bloomberg.com/news/articles/2011-04-07/its-andy-cohens-reality-at-bravo.

12. Ann Oldenburg, "'Radio Andy' Cohen plans SiriusXM channel," March 17, 2015, http://www.usatoday.com/story/life/people/2015/03/17/andy-cohen-new -siriusxm-radio- channel-fall/24857469.

13. Susan Sontag, "Notes on 'Camp,'" accessed September 13, 2024, https:// monoskop.org/images/5/59/Sontag_Susan_1964_Notes_on_Camp.pdf.

14. Denise Petski, "*Watch What Happens Live with Andy Cohen* Renewed through 2021 by Bravo," December 29, 2019, https://deadline.com/2019/12/watch-what -happens-live-with-andy-cohen-renewed-through-2021-bravo-1202804932.

15. Initially, the After Show was available only through Bravo's proprietary website, but it has since moved to X (formally Twitter).

16. Magder, "Television 2.0," 142–64.

17. Magder, "Television 2.0," 142–64.

18. Grindstaff, *Money Shot*.

19. The nine active domestic cities/regions include Atlanta, Beverly Hills, Dubai, Miami, New Jersey, New York City, Orange County, Potomac, and Salt Lake City.

20. Dubrofsky, "Surveillance on Reality Television and Facebook," 111–29.

21. Sears and Godderis, "Roar Like a Tiger on TV?," 183.

22. Foucault, *Discipline and Punish*.

23. Hearn, "Variations on the Branded Self," 194–210.

24. Hearn, "Variations," 194–210.

25. Marc Berman, "Fans Gather in Droves for BravoCon 2022," October 19, 2022, https://www.forbes.com/sites/marcberman1/2022/10/19/fans-gather-in-droves -for-bravocon-2022/?sh=33f3015d51b1.

26. Gabriela Barkho, "'We're Going to Get in on Every Square Inch of This Space': Branded Sponsorships Took over BravoCon," November 6, 2023, https://www.modernretail.co/marketing/were-going-to-get-in-on-every-square-inch-of-this-space-branded-sponsorships-took-over-bravocon.

27. The author attended BravoCon 2023 in Las Vegas.

28. Barkho, "'We're Going to Get in on Every Square Inch of This Space.'"

29. Barkho, "'We're Going to Get in on Every Square Inch of This Space.'"

30. Krystie Lee Yandoli, "'So Much Joy': How BravoCon Became the New Comic-Con," November 18, 2023, https://www.rollingstone.com/tv-movies/tv-movie-features/bravocon-new-comic-con-reality-reckoning-andy-cohen-las-vegas-fan-convention-1234886463.

6 Domestic Lives as Commodity

The History of Housewifery as a Consumer Good from Early America to Bravo's *Real Housewives*

SERENITY SUTHERLAND AND JENNIFER M. FOGEL

The public housewife has long existed in the consciousness of America, propelled by a variety of media texts that helped to construct its image—many of them conceived of by women. Most often in the form of books, cookbooks, and pamphlets, these texts advised women on how to establish and maintain expertise within the home, thus vaulting these authors onto the public stage and making them household names. The public housewife has gone by numerous designations throughout history, ranging from domestic science advisors, domestic economy experts, home economics professionals, and efficiency engineers.[1] Since the early nineteenth century, one of the consistent ideals for the housewife has been one of economic consumption and power in the home through decision-making in the marketplace. While the amount of power available to women through consumption—and the rates and meaning of consumption itself—have varied and shifted in significance throughout American history, consumption has been an integral component of American housewifery since the nineteenth century. In all cases, even up until today's *The Real Housewives*, this has been a very public-facing role and often vaults these women into popular personas and celebrities. Media shapes what we aspire to, and the ideal of the housewife is no different. Historical media that defines the housewife's role has long been promoted by domestic writers such as Lydia Maria Child (1802–80), Catherine Beecher (1800–1878), Ellen Swallow Richards (1842–1911), Christine Frederick (1883–1970), and Lillian Gilbreth (1878–1972). Historically, books, pamphlets, magazines, advice manuals, and cookbooks have prescribed an ideal of white and often middle-class housewifery that was restrictive in its assumptions of whiteness.

Since its inception, television has played a prominent and unique role in aspiring and affirming audiences' domestic expectations. Its narratives often focused on domestic relations, centered mostly on the idealized place of women in the home and a pervasive image of the housewife. The mythologized housewife has been immortalized in the domestic sitcoms of the 1950s and 1960s, mocked and retooled in the relevancy sitcoms of the 1970s and 1980s, and restored and modernized in the postfeminist prime-time melodramas of the 1990s and 2000s. However, the valorization of the American housewife, and by extension the nuclear family, shifted with the debut of the spectacle families of modern-day reality television, particularly docusoaps and reality sitcoms such as *An American Family* (PBS, 1973), *Jon and Kate Plus 8* (TLC, 2007–9), and *19 Kids and Counting* (TLC, 2008–15). While often pandering to the salacious, these series often edified through voyeurism the necessity of harmonious suburban domesticity and centralized housewifery and motherhood as its key component.

It was the American cable network Bravo that inaugurated a relative shift in housewifery and its connection to consumption beyond the advertisements that punctuated television programming. The evolution of the network from an indie arts channel to a "premiere lifestyle destination" populated with reality programming courted viewers by featuring series that were prescriptive of society's modern-day consumption ethics in a number of aspirational categories, from food to travel to fashion.[2] Bravo's popular reality franchise *The Real Housewives*, in particular, became the perfect amalgamation of over a half century of depictions of traditional (fictional) housewives and their associated gender roles with the essence of the old reality series *Queen for a Day* (NBC/ABC, 1956–64), come to life and augmented in a glorious high-definition docuseries set in different affluent enclaves.[3] The women of *The Real Housewives* may not be competing to alleviate some morose hardship, but like the books, advice manuals, and magazines of the past, they offer a new paradigm of commodifying housewifery.

This chapter focuses on the idealized depictions of the housewife and housewifery. Wrapped up in the trappings of domesticity, the ideal housewife is and always has been part of gendered mythmaking about women's roles in society. Ideals about women's place have held power and saliency within popular American culture since early in the nineteenth century, and it is this power of the housewife as consumer that we explore here. The American housewife's public stage has shifted dramatically from the time of early America into the 1970s to today's reality television, and yet there is the connecting theme of women's role as first, experts within the home, and second, powerful consumers outside the home. The consuming housewife is just one of many roles for women in the home and has been an ideal of housewifery from the early stages of American writers to *The Real House-*

wives on Bravo. Many aspects of housewifery have changed—household technology, the stage from which public housewives speak, the opening of the housewife ideal to include women of color, and the media types from which the rest of the world adopts or rejects the current portrayal of what it means to be a housewife—but one thing remains constant: the preeminence of the housewife's role in consuming goods and services.

As public housewives moved into the twenty-first century, the scale of consumption massively shifted toward more and more affluence, but the root of consumption and the idea that the housewife had a national duty to support the economy through her household purchases has been part of the American ideal of the housewife since Catherine Beecher's mid-nineteenth-century writings. This is not to say that the rate and style of consumption, or the security that such home consumerism promised, has always been the same. The very concept of a consumer and the dictates of a modern consumer society were only just being defined in the early twentieth century. As scholars Lizabeth Cohen, Lawrence Glickman, and Carolyn M. Goldstein suggest, the consumer was shaped, even created, by market forces in the early twentieth century at a dizzying rate.[4] Even as the consumer is a role that has shifted and changed based on historical context, so too is the housewife. Historian Catherine Hall has shown that being a housewife is "a condition which is socially defined and its definition changes at different historical moments."[5] Nancy Cott, in her analysis of women's spheres in New England, also helps demonstrate the ways in which "separate sphere" ideology was socially constructed using the ideals of domesticity, which is and always has been a culturally defined phenomenon. Women, as well as men, have been active participants in creating a "discourse of domesticity" from as early as Revolutionary America's "Republican Mothers," to the formation and perpetuation of women's spheres in 1780–1835, and the spread of essentialist ideology in the late nineteenth and early twentieth centuries.[6]

What follows in this chapter is a historical discussion about how discourses of domesticity proliferated by public housewives' prescribed expertise entwined the ideal of the housewife with consumerism. In addition to this historiography, we examine how *The Real Housewives* have fashioned the very gendered private domain of the home into a calculated opportunity for entrepreneurship and self-branding that is a result of a fabricated performance of reproducing traditional gender roles.[7] In fact, the women of *The Real Housewives* are not just providing an instructional performance on domestic skill and knowledge but are using these series as a way to brand themselves as experts in both domesticity and womanhood. The heightened version of wives and motherhood on display in *The Real Housewives* is, in essence, a pathway for capitalizing on the consumer ethos that has surrounded domesticity since the post–World War II era.

History of the Public Housewife and Consumerism

One of the first public housewives, Lydia Maria Child, gave advice that was opposite that of consumption in her 1829 manual *The American Frugal Housewife*, emphasis on "frugal." Married to struggling Boston-area lawyer David Lee Child, the financial success she found with her writings allowed her to provide basic necessities for her family. Child's economic reality set the tone for her advice to save and be frugal. Within this focus, she set up a moral imperative for a housewifery built around economy and responsibility to the nation: be frugal and you will be a good, moral citizen. "The consideration which many purchase by living beyond their income, and of course living upon others, is not worth the trouble it costs. The glare there is about this false and wicked parade is deceptive; it does not in fact procure a man valuable friends, or extensive influence. More than that, it is wrong—morally wrong, so far as the individual is concerned; and injurious beyond calculation to the interests of our country."[8]

According to one of the first in America's long line of public home figures, economy, morality, and nation become wedded: the three pillars of the good housewife. Future writers shifted away from Child's frugality and focused on logic related to productivity. Economic consumption for the good of the home and family was acceptable, and this new productivity-based logic maintained the moral imperative to consume for the good of the nation and its economy.

Never married and without children, Catherine Beecher became an unlikely public housewife when she published her *Treatise on Domestic Economy* (1841), which became one of the most well-known domestic advice manuals. Beecher was from a well-educated family, and she dedicated her life to teaching—first in Hartford, Connecticut, and then on the Ohio frontier. As a single woman, Beecher supported herself with teaching, lectures, and book publications. According to her biographer, Kathryn Kish Sklar, Beecher presaged the shift in the American housewife's significance as a consumer of goods for the sake of the economy. According to Sklar, "Not fully complete, this shift [toward consumerism] might have been far enough along to compel people to be conscious of keeping up appearances, but not sure enough of the mechanisms for doing it."⁹ In Beecher's own words from her *Treatise on Domestic Economy*, she invites her reader to imagine "two millions of the people in the United States" who stopped consuming all but those things "absolutely necessary to life and health," which would produce mass unemployment in trades, such as "manufacturers, mechanics, merchants, agriculturalists, and all the agencies they employ." Thus, consumption of what Beecher calls "superfluities," or seeming luxuries, are "as indispensable to promote industry, virtue, and religion, as any direct giving of money or time."¹⁰

Child's *Frugal Housewife* and Beecher's *Treatise on Domestic Economy* were read by New England women and informed the makeup of the genteel Northern housewife, but within antebellum America, one of the most visible yet uncredited aspects of Southern households was the labor of enslaved women. Beecher and Child focused on the housewife—a woman laboring in her home for her family, likely with minimal help from other labor sources, such as servants and enslaved women. The concept of housewifery begins with the housewife herself but also captures the entire retinue of labor in homes where extended family members, servants, or enslaved persons were overseen by the mistress of the home. Historians such as Elizabeth Fox-Genovese, Stephanie McCurry, and Thavolia Glymph have noted the complex way ideals of the nation, whiteness, and gender constructed the notion of domesticity in the South.¹¹ Thus, according to Glymph, while the vocabulary and ideology of domesticity shared much across the North and South, the implementation drastically differed in households where slaves labored to meet their enslaver's expectations while negotiating, enduring, or resisting their bondage. Consumption played a role in establishing Southern and national identity: "Women of the South's ruling class defined themselves in part by their consumption of luxury goods, from household furnishings to clothing. . . . Yet, there remained in the South, as in the North, though with vastly different consequences, a sense that the pursuit of worldly trappings undermined the larger task of building the republic and sustaining republican mothers."¹² Household consumption and violence against Black bodies were entwined within ideals of Southern domesticity in ways that permeated through Reconstruction and the Jim Crow–era South. This is best represented by Mary Ann Mason's advice manual, *The Young Housewife's Counsellor and Friend*, which was "expressly for the benefit of residents of the Southern States" prior to emancipation, yet according to the author, it needed no changes after emancipation given that it would be "easy to make allowance" for the change in labor circumstances.¹³ Indeed, well into the twenty-first century, Black and Brown women continue to be employed as housekeepers for Southern white households, in addition to maintaining their own homes.

Unlike both Child and Beecher, who discussed women's economy within the home as a signifier of religious or moral duty, Ellen Swallow Richards in the late nineteenth and early twentieth century presented the housewife's responsibilities to consume as a reflection of the scientific and technological know-how of America's women. Just as their husbands and brothers used the new technical arts and sciences of the post–Civil War to rebuild a nation as engineers and scientists, women could modernize the home and fight against disease and dust all while keeping their families fed and clothed according to the best scientific principles. Richards helped to spread this message with her many pamphlets, books, and exhibits, and even a model kitchen—The New England Kitchen—to promote the best scientific cooking tools and techniques, all in the name of efficiency and productivity.

While Richards did exhibit enthusiasm for consuming scientific and technological tools in the home, she moderated her advice to encourage purchasing only pragmatic devices and dismissed the more frivolous popular fads. Still, she found society's increased consumerism troublesome and attempted to balance her infatuation for scientific tools with a more prudent belief that the homemaker was to employ practical logic regarding the family's cost of living. In her view, uninformed consumerism failed to meet those practical standards. Elisa Miller argues that Progressive Era women working in the field of home economics pursued "disparate, and often incompatible, objectives" in that middle-class white women saw home economics as a way to contain the disorderly processes of modernity, such as urbanization, immigration, and industrialization, while African American, Native American, and working-class immigrant women used domestic science training as a vehicle for accessing economic gain, citizenship, or expression of Christian values.[14] It was during the Progressive Era that domestic science itself became an object of consumption through the purchase of advice manuals, domestic training institutes, and higher education focused on the home and housewifery.

Richards reflected on the turn-of-the-century woman's need for education about "what science might do for the housewife in her daily home keeping, in making her work both easier and more efficient."[15] According to Richards, housewives of the time were skeptical about the promises made by the "fanatical scientist," who advocated tools and techniques for science's sake, and not for the sake of the housewife's considerations regarding time and labor. "Bread mixers and washing machines were, in her [the housewife's] experience, thrown out on the dump heap, chemical foods were a delusion and new laundry powders a snare. How could she be induced to look with serious eyes upon the new century motor bearing down on her with irresistible power? How could she be rescued from sinking lower in the controlling plane and rise to her rightful place?"[16]

The housewife's duty was to lead the home with deft productivity. She should conquer the machines of industry and the science of food preparation to make her life more efficient. Consumption for the sake of status was the enemy of Richards's ideals. She cautioned against fads that had little scientific basis and only caused women to spend money needlessly, while maintaining that purposeful consumption, in service to the cleanliness or safety of the home, was money well spent: "Before a purchase is made, the labor involved in caring for it, or in cooking it, should be considered," and "There is a constantly growing temptation to unnecessary expenditure for things small in themselves and pleasant enough, but not worth while."[17] Richards's logic resembles scholar Carolyn Goldstein's definition of "rational consumption," in which an idealized version of the housewife relied on science and technology to solve practical problems.[18]

As women increasingly undertook home economics training, universities began promoting household equipment. Amy Sue Bix illustrates that household equipment and home economics became entwined at institutes like Iowa State College (later University), where by 1928, the study of home equipment was part of the curriculum. Educators at Iowa State imagined that information about household goods would trickle down to consumers, thereby transforming women's interactions with fancy gadgets so that they would be able to "look inside" and assess an appliance's value, even maintain its upkeep. Women students at Iowa State celebrated the new engineering of household technologies, initially coveting and eventually purchasing the appliances as informed yet motivated consumers.[19]

Efficiency expert and engineer Lillian Gilbreth also viewed the American housewife as a rational consumer rather than a pocketbook to be manipulated. According to Gilbreth's biographer, Gilbreth's "interventions into domestic consumption were aimed at minimizing routine household activities rather than encouraging a desire to spend."[20] Vaulted to popularity through the book *Cheaper by the Dozen* (1948), the public image of Gilbreth in the book is as a stay-at-home mother whose chief interest was ministering to the family's twelve children. This image was quite distorted from Gilbreth's own accomplishments, however. She worked professionally throughout her time caring for her large family as an engineer and efficiency expert. This is another key point to the public housewife of the mid-twentieth century: often their public image was a throwback to a more nostalgic nineteenth-century domestic ideology despite their professional commitments outside the home. In Gilbreth's case, this seems to be part personal preference and part professional strategy—she continuously supported her husband Frank and treated her accomplishments as intrinsic to his success. Yet she also endeavored professionally to contribute to her fields of efficiency and engineering. Gilbreth's looking back to nostalgic gender roles while engaging in professional work as a "modern" woman exemplifies how Nancy Cott characterizes women's involvement in the New England home as a "Janus-faced conception of women's roles: it looked back, explicitly conservative in its attachment to a traditional understanding of women's place," while promising modern results.[21] In many ways, Lillian Gilbreth represented this tradition, as did her contemporary Christine Frederick.

A home efficiency expert, advertising consultant, and consumer advocate, Christine Frederick fused the promises of twentieth-century efficiency technologies with the housewife's mission as a consumer. Her most well-known publication, *Selling Mrs. Consumer* (1929), painted the American housewife as the "quartermaster" of the home, who took charge of purchasing supplies for the "mutual organization" of her family. According to Frederick, the American woman had executed quite the accomplishment: "She has struck up a closer entente cordial and co-partnership with industry and trade (even if it is so largely unconscious), than has ever been known in the history of trading."[22] The housewife's spirit of "consumer acceptance" was essential to the booming economic prosperity of the 1920s, although increasingly throughout the decade the middle-class housewife bought these supplies on store credit and installment plans. As the economic depression of the 1930s brought the consumption of household gadgets on credit to a halt, a woman's identity as a "good" housewife was still tied to consumption. It was in the kitchen, cooking thrifty meals and devising do-it-yourself work-arounds, where women would help their middle-class family weather the economic upheaval. Once again, women's consumption habits were closely linked with a moral imperative: be thrifty to be a good housewife, and your family will weather the storm.[23]

Frederick vigorously promoted the tools of twentieth-century modernity while ironically, according to her biographer Janice Williams Rutherford, embracing nineteenth-century traditional ideologies of women's role in the home as caretakers for their families. Frederick had no qualms about using her voice as a public housewife to closely weave the identity of the consumer with that of married middle-class white womanhood. Frederick used advertising to promote modern gadgets and technology with two simple claims: they would save both time and money. As Ruth Schwartz Cowan and Susan Strasser have shown, however, increased mechanization of the home did not actually result in women spending less time doing domestic work. Technologies such as the hand-cranked laundry wringer, and eventually washing machines, certainly lightened the physical challenges of cleaning clothes by hand with lye, but for women, domestic labor was still time-consuming, although they were now engaged in a different type of work: transporting children via the station wagon (at the turn of the twentieth century) to school and practices, picking up prepared groceries, planning and preparing dinners, and maintaining spotless homes.[24]

Eventually, much of the work outlined by these public housewives would culminate in an entire ideological system after World War II. Known as the *nuclear* family, this domestic ideal became emblematic of the postwar nation-state in both political rhetoric and consumer advertising, characterized by the companionate marriage, the breadwinner-housewife dyad, and the delineation of childhood as well as adolescence.[25] The mass media, particularly the emergence of television, was influential in disseminating this hegemonic family and rarely deviated from a picture of blissful domesticity and consumption. Consequently, the housewife became a rigid archetype of conventional femininity, patriarchal subservience, and familial nurturance. While the cultural upheaval of the decades following the postwar era would test the resoluteness of this picture of womanhood and domesticity, the hegemonic definition of the housewife persists.

With the 1970s feminist movement, women intellectuals began to look on home economics with skepticism as a field that had, even if unintentionally, contributed to Betty Friedan's "problem with no name" and imprisoned middle-class women in the domestic space with their homemaking gadgets. According to Friedan, the very consumption in the name of freedom that housewives had been encouraged to pursue was confining: "She was free to choose automobiles, clothes, appliances, supermarkets; she had everything that women ever dreamed of."[26] Yet this liberation and privilege to consume for her home, according to Friedan, left many women feeling unfulfilled: they had been educated, worked during World War II, and yet were relegated to their homes in the 1950s and beyond. As white middle-class women rebelled and became part of a bourgeoning feminist movement, the figure of the public housewife and their advice manuals became suspect within women's intellectual and educational circles—an artifact of the past to be studied, rather than emulated. Thus, a gap for public housewifery advice was largely left open, and television media filled it in with domestic sitcoms such as *The Adventures of Ozzie and Harriet* (1952–66) and *Leave It to Beaver* (1957–63). However, conceptualizations of domesticity were not stagnant after the postwar era, and television was there to mark the evolution of the housewife from the 1960s to the 2020s. Still, despite any hegemonically anomalous turns of the housewife on television, one characteristic remains: the necessity of consumption practices. This is certainly on display with the debut of *The Real Housewives* in 2006, which promoted luxurious affluence, the myth of self-actualization, and hyperconsumption.

The Role of Television Media in Creating the Housewife Image

Television has long imparted knowledge or instructed its audiences on how to think about and configure domestic life. Media scholars John Fiske and John Hartley note that television's "bardic function" represents our everyday cultural perceptions, thereby "articulating the established cultural consensus and implicating the dominant value-system."[27] A confluence of economic and social circumstances after World War II led to the reaffirmation of the white patriarchal nuclear family as the dominant ideal in America, composed of the breadwinning patriarch and the nurturing mother and homemaker. This model family was a key piece of the American dream for those searching for security and stability in postwar society and the consumption ethos that permeated it. Constructed as the cultural norm, the emulation of this soon-to-be iconic patriarchal nuclear family coincided with the birth and infancy of television, which conveniently and strategically used familial imagery—particularly that of the domestic housewife—to develop and market products and values that would encourage families to mold themselves after the nuclear ideal for the betterment of the private and public spheres.[28]

Fast-forward to today, and we can see much of this same utilization of familial imagery to proselytize consumption in reality television. Many reality series focus on the "unscripted rhythms of daily life" and how domesticity itself becomes the spectacle.[29] Reality TV is not simply "real" life recorded for the small screen, but "real" life produced and constructed for the entertainment of the audience. Within the explosion of reality TV series over the last two decades, "images of 'real' family life now permeate all areas of the TV landscape, presenting a variety of representations of marriage and child rearing" that still function as a guidebook for women and domesticity.[30] However, today, this is not simply a matter of offering a how-to on domestic service in the private sphere but an industrialized mechanism of entrepreneurship through which women can capitalize on self-branding a particular domestic lifestyle.

This new enterprise of domestic entrepreneurship being sold via reality TV is on full display in each series of Bravo's *Real Housewives* franchise. The first installment of the franchise, *The Real Housewives of Orange County*, debuted in 2006 and was an amalgamation of a traditional soap opera and a "real-life" version of the ABC network's *Desperate Housewives* (2004–12). Often overly dramatic, salacious, and heartwarming all at the same time, *The Real Housewives* takes viewers behind gated communities and upper-class enclaves of wealthy housewives in a variety of American cityscapes. A highly profitable and successful television series for Bravo and its creator Andy Cohen, *The Real Housewives* angles to capture the zeitgeist of a bourgeoisie domesticity by documenting these so-called ordinary women's day-to-day lives for audiences' voyeuristic pleasure.

Television offers viewers a glimpse into the lives of others; today, reality TV not only allows viewers to enter into the confidential space of one's home but invites them to examine and wax nostalgic over the behaviors and emotions they witness. The success of *The Real Housewives*, in essence, is premised on the negotiation of gender roles and codes of femininity. Furthermore, as noted by gender studies scholar Suzanne Leonard, "The housewives' public perch grants them the access and legitimacy to turn their professionalization of wifedom into a profitable business enterprise."[31] Thus, not only has the series become an outline for a "performance" of high-class womanhood and domestic engineering, but it also now capitalizes on this instruction as a consumer product in its own right, with many of the Housewives throughout the series turning their respective domestic tips and tricks into certified cash cows. For many of the cast members of *The Real Housewives*, domestic entrepreneurship is both a form of financial independence and a valorization of consumerism and conspicuous consumption.[32]

While the premise of *The Real Housewives* is to offer up an authentic experience of bourgeois wifedom and motherhood, the performance of domesticity—though still ideologically conservative—is dispossessed of many of the traditional trappings viewers are accustomed to in sitcoms. Instead, as noted by historian Peter Bjelskou, "These women engage in extravagant consumption to acquire signifiers of wealth and status."[33] In doing so, this menagerie of women manifest domestic success through the purchasing and creation of a variety of consumer products that essentially develop into a legitimated lifestyle brand. In *Consuming Reality*, media scholar June Deery suggests that series such as *The Real Housewives* encapsulate a basic formula of reality television, that being "the privatization of private lives for public consumption and commercial profit." In fact, Deery also argues that "reality TV's contribution to a public imaginary around homes and bodies is to position both spaces within market capitalism as projects, as commodities, and as forms of property."[34] Thus, *The Real Housewives* has become an exemplar not just of television's storied history of engagement with the domestic space but also of its push toward consumption.

The series is the ultimate continuation of the postwar television landscape that promulgated the suburban housewife as the archetypal consumer. In an effort to reinforce the economic imperative of postwar consumption, the media targeted the housewife "as the main point of access to household consumption practices and the chief shopper for the family."[35] However, it was not just the idea of conspicuous consumption being sold to women but also advice about home management and care, thereby reaffirming consumption as a gendered activity.[36] This promotion of consumption as home management also perpetuated a kind of privilege afforded to women within the domestic sphere as they wisely purchased goods that could grant them more efficiency in their domestic work. Still, the advertising propaganda that touted easing the burden of domestic practices was simply a transference of consumption practices as a postwar ethos to the self-actualization of domesticity as a lifestyle women could purchase for themselves, as well as become experts at.[37]

The lives of fictional white women reified an idealized domesticity that only women could achieve. For example, *I Love Lucy* hilariously implemented a role reversal between Lucy and Ethel with their righteous husbands, leaving the two men to complete domestic chores as the ladies went to work at the candy factory.[38] The men terrorize domesticity by dropping dishes on the floor, burning iron marks into the laundry, and ruining dinner—a testament to their domestic ineptitude. A similar theme propagating the centrality of women to the domestic space occurs in *Leave It to Beaver*'s "Mother's Helper," when June Cleaver hires teenager Margie Manners to help around the house.[39] Young Wally Cleaver becomes smitten with the helper and skips track practice and doing his homework to "help"

Margie with housework. This distresses his parents, who worry that Wally should be focusing on his own work, unrelated to housekeeping—thereby perpetuating the gender-specific domestic ideology.

Whereas postwar television encouraged the consumption of goods and services to shore up a woman's domestic knowledge, today's reality television often centers on this entrenched idea of privatizing domesticity for commercial profit. Reality television series, from competition to docuseries to home and garden informational series, now capitalize on repositioning experts as "friendly guides" and "the blurring of the boundaries between media celebrity and ordinariness."[40] According to media and cultural studies scholar Tania Lewis, these so-called experts "tend to place an emphasis on domestic style and the acquisition of consumer choice-making skills." She further argues that the "domestic space is presented as a site that can be rationalized, managed, and controlled."[41] In concert with Lewis's assessment of the confluence of the domestic space as commercial enterprise, sociologist Arlie Hochschild has noted that "in the marketization of personal life, acts that were once intuitive and ordinary . . . now require the help of paid experts."[42] Thus, we have seen a massive shift in the documentation of domestic skills and advice, as well as the capitalization of "ordinary" people as lifestyle experts.

The Real Housewives franchise has become a launching pad for the self-promotion of a variety of product lines, ranging from cosmetics to cookbooks, epitomizing Lewis's observation of the "growing commoditization of information and advice whereby everyday life skills and expertise have become professionalized and incorporated into the market."[43] Hence, the "domestic goddesses" of reality television are now contemporary counterparts to the advice columnists and medicinal authorities of the previous century. What differentiates these women from commercial spokeswomen in advertisements is precisely what makes them so appealing as a new format of lifestyle gurus: their supposed authenticity. Moreover, the surveillance of the lives of the Housewives—although early on simply a measure of documentary interest—has become a finely crafted performance of self-branded womanhood and motherhood.[44] Each iteration of the franchise features Housewives "who corporatize domestic, aesthetic, and affective labors and simultaneously manage taste cultures."[45] As a result, the "housewives commercialize wifedom at the same time that they are commodified by it."[46] While this reinforced commercialization of both products and the ideological figure of the housewife was not a new phenomenon, as discussed in our historical examination of the public housewife, the immediacy of the televised medium and the combination of celebrity culture has fashioned a popular and widely pervasive image of what it means to be a housewife.

More Than Just a Housewife

Just as Judith Butler acknowledged that gender is performative and constructed as though one "true" iteration or *norm* exists, the housewife, in particular, is a cultural fiction endlessly reproduced to sanction a particular kind of domesticity—one that often obscures alternative iterations of wife and mother that might contradict it.[47] *The Real Housewives*, like many reality television series, is premised on the spectacle and eccentric to draw viewers in, yet it is finely crafted to be in lockstep with numerous hegemonic cultural values concerning motherhood and domesticity. However, as noted by communication scholar Ragan Fox, "Bravo's rendition of the homemaker gains much of its appeal by caustically stretching conceptualizations of housewives." Thus, the series and its appeal to capitalize on the iconicity of the housewife actually legitimates that the visualization of women and domestic life is simply a "performative construct."[48] These women are not just wives and mothers—and some cast members are not even either of those things; they are entrepreneurs using the artifice of the ideal housewife, as well as their own accruing celebrity, to launch savvy branding opportunities for products to educate housewives "just like them." It is not surprising that reality TV—a genre of television that has cemented the relationship between surveillance narrative and product placement—has now become populated with individuals intentionally choreographing their fifteen minutes of fame into a commercial branding opportunity.

According to media scholar David Escoffery, "On the one hand, [the domestic setting of many reality series] draws the viewer in by offering them a glimpse of the good life, giving them a chance to see how the other half lives. On the other hand, it simultaneously humanizes that other, presenting him or her as 'a regular person, just like me.'"[49] Reality TV changes the way we come in contact with so-called celebrity and, importantly, perceive the distinction between the real and what Baudrillard terms the simulacra.[50] Celebrity has always been heavily constructed and marketed to provide a clear-cut distance between the star, their "real" life, and the fans. Fan connection to celebrity was built on admission to the performance, consumption of commercial items, and behind-the-scenes access to the star. Each offered fans simulated experiences of attachment to their idols, a kind of parasocial relationship or intimacy with fame unlikely to occur in reality. Today, reality television blurs the lines between the "real" and the inauthentic, all while transforming the cultural capital earned in other areas by the Housewives (film/television, socialite society, business) into an extension of a manufactured parasocial relationship driven by the seemingly ordinary lives of these women. In doing so, the women who inhabit *The Real Housewives* become entrepreneurs, tirelessly attempting to brand and commercialize their "real" lives and redefine what it means to be a "housewife."[51]

Although it may not be labeled as such by the television industry, *The Real Housewives* is a form of lifestyle programming, one that conflates celebrity culture with a more nuanced aura of prescribed expertise in a variety of domestic areas. As suggested by Tania Lewis, "What lifestyle programming sells to the audience are not just products but ways of living and managing one's private life." In particular, she argues, "Celebrity lifestyle experts take this process one step further—embodying and enacting models of consumer-citizenship through their own much publicized and idealized domestic and personal lifestyles."[52] Furthering Lewis's analysis, it is possible to see how the twenty-first century's culture of celebrity has taken over and subsumed the traditional public housewife figure: to be a public housewife in the twenty-first century is to be a celebrity and social influencer. Instead of advertisements selling concepts of success and self-worth, messaging that internalizes domestic values is now materializing as a performance of housewifery and its trappings embedded in a reality television series about upper-class women. As a new type of commercial synergy, *The Real Housewives* embodies and engineers a new expertise in selling domesticity.

Selling Domesticity

As highlighted by Suzanne Leonard, the women of *The Real Housewives* "commercialize wifedom at the same time that they are commodified by it."[53] Indeed, Peter Bjelskou categorizes these women as "personified corporations."[54] In concert with much of today's reality television series that center on celebrities, workplace surveillance, or transformative lifestyle redesign, *The Real Housewives* has far surpassed the straightforward documentation of observing "regular" individuals in the strange yet also humdrum spectacle of navigating real life. Audiences have already been privy to the ways in which reality TV can launch entire careers and create lucrative business opportunities with the success of the Kardashian-Jenner family. While the Housewives—aside from the indomitable triumph of Bethenny Frankel's Skinnygirl—have not achieved this same level of household acclaim, the series has become singularly recognized as much for self-branding opportunities as for its overdramatic antics and interpersonal hostilities. These savvy women are not lending their name to just any product; the commodity must be fundamentally wed to their lifestyle as an upper crust and cultured housewife. *The Real Housewives*, as a series, offers a prime opportunity for women to develop a particular personality that they can then leverage in order to self-promote the products that they have identified (or loosely conceived of) as integral to performing and maintaining their domesticated lifestyle—be that wine, eyelashes, or handbags.

Whether or not we are to believe that the Housewives are so-called experts on spirits because they regularly consume alcohol (e.g., Ramona Singer's personalized Pinot Grigio) or that they possess culinary competence from decades of re-creating family recipes (e.g., Teresa Giudice's cookbooks and Kathy Wakile's cannoli kits), *The Real Housewives* has been perfected into an avenue by which women can commodify the performance of the housewife. Media studies scholar Jacquelyn Arcy defines the symbolic branding of the distinctive qualities of the housewife as "affective enterprising."[55] Although fostering the personality of a lifestyle expert is inherently common to the genre of reality television, *The Real Housewives* more fully exploits the ways in which women colonize "the realm of domestic advice" through their branded merchandise.[56] As Arcy argues, the "calculated convergence of emotional spectacle and branding occasions operates as a particularly gendered strategy that harnesses the ongoing activity, innovation, and flexibility of women's affective labor." She continues, "Affective enterprising reconfigures women's private affects into modes of capital accumulation."[57]

To illustrate just how ingrained this affective enterprising is within the series, a 2013 article in *HuffPost* revealed that "42 percent of the housewives launched their own product lines and brands," and that does not even include the two franchises to debut afterward or new cast members joining the "OG" housewives elite.[58] The stellar success of Bethenny Frankel's rise from aggrieved Manhattan girlfriend and personal chef to billionaire brand mogul is continually used to pinpoint the transition of *The Real Housewives* from narrative spectacle to vehicle for commodifying the performance of domesticity, thereby encouraging more of these women to "monetize their so-called 'personal lives.'"[59] As noted by Suzanne Leonard and Diane Negra,

Frankel's product development hinged on the alignment of her everywoman product line with her own domestic lifestyle of fitness, health, and self-assurance; thus, her message was "read in affective terms, a string of associations that lump psychological and spiritual well-being in with purchasing power."[60] Frankel, along with some of the other successful Housewives, is the new reincarnation of the domestic science advisor of the twentieth century, happily commodifying her attempts to move within society's elite while "visibly marking the social status" of the American housewife.[61]

Similar to the taste and advice manuals of the nineteenth century, *The Real Housewives* uses the documentary style format as a way to democratize consumption and class mobility, "making the role of consumption practices as a marker of taste and status even more pivotal."[62] These women clearly require high-end consumer products, can afford first-class travel, and wear couture; their luxury lifestyles necessitate consumption in order to perform as Housewives. The performance is not only instructive but also meant to be emulated. And yet the business success some have achieved is less about reifying a privileged lifestyle than it is about offering a means for all women to participate in the performance at an affordable price. Whether they are selling clothing, work-out accessories, or cookbooks, the bourgeoisie accoutrement of the "aspirational femininity" they are selling can (mostly) be had at bargain rates. For example, Gizelle Bryant, from *The Real Housewives of Potomac*, started an affordable luxury cosmetic line (Everyhue Beauty) for women of color to be sold at Target and thus be accessible regardless of a woman's budget. As Suzanne Leonard argues, the products being sold by the Housewives connect "the sort of appearance or activity that a well-heeled woman might enjoy to a marketable item that allows purchasers to indulge in the fantasy of a high-end life."[63] Although the premise of *The Real Housewives* may have initially been to observe the luxe lifestyles of upper-class women, within the past few years the women of the franchise are more set on mainstreaming their own upscale brands to "emphasize versatility and affordability."[64] The Housewives who have found the most financial success (Bethenny Frankel, Skinnygirl; Teresa Giudice, cookbooks; Kim Zolciak-Biermann, cosmetics; Kenya Moore, hair care; Lisa Rinna, clothing) have sought to marry traditionally feminine domestic necessities and maintenance with budget thriftiness, often selling these commodities at bargain retailers such as the Home Shopping Network, Sally's Beauty Supply, and grocery stores. Thus, those Housewives who have pitched, marketed, and sponsored products on the show are now as inextricably linked to pushing an affordable consumerist ethos for ordinary housewives as they are to providing the spectacular clashes between various women that is a key attribute of the series.

Conclusion: The Domestic Goddess and Hyperconsumption

In propagating a specific lifestyle of domesticity, television—whether it was through programming or advertising—distinguished domesticity as a skill that women could learn. The professionalization of the unpaid and hidden labor of housework encourages women to seek out mechanisms of compliance to a particular ideal of domesticity enacted in soap operas and sitcoms and now, reality television.[65] Although the taxonomy of domesticity, and thereby housewifery, as visualized on the television screen has changed, its prescriptive intention has not. Today's public housewife, adept at the nuances of performing housewifery and championing the consumer products and other accoutrement it entails, has largely been instigated by Bravo's brand of lifestyle reality programming. The new portrait of the American housewife is no longer epitomized by the bucolic mothers of *The Adventures of Ozzie and Harriet* or *Leave It to Beaver* or the dysfunctional but lovable "domestic goddess" *Roseanne* (ABC, 1988–97). Instead, Bravo offers viewers the women of *The Real Housewives* franchise, each a fusion of American opulence, entrepreneurism, and domestic influencer. In exchange for their own personal treatises on the professionalization of housewifery, viewers are given unfettered access to their lives.

The saturation of self-branding that now permeates the various iterations of Bravo's *The Real Housewives* has pushed the series in a new direction of hyperconsumption. In *Branded Women in U.S. Television*, Peter Bjelskou discusses the connection between the cultural significance of the term "housewife" and the hypercommercial representation that was afforded to the domestic sphere in postwar era television.[66] This "gendered connoisseur-consumer" is no longer simply an attempt to manifest traditional gender roles and conservative domestic ideology but a persona commodified for contemporary women as they seek to emulate a particular domestic ideal that continues to be the subtle bedrock of fictional and nonfictional programming. As previously discussed, reality TV and its pervasive consumerist ethos has moved audiences "beyond straightforward advertising to consuming reality in the form of commercializing and commodifying everyday life."[67] This new perception of the domestic goddess and her domestic efficiency and idealism is integrated into numerous versatile consumer products that are now created and promoted by a group of women trading on the capricious reputation of their reality TV housewife personas. Teresa Giudice from *The Real Housewives of New Jersey* transformed her Italian heritage into multiple *New York Times* best-selling cookbooks, thereby securing her family's financial future amid legal troubles. Bethenny Frankel may have sold her line of Skinnygirl Cocktails for millions of dollars in 2011, but she retained the Skinnygirl name and has since spun the brand into a variety of successful products from food to apparel. As she notes on the Skinnygirl website: "Skinnygirl is you. We believe every woman deserves to feel confident and live life free from judgments. It's not about a shape or size, it's about every shape, every size, and every woman." Kim Zolciak-Biermann may have had a salacious and confrontational persona on *The Real Housewives of Atlanta*, but her Kashmere Kollections is a luxury beauty and lifestyle brand that encourages women "to pamper yourself to a spa-like experience right from the comfort of your own home." Finally, Shannon Beador from *The Real Housewives of Orange County* managed to rejuvenate her life after a messy divorce to embrace a healthier lifestyle by launching Real for Real Cuisine in 2018, which sells on QVC. Yes, these women are clearly exploiting the surveillance of their day-to-day lives as a ploy to sell self-branded products, but reality television had already normalized these types of marketing techniques.[68]

In the end, the constellation of products being sold within *The Real Housewives* franchise fashion an expedient formulation of an ideology of the new domestic goddess through hyperconsumption. Today's wives and mothers may not necessarily be outright searching for domestic instruction as they had in the Victorian and postwar eras, but they are certainly willing to purchase the commodities that can offer them a pathway to domestic success, as well as imbibe the ideal of the hyperconsuming twenty-first century housewife. The women of *The Real Housewives* who have successfully leveraged the platform to financial success are those who understand women as "cosmopolitan consumers," seeking self-assurance and self-actualization as much as they wish to be economically stable.[69] This notion that "commodities contain value beyond their aesthetic significance" is reminiscent of early American domestic discourse that sought to teach housewives the discriminating skills of the economical archetypal housewife, whose consumption was of national importance.[70] The public housewife—no longer just a public figure of instructional import but a bona fide symbol of celebrity and social influence—has now become thoroughly commodified through the reality television format.

Notes

1. On naming and home economics experts, see Weigley, "It Might Have Been Euthenics"; Hayden, *Grand Domestic Revolution*; Stage and Vincent, *Rethinking Home Economics*.

2. Leonard, "Real Housewives of Beverly Hills," 280–81.

3. *Queen for a Day* was a precursor to traditional reality television. Women, portrayed as down in their luck in some way, competed to be named "Queen for a Day" and have their troubles alleviated by things they needed—typically some kind of consumer appliance or other materialistic desire.

4. Cohen, *Consumer's Republic*; Glickman, *Buying Power*; Goldstein, *Creating Consumers*. See also the collection of essays in Fox and Lears, *Culture of Consumption*.

5. Hall, *White, Male and Middle Class*, 43.

6. Cott, *The Bonds of Womanhood*, xxv.

7. Leppert, "Keeping Up with the Kardashians, 215–31.

8. Child, *The American Frugal Housewife*, 5–7.

9. Sklar, *Catherine Beecher*, 307.

10. Quoted in Sklar, *Catherine Beecher*, 307.

11. Fox-Genovese, *Within the Plantation Household*; McCurry, "Producing Dependence"; Glymph, *Out of the House of Bondage*.

12. Glymph, *Out of the House of Bondage*, 77.

13. Mason, *Young Housewife's Counsellor and Friend*.

14. Miller, "In the Name of the Home," 4–6.

15. Richards, "Ten Years of the Lake Placid Conference on Home Economics," 19–20.

16. Richards, "Ten Years," 19–20.

17. Richards, *Cost of Living as Modified by Sanitary Science*, 51, 55.

18. Goldstein, *Creating Consumers*, 3.

19. Bix, "Equipped for Life."

20. Lancaster, *Making Time*, 255.

21. Cott, *The Bonds of Womanhood*, 3.

22. Quoted in Rutherford, *Selling Mrs. Consumer*, 146.

23. Inness, *Dinner Roles*, 110.

24. Cowan, *More Work for Mother*; Strasser, *Never Done*.

25. May, *Homeward Bound*; Mintz and Kellogg, *Domestic Revolutions*.

26. Inness, *Dinner Roles*, 145; Friedan, *The Feminine Mystique*.

27. Fiske and Hartley, *Reading Television*, 66.

28. Television scholar Mary Beth Haralovich wrote a defining piece pertaining to the family as it was presented on television in the 1950s and early 1960s—particularly television's persistent depiction of distinct gender roles (i.e., "separate spheres" ideology). Analyzing suburban domestic sitcoms such as *Father Knows Best* (1954–60) and *Leave It to Beaver*, Haralovich explained how these series mediated the importance of the suburban housewife and "realigning family gender roles" to middle-class family life. The portrayals of paterfamilias and suburbia in the domestic sitcoms of the period instructed viewers on how to assimilate and achieve "the

comfortable environment and middle-class lifestyle that housing and consumer products sought to guarantee for certain American families." Haralovich, "Sit-Coms and Suburbs," 113–14.

29. Andrejevic, *Reality TV*, 3, 8.
30. Matheson, "Cultural Politics of *Wife Swap*," 33.
31. Leonard, "*Real Housewives of Beverly Hills*," 279.
32. Cox and Proffitt, "The Housewives' Guide to Better Living."
33. Bjelskou, *Branded Women in U.S. Television*, x.
34. Deery, *Consuming Reality*, 10.
35. Lewis, *Smart Living*, 36.
36. Bjelskou, *Branded Women in U.S. Television*, 27.
37. Bjelskou, *Branded Women in U.S. Television*, 27; Lewis, *Smart Living*.
38. *I Love Lucy*, season 2, episode 1, "Job Switching," aired September 15, 1952, on CBS.
39. *Leave It to Beaver*, season 4, episode 23, "Mother's Helper," aired March 4, 1961, on ABC.
40. Lewis, *Smart Living*, 3.
41. Lewis, *Smart Living*, 8, 13.
42. Hochschild, *Outsourced Self*, 209.
43. Lewis, *Smart Living*, 2–9.
44. Fox, "Queering *Housewives*," 13–25.
45. Leonard and Negra, "After Ever After," 200.
46. Leonard, "*Real Housewives of Beverly Hills*," 278.
47. Butler, *Gender Trouble*.
48. Fox, "Queering *Housewives*," 13.
49. Escoffery, "Domestication Incorporation," 101.
50. John Fiske interprets Baudrillard's *Simulacra and Simulation* (1985) for television, specifically referring to the way television constructs a hyper-reality, which invariably "collapses the binary concepts of reality and representation into a single concept" (2). In other words, as Baudrillard noted, we have become so reliant on the media's perception of reality (i.e., the simulacra) that the distinction between reality and representation has broken down. Fiske, *Media Matters*.
51. Silverman, *Fantasy of Reality*.
52. Lewis, *Smart Living*, 138.
53. Leonard, "*Real Housewives of Beverly Hills*," 279.
54. Bjelskou, *Branded Women in U.S. Television*, 4.
55. Arcy, "Affective Enterprising: Branding the Self through Emotional Excess."
56. Lewis, *Smart Living*, 143.
57. Arcy, "Affective Enterprising: Branding the Self through Emotional Excess," 76.
58. Lee and Kornowski, "*The Real Housewives* of Bankruptcies, Businesses and Divorces by the Numbers."
59. Leonard and Negra, "After Ever After," 196.
60. Leonard and Negra, "After Ever After," 203.
61. Bell and Hollows, *Ordinary Lifestyles*, 8.
62. Lewis, *Smart Living*, 28.

63. Leonard, "*Real Housewives of Beverly Hills*," 279.
64. Leonard and Negra, "After Ever After," 205.
65. Lewis, *Smart Living*; McRobbie, "Notes on *What Not to Wear* and Post-Feminist Symbolic Violence."
66. Bjelskou, *Branded Women in U.S. Television*.
67. Deery, *Consuming Reality*, 45–46.
68. Deery, *Consuming Reality*.
69. Leonard and Negra, "After Ever After."
70. Bjelskou, *Branded Women in U.S. Television*, 83.

7 Behind the Scenes

Housewives' Strategies for Reclaiming Control in Intimate Partner Violence Narratives

ROSEMARIE JONES

Taylor Armstrong. Bethenny Frankel. Kenya Moore. Shereé Whitfield. Stassi Schroeder. The list goes on and on. Not only are these women famous for their personalities on reality television, but they have all shared their experiences of abuse or harassment with the world on Bravo programming. While watching any of *The Real Housewives* series, it can be tempting to separate the women featured from most of society's daily realities. Their cars, personal assistants, traveling makeup and hair teams, dogs depressingly dressed in furry pink coats, and other notes of class and privilege separate their lives (and relationships) from typical social norms. However, elements of power and control within their interpersonal relationships showcase that intimate partner violence (commonly referred to as domestic violence) is pervasive across class, race, gender, location, religion, and status. Indeed, intimate partner violence (IPV) occupies a space in many of the women's lives, although they react differently to it.

Notably, it can be easy for viewers watching these programs to get lost in the fortune and fashion of the shows. However, in the deeply vulnerable moments, when cast members share their lived experiences of violence, harassment, and abuse, many viewers can find a real-world connection to the stars. In these stories, many viewers find commonalities and shared experiences. Unfortunately, the reality of IPV is that it affects a significant portion of the U.S. population. These stories may be the closest to reality many of the viewers ever witness from the presented storylines of the shows.

This chapter will provide layered case studies of intimate partner violence as showcased across *The Real Housewives* franchise and other Bravoverse series. Ultimately, the deep dive into these examples will work to analyze the range of socially constructed myths IPV survivors often navigate in an effort to protect their own physical, emotional, mental, and financial safety. Moreover, it must be recognized that these myths rely on social norms to flourish. Institutions that uphold these norms often benefit from the norms themselves and therefore have little incentive to deconstruct them. However, this chapter will argue that using spaces that have been socially constructed as "other" might be a possible venue for revolutionary change from within the system itself. That is, spaces that society often doesn't deem serious, such as reality television, may serve as a way for the public to connect with stories not told elsewhere but that still have the power to affect lives and norms.

Understanding Intimate Partner Violence and Power

Intimate partner violence is first and foremost about power. An abuser may use their power to enact control over their victim's autonomy. This power can range from visible to invisible in its expression; an abuser may use their positions of power (both inside and outside the relationship) to control their partner and limit their choices. To most fully analyze power and control, it is vital to unpack power dynamics within the relationship and social constructions of identities within broader society to more clearly understand cycles of abuse. For example, community attitudes toward law enforcement may seriously affect whether a victim calls a police agency to report abuse. Therefore, the victim may feel that their lack of power in the situation is controlling, or limiting, their options. Elements of power and control cannot be ignored or undervalued in analyzing abusive relationships. Both public and private power can be used to intimidate and control victims and must be taken seriously as a strategic abusive method to silence victims.

According to the National Coalition Against Domestic Violence, "an average of 24 people per minute are victims of rape, physical violence, or stalking by an intimate partner in the United States—more than 12 million women and men over the course of a single year."[1] IPV is a social epidemic that is heavily rooted in society's constructions of gender, which are influenced by both institutions (media, religion, educational systems, political systems) and individuals (peers, family). For example, gender norms are so deeply rooted in society that many people automatically link pink to girls and blue to boys without questioning the why behind these norms. Moreover, gender expectations are typically viewed in opposition of each other: society says that men are rational, while women are irrational or emotional; men should be strong to protect the "weaker" sex (women); and men should focus on the financial needs of the family so that women can focus on child-rearing and household organization. In other words, using a separate sphere approach, women are relegated to the private (home) sphere, while men are afforded power in the public (business, political, religious) spheres. Melissa and Joe Gorga from *The Real Housewives of New Jersey* showcase gendered roles and expectations in an extremely binary manner and map easily onto this ideology. For example, Joe pointedly discourages Melissa to open Envy, her future boutique, because it would cause her to neglect her "wifely duties." This line of thinking is reinforced when he tells her he married her to "raise [his] kids" as her primary responsibility. Coupled with discouraging her from working outside the home, Joe clearly works to place Melissa's gendered role as primarily "in the house."[2] Though these social constructs may help to organize society, they can also promote dangerous norms about who is afforded power—both in society at large and within relationships. Real-world examples showcase the importance of unpacking these dangerous norms, as they are often codified into law, formalizing inequities into the legal system.

When examining power in relation to the social constructs of gender, it is vital to understand the public–private divide. Ideologies about gender in early American colonial times "affirmed that women's place was within the realm of the family, where they were to be docile. . . . Women's domain was the home, or the *private sphere*, while men's domain was the workforce, or the *public sphere*."[3] Clearly this divide had implications relating to individuals' abilities to be autonomous. These ideas directly influenced legal policies and writings, creating a system of gendered justice. Historically, it is easy to see that women's lives, safety, and aspirations were not valued in the same regard as men's. This ideology was underscored by the Victorian construction that women needed to be protected by men, as women's morality was based on their ability to be docile, passive, and delicate.[4] There are many examples of men attempting to be protective of women in the Bravoverse. For example, Ken Todd attempts to protect the reputation of his wife, Lisa Vanderpump, when Kyle Richards is unsure of a rumor she hears about Vanderpump.[5] It should be noted that more often than not, these instances result in men working to protect their partners at the price of being hostile and intimidating to other women in the group.

Not only did these aforementioned laws fail to protect women from abuse, but they sought to condone intimate partner violence—as long as it was in "moderation." For example, *Bradley v. The State of Mississippi* ruled in 1824 that a husband could "moderately chastise his wife in cases of great emergency, without subjecting himself to vexatious prosecutions for assault and battery, resulting in the discredit and shame of all parties concerned."[6] While "moderation" was not clearly defined in the decision, the notion that *any* amount of abuse is permissible is troublesome. Legalizing abuse in moderation in an effort to control or reprimand women clearly shows that the law favored men's autonomy and personhood over women's. Additionally, it encourages men to internalize understandings of entitlement over their wives' bodies. Roughly fifty years later, *Fulgham v. The State of Alabama* (1871) rejected a husband's right to beat his wife, with other states to follow. However, abused women had little success overall in using the legal system as a means of protection and justice.[7] Rather than reducing IPV rates, it can be argued that the handling of abuse by the justice system continues to misunderstand abuse as a "private, family matter" as opposed to a social epidemic influenced by institutions and norms.

Women's movement into the public sphere during World War II encouraged a split in the public–private divide.[8] The second wave of feminism in the 1960s challenged traditional social norms of the family, paying particular attention to divorce and women's autonomy in marriage. It wasn't until 1984 that police had a responsibility to respond to IPV calls and protect the victims. Tracey Thurman successfully sued the city of Torrington, Connecticut, after police officers failed to properly protect her from her abuser based solely on her domestic (intimate) relationship with him.[9] The District Court for the State of Connecticut's decision was a major shift in understanding IPV as both a social problem and a crime, as opposed to a private dispute between two individuals that should be handled in the manner they (usually the person with the most power and control) see fit. However, it is important to note that while laws and attitudes toward IPV have changed, they are still based in socially constructed myths of who is an "ideal victim." It is important to note that the myth of the ideal victim is raced, classed, and gendered. The ideal victim is a middle-class, heterosexual, cis-gender white woman who does not use drugs, does not engage in any physical methods of defense, and cooperates with law enforcement and the criminal justice system. As a result, it is important to understand IPV through an intersectional lens, with a distinct effort to bring those on the margins into the center of the analysis.[10] Though raced, classed, and gendered, Bravo programming allows the viewer to have a unique glimpse into the often hidden private realm of the public–private divide. Such portrayal of experiences may serve to showcase how myths are made surrounding what is considered "normal" and "not-normal" in cases of intimate partner violence. The inner workings of romantic and platonic relationships are exposed and investigated, thus removing the often distinct divide created between public and private spheres. Thus, a feminist reading may argue that Bravo creates a new space that encourages the private to move public, dispelling many socially constructed myths (e.g., the myth that survivors must engage with the police to be "true victims"). Moving IPV from behind the gates of elite communities to the public realm under certain circumstances, which would notably underscore survivor-centered autonomy, may create an empowering platform for Bravolebrities and in turn Bravo fans who routinely connect with meaningful storylines. In other words, by showcasing the behaviors behind the gates of exclusive communities on the screens of everyday viewers, we may disrupt social norms that don't talk about abuse, violence, or harassment. Instead, viewers may more readily understand power and control dynamics and how to support survivors. Reasonably, after watching the complicated dynamics of abuse, viewers may better understand why a survivor "doesn't just leave." Rather, they may see the complicated layers that are involved in relationships where abuse is present; they may start to question easy answers and analyze the deeper individual and institutional dynamics of abuse.

The following sections of this chapter will aim to do just that. Each case study will not only describe the situation but also underscore how its nuances showcase the need to analyze intimate partner violence from an intersectional lens that highlights a critical analysis of race and gender, thus exposing how myths are made around IPV. Additionally, each case study will be grounded in the understanding that intimate partner violence is not always physically observed. In fact, an important dynamic in abusive relationships is the power and control the abuser attempts to hold over their partner and which is reinforced by the norms in greater society. Interestingly, even over the time span of Bravo's programming, we can examine changes in norms surrounding IPV, how survivors are cared for, and the obligations of bystanders.

The analysis provided will unpack strategies used by women to navigate social constructions and myths of intimate partner violence, and how these choices and others' reactions incorporate the myths held about IPV. For example, the chapter will explore how methods of resistance, such as reclaiming the mainstream narrative, are used in an attempt to regain the power victims often lack in relationships and to exert control and autonomy over how their lived experiences are discussed in the media. The themes of mythmaking and race and gender will be used as foundational elements to the critical intersectional feminist analysis in this chapter. The relationships between these themes should be noted: they rely on each other to thrive. The making of myths surrounding intimate partner violence is informed by social constructions of race and gender, and in turn racialized and gendered expectations are affected by widely held myths. It is my hope that the following analysis works toward highlighting the importance of unpacking mythmaking, especially in connection to race and gender, when discussing how society can better support survivors of IPV.

Taylor Armstrong: Managing the Public-Private Divide

One of the most striking examples of IPV on any Housewives franchise is Taylor Armstrong. When watching season 1 of *The Real Housewives of Beverly Hills*, it becomes apparent that Taylor's marriage to Russell won't be portrayed in a romantic sense, especially when contrasted with the pink, frill, and puppy-filled marriage of Lisa Vanderpump and Ken Todd. Instead, it is poised as a business exchange, wherein Taylor's work is belittled by her partner. In the first episode of the series, Russell asks, "So what's the latest with your little company?" Later, Taylor expresses deep concern that Russell will leave her for a "younger, better thing," but also knows she "signed-up" for this relationship.[11] Thus, from the very first episode, production sets the stage for viewers to see Taylor and Russell's relationship as a foil to Lisa and Ken's.

Taylor and Russell's marriage showcases how the public and private divide, or the separate spheres ideology, can influence dynamics within a relationship; this is a prime example of needing to understand how concepts of power and status on a macro level (societal ideologies) affect those on a micro level (interpersonal relationships). Foremost, we can see that Taylor has rooted her power in her ability to be viewed as attractive. By suggesting that Russell might leave her for a "younger, better thing," she is suggesting that her worth or value in this relationship is defined by her ability to be sexually and socially attractive in a patriarchal society. In other words, her power in the relationship is defined by Russell's (and society's) parameters of beauty. When referencing her "little company," Russell further minimizes her status as a businesswoman, and actor in the public sphere. Thus, even when Taylor attempts to exercise autonomy and power in the public realm, Russell minimizes her abilities and efforts—though the cues may be subtle. As a result, it is clear that Taylor has perhaps internalized such messaging.

Unfortunately, Taylor's summation that she "signed-up" for such a relationship encapsulates historical, social, and political efforts to victim blame and shame women in unequal relationships. And by signing up for the show, she opened her private life to the public. Viewers can assume, and are later told, that the abuse had already started by episode 1. While Taylor does not explicitly say that she "signed-up" for the abuse, she makes it clear that she did sign up for a relationship in which she is dominated and holds little autonomy or power. In fact, it may be speculated that Taylor joined the show to regain the confidence that was perhaps undermined within her relationship before filming. Indeed, emotional abuse, such as gaslighting, can lead to anxiety, depression, suicidal thoughts, and post-traumatic stress disorder.[12] As the cycle of abuse repeats and intensifies, the survivor's self-image and confidence may be negatively affected.

Feminist research argues that abusive relationships are centered around the abuser's ability to exert power over the victim in an effort to control their ability to make choices and practice autonomy.[13] Relationships in which one person holds a majority of the power and controls the movements and choices (physical, financial, emotional) of another is abusive. Clearly, it can be analyzed that Taylor's marriage is not one in which there is an equal power dynamic; moreover, her partner uses that imbalance to control her decisions. Yet perhaps a combination of normalization of abuse and internalized victim blaming suggested to Taylor that she did in fact "sign up" for the dynamics of this relationship. Although she may have known about this aspect of Russell's personality, victims do not "sign up" to be abused or stay in relationships because they enjoy being abused. Rather, they are often strategically staying with an abuser for a variety of reasons. Foremost, they most likely love their abuser; abusers are not always abusive and usually solidify meaningful relationships with their partners. Additionally, the most dangerous time in an abusive relationship is when the victim/survivor attempts to leave the relationship.[14] As a result, they need to be strategic about making this choice and often stay out of fear and the belief that they can manage their abuser's dangerous behaviors better while they are in a relationship than they would be able to after it is over.

While Taylor has shared that the abuse was present in season 1, it became more noticeable in season 2. In addition to a heightened sense of internalized self-blame, the audience is able to view how intimate partner violence often affects other relationships in the victim/survivor's life. For example, her bizarre behavior in season 2's second episode is similar to the exhaustion many survivors feel as a result of the mind games their abusers force them into. While on a trip, Taylor attempts to hide in a suitcase, admits to self-medicating with alcohol, and then has a serious discussion with Kim Richards.[15] Taylor's dynamic highs and lows in the episode paint her as unstable. This is a common trope attributed to women in abusive relationships. Abusers often benefit from gaslighting their partners and constructing them as the unstable party.[16] As a result, victims routinely have their experiences questioned. Moreover, the brain doesn't process trauma in a linear fashion. Therefore, expressions of trauma and the detailing of events are not often accomplished smoothly. Rather, they lead to jumbled outbursts after victims/survivors repeatedly try to maintain normalcy. The difficult-to-follow narrative of a victim/survivor often leads her confidants to question her situation. Taylor's perceived erratic behavior comes to a head at Lisa Vanderpump's house later in the season.

Tension on-screen—both within Taylor's relationship and among the women—builds when the simmering gossip about Taylor's abusive relationship is brought forward. Until then, the women say that Taylor has only individually told them about the abuse off-screen. However, due to Taylor's "unpredictable" behavior and narrative, they don't appear to believe her accounts. The ladies discuss their disbelief that Taylor is actually being abused, as "[Russell] has always been lovely to [them,]" so perhaps Taylor is "exaggerating."[17] This is extremely problematic, as abusers are often charming people to their friends, families, coworkers, and community members. In fact, they are typically still charming at moments toward their victims. Later, Camille confronts Taylor, as she's never seen signs of abuse, suggesting that Taylor is lying. Ultimately, Camille storms out of Lisa's house.

This conversation mirrors many messages IPV survivors receive from society. In fact, Camille disclosing Taylor's abuse to a public audience most likely put Taylor at more risk of physical harm. The ladies also discuss why Taylor hasn't left yet if the abuse is really so bad, ignoring the fact that leaving is when IPV victims most likely experience violence.[18] (It should also be noted that, on average, it takes seven attempts to successfully leave an abusive relationship.)[19] Additionally, it discounts the trauma of psychological, mental, emotional, verbal, financial, and other invisible forms of abuse. It becomes quite clear that the housewives align themselves with the socially constructed myths and misunderstandings of intimate partner violence when assessing Taylor's relationship. The social construction of masculinity is also at play when the women evaluate the likelihood of Taylor's abuse. For example, Lisa Vanderpump often refers to Russell not fitting into a hypermasculine image. As a result, he is not viewed as an abuser—solely based on social constructions. This may also indicate that Lisa subscribes to an older version of what constitutes masculinity. Ultimately, these myths, which rely on manufactured norms, reinforce abusive patterns and reduce victim/survivor autonomy and support.

While these myths isolate Taylor from her friends, she is further separated when Russell begins threatening legal action against several of the Housewives. As a result, Taylor and Russell are disinvited from Kyle Richards's white party.[20] After arriving at the party and learning they are no longer welcome, the couple continues to be recorded in their limo. Taylor ultimately apologizes to Russell for "talk[ing] about [their] marriage, at times" and attempts to normalize the situation by saying "all couples fight."[21] Perhaps this was Taylor's attempt to protect her safety by placating her husband and normalizing his behavior, while simultaneously allowing Russell to drive a deeper wedge between his wife and her friends. Often abusers calculate how to isolate their partners from their support circles, and Russell uses his power and control in public spaces to do just that.[22]

After the season finished shooting, Russell died from suicide, which is discussed at the season's reunion.[23] Russell's suicide perhaps led to even more intensified feelings of self-blaming for Taylor, in addition to complex and compounded trauma. While Russell's suicide should be discussed with its own analysis since that is not the purpose of this chapter. Instead, it should be noted that one can simultaneously be saddened by the suicide and continue to recognize Taylor's lack of autonomy in the relationship. After his death, Taylor was left to navigate his business debts and social implications. It might be analyzed that even if Russell did not intend to, his act of suicide was another way to continue controlling Taylor. It is a common tactic for abusers to attempt to maintain control even after a relationship is over, especially if children are involved.[24] In fact, it may have served as both the ultimate form of control and the ultimate method of escape for Taylor.

During the season 2 reunion, Taylor admitted to joining the cast because she thought it would perhaps minimize the abuse, as their relationship would be public, or force them into a divorce. Taylor again recognizes the public–private dynamic of intimate partner violence. By attempting to make their relationship more public, she thought she was protecting herself and her child. However, she detailed that Russell became more creative in his methods of abuse in private in an attempt to leave few marks that were easily visible to the eye. For example, in an interview with *Entertainment Tonight*, Taylor said she would often have wounds on her head, as he knew her hair would easily hide the contusions.[25] Recognizing the public–private dynamic of intimate partner violence showcases the remarkable way Taylor attempted to regain autonomy and mitigate dangers in her relationship. Although she stated that Russell continued to abuse her, this is a strong example of using creative resources to try to exit a relationship and strategize methods of reducing harm using social constructions. Furthermore, the lack of social understanding of the dynamics of abuse—particularly in the early 2000s, when the seasons were filmed—highlights the multiple layers of difficulties abuse survivors must navigate when coming forward; not only must survivors find safety from their abuse, but they must also carefully calculate who is and isn't safe to confide in. This calculation can become extremely complex when social norms do little to support survivors.

Bethenny Frankel: Growing Up Viewing IPV

The Real Housewives of New York City also holds multiple examples of domestic violence, with particular regard to parents. Both Bethenny Frankel and Ramona Singer disclose having abusive parents.[26] Their disclosures of past abuse are seemingly done to try to bridge the gap between private and public spaces of domestic family violence, which has very similar dynamics to intimate partner violence. These conversations, while problematic, may contribute to a more developed and nuanced understanding of abuse, which wasn't previously showcased. Frankel and Singer attempt to use their platforms on the show to discuss how experiencing violence and abuse in the home while growing up can affect victims/survivors throughout their lives.[27] Such disclosures of abuse are often done in an attempt to break the cycle of abuse.

Interestingly, Bethenny seems to argue that the abuse she experienced helped make her stronger. In season 7, episode 7, she visits her stepfather and discusses how she reflects back on her childhood.[28] First she meets with a friend, who echoes comments we commonly hear about IPV survivors in reference to Bethenny's mom "making" her stepdad act crazy. As detailed earlier, this conversation represents multiple socially constructed myths about intimate partner violence. First, it suggests that Bethenny's mother is to blame, at least partially, for the abuse. While we do not know the inner workings of their relationship and whether theirs was, in fact, mutual abuse, this is a common trope that victims of abuse have to face.[29] Often their actions are questioned, with outsiders wanting to know why they couldn't have simply acted how their partner wanted them to act. In this case, this line of thinking suggests that women are in control of men's emotions and actions. If a man behaves inappropriately, it's because a woman has led him astray. Patriarchal Christian societies often encourage men to assume this view through a clear connection to Adam and Eve, wherein Eve led Adam to act against God's orders, thus tempting Adam through her own "immorality."[30]

Later in the episode, Bethenny meets with her stepfather, John. During her conversation with John, she says she holds no anger. While she may not hold anger, it's important to put the emotion of anger in social context. Often women are told they cannot be angry, as it doesn't align with how a "good" woman or girl should act. Instead, good women and girls should be polite, comforting, and respectful, and should minimize their own needs so they can serve others—often men. Furthermore, gendered dynamics come into play quite commonly for victims/survivors regarding their relationships with their abusers. Holding anger toward abusers is often a difficult space to navigate. They may very much love their abusers and feel their anger might negate that love. It might also inhibit their ability to fit neatly into the "ideal victim" narrative, as ideal victims must follow gender norms. Thus, an angry woman is not following the gender norms to be a "good" woman and would not be an ideal victim in society's eyes.

Bethenny explains that she doesn't hold anger because the abuse "made [her] who [she is]." She credits her success to the abuse she endured. Many survivors use this narrative to justify the abuse that happened to them. Additionally, John apologizes "for what [she] experienced" as opposed to apologizing for the abuse. While this might be a comforting gesture, further analysis argues that such phrasing dismisses Bethenny's experiences and minimizes John's responsibility. Abusers often sidestep accountability and avoid taking full blame for the pain, fear, distrust, and other effects they created for their victims/survivors.[31]

Finally, Bethenny and John agree that other people have experienced much worse than what Bethenny experienced. This is problematic, as it places abuse into a hierarchical system. Different experiences of abuse affect people in very different ways; therefore, there is no scale of abuse or victimhood. Nevertheless, many victims/survivors use this rhetoric when discussing their traumatic experiences; by saying that they didn't have it "so bad," they are minimizing their pain and trauma. This rhetoric can make it difficult to accept the effects of abuse, as it essentially suggests the victim/survivor should get over it because it could have been worse. This mentality doesn't allow for the experience to be processed fully and accurately. Even the rhetoric surrounding victims' ability to feel grief and anger removes their autonomy, especially when constructions of gender are intertwined.

Social Constructions of Gender and IPV

Social constructions of gender also influence how we view intimate partner violence when a woman is the alleged perpetrator.[32] *The Real Housewives of New York City* provides a case study. For example in the season 8 reunion, Jules Wainstein is asked about her alleged abuse toward her then husband Michael.[33] Andy Cohen says there's been speculation that she "somehow" abused her husband. An analysis of this interaction shows gendered dynamics at work. First, the phrasing suggesting that Jules "somehow" abused Michael points to beliefs that women cannot be abusive toward men. This construction is most likely rooted in ideologies of femininity and masculinity. According to social norms, women are supposed to be dainty, submissive, and pleasant. This contrasts with men being told that they should take up space, hold authority, and exert power both privately and publicly. As a result, a woman abusing a man doesn't fit neatly into society's gender norms. Therefore, as a product of his environment, Cohen uses the word "somehow," reinforcing the myth that IPV always includes a male perpetrator. Additionally, after Jules declines to talk about it, they move on with the reunion. This is in stark contrast to how abuse is portrayed elsewhere on the show; typically, if a woman is suspected of being abused, it is fully covered. However, because society has a hard time accepting that women abuse men, the storyline does not go any further. For example, after NeNe Leakes's husband, Gregg, announced that he was cancer-free, she posted on Instagram, "Now I can go give Gregg a black eye ["punch" emoji] since so many think he's abused."[34] In this situation, it might have been valid to ask what the public response might have looked like if a man had said that. For NeNe, the comments were mostly cast aside and did not interfere with her celebrity standing. While the couple's relationship dynamics during Gregg's illness were certainly complex, it may be analyzed that Leakes's comments were dismissed due to cultural myths that women aren't abusers.

LGBTQ+ Relationships and the Erasure of IPV

Dismissive treatment of women's alleged domestic violence, and violence in nonheterosexual relationships, can be viewed in an analysis of *Below Deck*'s

Kate Chastain. For example, Chastain was arrested in Florida in 2016 for domestic battery by strangulation toward her then girlfriend. The charges were eventually dropped. However, court documents allege that Chastain bit her girlfriend, Rocio (Ro) Hernandez. Hernandez alleged "that Chastain sat on top of her, put a knee to her head and pulled her hair. Hernandez also told officers that Chastain covered her mouth and nose so that she couldn't breathe."[35] Although her alleged abuse was briefly discussed on *Below Deck*, there were no serious public discussions regarding her casting. This contrasts with Thomas Ravenel on *Southern Charm*, who has not been included in more recent seasons of the show after pleading guilty to third-degree assault and battery toward his daughter's former nanny.[36] While there should be a noted difference in Chastain dropped charges, compared to Ravenel's plea agreement, it is also important to underscore the seeming lack of awareness or concern toward IPV that occurs outside heterosexual relationships. In fact, our "climate of structural violence against [gender and sexually diverse] persons creates specific risk factors for domestic violence."[37] However, because folks in the LGBTQ+ community do not fit the aforementioned "perfect victim" narrative, society often does not take LGBTQ+ IPV as a serious issue that needs to be addressed in policies, social services, and cultural attitudes. It is unknown why the charges against Chastain were dropped (perhaps lack of evidence, or the survivor did not wish to participate), and an analysis of power that includes race, class, gender, and sexuality would work to provide insight into the situation. Often, survivors who have relatively little social capital and power do not feel safe confronting their abuser in the public sphere, especially when their abuser holds more social capital and power than they do. Additionally, Chastain has been able to salvage her image and expand her career, perhaps because she often showcases "normative" standards of whiteness and femininity, the latter of which was reinforced by her interior role on *Below Deck*.[38] Until an intersectional, nuanced understanding of IPV is undertaken by individuals and institutions, our support and empowerment toward IPV survivors will be drastically limited in its scope and fail to be fully successful or inclusive. Thus, we can see how Chastain is able to continue her successful career despite allegations of abuse that were informed by race, class, and gender norms. Ultimately, these norms might have worked in her favor, as they discredited Hernandez from being the "ideal victim."

Roughly half a decade later, *Below Deck*'s depiction of abuse demonstrates a substantially increased understanding of the dynamics of power, gender, and bystander responsibility. On the second season of *Below Deck Down*

Under, viewers see Luke pursue Margot for multiple episodes. As bosun, Luke holds significant power over Margot, who is the ship's third stew. After a night of drinking, at which time Margot very clearly states she does not want to engage in any sexual relations, Luke lets himself in to Margot's cabin following an electrical malfunction. Margot "was fully either asleep or passed out, depending on how you choose to describe the heavy sleep that follows heavy drinking. Fully naked, he hoisted himself up and crawled into her bed."[39] Producers intervene, and an angry Luke eventually returns to his room. Ultimately, Captain Jason fires Luke, and the crew largely supports Margot as she navigates her experience. One fellow stew, Laura, does not offer much support to Margot and instead engages in victim blaming. Laura is also fired by Captain Jason for this behavior *and* for making sexual advances toward a deckhand named Adam, who has repeatedly told Laura that he is only interested in a platonic relationship, though Laura continues to make physical advances. These advances culminate in her climbing into his bunk uninvited and subsequently being removed by producers. Like Margot, Adam engages in some self-blaming for the dynamics. However, the support they both receive from producers and staff alike demonstrates an extremely significant shift in how harassment and assault is viewed. Additionally, producers breaking the fourth wall highlights the role that bystanders play in these situations as well as the responsibility we all have in promoting the importance of consent. Interestingly, *Below Deck* showcases personal lives and workplace dynamics, a mixture that can lead to complicated tensions when it comes to creating a supportive environment, particularly when mixed with the complexities of reality television. *Vanderpump Rules* is also a strong example of how these multiple dynamics, including abuse, power, and control, can all converge.

Stassi Schroeder: Revenge Porn and Power and Control

In mainstream discussions of intimate partner violence, it seems that physical violence is at the center. However, as stated earlier, there are many forms of intimate partner violence. Much like patriarchy, abuse has been able to adapt and take on new forms throughout history. Two examples of this are cyber-harassment and revenge porn. These types of abuse are covered on more contemporary Bravo shows, such as *Vanderpump Rules*. Most notably, Stassi Schroeder navigates becoming the victim/survivor of revenge porn. Revenge porn refers to abusers who obtain consensual sexual content (videos, photos) and then nonconsensually release it.[40] The release of the private information typically comes after a breakup or in an effort to blackmail or control the victim.

For example, it's revealed that Stassi's ex-boyfriend attempted to extort Stassi (and then Lisa Vanderpump) for $900 in exchange for not releasing a sex tape of Stassi. It's also revealed that Lisa paid the individual to not release the tape without Stassi's knowledge of the deal. Subsequently, Stassi apologizes to Lisa for being ungrateful regarding the situation.[41] Additionally, Lisa tells Stassi that she warned her about the abuser and that he was "sleazy." It isn't until Stassi releases *Next Level Basic* in 2019 that she reveals the identity of the abuser (Frank, from season 1). Stassi's autonomy is further diminished when Lisa decides that she alone knows how to handle the situation. Additionally, Stassi notes that Lisa failed to get anything in writing or pay with a check to have a record of the transaction. Stassi is then victim blamed for engaging with this man because she should have known better and heeded Lisa's warnings. Stassi attempts to regain control of her narrative in her book and jokes in interviews that if someone is going to send a nude, they should make sure not to have their face in it.[42] While this may seem like helpful advice, a more powerful sentiment might be "Don't share others' nudes/sex tapes that were only meant for a specific audience." The first sentiment focuses on the victim's behavior as problematic, whereas the second places accountability on the abuser.

Kathryn Dennis: The Manipulation of IPV

Southern Charm highlights a wide variety of abusive dynamics between Thomas Ravenel and Kathryn Dennis. Throughout the series, the audience sees how Ravenel uses his power and influence to control Kathryn and others' opinions of her. Dennis and Ravenel have two children together; it can be analyzed that Ravenel uses court orders pertaining to custody to further control Dennis. Most notably, it seems that Ravenel uses his ability to influence others in an effort to isolate Kathryn from her friends and children. Ravenel works to characterize Kathryn as erratic, irresponsible, and unstable. These characteristics are in direct opposition to social constructions of motherhood, a disconnect others on the show repeatedly discuss. When analyzing Ravenel's attempts to isolate Kathryn, viewers can observe this physically and socially. For example, Thomas sequesters Kathryn in a country house, far away from her friends, while he continues his public life and engagements downtown. Thomas also paints a negative picture of Kathryn to Patricia Altschul. This is especially noteworthy, as Altschul is a makeshift gatekeeper for Charleston social elites. Kathryn is portrayed as creating "too much drama," and even though Thomas is an equal participant in the relationship and dynamic, fellow cast members sanction Kathryn more harshly. Again, we see how power is a vital element in abusive relationships. Through his use of power, Ravenel is able to construct Dennis as the "bad" apple, suggesting to others that her behavior perhaps led to Thomas's controlling behavior. Although Ravenel is not featured on the sixth season of the show due to rape allegations that have since been dropped, Kathryn continued to have her autonomy limited.

At the season 6 reunion, Kathryn, when asked about her relationship, states that she is not able to comment due to ongoing legal issues. She also warns her cast members that Thomas would be using any negative remarks made about her against her in their custody case.[43] This is a prime example of how abusers continue to control their victims/survivors even after relationships have ended. As a result, friends and family may continue to isolate themselves from victims/survivors because it's "messy" or too complicated. Multiple times in the show, cast members remark that they do not want to comment because they don't want to get involved. Thus, despite not being in the season, Thomas was able to continue influencing Kathryn's ability to create a support network and exercise full autonomy in creating her own narrative.

Southern Charm: Patriarchy and IPV

Southern Charm has a history of engaging in double standards for women compared to men. Women's behaviors are judged much more harshly, while men are referred to as having Peter Pan syndrome. As a result, men rarely take accountability for their actions, as it is assumed they are entitled to whatever (and whomever) they want. Locating *Southern Charm* in a system of patriarchy (as are all the shows) helps to uncover a deeper pattern of misogyny that underscores society's failure to take violence against women seriously. It isn't until later seasons of the show that the women begin to call out this behavior. However, when they do, they are characterized as women scorned by former lovers. For example, in season 5, the newly single women are referred to as "the break-up bunch." When they challenge men about their behavior, the men laugh, suggesting that their disdain is not taken seriously.[44] The men have been told they are right in not taking the criticism seriously, as they are entitled to act however they please. This is showcased in particular by Shep's attempt to kiss Chelsea when she is dating Austin. Chelsea tells Austin that while he was in a different part of a restaurant, Shep grabbed her arm and attempted to kiss her. After confronting Shep, Austin receives an apology before Chelsea does, suggesting that Shep disrespected Austin more with his actions than he did Chelsea. This fits into the patriarchal and misogynistic narrative that women are men's property, not subjects in their own right—an ideology that is the supporting foundation upholding intimate partner violence. Interestingly, the women's reactions showcase internalized patriarchy too. Chelsea tells Shep that she did not like his actions because they made her feel like she was "that kind of girl," perhaps suggesting a "slut."[45] We see Chelsea enforce a virgin-whore double bind in this situation, which creates little room for her own feelings and instead leaves her to avoid being viewed as someone who doesn't fit the "good" woman image. When Shep tells Cameron about the incident, he details that grabbing a girl by the arm and trying to kiss her usually "works." By suggesting this, it's apparent how normalized sexual assault is. Consent and autonomy are not valued in this picture; instead, power and patriarchy define the rules of what is right and what is wrong—with few repercussions for the latter. It should be noted, however, that in more recent seasons of the series, newer cast members have labored to call out Shep and Austin for their womanizing ways. Newer male cast members have gained traction in identifying and condemning this behavior, perhaps using their male privilege in these circumstances so that these concerns would be taken more seriously than when other women on the cast identify problematic behavior and double standards.

Real Housewives of Atlanta: IPV and Social Change

The women of *The Real Housewives of Atlanta* (*RHOA*) perhaps detail intimate partner violence in the most specific manner compared to the women of all other Bravo shows. In season 10, Kenya Moore creates a public service announcement (PSA) about domestic violence.[46] It features the other women reading statistics and Shereé Whitfield and Cynthia Bailey's mother recounting their own stories of abuse. Kenya Moore reveals that she was stabbed by an abusive ex when she was sixteen. NeNe Leakes outlines her experience being abused by a partner at a young age. The candid format of both the PSA and the confessionals of the episode highlight important patterns in abusive relationships. Whitfield and Leakes talk about what drew them to their abusers' charming personalities and assurance of love. However, abusers are often able to use these charms to manipulate their partners into thinking their abuse equals signs of love. Conflating love with abuse happens very frequently in our society. For example, girls who report being bullied by boys are routinely told that "he's doing that because he likes you." Thus, girls can rationalize that line of thinking to believe that abuse is a form of love, similar to jealousy. However, jealousy, combined with abusive control and perceived "ownership" over partners, can lead to lethal violence.[47] Abusers tend to react more dangerously when their partners deny or reject them, thus reinforcing that the most dangerous time in an abusive relationship is when the victim/survivor is attempting to leave.

In the PSA, Whitfield shares her account of abusive episodes with an ex wherein he accused her of cheating. While cheating might be considered breaking the trust of a monogamous relationship, it is not an excuse for abuse—as nothing is. Possibly her abusive partner believed she was his property. It should be noted that this line of thinking, as earlier discussed, is supported through historical, social, and legal norms concerning marriage and patriarchy. Whitfield had previous experience discussing the abuse she's navigated during season 9 of *RHOA*.

While on vacation with the cast, Shereé and her ex-husband, Bob, share a car with Kenya and Phaedra. During the car ride, they discuss Cynthia and Peter being on the trip after separating. Bob recounts that after he and Shereé split, they were driving in Las Vegas, and while she was sleeping, he contemplated taking her seat belt off and slamming the brakes so that she would go through the windshield. After receiving questioning looks from the others in the car, he proclaims that he "never hit her." However, Shereé argues that there was physical abuse, including strangulation. Strangulation is one of the most lethal tactics of physical abuse and is often used by police, shelter advocates, and judges to assess the level of potential imminent harm in a relationship.[48] Bob says that he doesn't remember choking her, but if he did, he's sorry. He then goes on to say he's sorry because "maybe he didn't choke [her] hard enough."[49] Through the entire conversation, it seems that Bob is not taking his abuse of Shereé seriously; this is punctuated with his suggesting that he should have killed her. By saying this, he is being cavalier about the situation while wielding power under a new threat. While some might analyze the situation as Bob joking about repeatedly engaging in attempts or considerations of murder, it is important to note that Black women are twice as likely as white women to be victims of IPV homicide.[50] In her confessional, Shereé notes how Bob showcased both a charming personality and a dangerous, violent side. Often men who are abusers but who have support in the community are not looked at as true abusers. Victims/survivors' narratives are dismissed because he "seems like such a good guy." This concept is present in many abusive intimate partner situations, as it reinforces many socially constructed myths of abuse. It's also worth noting that Shereé was hesitant to speak up because she was concerned with how her children would view Bob. In essence, she was still invested in protecting Bob.

In the PSA in season 10, victims/survivors are encouraged to "leave before it's too late." While the sentiment of this phrase is well intentioned, it is important to discuss why victims/survivors don't leave. Victims/survivors know their partners the best; they have had the most experience in keeping themselves and their families safe. Additionally, victims argue that one of the reasons they don't call the police or leave is because they fear community backlash. This is especially true in communities of color, which already have reasonable distrust of law enforcement as an institution. As a result, they are the experts of their own experience. It is important to note the need to support victims/survivors if they are not ready to leave their abusive relationship—no matter the reason. They might not leave for a flurry of reasons, with their safety being an important one. Victims/survivors might know that it's more dangerous to leave an abusive situation than stay at a particular time. Instead, intimate partner violence should be tackled as a social problem that relies on institutional norms and policies to perpetuate. As a result, we must dismantle these norms and build new policies in their places that better support survivors, such as funding for shelters and deconstructing myths about intimate partner violence.

Conclusion: Using Bravo Reality TV to Transform Reality

A range of dynamics relating to intimate partner violence and abuse are showcased on reality television. Perhaps in these narratives, society can begin to start viewing IPV as a social problem and not as a personal failing, a common myth exemplified throughout this chapter. Similar to consciousness-raising groups, reality television (with particular regard to *The Real Housewives*) focuses on women's experiences; as a result, these spaces are often discounted by mainstream society as frivolous, flighty, and lacking meaning. While it should be noted that the IPV experiences and dynamics on reality TV must be analyzed through an intersectional lens that accounts for race, class, gender, sexuality, religion, ability status, location, and other identity markers, it is also intriguing to wonder if these spaces can be used to publicize the private. The Housewives franchise provides a rich landscape for analysis, using a critical lens to make institutional and conceptual connections about intimate partner violence. Additionally, these spaces may serve as a productive site to question the myths concerning IPV, which often disempower anyone who is outside the "ideal victim." For example, Taylor Armstrong dispels the common myth that "if abuse is truly bad, the survivor will leave." This chapter showcased how this myth was reiterated by her castmates on the show, potentially placing her in increasingly more dangerous situations; thus, the making of the myths doesn't simply stay in a theoretical space. Rather, these myths come to life and directly affect the lived experiences of survivors. Therefore, I argue that the Bravoverse be employed as a site to dismantle these myths. After all, if these myths were socially made, they can be unmade.

However, rewriting myths is not an overnight process. Creation of new social constructions, norms, and ideologies should be thoughtfully crafted with respect toward recognizing the impacts of race, gender, class, and other social markers. As viewed in this chapter, new social norms are incrementally created but can have substantial influence on the support survivors receive. Using an analysis that incorporates intersectional themes, such as race and gender, when discussing intimate partner violence helps to unpack why IPV continues to affect so many individuals and lets us imagine how we might respond in a more empathetic and supportive fashion. For example, understanding how ethnicity and sexuality combine in marginalizing certain survivors of IPV helps us to better understand why Kate Chastain's career may have continued to thrive despite allegations of abuse. Recognizing that survivors with varying identity markers might need different modes of support is crucial in creating an inclusive and equitable movement toward eliminating intimate partner violence.

Once IPV is recognized as a social problem that relies on institutions to uphold it, perhaps these institutions might be viewed through a more nuanced scope. Recognizing how social constructions and myths normalize abuse might help viewers make connections between the public and the private and the individual and the institution. Additionally, viewing experiences of intimate partner violence that are portrayed in an intersectional feminist, well-informed light could be extremely empowering for victims/survivors in seeing shared experiences and removing the societal shame that is often aligned with victimhood status. Though Bravo programming still has significant work to do if it is to highlight narratives using an intersectional feminist lens, perhaps it can provide a space to start the discussion. Indeed, in the wake of the #MeToo movement, Bravo has taken more editorial responsibility in showcasing dynamics of consent, as evidenced in *Below Deck Down Under*. This provides hope that the future of Bravo programming will grow in its support of survivors and the responsibility of bystanders.

Displaying positive examples of how bystanders, friends, and family can support survivors of abuse and harassment is truly one of the most meaningful depictions of reality that the network could showcase. While shows often draw viewers into lives of luxury, many viewers may find connections with the cast members and their personal experiences of intimate partner violence. We know that many Bravo fans will never fly on a private jet, stay on a yacht, or casually spend thousands of dollars shopping. However, viewers will likely support a family member or friend through an abusive relationship or may even experience violence themselves. Therefore, it is in these raw moments of reality television that viewers see themselves represented and can even gain skills in how to support their own well-being and safety, in addition to that of others.

Resources for Survivors

National Domestic Violence Hotline
Phone: 1.800.799.SAFE (7233)
Website: https://www.thehotline.org

National Sexual Assault Hotline
Phone: 800.656.4673
Website: https://www.rainn.org/resources

Notes

1. "Domestic Violence Statistics," National Domestic Violence Hotline, accessed August 26, 2024, https://www.thehotline.org/stakeholders/domestic-violence-statistics.

2. *RHONJ*, season 7, episode 9, "Driving Miss Siggy," aired September 11, 2016, on Bravo.

3. Garcia and McManimon, *Gendered Justice*, 7.

4. Garcia and McManimon, *Gendered Justice*, 7–13.

5. *RHOBH*, season 9, episode 8, "Showdown at Villa Rosa," aired April 2, 2019, on Bravo.

6. Stedman, "Right of Husband to Chastise Wife."

7. Garcia and McManimon, *Gendered Justice*, 71.

8. *Oxford Research Encyclopedia*, s.v. "Women, Gender, and World War II," accessed April 5, 2020, https://doi.org/10.1093/acrefore/9780199329175.013.55.

9. Garcia and McManimon, *Gendered Justice*, 88–89.
10. Bograd, "Strengthening Domestic Violence Theories," 25–28.
11. *RHOBH*, season 1, episode 1, "Life, Liberty and the Pursuit of Wealthiness," aired October 4, 2010, on Bravo.
12. "Domestic Violence Statistics," National Domestic Violence Hotline, accessed August 26, 2024, https://www.thehotline.org/stakeholders/domestic-violence-statistics.
13. "FAQs: About the Wheels," Domestic Abuse Intervention Programs, 2017, https://www.theduluthmodel.org/wheels/faqs-about-the-wheels.
14. Eckstein, "Reasons for Staying in Intimately Violent Relationships," 23.
15. *RHOBH*, season 2, episode 2, "Blame it on the Altitude," aired September 12, 2011, on Bravo.
16. Gillig et al., "Humiliation, Manipulation, and Control," 342–49.
17. *RHOBH*, season 2, episode 11, "Tempest in a Tea Party," aired November 14, 2011, on Bravo.
18. "Why People Stay," National Domestic Violence Hotline, accessed September 15, 2024, https://www.thehotline.org/support-others/why-people-stay-in-an-abusive-relationship.
19. "50 Obstacles to Leaving," National Domestic Violence Hotline, 2013, https://www.thehotline.org/2013/06/10/50-obstacles-to-leaving-1-10.
20. *RHOBH*, season 1, episode 16, "Uninvited," aired December 19, 2011, on Bravo.
21. *RHOBH*, season 1, episode 17, "Leis and Lies in Lanai," aired January 2, 2012, on Bravo.
22. Lorenzetti et al., "Understanding and Preventing Domestic Violence," 177–80.
23. *RHOBH*, season 2, episode 21, "Reunion: Part One," aired January 30, 2012, on Bravo.
24. "Dynamics of Abuse," National Domestic Violence Hotline, accessed August 26, 2024, https://www.thehotline.org/resources/dynamics-of-abuse.
25. APB Speakers, "Taylor Armstrong: The Physical Signs of Abuse," YouTube video, 2:53, January 8, 2015, https://www.youtube.com/watch?v=3ifHqon4iCM.
26. Rosie Jones, interview by Kacey Calahane, Jessica Millward, and Max Speare, *Historians on Housewives*, podcast, June 27, 2020, https://podcasts.apple.com/us/podcast/i-dont-play-victim-i-help-empower-them-survival-stories/id1475184480?i=1000479953437. This interview provides additional conversation regarding how children's trauma might affect adult relationships.
27. *RHONY*, season 11, episode 12, "Luann Land," aired May 22, 2019, on Bravo.
28. *RHONY*, season 7, episode 7, "Family Matters," aired May 19, 2015, on Bravo.
29. Garcia and McManimon, *Gendered Justice*, 47–54.
30. Garcia and McManimon, *Gendered Justice*, 53.
31. "Abuser Accountability," Center for Relationship Abuse Awareness, accessed April 5, 2020, http://stoprelationshipabuse.org/professionals/social-workers-and-therapists/working-with- perpetrators-of-abuse/abuser-accountability.
32. Kernsmith and Kernsmith, "Treating Female Perpetrators," 342.

33. *RHONY*, season 8, episode 22, "Reunion, Part 2," aired September 7, 2016, on Bravo.

34. Kiersten Willis, "'Absolutely Uncalled For': Nene Leakes Finds Herself in a Firestorm over Joke concerning Gregg after He's Revealed to Be Cancer-Free," Atlanta Black Star, May 14, 2019, https://atlantablackstar.com/2019/05/14/absolutely-uncalled-for-nene-leakes-finds-herself-in-a-firestorm-over-joke-concerning-gregg-after-hes-revealed-to-be-cancer-free.

35. Jodi Guglielmi, "*Below Deck*'s Kate Chastain Opens Up about Dating Again after 2016 Domestic Violence Arrest," last modified October 2, 2018. https://people.com/tv/below-deck-kate-chastain-dating-after-domestic-violence-arrest.

36. Dave Quinn, "*Southern Charm*'s Thomas Ravenel Apologizes to Nanny in Sexual Assault Case Settlement," October 11, 2019, https://people.com/tv/thomas-ravenel-apologizes-to-nanny-in-sexual-assault-case-settlement.

37. Lorenzetti et al., "Understanding and Preventing Domestic Violence," 181.

38. The connection between interior spaces and femininity serves to highlight traditional notions of femininity as domestic, pleasant, serving, and socially attractive as defined by contextual standards. Furthermore, on *Below Deck*, women deckhands are often treated as more masculine than their interior counterparts. This is in no way arguing that interior work is not inherently valuable or laborious; rather, it works to highlight the social constructions placed on such work.

39. Linda Holmes, "*Below Deck*, Reality Producers Stepped In to Stop a Drunken Assault—This Time," NPR, August 12, 2023. https://www.npr.org/2023/08/12/1193446744/below-deck-down-under-sexual-assault.

40. McGlynn and Rackley, "Image-Based Sexual Abuse," 535–37.

41. *Vanderpump Rules*, season 4, episode 14, "Sex, Lies, and Stassi's Videotape," aired February 1, 2016, on Bravo.

42. Schroeder, *Next Level Basic*, 62.

43. *Southern Charm*, season 6, episode 15, "Reunion, Part 1," aired August 21, 2019, on Bravo.

44. *Southern Charm*, season 5, episode 1, "The Break-Up Bunch," aired April 5, 2018, on Bravo.

45. *Southern Charm*, season 4, episode 11, "Boys Gone Wild," aired June 12, 2017, on Bravo.

46. *RHOA*, season 10, episode 8, "A Mad Tea Party," aired January 7, 2018, on Bravo.

47. For example, in 2014, about fifty miles outside St. Louis, Jessica Powell told her estranged husband, Shawn Kavanagh, to leave her friend's residence. Powell had an active order of protection against Kavanagh, but he returned to the residence and stabbed Powell, her friend, and two children. Powell survived the attack after being severely wounded, but the three other victims did not. See Adam Rollins, "Kavanagh Murder Trial Moved to October," March 27, 2020, https://www.warrencountyrecord.com/stories/kavanagh-murder-trial-moved-to-october,1851?

48. Messing, "Risk-Informed Intervention," 107.

49. *RHOA*, season 9, episode 16, "Maui Mayhem," aired March 12, 2017, on Bravo.

50. Garcia and McManimon, *Gendered Justice*, 1.

8   Politics and *The Real Housewives*
The 2016 Election and the Increase in Political Conversations on Bravo

NICOLE L. ANSLOVER

In 2020, the world grappled with the devastation wrought by the COVID-19 pandemic. The United States had been especially ravaged, largely because of a dereliction of duty by the president of the United States and other leadership. And yet as one might expect on a reality television show, there was a plot twist. It was also an election year, and a wild one at that. As one historian noted near the end of the year, as the death toll continued to break records each day, "Despite the coronavirus crisis, the Trump administration continues to put its energy into overturning the 2020 election."[1] Joe Biden won the 2020 presidential election by more than 7 million votes, yet a shockingly high number of Americans and current president Donald Trump did not accept the results of this free and fair election. In fact, Trump held rallies assuring his supporters that they were the victims of a sinister plot to steal the election from them.[2]

On January 6, 2021, one of these rallies turned deadly, as a violent mob of protesters attacked the U.S. Capitol as Congress was in the process of certifying the electoral votes from the election. President Trump spoke to a crowd of thousands of supporters shortly before the insurrection erupted and urged them not to accept the results of the election, calling it a "fraud," "corrupt," and "stolen." He exhorted the crowd to make their voices heard and make sure that Congress and Vice President Mike Pence do "the right thing," meaning to overturn the results of the election.[3] His supporters did head to the Capitol, but what resulted was not a peaceful protest. Rioters stormed the building, fought with the police, and ruthlessly hunted for lawmakers.[4]

If this were being shown on any television show, reality or scripted, viewers might wonder if this was the season where the show had jumped the proverbial shark. But this is reality, and it provides an excellent opportunity to analyze how politics have been and will be portrayed on reality television. We seem to have reached the point in the American experiment where reality is stranger than fiction—or, in this case, stranger than reality television. It is therefore not surprising that since this era is truly incredible and illuminates a democracy that is more precarious than many would like to believe, the way that politics is dealt with on reality television has radically changed too. And with that comes a change in how politics itself and political issues such as race, voting, and police brutality are shown on TV. As the public mood has shifted on issues of politics, so has its tolerance for what its willing to see on reality shows. The previous presidential election year, 2016, showed a marked increase in political conversations on Bravo, which intensified over the next several years. The elections of 2020 and 2024 illustrate that reality television and politics will continue to be intertwined.

On December 6, 2020, *The Real Housewives of Atlanta* (*RHOA*) premiered season 13 with what is probably the rawest and most impactful episode of any of *The Real Housewives* entries. The central focus of the episode was the activism of Porsha Williams, the granddaughter of famed civil rights activist Hosea Williams. Viewers are thrown right into the emotional events of recent months as images of Breonna Taylor, the murder of George Floyd, and Black Lives Matter protests flash across the screen, accompanied by stories of rising COVID-19 cases.[5] The images likely provoke visceral memories and emotions in viewers, and Porsha is there to tell them why it matters. She explains that she was moved to act because she was "furious . . . offended at the blatant racism that was happening to my people." The episode follows Porsha as she protests on behalf of Breonna Taylor in both Atlanta and Lexington, Kentucky (with her arrest in the latter). Porsha tells viewers that action against racism and violence is urgent and necessary: "We need to yell this from the rooftop that 'no justice, no peace.' We got to get busy. Period."[6]

While Bravo and other networks will not likely be able to stay away from politically driven storylines moving forward, that has not always been the case. The shift toward starting to cover politics began only a few years earlier in 2016, a watershed year in American politics, with traditional campaigning seeming to fall by the wayside, the media stumbling to figure out how to cover the constant accusations and mudslinging, and pollsters seemingly getting everything wrong. It was also the year that politics became the topic of virtually every conversation. It makes sense that once America elected a former reality star in Donald Trump, politics became much more prevalent on certain reality shows. *The Real Housewives of New York* (*RHONY*) centered much of season 9 around the 2016 presidential election, signifying that the line between reality and reality television had become even less clearly defined. With her tagline "In the politics of friendship, I win the popular vote," Carole Radziwill signaled that politics would be a major theme.[7] Like many Americans, the stars of *The Real Housewives* franchise, which began airing in 2006, mainly avoided talking about politics, at least publicly, before 2016. As the 2016 election approached, many of the Housewives became more vocal about politics, a trend that has somewhat continued on the shows. This is a similar trend in the country as a whole, which illustrates that these reality shows do mirror actual reality, at least in some cases. A month after the election, 64 percent of American adults reported that they regularly discussed politics.[8]

This chapter explores the various ways that individual Housewives express their political views and how they participate in politics, with one of the central themes being the 2016 presidential election. Of particular interest are the New York City Housewives' connections to Trump and how many of them voted. Embedded in this discussion is the juxtaposition of Carole Radziwill and her passion for Hillary Clinton with some of the other New York Housewives and their ties to Donald Trump and refusal to discuss their votes. This discussion can be used as a lens through which to view the emotions involved with voting in 2016 and compare the Housewives' voting behavior to patterns among women nationwide. The women of Atlanta and their political activism will also be a key component of this analysis, especially Porsha Williams. In 2016, Williams and Phaedra Parks traveled to the Democratic National Convention. Part of what drove them to attend was the desire to participate in conversations about police brutality. By using examples of political action and discussion from several of the franchise's entries to fully explore the importance (or lack thereof) of politics in the Bravoverse, we can come closer to understanding the relationship between politics and public discourse.

Many people dismiss *The Real Housewives* as "trash television" or mindless entertainment. In her analysis of the Black image and popular culture, Raquel Gates notes that influential people have publicly disparaged the show: "References to the show magically appear in Shonda Rhimes's discussion of *Scandal* as a 'guilty pleasure' (a term she uses pejoratively) and in Barack Obama's imperative to America's young people that they need to work harder at school rather than sitting at home and 'watching *The Real Housewives*.' In both cases, the subjects of Rhimes's and Obama's speeches were not *The Real Housewives*, but each used the unquestioned 'trashiness' of the show as a point of comparison for the questions at hand."[9] Rhimes's and Obama's derision has certainly been echoed by media elites and members of the general public. But the reality of certain reality shows is that there is significant political relevance to many of them. For example, the argument can be made that *The Apprentice* played a major part in Donald Trump's 2016 electoral victory.[10] While not all reality shows have quite that impact, many of the iterations of *The Real Housewives* do shine a light on the political pulse of the nation.

But as Gates argues, reality television can actually contribute to culture on several different levels. It does, of course, entertain and offer viewers a way to escape their own reality and take pleasure in watching someone else's reality. In their edited volume *Reality TV*, Susan Murray and Laurie Ouellette offer several valuable insights on the different layers of reality TV, as well as a good working definition of the genre: "We define 'reality television' as an unabashedly commercial genre united less by aesthetic rules or certainties than by the fusion of popular entertainment with a self-conscious claim to the discourse for the real." Murray and Ouellette further argue, "This coupling, we contend, is what has made reality TV an important generic forum for a range of institutional and cultural developments."[11]

But why, exactly, is it so important? Murray and Ouellette argue that there is an important connection between the viewers and the people who share their lives on reality TV. At the crux of it, "Reality TV promises its audience revelatory insight into the lives of others as it withholds and subverts full access to it. What results is an unstable text that encourages viewers to test out their own notions of the real, the ordinary, and the intimate against the representation before them." Murray and Ouellette also contend, "Far from being the mind-numbing, deceitful, and simplistic genre that some critics claim it to be, reality TV provides a multilayered viewing experience that hinges on culturally and politically complex notions of what is real and what is not."[12] So when viewers in 2016 began seeing politics become a central storyline for some episodes of *The Real Housewives*, they were actually being given another way to view politics and participate in meaningful conversations about the subject.

It is important to note that reality TV and politics became more closely intertwined in 2016 not just because a large majority of Americans were regularly discussing politics, but because one of the candidates and the eventual winner of the 2016 presidential election was himself a reality television star.[13] Donald Trump presided over the boardroom for fourteen seasons of *The Apprentice* and several seasons of *The Celebrity Apprentice*. Scholar Ruth Deller notes of Trump, "Having spent over a decade honing his public image through this programme (and associated media like autobiographies and self-aggrandising interviews), Trump was able to create and stage his image to give the impression he was a successful businessman . . . shrewd judge of character and talent, a confident leader."[14] In other words, Trump was able to translate his reality TV persona into performing the role of a real-life candidate that many believed was qualified to be the president. Since reality television is likely to be at least partially responsible for the Trump presidency, it is even more important to look at how politics is portrayed on other reality TV programs. Deller continues, "Trump presents an extreme example of the (perceived) impact of reality television on global politics and culture—and it should be noted that reality TV is just one of the many possible factors contributing to his success—but it highlights the range of key debates about the role of reality television in public life, including its relationship with politics and governance, its influence on its audience, and its power to create celebrity."[15] It was perhaps inevitable that other reality stars began to discuss politics on-camera.

Since it began airing in 2008, *The Real Housewives of New York* has been one of the most popular iterations of the franchise. Viewers are drawn to the women's luxurious lifestyles, glittering social lives, and, of course, drama. Like many reality shows, *RHONY* is aspirational. It certainly doesn't reflect the reality of most people actually living in New York City, and it absolutely does not reflect the diverse makeup of the city's population.[16] Viewers often watch television shows as a form of escapism, and for nearly a decade, *RHONY* fit the bill. But as the presidential election of 2016 drew near, many of the women in the cast began to discuss politics while filming. The election was a central storyline throughout season 9, which marked a clear departure from the show's typical storylines, such as marriage, divorce, dating, and social snubs.

Carole Radziwill brought the election storyline to the forefront of the season in the very first episode. In the premiere, there is a lengthy scene in which Carole brings over a present for pal Bethenny Frankel's new puppies: a chew toy made to look like Donald Trump, then candidate for president. Carole proceeds to engage Bethenny in a discussion of the election, which irritates Bethenny, who claims that all Carole talks about anymore is politics. Carole doesn't let it drop and carries the subject into a short interview clip. Here, Carole talks openly about her disdain for Trump and compares him to another cast member, Luann de Lesseps: "For both the candidate and Lu, it's as if 'the bigger the lie, the more people believe it.'"[17] It's a light scene, perhaps meant to give viewers a laugh while reacquainting them with the cast members. But it also serves to let viewers know that they should expect a new type of storyline this season, one that might make some viewers uncomfortable. Season 9 illustrates how all-consuming politics became for many Americans in 2016, extending as it did into reality television. It may not have been that more people were discussing politics than had in the past, but rather that those who were talking were more partisan, passionate, and vocal. People who identified as either Republican or Democrat were more likely to hold extremely negative views of members of the other party than they had in the past. Consequently, there was greater partisanship when discussing the candidates. Rising partisanship almost certainly contributed to the negative tone of the campaign and led large numbers of Americans to claim that they felt extremely frustrated when trying to talk to a member of the other party.[18]

This trend is an important part of the politics storyline on season 9 of *RHONY*. In nearly every episode of the season, politics—particularly the candidacy of Donald Trump—is a topic of conversation. While Carole continues to be extremely critical of the Republican nominee, other castmates either don't understand her keen interest in the election or don't understand her dislike of Trump. For some, their defense of Trump is personal. Sonja Morgan worked as a "former brand consultant for Trump."[19] Her close friend and fellow Upper East Sider Ramona Singer has also mentioned several times throughout the series that she knows Trump personally. Carole once again makes a comparison to Trump to insult one of the women, noting that Ramona "reminds me of Trump, she just sticks her foot in her mouth, her timing is off."[20] The one castmate who openly aligns politically with Carole is Dorinda Medley, who mocks Sonja for having worked for Trump. Sonja feigns ignorance and claims that she does not understand the insult. Or perhaps Sonja is actually confused. She is one of many wealthy white women who supported Trump in 2016.[21]

The politics storyline peaks in episode 5, titled "The Politics of Friendship," which opens with Carole and her mother driving to Pennsylvania to canvas for Hillary Clinton. Carole explains to the viewers that Pennsylvania is a swing state and why that makes it so important during the 2016 election. This season aired in April 2017, so viewers obviously knew the outcome. That fact makes it even more interesting that both the cast and the producers chose to center much of the season's drama on an event whose outcome was far from surprising. Yet this episode, which is mostly about Carole's election party, did have a sense of drama. Regardless of who the viewers voted for, watching the Housewives and their friends watch the election results come in was probably something that a large percentage of viewers could relate to. Perhaps this is one of the reasons that politics became a central feature of the season 9 storyline; it's probably one of the first dramatic storylines that many viewers had experienced in a similar way themselves.[22]

The footage of Carole and her mom canvassing is interspersed with one of Carole's interview sessions. Viewers hear her explain part of why she is working so hard to elect Democratic nominee Hillary Clinton. Not only does Carole want to elect the first female president, but she sincerely believes that Clinton is the most qualified and experienced candidate. She elaborates, saying, "I've just had a visceral reaction to Donald Trump potentially being president of the United States. Men like Trump are a dime a dozen in New York. They have a nickel in their pocket, they think they're hot shit, that they can take advantage of women. On a national stage, magnified, he stands for everything I am against."[23] This further sets up the drama for the episode—the election results. The viewers now understand a little more about Carole's politics. And, like almost all discussion of politics during and after 2016, her statement likely provoked a reaction in viewers. Most viewers probably either strongly agreed or strongly disagreed with her reaction.

The climax of the episode is Carole's election party. She has invited several friends, including some of the other Housewives, to a bar in Manhattan to watch the election results on television. She pointedly uninvited Ramona after they had several arguments about politics, culminating in Carole telling Ramona that she was uninformed. Bethenny, who consistently mocked Carole for her obsession with politics, arrives with several friends. Dorinda arrives in a pantsuit and explains to the audience that she has a personal connection to Hillary due to her late husband's work with the Democratic National Committee. There is a festive air at the beginning of the party; the excitement is palpable through the screen. As the evening progresses, it becomes clear that a Trump presidency is becoming an increasing reality. Most of the attendees at the party cycle through the emotions of disbelief, anxiety, shock, and grief. The party uncomfortably breaks up; the next scene is of Carole on the phone with her mom the next morning, crying and trying to articulate how "devastated" she feels.[24] This emotional reaction was one felt by women around the world, particularly ardent Clinton supporters.

Later in the season, the political storyline continues by showing some of the women attending the Women's March in Washington, D.C. The Women's

March on Washington took place on January 21, 2017 with more than a million people filling the streets of the nation's capital. The crowd was estimated to be two to three times the size of the turnout for President Trump's inauguration the day before, and millions of other people participated in similar events around the country and the world. After some initial criticism, the organizers of the event committed to making the event more about inclusivity and intersectionality, issuing an invitation to "Black women, Indigenous women, poor women, immigrant women, disabled women, Muslim women, lesbian, queer, and trans women" to join in the movement to signal unity among women and push for change. The election of Donald Trump, who repulsed many women by speaking about grabbing women by their pussies, among other egregious actions and statements, was the impetus for the march.[25]

The Women's March would have made a compelling storyline on *RHONY*. It was clearly something that was important to millions of women (and other people) in the country, and as Bravo's core audience is women, it likely would have been interesting for viewers to see how several of the Housewives felt about the march. Instead, we see only Carole and Dorinda, the vocal liberal Democrats, traveling to the march in Washington D.C. While Bravo does send cameras to follow the two women, along with Dorinda's daughter, as they participate in the event, it is not the main focus of the episode. Instead, we see only a few minutes of clips.[26] It would have been interesting to hear more about Carole and Dorinda's experience, if they planned to continue actively participating in the movement, and what really compelled them to attend. It would also have been a great opportunity to spark additional debate by asking other cast members (namely Ramona, Sonja, and Tinsley) about their views. While lauded by many, the Women's March was not without controversy or critics. Debates about it could have made for compelling television and perhaps made reality TV feel a little more like reality.

The season reunion continues to highlight the election and politics. One caller asks the women to say whether they've ever met either Donald Trump or Hillary Clinton and to state who they voted for. The question highlights clear divisions in the cast as the group responds as such: Ramona states that she has met Clinton and traveled to Trump's Mar a Lago estate, but then declines to say who she voted for; similarly, Luann acknowledges meeting both candidates and chooses to plead the Fifth regarding her vote. Sonja reiterates the fact that she knows Trump and his family, but also declines to reveal her vote. Dorinda and Carole proudly declare themselves as

Hillary voters, while Bethenny describes herself as a reluctant Hillary voter who didn't like either candidate. Tinsley states that she didn't vote because "it's not my thing." Carole argues that not saying who you voted for indicates a vote for Trump.[27]

The women being directly asked about their vote (or lack thereof) is an interesting development for several reasons. For one thing, this is not the typical topic of discussion on any of the iterations of *The Real Housewives* franchise. It also reveals a clear divide among the cast, with three Clinton voters, three Trump voters, and one abstention. While there isn't definitive information on the votes cast by all of the Housewives in other cities, there is enough anecdotal evidence, based on social media posts and other statements, to get a pretty good idea of how the women on the other casts voted. *Bitch Media* wrote an article about Housewives and their votes in which the author makes a useful point, noting that while it is understandable that many of these reality stars don't want to alienate their fans, their social media accounts perhaps tell more than they would like. In a study of tweets by the Housewives, it is true that "being virtually silent about the 2016 election speaks volumes."[28] The assumption is that people who don't like to talk about who they voted for most likely voted for Trump, as Carole was quick to point out.

The author of the *Bitch Media* compilation posits some interesting ideas, which she precedes with the following disclaimer: "I don't actually know who the Real Housewives voted for. What follows are best guesses based on public statements, campaign contribution records, tweets." Unsurprisingly, the all-Black casts of *RHOA* and *Real Housewives of Potomac* (*RHOP*) were likely Clinton voters, with several of the women being vocal about their positions. Although several women on the *RHOBH* cast have ties to Trump (both Kyle Richards and Lisa Rinna competed on *The Celebrity Apprentice*, for example), public statements, although brief and often vague, indicate that this cast also all voted for Clinton, with the exception of British citizen Lisa Vanderpump, who is ineligible to vote. Not surprisingly, many of the women on the *Real Housewives of Dallas* (*RHOD*) cast, based deep in the heart of conservative Texas, fairly openly supported Trump, even appearing at fundraising dinners with him.[29]

In the Garden State, *Real Housewives of New Jersey* (*RHONJ*) cast member Teresa Giudice was one of the few Housewives across the board to openly support Trump, revealing on *Watch What Happens Live*, "Of course I'm going to vote for Donald Trump. I think he's amazing. I think he'll make a great president."[30] It's likely that many of her conservative castmates cast the same ballot but were not as vocal about it. In Orange County, Vicki Gunvalson was very open about being a Republican. The other women were not forthcoming, but it was likely a somewhat split cast. That leaves viewers to surmise that out of all the Housewives on the air in 2016, twenty-five of them were likely Clinton voters, fifteen were likely Trump voters, and the others were too close-lipped to properly speculate about.[31]

Why does this matter? It matters because 2016 signals a shift in Americans' willingness to engage in politics to an extent that they previously were not. Although *The Real Housewives* specializes in allowing viewers a glimpse into an aspirational world full of luxury, gossip, and social drama, the 2016 election caused some viewers to want to know a little more about the Housewives and their views. The fact that a quick Google search for "who did the Housewives vote for" returns millions of results indicates that this is something a lot of viewers are actually interested in knowing. Perhaps this signals that while Bravo viewers definitely want glamour and petty fights, they might also be ready for a little more reality in their reality TV. As a *Jezebel* article from 2017 noted, "With the *Housewives* being one of the few popular culture phenomena that seems nonpartisan (in that its fan base includes both liberals and conservatives), the voting records of cast members are more intriguing than ever." The author also reiterates that "reality TV occasionally does intersect with actual reality—and like reality, it's uncertain and terrible."[32]

While Bravo took a step toward airing more important topics on season 9 of *RHONY*, politics did not become a central storyline in other cities, even though they had compelling and interesting material from which to work. Cast members on *RHOA* were very involved and invested in the 2016 election and antiracist movements. During season 8, which aired in 2015–16, several cast members traveled to Washington, D.C., to meet with leaders to discuss Housewife Phaedra Parks's organization, Save Our Sons. Save Our Sons' mission statement notes, "African-American boys and men, particularly ones who have grown up fatherless and without positive male role models, are often in need of guidance, information and resources to be successful in life.... It is important for individuals, businesses and local organizations to support the needs of African-American males who want to better their lives and become productive and positive members of their communities."[33]

Many seasons on *RHOA* have featured casts composed solely of Black women. Issues like police brutality and high incarceration rates are important topics, particularly in the Black community. One episode of season 8 covers Phaedra's activism and gives us a glimpse of some of her castmates supporting her. Along with Phaedra, Porsha Williams, Shereé Whitfield, and Kim Fields travel to the capital to meet with Congresswoman Frederica Wilson of Florida to discuss issues affecting Black males and how Save Our Sons can help make a difference. *RHOA* is known for being one of the more humorous groups of Housewives, and this compelling episode offers a stark contrast to the usual light tone of the series. The women have a serious, productive conversation with Congresswoman Wilson and also attend a series of speeches by well-known Black leaders.[34]

The 2016 presidential campaign was also featured on *RHOA*, but not nearly as extensively as on *RHONY*. During season 9, some of the women continued to be openly politically active. In an early episode, Porsha and Phaedra discuss the upcoming election and make plans to attend the Democratic National Convention in Philadelphia. They are clearly excited about the trip and add in some humor by making fun of Melania Trump (humorous to some, anyway). As one reality TV critic opined, "Phaedra and Porsha talk some delightful shit about First Lady-elect Melania Trump. It's not the civil disobedience that we need; it's the civil disobedience that we *desperately* need. Read the Trumps to filth."[35] For some viewers, this would have landed as either funny or disrespectful. Many might not have even paid much attention. But it is notable, again, that 2016 is one of the first times that we really see Housewives willing to be open about their electoral political beliefs.

Later in the episode, Porsha and Phaedra travel to the Democratic National Convention to engage in more discussions about ongoing racism in America. While there, the two listen to such speakers as former attorney general Eric Holder, and Phaedra helps lead a panel discussion on police brutality. The two cheer in the convention center as they wait for the nominee, Hillary Clinton, to take the stage and address the excited crowd.[36] What these women were talking about and doing was significant and interesting, making it notable that politics was not a main theme of the season, as it was on *RHONY*. In fact, it was not even the main theme of the episode. While Bravo chose to highlight political discussions among the women of New York, the women of Atlanta are shown discussing what is traditionally considered politics for only a couple of brief segments during this one episode. It could have been powerful to more fully develop this political storyline, particularly if Bravo chose to focus on broader conceptions of what counts as political.

Politics cannot be defined as simply electoral politics and voting. It would serve us well to instead rely on the feminist slogan "the personal is political" to gain a better understanding of what actually constitutes politics. The women of *RHOA* (and *RHOP*), for example, are always dealing with a lot of political issues. They have to contend with what it means to be Black in America, as we see with Porsha's activism with her Save Our Sons organization, and grapple with important issues like domestic violence, police brutality, and the legacies of slavery. While the Atlanta housewives may not be shown on-camera discussing elections, they do have frequent conversations about race and activism. One example is when the women travel to cities like Houston to help with disaster relief. While they are explicitly helping Black communities that have been hardest hit by natural disasters and inadequate government help, these haven't typically been the storylines to which Bravo devotes the most time. It seems that the network has made a specific choice to cut the instances of activism by these women. What might reality television look like if it actually showed more of the actual reality that women of color live with every day? It would look more real. It would help people understand, or at least acknowledge, complex issues. And yes, it would still be entertaining.

If white women were the activists, would scenes like this be highlighted more on these shows? That's an easier question to answer: Yes, when white women are engaged in activism, it is typically a significant focus on Bravo shows. Bethenny Frankel's BStrong foundation has been the focus of many *RHONY* episodes and storylines. And while Bethenny's activism deserves to be highlighted, it is not more deserving than the activism that is only briefly touched upon on *RHOA*. It would be powerful to get to discuss some of these topics during reunion shows or on *Watch What Happens Live*. Instead, the activism of Black Housewives receive very little camera time or attention, much like their electoral and grassroots politics and the important race-related issues they deal with every day. Whether or not this is a conscious decision, it speaks volumes about whose voices are heard the most on Bravo and in many segments of American popular culture.

After the 2016 election and inauguration, politics didn't necessarily remain at the forefront of many new seasons of *The Real Housewives*, regardless of the city or cast. Politics did, however, continue to be discussed more openly and more frequently than it had before. One such example is the discussion of the appointment of Brett Kavanaugh to the U.S. Supreme Court on *RHOBH*. Season 9 began airing during the winter of 2019, a few months after the October 2018 Senate confirmation hearing on Kavanaugh.[37] Shortly after President Trump nominated Kavanaugh for a seat on the highest court in the land, allegations of sexual misconduct by the nominee became public. The most high-profile accusation came from Dr. Christine Blasey Ford, a professor of psychology. After much deliberation, Ford came forward, stating that Kavanaugh had attempted to force himself upon her sexually during the late 1980s and that she was gravely concerned for her safety.[38]

The Kavanaugh hearing turned into one of the most hotly contested Supreme Court appointments in American history, and there were many clear parallels to another controversial nomination hearing, that of Justice Clarence Thomas in the 1990s. The American public and the Senate were deeply divided as they watched the testimony of both Kavanaugh and Ford. The compelling testimony of Dr. Ford compared with the outrage and righteous indignation of Kavanaugh's response sparked heated debates across the country. The women of *RHOBH* mirrored the public in that the women were both intensely passionate about the issue and deeply divided among themselves.

During an episode titled "A Supreme Snub," the Beverly Hills women attend a dinner party hosted by Lisa Rinna. Filmed in the fall of 2018, this dinner occurred in the context of the #MeToo movement, which began in earnest in 2017 following the accusations of sexual abuse against media mogul Harvey Weinstein.[39] It was during this time of heightened awareness of sexual abuse toward women that America emotionally followed the Kavanaugh hearings. When Rinna arrives at the dinner, she announces that her husband, the actor Harry Hamlin, isn't able to attend because it's a "pretty big day politically," meaning that he's monitoring the Kavanaugh hearing. Rinna goes on to say that Dr. Ford is "changing everything with her courage." The calm atmosphere erupts when Housewife Camille Grammer vehemently disagrees, saying that Dr. Ford doesn't have enough evidence and that she is ruining a potentially innocent man's life.[40]

Grammer's statement is met with shock and revulsion by several of the Housewives. Teddi Mellencamp seems particularly disgusted, telling Grammer that her comments were "a sick thing to say." For her part, Rinna raises her voice at Grammer, arguing that women should be believed, while Grammer refuses to back down from her strong statements. While several of the women are very willing to engage in this important debate, some of them are demonstrably reluctant to participate. Dorit Kemsley mainly responds by closing her eyes as if she wishes she were someplace else. Kyle Richards attempts to close down the conversation by saying, "My mom told me not to talk about religion or politics or sex in public."[41]

RHOBH seems to be one of the *Real Housewives* shows that is perhaps the least realistic, at least for the average viewer. The storylines focus a lot on high-end fashion, mansions, possessions, and living a fabulous lifestyle, even more than the shows in the other cities do. This is why it is even more striking that this politics-centric episode was one of the most dramatic of the season, if not the series. The passion that these women displayed while discussing current events was palpable and likely very relatable to viewers. Like the 2016 election, the Kavanaugh hearings and appointment did not leave much room for neutrality. This was a hotly debated moment in American history, and it was reflected by the debate on-screen.[42]

However, there was little to no follow-up on this dramatic episode and important topic. This fight was only briefly mentioned during the third reunion episode of the season, and host Andy Cohen appeared very reluctant to broach the topic. He allowed both Grammer and Rinna to quickly reiterate their points (with Rinna again asserting that victims must be believed) and then moved on to another subject within moments. This could have been an important discussion not only of the Kavanaugh hearings and the aftermath but of the #MeToo movement in general.[43] By the time this season was filmed, more evidence of sexual assault in all industries, but particularly entertainment and politics, was coming to light, and the subject was being discussed more and more. It did not, however, remain a storyline in the following season of *RHOBH*.[44]

The year 2020 was another election year and, with the trauma of COVID-19, was more emotional and partisan than the 2016 election cycle. It will be interesting to see if the increase in the number of political discussions continues to be a trend on some seasons of *Real Housewives*. Unfortunately, the pandemic has been turned into a political issue in the United States and has been treated as such on many of the Bravo shows. Coming seasons will show some Housewives treating the pandemic seriously while some will go so far as to mock the people who took the proper precautions. The COVID-19 pandemic caused many shows to either delay or cancel shooting, but for the most part, filming resumed in the late summer and fall of 2020. Fans who follow the Housewives on social media continued to get at least a glimpse of many of their political opinions. Some Housewives had been openly participating in Black Lives Matter (BLM) protests ignited by the murder of George Floyd, Breonna Taylor, and other Black people killed by police brutality. As the summer of 2020 continued, the protests continued, and more and more peaceful protesters were being arrested and even harmed. Because of hateful, misleading, and false rhetoric from President Trump and senior GOP leaders, racism, protests, and the BLM movement became even more of a partisan issue.[45]

As noted at the beginning of this chapter, the most notable activist on Bravo has been Porsha Williams of *RHOA*, the granddaughter of civil rights activist Hosea Williams, who marched with Dr. Martin Luther King Jr. Porsha participated in antiracism marches in June 2020 and appeared on *Watch What Happens Live* to discuss issues of race. As the summer progressed, Williams's activism and her public profile increased. She was arrested in Louisville, Kentucky, for protesting the murder of Breonna Taylor by police, and has since used her platform to increase awareness about racism, police brutality, and BLM. In August, the *New York Times* profiled the reality TV star's activism, exploring her family roots in the civil Rights movement and giving Williams a chance to explain why she has been so moved to action over the past several months. Williams noted, "When I saw that video of George Floyd being murdered, I knew that I had to change the way I was moving. . . . That meant now I have to sacrifice myself, my finances, my brand, my everything, and put it all on the line for change."[46]

So far, Bravo has championed Williams and her work, airing multiple episodes on race on the network in the summer of 2020. In one special, the comedian W. Kamau Bell joined Williams to discuss racism in America and the damage it has done to society. Later, Bravo aired a roundtable discussion of race in America featuring Williams and other Bravolebrities, both white and Black.[47] Williams has stated that she expects future seasons of *RHOA* to continue to address these important issues.[48] In the season 13 premiere, several of Porsha's castmates, including Kandi Burruss and Cynthia Bailey, expressed pride in her activism and also noted their vocal support for BLM. The scenes for future episodes indicate that the movement will be a key storyline for the entire season.

Whether Bravo chooses to air more political discussions or not remains to be seen. It will, however, be much harder to avoid them, particularly as the pandemic has become political. On *RHONY*, Ramona Singer's refusal to wear a mask or closely follow pandemic protocols caused several heated arguments at the season 12 reunion. Her casual attitude angered several of her castmates, particularly Leah McSweeney, and seemed to exasperate host Andy Cohen, who had contracted COVID-19 a few months prior. As the pandemic and masks continued to grow more political, trailers for the new season of *Real Housewives of Orange County* began airing, and another housewife began causing real life drama. Housewife Kelly Dodd's public COVID-19 denials and racist behavior have already garnered attention in the press and on social media.[49] And it is likely that Dodd will not be the only reality star on Bravo to face public fire for abhorrent actions.

The years 2020 and 2021 continued to see tensions heightened not just over COVID-19 but due to the growing anger over systemic racism and police brutality in America. Movements like Black Lives Matter grew as more and more people became aware of the need to fight for justice. Even Bravo couldn't remain in its bubble of wealth and pettiness. The network and Andy Cohen began to face backlash over some of the content on the shows and certain cast members in particular. Kelly Dodd, with her ignorant statements about COVID-19, was an easy target for irate fans and was let go, at least partly due to public demand. Several cast members of the popular *Vanderpump Rules*, such as Stassi Schroeder and Kristen Doute, were fired for unacceptable behavior (in this case, racism).[50]

While some might have expected a wave of firings to follow, Bravo went in the opposite direction and opted to hire new cast members. The network tried to add diversity to some of the all-white casts and hired Leva Bonaparte, who is Persian, as a main cast member on *Southern Charm*. Some of the *Real Housewives* series also saw newcomers, including Dr. Tiffany Moon, who was *RHOD*'s first Asian American cast member, and Eboni K. Williams, who was the first Black cast member on *RHONY*. Bravo has also added new diversity training for all employees, including cast members. While it is shocking that it has taken this long for Bravo to add diversity to its casts (particularly in a city as diverse as New York City), this is a positive change. Plus, it seems that like many other Americans, Bravo viewers are ready for it. Yes, they still want the old standbys of a good Bravo show—wealth, petty fights, and bad behavior, to name a few. And, as one journalist cannily observes, "there must be a borderline-narcissistic blend of self-awareness and unself-consciousness, and there must be a cast we care about that comes together, falls apart, and comes back together again." But the one thing about these standbys that has changed? "Viewers have rejected the idea that this can happen devoid of a broader societal context."[51]

The January 6 insurrection also caused rifts between Housewives and left many fans even more aware of the politics of the women. Sara McArthur Pierce, who appeared on *The Real Housewives of Salt Lake City* as a friend of cast member Whitney Rose, participated in the rally, and Bravo viewers immediately clamored for her never to appear on their screens again. Sara took to social media to defend herself, claiming she was entirely peaceful while in Washington, D.C. But for many Bravo viewers, her MAGA ties were too much to overcome. Whitney Rose publicly distanced herself from Pierce after the backlash from fans.[52]

The ramifications of appearing to support anything related to January 6, 2021, continued to cause problems for Housewives past and present years after the event. Once she was cast as a member of the new iteration of *RHONY*, real estate maven Erin Lichy saw her political donations become a hot topic of debate and criticism from much of the Bravo audience. A Reddit post revealed the information that Lichy had donated to Trump's "Stop the Steal" campaign, which signaled to many that she was a MAGA supporter. The outcry was loud enough that Lichy released a statement in an attempt to defend herself, stating, "Regarding the hateful and misinformed social commentary going on about me, I'd like to dispel these false narratives before they continue any further. I do not deny the election and have never supported stop the steal. I unequivocally believe that the 2020 Presidential election was fair and the President was rightfully elected." However, neither she nor her representatives explained her post-election financial contributions to Trump.[53]

Former *RHONJ* star Siggy Flicker has not appeared on Bravo since 2018, but the media and fans of the network are still critical of her political opinions and activities. Flicker first voiced her support for Donald Trump in 2016 and has continued to do so into 2024, making frequent social media posts thanking him for his words and actions. Her actions have caused vocal criticism from many fans, and she even found it necessary to publicly deny that she was at the Capitol on January 6, 2021.[54]

Clearly, political discussions are not going away from Bravo anytime soon. But in a reality television–worthy twist, Bravo has entered the lexicon of discussing politics on a national scale. A *Vox* headline declared, "The Trump Presidency Was a Reality Show. The January 6 Hearings Are the Reunion Special." Journalist Emily St. James made an apt comparison between the often-chaotic reunion specials that are a staple of each *Real Housewives* franchise and the congressional hearings to investigate the insurrection of January 6, 2021. St. James compares the witnesses in the hearing, like Cassidy Hutchinson, to Housewives showing up at the end of the season to talk about what happened during filming and to set the record straight on any fights. In this article, Trump is cast as a reality star who is estranged from his castmates and declined to even show up to film the end-of-season special.[55] But like most reality stars, Trump didn't stay away from the cameras and spotlight for long. At the time of writing, he was reelected president in 2024.

Conclusion

So, does this intersection between reality television and politics matter? Yes, for several reasons. Reality TV is important in reflecting and driving cultural conversations. And research indicates that it might have other impacts. A *New York Times* article suggests that the behavior of Housewives could actually impact public health. One expert noted, "I think that if these characters modeled good behavior, or at least indicated they were concerned about mask wearing and the virus, that would have a positive effect on viewers."[56] That is not to suggest in any way that reality TV stars are personally responsible for the health of millions of people. But it is not a stretch to imagine that those with a public following should perhaps think carefully about how they use their platform. And the pandemic is certainly not the only way that people can use their voices to make a positive change. Porsha Williams is an excellent example of that, and other Bravo stars should follow suit. As one Bravo commentator notes, times have changed, the Bravo audience has changed, and the reality stars must change with them. Brian Moylan writes, "Previously I thought it was easy to ignore the political beliefs of the Housewives," and many people certainly agreed with him. But, he continues, "Things are different now. If not for a divisive political landscape, national protests, and a pandemic, our favorite awful women may have been free to continue behaving badly forever."[57] There may be a time when viewers once again turn to reality TV for pure entertainment. But in the current climate, Moylan is correct. Bravo could use *The Real Housewives* to contribute to an important national discussion on politics. Or they could shy away from it, as many Americans have tried to do.

Notes

1. Heather Cox Richardson, "December 7, 2020," *Letters from an American*, December 8, 2020, https://heathercoxrichardson.substack.com/p/december-7-2020?r=36hiy&utm_campaign=post&utm_medium=email&utm_source=copy.

2. Heather Cox Richardson, "December 5, 2020," *Letters from an American*, December 6, 2020, https://heathercoxrichardson.substack.com/p/december-5-2020?r=36hiy&utm_campaign=post&utm_medium=email&utm_source=copy.

3. Donald J. Trump, "Remarks to Supporters prior to the Storming of the United States Capitol," American Presidency Project, January 6, 2021, https://www.presidency.ucsb.edu/node/347341.

4. At the time of writing, there has understandably been very little academic scholarship completed on January 6, 2021. However, one can look to the reports of Congress and several good media sources to understand the scope of the event and

its continuing ramifications. See the archived committee reports of the Select Committee to Investigate the January 6th Attack on the United States Capitol at https://www.congress.gov/committee/house-select-committee-to-investigate-the-january-6th-attack-on-the-united-states-capitol/hlij00.

5. For information on these events, see Richard A. Oppel Jr., Derrick Bryson Taylor, and Nicholas Bogel-Burroughs, "What to Know about Breonna Taylor's Death," *New York Times*, October 30, 2020, https://www.nytimes.com/article/breonna-taylor-police.html; Jelani Cobb, "The Death of George Floyd, in Context," *New Yorker*, May 28, 2020, https://www.newyorker.com/news/daily-comment/the-death-of-george-floyd-in-context; Michael D. Shear, Noah Weiland, Eric Lipton, Maggie Haberman, and David E. Sanger, "Inside Trump's Failure: The Rush to Abandon Leadership Role on the Virus," *New York Times*, September 15, 2020, https://www.nytimes.com/2020/07/18/us/politics/trump-coronavirus-response-failure-leadership.html.

6. *RHOA*, season 13, episode 1, "No Justice, No Peace, aired December 6, 2020, on Bravo.

7. *RHONY*, season 9.

8. J. Baxter Oliphant and Samantha Smith, "How Americans Are Talking about Trump's Election in 6 Charts," Pew Research Center, December 22, 2016, https://www.pewresearch.org/fact-tank/2016/12/22/how-americans-are-talking-about-trumps-election-in-6-charts.

9. Gates, *Double Negative*, 22.

10. Emily Nussbaum, "The TV That Created Trump: Rewatching *The Apprentice*, the Show That Made His Presidency Possible," *New Yorker*, July 24, 2017, https://www.newyorker.com/magazine/2017/07/31/the-tv-that-created-donald-trump.

11. Murray and Ouellette, *Reality TV*, 3. For more on different forms of media and culture, see Couldry, *Media, Society, and World*.

12. Murray and Ouellette, *Reality TV*, 8.

13. For an analysis of political engagement in 2016 compared to previous elections, see Prior and Bougher, "'Like They've Never, Ever Seen in This Country'?" While voter turnout wasn't necessarily larger, there was markedly higher political engagement during the primary.

14. Deller, *Reality Television*, 19.

15. Deller, *Reality Television*, 20.

16. Tracie Egan Morrissey, "When Will a Reckoning on Racism Catch Up with Reality TV," *New York Times*, October 29, 2019, https://www.nytimes.com/2019/10/29/style/bravo-real-housewives-race.html.

17. *RHONY*, season 9, episode 1, "Talk of the Town," aired April 5, 2017, on Bravo.

18. "Partisanship and Political Animosity in 2016: Highly Negative Views of the Opposing Party—and Its Members," Pew Research Center, June 22, 2016, https://www.people-press.org/2016/06/22/partisanship-and-political-animosity-in-2016. For further analysis of changing political trends in 2016, see Susan Milligan, "One Crazy Year: Does Donald Trump's Victory Signal Politics as We Know It Changed in 2016?," *U.S. News and World Report*, December 30, 2016, https://www.usnews.com/news/the-report/articles/2016-12-30/2016-a-crazy-year-in-american-politics.

19. *RHONY*, season 9, episode 4, "The Etiquette of Friendship," aired April 26, 2017, on Bravo.

20. *RHONY*, season 9, episode 3, "A New Low," aired April 19, 2017, on Bravo.

21. Katie Rogers, "White Women Helped Elect Donald Trump," *New York Times*, November 9, 2016, https://www.nytimes.com/2016/12/01/us/politics/white-women-helped-elect-donald-trump.html. For an analysis of how sexism factored into the 2016 election, see Knuckey, "I Just Don't Think She Has a Presidential Look."

22. Many women experienced a very emotional reaction to the election results. See Christina Asquith, "Shock. Anger. Grief: How Women Worldwide Reacted to Hillary Clinton's Defeat," *Newsweek*, November 11, 2016, https://www.newsweek.com/election-hillary-clinton-defeat-donald-trump-misogyny-women-worldwide-520137.

23. *RHONY*, season 9, episode 5, "The Politics of Friendship," aired May 3, 2017, on Bravo.

24. *RHONY*, season 9, episode 5.

25. Moss and Maddrell, "Emergent and Divergent Spaces in the Women's March."

26. *RHONY*, season 9, episode 12, "Regency Reunion," aired June 21, 2017, on Bravo. Ramona Singer continued to be an avid Trump supporter in 2020, regularly attending social events with Trump insiders and family members. She also attended a party held at well-known Trump fundraiser Joe Farrell's house on-camera in season 12. While some cast members, such as Luann and Sonja, didn't comment publicly on this behavior, Dorinda did let it be known that Ramona's political behavior and reckless socializing during COVID-19 was part of the reason for their rift during 2020. Chris Murphy, "Dorinda Medley Says Ramona Singer Needs a Coronavirus Test 'ASAP' after Attending Hamptons Party," *Vulture*, July 4, 2020, https://www.vulture.com/2020/07/dorinda-medley-says-ramona-singer-needs-a-coronavirus-test.html.

27. *RHONY*, season 9, "Reunion, Part 2," aired August 23, 2017, on Bravo.

28. Dahlia Balcazar, "Who Did the Real Housewives Vote For?," *Bitch Media*, September 18, 2017, https://www.bitchmedia.org/article/who-did-real-housewives-vote.

29. Balcazar, "Who Did the Real Housewives Vote For?" Brandi Redmond appeared at a fundraising dinner with Donald Trump, and D'Andra Simmons speaks very proudly of her deep connections to the Republican Party, noting her work as a communications official in the Department of Energy during the George W. Bush administration. Tamara Palmer, "The Real Housewives of Dallas' D'Andra Simmons Defends Her Work History," Bravo, September 26, 2018, https://www.bravotv.com/the-daily-dish/dandra-simmons-career-before-the-real-housewives-of-dallas-video.

30. Ryan Gajewski, "Teresa Giudice Reveals She's Voting for Donald Trump: 'He's Amazing,'" *US Weekly*, February 10, 2016, https://www.usmagazine.com/entertainment/news/teresa-giudice-reveals-shes-voting-for-amazing-donald-trump-watch-w163937.

31. Balcazar, "Who Did the Real Housewives Vote For?"

32. Madeleine Davies, "Most the Cast of *RHONY* Is Personally Acquainted with Donald Trump, but Did They Vote for Him?," *Jezebel*, August 24, 2017.

33. Jocelyn Vena, "Phaedra Parks Announces 'Save Our Sons' Event," Bravo, November 19, 2014, https://www.bravotv.com/the-daily-dish/phaedra-parks-announces-save-our-sons-event#:~:text=Phaedra%20Parks%20Announces%20'Save%20Our%20Sons'%20Event,place%20this%20weekend%20in%20Atlanta.

34. *RHOA*, season 8, episode 11, "Ms. Parks Goes to Washington," aired January 17, 2016, on Bravo.

35. Ali Barthwell, "*The Real Housewives of Atlanta* Recap: I'm with Her," *Vulture*, December 5, 2016, https://www.vulture.com/2016/12/real-housewives-of-atlanta-recap-season-9-episode-5.html.

36. *RHOA*, season 9, episode 5, "Shade Grenade," aired December 4, 2016, on Bravo.

37. Ezra Klein, "The Ford-Kavanaugh Sexual Assault Hearings, Explained," *Vox*, September 28, 2018, https://www.vox.com/explainers/2018/9/27/17909782/brett-kavanaugh-christine-ford-supreme-court-senate-sexual-assault-testimony.

38. Emma Brown, "California Professor, Writer of Confidential Brett Kavanaugh Letter, Speaks Out about Her Allegation of Sexual Assault," *Washington Post*, September 16, 2018, https://www.washingtonpost.com/investigations/california-professor-writer-of-confidential-brett-kavanaugh-letter-speaks-out-about-her-allegation-of-sexual-assault/2018/09/16/46982194-b846-11e8-94eb-3bd52dfe917b_story.html.

39. For analysis of Weinstein and the #MeToo movement, see Farrow, *Catch and Kill*; Kantor and Twohey, *She Said*.

40. *RHOBH*, season 9, episode 10, "A Supreme Snub," aired April 16, 2019, on Bravo.

41. *RHOBH*, season 9, episode 10.

42. For analysis of the hearings, see Elizabeth Jensen, "Reflecting on the Ford-Kavanaugh Hearings Coverage," NPR Public Editor, October 10, 2018. https://www.npr.org/sections/publiceditor/2018/10/10/654142555/reflecting-on-the-ford-kavanaugh-hearings-coverage; Pollino, "(Mis)Representations of Sexual Violence."

43. See Farrow, *Catch and Kill*; Kantor and Twohey, *She Said*.

44. Orange County, California, has traditionally been a conservative enclave. During the 2018 midterms, Democrats brought down the so-called orange curtain by making major gains in the former Republican stronghold. This was a significant political happening yet was not a main theme on the *Real Housewives of Orange County*, with one exception. Tamra Judge's storyline at times centered on family strife brought on by her two sons, Ryan Vieth and Spencer Barney, who hold very different political views. In one episode, viewers learned that the two had been fighting and ultimately stopped speaking. Ryan claimed that Spencer called him a racist for supporting Donald Trump, specifically his efforts to build a wall. Bravo could have explored this in depth, but it did not. See Tamara Keith, "Democrats Demolish the 'Orange Curtain' in Orange County," *Morning Edition*, NPR, November 20, 2018, https://www.npr.org/2018/11/20/669330214/democrats-demolish-the-orange-curtain-in-orange-county.

45. Jennifer Agiesta, "CNN Poll: Views on Racism, Protests Grow More Partisan This Summer," CNN, September 4, 2020, https://www.cnn.com/2020/09/04/politics/cnn-poll-racism-protests/index.html.

46. Caity Weaver, "Porsha in Protest," *New York Times*, August 10, 2020, https://www.nytimes.com/2020/08/10/style/porsha-williams-real-housewives-atlanta.html.

47. Weaver, "Porsha in Protest."

48. Kellee Terrell, "Porsha Williams Won't Back Down: 'It's Life or Death in America Right Now,'" August 28, 2020, https://www.elle.com/culture/movies-tv/a33808366/porsha-williams-interview.

49. Gabrielle Chung, "*RHOC*'s Kelly Dodd Responds to Backlash over 'Drunk Wives Matter' Hat and Lack of Masks at Bridal Shower," *People*, October 5, 2020, https://people.com/tv/kelly-dodd-responds-backlash-bridal-shower-drunk-wives-matter-hat.

50. Anna Peele, "The Soul of Bravo: A Year of National Reckonings on Race and Inequality Has Tested How Real the Housewives Should Be," *Vulture*, April 14, 2021, https://www.vulture.com/article/bravo-real-housewives-reckoning.html?fbclid=IwAR0mhMh_a0TcgMv5u6Ux31XR2W6UzTYLJTZ0sJU9KQM74mL4uzQJl5Vzr94.

51. Peele, "Soul of Bravo."

52. Bryan Brunati, "'GET HER OFF THE SHOW:' *RHOSLC* Fans Demand Bravo Fire Sara McArthur Pierce after Attending Capitol Riot but She Says She 'Peacefully Protested,'" *US Sun*, January 10, 2021, https://www.the-sun.com/entertainment/2116490/rhoslc-fans-bravo-fire-sara-mcarthur-pierce-capitol-riot.

53. Kate Aurthur, "*Real Housewives of New York City* Cast Member Erin Lichy Disputes Trump Donations: 'I Do Not Deny the Election,'" *Variety*, July 31, 2023, https://variety.com/2023/tv/news/rhony-erin-lichy-explains-trump-stop-the-steal-donation-1235683632.

54. Shannon Power, "Siggy Flicker's Relationship with Donald Trump," *Newsweek*, September 19, 2023, https://www.newsweek.com/siggy-flicker-real-housewives-donald-trump-1828071.

55. Emily St. James, "The Trump Presidency Was a Reality Show. The January 6 Hearings Are the Reunion Special," *Vox*, July 12, 2022, https://www.vox.com/culture/23188617/jan-6-committee-hearings-testimony-cassidy-hutchinson-trump-reality-show-reunion.

56. Jessica Grose, "Watch What Happens When *Real Housewives* Don't Wear Masks," *New York Times*, October 27, 2020, https://www.nytimes.com/2020/10/27/style/reality-tv-real-housewives-coronavirus.html?fbclid=IwAR1p7qUUtSAxfc2WAMkMuO092SIP4-I2-87_J5GJeXXK3Vg6JANYAbur1q0.

57. Brian Moylan, "The Real Housewives versus Reality," *Vulture*, October 7, 2020. https://www.vulture.com/article/the-real-housewives-vs-reality.html.

Part III **The Realities of Race and Space in Historical Memory**

....

Building on the themes presented in part 2 that grappled with the myths versus realities in the premise of Bravo shows, this final part delves further into the ways that historical memory around race and space inform narratives on *The Real Housewives of Potomac (RHOP)*, *Southern Charm*, and *The Real Housewives of Atlanta (RHOA)*. From the D.C.-Maryland-Virginia area to Charleston and Atlanta, the following chapters investigate the multilayered histories and legacies of race and slavery that shaped Black communities and forged the New South. Furthermore, these chapters emphasize the way that Bravo storylines manage tensions related to racial uplift and Black philanthropy, Black freedom struggles, American capitalism, and ongoing white racism with the Lost Cause narrative.

Analyzing the way that the invisible hand of Bravo magic presents reality, Tanisha Ford explains the ways that Potomac as a place offers historical contrast to story arcs seen on *RHOA*. Producers transform the suburb of Potomac by mapping the social dynamics of D.C. onto the show. While Potomac is situated as an enclave of old Black money on Bravo, it is not a Black enclave like Bethesda or Prince George's County, Maryland, and the cast members mostly reside outside the city. This fictionalization of Potomac highlights battles over historical memory surrounding histories of Black philanthropy, and the class dynamics influences how Black fundraising is typically narrated. Unpacking notions of family legacy, colorism, and wealth, Ford situates histories of foundation-model and grassroots Black philanthropy using *RHOP* as an entertaining and educational entry point into what she terms *The Real Housewives* gospel of wealth.

Moving farther south, Kristalyn Shefveland explores the tensions in Charleston's history through analysis of *Southern Charm*. The city's Confederate past melds with persistent Lost Cause mythology, entrenching the racial, gendered, and class power structures from the nineteenth century's plantation elite. Shefveland emphasizes the ways that the show implements *Gone with the Wind* metaphors as a shorthand for female stereotypes that uphold the Old South and Lost Cause nostalgia. In this way, we see examples in Shefveland's work that builds on Baldwin's and Jones's earlier discussions of production seeking to appeal to viewer critique, as they avidly follow the media around the show to condemn various acts of abuse and racism. Shefveland contends that *Southern Charm* presents a town that embodies slavery's legacies, complete with cast members steeped in family histories of Southern dynastic elites and gendered double standards.

Finally, Marcia Chatelain examines histories of Black excellence in the reverse migration of Blacks back to the South beginning in the 1970s through an analysis of Porsha Williams and her entrepreneur co-parent Dennis McKinley on *RHOA*. Together, Williams and McKinley demonstrate Black precarity and Black achievement in the New South, representing two visions of Black progress rooted in the civil rights movement. Williams embraces her heritage as the granddaughter of Hosea Williams to engage in civil disobedience and political activism to fight for Black equality, while McKinley—as "the Hot Dog King" of Atlanta—looks to realize "silver rights" of Black economic mobility by selling franchises. These civil rights movement histories and legacies are deeply connected to Atlanta as a place and to notions of Black womanhood in the South. The multifaceted layers of historical memory reflected through Williams and other cast members capture the legacies of slavery and Jim Crow while projecting the possibilities for political and economic freedom for Black futures.

9 Old Money and Champagne Taste
The Real Housewives of Potomac and the History of Black Philanthropy

• •

TANISHA C. FORD

"Anyone who wants to be taken seriously in philanthropy in this community *has* to go through Potomac," Ashley Darby says in her confessional. It's episode 3 ("What a Little Whiskey Can Do") of *The Real Housewives of Potomac* (*RHOP*), and twenty-six-year-old beauty pageant queen Ashley and her Australian spouse, Michael Darby, are seen sipping wine with socialite Katie Rost and her Jewish boyfriend, Andrew. Ashley manages an Australian-themed restaurant called Oz (financed with Michael's money). But she's hoping to expand her social reach and create a name for herself in the D.C.-Maryland-Virginia (DMV) area. It is a region that, among other things, is a hub of old money. Ashley believes the route to social power is through philanthropy—that is, using Michael's money for the public good. Katie is a self-proclaimed "ball and gala girl," meaning she grew up attending all of high society's formal events. Her family is prominent in DMV philanthropic circles. Ashley, an outsider with no pretense of pedigree, believes that networking with Katie and the other Black women in the Potomac circle will help her vault from being a former bartender—who happened to snag a wealthy real estate developer of a husband—to being a power broker and socialite in her own right.

The rest of the cast is a scintillating mix of personalities: mean-girl Gizelle Bryant, ex-wife of megachurch pastor Jamal Bryant; Robyn Dixon, a daughter of the DMV Black elite and kinda-sorta ex-wife of now broke NBA player Juan Dixon; Karen Huger, the farmer's daughter who married "the Black Bill Gates"; and socialite Charrisse Jackson Jordan, the estranged wife of retired NBA player/coach Eddie Jordan. Collectively, they represent Black women born into old money and prestige, those who married into it, and those who have recently lost the new money they'd once acquired. The social lives they live on-screen are dominated by major themes of contention:

Who keeps the gates of the sisterhood? Who is the *most* philanthropic—the queen of giving? And who is the biggest social fraud?

In sharing her ambition to acquire influence in the DMV, Ashley establishes one of the central story arcs of the season and offers viewers a peek at Black philanthropy in action. Black philanthropy, and the webs of power around it, is rarely the focus of mainstream scholarship, let alone mainstream television. Our introduction to *RHOP*'s particular brand of catty housewives sets the stage with this internecine struggle over the level of status that being a philanthropic woman affords and projects. For example, the big-dollar foundation-style philanthropy that Katie in particular (unsuccessfully) engages in is meant to replicate a top-down giving model that always makes people of color and the poor the recipients of charitable gifts—never generous givers. Others in the cast, Gizelle, for example, represent the long history of grassroots Black philanthropy, which has sustained African American social justice efforts since the eighteenth century. It is this tension, of seeing Black women operate in a grassroots tradition of philanthropy while simultaneously reproducing the giving logics of white capitalists, that would provide great fodder for the classroom. What does it mean to be Black, a woman, and philanthropic while also trying to fit into a *Real Housewives* brand that was not initially modeled to reflect the lived experiences of an all-Black cast? In other words, the sisters of Potomac offer an introduction to what we might call *The Real Housewives* gospel of wealth. It is a frothy, made-for-television take on philanthropy that has enough real roots in African American history to be both entertaining and educational.

Atlanta's African American ensemble cast were the reigning queens of the *Housewives* franchise at the time *RHOP* premiered, in January 2016. People connected with OG NeNe Leakes and the *The Real Housewives of Atlanta* (*RHOA*) cast. I have lived in Atlanta. I can taste and feel the specific new-money vibe: the gaudy, oversized handbags, houses, and designer sunglasses; the plebeian knowledge of all things *fine*, such as wine, dining, and art, which the Atlanta housewives reveal to the camera. The "BET dream," I call it. Something about their lifestyle feels at once aspirational and accessible. These Potomac women were a different kind of cast, representing a lifestyle that most viewers did not have much context for understanding and interpreting. These were the women who lived on the pages of Lawrence Otis Graham's *Our Kind of People: Inside America's Black Upper Class* (1999), where they are portrayed as respectability monsters who will cling to the most elitist rituals and practices in order to maintain their own power. Their tastes are exquisite yet understated. Their palates are discerning and refined. I was curious to see how Bravo would portray this community, these "high-saditty" folks we all love to hate, and how they would make them relatable to Black and white audiences alike.

The Fictional Universe of Potomac

Why Potomac? It's a bit of a mystery, but we have some clues. It helps to know that *RHOP* was the second attempt to launch a *Housewives* show in the Washington, D.C., area. *The Real Housewives of D.C.* (2010) had been an instant flop. Five years later, the Bravo team decided to take another shot, but this time, with a couple of key differences. First, the plan for this show was to keep the focus away from the type of "big P" political drama one associates with D.C. Those politics might work well for a Shonda Rhimes thriller but do not quite stir up the soapy froth Andy Cohen loves.[1] The second difference would be a Black cast, hoping to draft off the energy and fanfare of *RHOA*. This new ensemble would be situated in an enclave of old Black money. And this is where the line between fact and Bravo fiction becomes blurry.

Potomac is a real place, in Montgomery County, Maryland. It is surely an enclave: the fact that one cannot get to it from the Beltway gives it an exclusive status. And its residents have got beaucoup money; its median household income is over $200,000. It probably helped that the town has a name that sounds like it belongs in one of the soap operas that Cohen loved as an adolescent, set in fictional towns such as Pine Valley, Port Charles, and Genoa City. However, it is not really a *Black* enclave. In fact, Black people make up little more than 5 percent of the population.[2] I interviewed people from the region who know these social circles well. "Potomac is not a place that is desirable for African Americans," says corporate executive Latisha Roberson, who currently lives in D.C. If you wanted to find the center of Black power in Montgomery County, Bethesda would make more sense.[3] There is a small but potent Black community in Bethesda, with the type of Black cultural infrastructure (churches, restaurants, and so forth) that make it far more amenable than Potomac to the African American professionals who live there.

If Bravo had truly wanted to tell this story of old Black money and power, they would have set the show in Prince George's County—PG County, as it is colloquially known to generations of Black doctors, lawyers, business executives, and professional athletes. At the time of emancipation, PG County had the highest number of enslaved Africans in the state; together with the free Black population, they far outnumbered white residents. Black people continued to be the majority into and throughout much of the twentieth century (despite treacherous Jim Crow laws), and the area became famed as a place where Black people of means could buy sizable tracts of land. By the late twentieth century, PG County had attracted an expansive elite Black population and had grown in prominence. Today it boasts some of the wealthiest predominantly Black towns in America, including Woodmore, Bowie ("Bourgie Bowie," as it is humorously referred to), Fort Washington, Upper Marlboro, and Accokeek. And its median income is only slightly lower than Potomac's.[4] The staples of the *Housewives* lifestyle—fancy cars, vacation homes, and frequent trips—are "nothing exceptional" in PG County, according to Roberson, who is a Bowie native. "It's the norm to make that much money in PG County, so the big deal they make of it on [*RHOP*] is extreme."[5]

It is unclear why Bravo went with Montgomery County and 75 percent white Potomac instead of an actual enclave of Black power and influence. Perhaps PG County's deep entanglements with the history of slavery seemed too fraught—they would have to address how and why so many people of African descent have settled there over the centuries. Or perhaps it was because Potomac is regularly named to lists of the wealthiest towns in the United States.[6] Or maybe, while they wanted an all-Black cast, they didn't necessarily want an all-Black town, since Atlanta is now seen as a Black mecca in the way D.C. used to be in the 1980s.

Based on the show's early promotional language, it is most likely that they set the show in Potomac to address issues of racial integration and assimilation. "Potomac will follow six wealthy, mainly African-American families living in the area full of rolling hills, gated mansions, prep schools and country clubs, breaking racial barriers to give their children the best lives possible."[7] With its small Black population threaded among a white majority, Potomac is better suited for this minority-struggle angle than is PG County, whose wealthy cities are 60 to 80 percent Black.

Roberson offers another, cultural possibility: "Women in PG are so accomplished. They likely wouldn't want to show up like a Housewife."[8] The two constants of Housewive-ry are (1) disposable income and (2) an abundance of free time. You do not have to be happily married, or even married at all, to star as a Housewife, but you do have to have the money and time to portray a leisurely lifestyle replete with drinks—in Potomac, champagne is preferred—vacays, shopping, tea spilling, and shade throwing.

Some women have the money but not the time. Roberson, for example, is a high-powered corporate executive with a spouse and a child; the grueling filming and social media promotion schedule would not be conducive to her already demanding lifestyle. Plus, the things that make for a really good Housewives performance—politically incorrect "reads," table flipping, and physical assault—do not mix well with the pursuit of a high-powered career. (Indeed, many thought a factor in the D.C. flop had been that reputational concerns kept cast members "a tad too proper to achieve Maximum Housewife," as *Washington Post* food reporter Emily Heil put it.)[9] Housewife-ry tends to appeal more to entrepreneurial women looking to use the huge platform of the show to launch anything from a podcast to a restaurant to a brand (Skinnygirl Margarita, anyone?). Perhaps Bravo chose Potomac because it is simply where they found the most willing recruits to form the nucleus of the cast.

The interesting twist: most of the cast does not reside in Potomac. The first episode ("Mind Your Manners") opens with Gizelle saying, "If you haven't heard of Potomac, that's fine because that means we've done a great job keeping it a nice little secret." Yet Karen and Charrisse are the only two who live in the "exclusive" town. Ashley resides in Arlington, Virginia; Robyn in Baltimore. In the first season, it is unclear exactly where in the DMV Gizelle and Katie reside, but according to the *Washington Post*, it was not Potomac. In a later season, Gizelle eventually buys a home in Bethesda. The jokes about her not residing in Potomac rage on . . . as does the shade-filled debate about whether it is better to *rent* a home in Potomac (as Karen and the Black Bill Gates do) or *own* a home in Bethesda.[10]

For people who have lived in/near big cities, this conversation about geography is not necessarily a shocker; it is merely the politics of place, or how people discuss where they live in relationship to another's knowledge base or point of reference. For example, it is common for someone to tell a nonlocal she lives in New York City when she lives in Yonkers. Likewise, few live in Atlanta (Fulton County) proper, but many describe their home in Cobb or Clayton Counties as Atlanta. But the fact that Bravo initially concealed and misrepresented where the cast lives in the first season feels particularly egregious because they are selling the Potomac zip code as prime socioeconomic real estate. In other words, if you have to import a cast to the town, to pretend as if they live there, it is a telltale sign that the premise of the show is more myth than reality.

"White Potomac" mostly disappears from view in the show. Early in the season, Gizelle and Charrisse inform viewers that very few African

Americans live in Potomac. What is implied here, and reinforced by Karen's insistence on adhering to the rules of proper etiquette, is that those select few have been invited within its gates because they have been properly acculturated into the Potomac way of life. In other words, they—or their family before them—are respectable and thus exceptional "Negroes" (W. E. B. DuBois's framing of "The Talented Tenth" comes to mind). This framing helps distinguish the show from the Housewives of decidedly new-money Atlanta, where a sense of ratchet sophistication is part of the series' brand. Moreover, it brings viewers into the mindset, the worldview, of a Black woman from Potomac. She recognizes that she is privileged to be there, and she is proud to have been "chosen." She will police the boundaries of its territory more than would any white person who believes they are entitled to be there. Yet racial politics in the United States being what they are, the reality is this: the only people to whom she could serve as gatekeeper are the handful of other Blacks who live there. Thus, the target of her ire is other Black women. To sidestep the tough realities of racism, the Bravo producers simply make the white folks disappear. In a bit of camera magic, there are rarely any whites at the center of the screen beyond some B-roll footage of white Potomac residents playing golf and tennis at local country clubs or the occasional white guest at one of the women's soirees.

Bravo seems to deliberately dial-in its focus to make the small and isolated community of "Black Potomac" appear to take up far more space than it actually does. For starters, most of the filming takes place in more culturally and racially diverse areas of the DMV—not in Potomac proper. This fish-eye effect makes it pretty easy for the stars of the show to map themselves as the center of the Potomac social world. In reality, "No one was in the running to become the queen of Potomac. That isn't a thing," says D.C. native and author of *Colored No More: Reinventing Black Womanhood in Washington, D.C.* Treva Lindsey.[11] Lindsey, who attended the elite Sidwell Friends School in Bethesda (which boasts presidents' daughters Chelsea Clinton and Malia and Sasha Obama among its recent alums), explains that Potomac is not known as a society hub for Blacks or whites. It is a sleepy residential community, whose denizens would head into the bustling District to engage in high-society life and the power theatrics of its world.

The producers clearly wanted to map all the power, class, and culture dynamics it had originally intended to portray in *RHODC* and imbricate that with the long history of Black philanthropy and cultural and material affluence that PG County represents. Since Potomac is unknown to most Americans, they could just call it a center of old Black money and most viewers would believe it. I myself had no inkling of the degree to which Bravo's Potomac had been fictionalized until I discovered I have a solidly working-class cousin who lives there. And he is not at all invested in bourgeois politics. Nevertheless, while the cameras are rolling, the women's focus is all about who gets in and who stays out of their gated community.

The *RHOP* Cast: New Adventures of the Old Black Bourgeoisie

RHOP is all about elite status, and each of the women illustrates a different strategy for attaining and maintaining it. In the first episode of the show, the cast members offer a grammar book on the Potomac Black elite: legacy, money, and social sophistication, and philanthropy. Only the first two get you in, but social sophistication (networking) and philanthropy build your personal reputation and influence. Historically, there has been plenty of debate over who makes up the Black elite. At the turn of the twentieth century, Black newspapers were obsessed with chronicling the lives of this group, much the way we now follow the personal exploits of reality stars from NeNe Leakes to Kim Kardashian.[12] Back then, certain qualifications of lineage were a factor in determining if one was "in." For example if your Black ancestor had been enslaved by, and bore the family name of, a signer of the Constitution or an important Revolutionary War or Civil War general, that gave the newly freed family status. Later, in the mid-twentieth century, having family roots in the civil rights movement and ancestors who worked alongside important Black historical actors, such as Dr. Martin Luther King Jr., functioned the same way.[13] *RHOA*'s Porsha Williams, granddaughter of Atlanta civil rights activist Hosea Williams, constantly refers to her family's activist roots for this very reason.

Other ways of getting in could vary from region to region. In the Midwest, particularly Chicago and Detroit, it was all about money. Old or new, especially during the transient years of the 1940s and 1950s, money got you in. In Boston—the bastion of refined New England life—it was all about family background. You had to come from a prestigious family who claimed that they had never been enslaved or whose money had come from business success immediately after slavery, giving them enough decades to have accumulated social and civic prominence by the middle of the twentieth century. In Atlanta, an advanced degree was the ticket to social success, not surprising given the number of historically Black colleges and universities in the city.[14] In Charleston and other parts of the coastal South, it was a color hierarchy. Having a complexion fair enough to pass for white could trump pedigree and wealth (at least for women). Having the magic combination of all these things (money, pedigree, education, and fair skin/"good" hair) could give one social status and mobility, no matter where they migrated.

Gizelle, for example, represents the coming together of all these markers of Black elite identity, and it is arguably why she wields so much power on the show. She resembles a 1980s R&B star (think Vanessa Williams or Pebbles), with her long honey-blond tresses, green eyes, and skin light enough to pass the dreaded paper bag test (it is said that certain high-caste Black social groups would compare a potential member's skin color to the color of a brown paper bag. If their skin was darker than the bag, they could not gain membership). Gizelle describes herself as being "from Potomac," meaning born and raised there, so her entrée into the community was through family legacy. Gizelle's father, Curtis Graves, marched with Dr. King and Andrew Young before, in the 1960s, becoming one of the first African Americans to be elected to the Texas House of Representatives. Like her father, Gizelle attended a historically Black college or university (HBCU)—the prestigious Hampton University—where she pledged Alpha Kappa Alpha. When she married Pastor Bryant, she became the First Lady of the most prominent Black church in Baltimore, which, in her own eyes and many others', is a natural position for someone of her ilk. Viewers can surmise that Gizelle's fair-complexioned bestie Robyn, too, is a Potomac native (though it has been said that her family is from Baltimore) because she descends from a family of "doctors and educators." She earned a degree in business marketing from the University of Maryland–College Park, joined Delta Sigma Theta, and married an elite athlete.[15]

Both Gizelle and Robyn represent another legacy of the region. The color caste system has a deep history in the Washington, D.C., area, where for centuries a fair complexion and loosely textured hair were required to gain acceptance into the upper social echelons.[16] Early reactions to the casting accused the show of upholding the region's notorious colorism. Gizelle and Robyn, nicknamed "the Green-Eyed Bandits," were particular targets of such criticisms.[17] The *RHOP* colorism debate reached fever pitch in season 7, once friendship lines seemed to cohere in ways that confirmed the color hierarchy. Viewers and social media commentators believed that newer cast members—Candiace Dillard Bassett and Dr. Wendy Osefo, both dark complexioned—were given the "angry Black woman" edit.

Nevertheless, Gizelle and Robyn position themselves as "it girls" who break social norms. Gizelle is a divorced mother of three daughters by the time the show airs, and Robyn is in an unconventional cohabitation with her ex-husband Juan and their two sons, Corey and Carter (named after rapper Jay-Z, born Shawn Corey Carter). One could argue that they are able to flout these norms because their status is secured by their legacy and by the traces of the color caste system still visible on their skin.

If legacy is one form of entry, then money is the other. Early on, the women make the priorities clear when they say that to get in, you need either old money or *a lot* of new money. For the women of new money in Potomac, there is no room to flout norms. New-money Charrisse is best friends with legacy-rich Robyn. Charrisse comes from a lower-middle-class family in New Jersey. She married Eddie Jordan, an NBA player who went on to coach the Washington Wizards and other teams. Charrisse and Eddie's move to Potomac was a way to mark their new status when he became the Wizards' head coach. (One of the players on the Wizards was Robyn's husband Juan; this was how Charrisse and Robyn met, in 2003, and formed their bond.) Charrisse remembers how painful those early years in Potomac were, as white residents assumed that she was "Section 8" because there was no way she could afford to live there otherwise.[18] But once they learned she was an NBA coach's wife (with coaches and owners being more revered among the old monied than players), she says, the lunch and dinner invitations started flooding in. By the time we meet Charrisse, she has been living in Potomac for eleven years. We learn that to solidify her status, Charrisse has branded herself as a leading socialite and philanthropist, hosting lavish events at her mansion. "Everyone in Potomac knows who Charrisse is," says Robyn in episode 1.

Karen, the self-proclaimed "Grand Dame of Potomac," is another outsider who married in. But she takes a different strategy than Charrisse and Eddie, claiming old-money status through the legacy of her husband, Ray Huger. Karen proudly refers to him as "the Black Bill Gates" because he's made his millions in the tech world, as president and CEO of Paradigm Solutions International. He built his tech company from a start-up to a $60 million business.[19] According to Karen, his family are doctors and Supreme Court judges, though Ray's family presents (sartorially and tastewise) like every day Black folks in the few times they appear on-screen."

Karen herself did not grow up in the area; she was raised on her family's farm in rural Virginia and met Ray while she was living in Baltimore.[20] Unlike several of the other Housewives, she did not attend college. But Karen is dedicated to keeping the Huger name and standards of living alive. Countering a typical view of her situation, she asserts to Ashley in episode 6 ("Beach Season") that she did not "marry into" the Potomac life; she and

Ray built that life together. When they first moved to Potomac, they were "the outsiders looking in." Ray's Lipton tea–loving Aunt Dot helped teach Karen the ins and outs of being a Black society woman. And, twenty years later, she has mastered it, which is why she feels like she has earned the title Grand Dame—though it is a title that the rest of the cast show scant respect for.

Katie's claim to Potomac comes from a blend of legacy and money. She was raised in what she describes as a "conservative and traditional" family that prized education.[21] Katie's mother Rynthia Rost descends from a family that established an HBCU (Fisk University). Rynthia married one of her law school professors, Ronald Rost, whose Jewish family came into wealth during the Prohibition era, bootlegging liquor, Katie reveals in episode 3. Katie earned a degree in broadcast journalism from Boston University and pursued a career in modeling, which took her around the world and saw her gallivanting with men such as the infamous Russell Simmons, before she settled down with a white New Jersey–based oncologist-hematologist and had three children.[22] Now divorced, Katie has returned to Potomac to do the philanthropic work that is "my legacy and my calling."[23]

At the start of the season, Katie is running her family's foundation. Rynthia, VP of Public Affairs for Geico, is a philanthropic powerhouse in the DMV area. After Katie's father, Ronald, passes away in 2000, Rynthia helps Katie set up a foundation to honor Ronald's legacy and social justice work. According to its website, the Ronald F. Rost Foundation's mission is to "help children in maximizing their life potential and realizing their highest dream of themselves through recreational, enrichment and leadership activities." The foundation fundraises for aligned organizations as well as for indigent families and individuals who need assistance in paying for physical wellness activities (associated with the upper classes): golf, tennis, and skiing lessons; hiking excursions; and yoga classes.[24] Katie's deep philanthropic roots are even co-signed by Gizelle, who notes in her confessional in episode 1 that Rynthia gives away "hundreds of millions of dollars" annually. Season 1 sees Katie hoping to follow in her mother's footsteps, establishing her own, individual reputation in DMV philanthropy.

Black Women's Long History of Philanthropy

In episode 10 ("Rules of Engagement"), Gizelle's dad, Curtis, tells her a story about a benefit concert fundraiser he organized with Dr. King. Those types of fundraisers were essential to the movement because the monies raised would help support bail campaigns, provide food and basic supplies for organizers, and so forth. Before the event, Curtis approaches King dismayed, telling him that he does not think they've sold enough tickets to make money for the fundraiser. He remembers that King started to pray fervently. King then looks at Curtis and tells him to "give away the tickets" to anyone who wants to see the concert and don't worry about the money. Just then, a limo pulls up and the man in the car says he wants to buy tickets—$25,000 worth of tickets in fact—and he wants the organizers to give them away to people who might want to attend. It was a miracle. They were able to raise the money they needed for the movement, and some local community folks got to attend a star-studded concert for free. Curtis tells Gizelle that he believes King's direct communication with God helped to prophesy that miracle. This cross-generational exchange about the grassroots movement for Black freedom throws light on a rarely told history of Black fundraising and philanthropy.

African Americans, particularly the poor and working class, have been written out of mainstream histories of philanthropy. Historian Kathleen McCarthy argues that this is because contemporary definitions of philanthropy center on the generosity of the extremely wealthy. In the early twentieth century, people in the nonprofit sector came to define philanthropy as a "voluntary action for the public good."[25] A handful of white families were seen as engaging in this form of generosity through their corporate family foundations. The word "philanthropist" conjured up images of some of the richest people in the world, from Andrew Carnegie and John D. Rockefeller to Bill Gates and George Soros. Thus, the stereotypical twentieth-century philanthropist came to be seen as white, male, educated, generationally wealthy, and a business owner or leader of industry, often with government ties. Many link the association of "lavish generosity with lavish wealth" to Andrew Carnegie's 1889 essay "Wealth" (republished in Carnegie's *Gospel of Wealth*): "This, then, is held to be the duty of the man of Wealth: . . . to consider all surplus revenues which come to him simply as trust funds, which he is called upon to administer . . . in the manner which, in his judgment, is best calculated to produce the most beneficial results for the community—the man of wealth thus becoming the mere agent and trustee for his poorer brethren, bringing to their service his superior wisdom, experience and ability to administer, doing for them better than they would or could do for themselves."[26] Carnegie conceived of charitable giving as a way the winners of capitalism would, as a moral duty and reflection of their demonstrated merit, administer wealth for everyone else.

Since Carnegie's mandate, we have come to think of philanthropy as a privilege (or duty) of the lavishly wealthy.[27]

Yet scholars of the African American experience, particularly of African American women's experience, have long understood philanthropy to have a different meaning and to take a different shape. In the eighteenth and nineteenth centuries, free Blacks, along with whites of all classes, defined philanthropy as both monetary giving and volunteerism (of time). In this sense, it was less about a vertical obligation where the upper classes must take care of the lower classes and more about a civic responsibility, a horizontal form of community care and mutual aid. In fact, Black abolitionists and activists often referred to themselves as "philanthropists and lovers of equal rights" in their pamphlets and newspapers. Thus, philanthropy was not considered the exclusive province of the wealthy. The poorest and most disenfranchised members of pre–Civil War America determined that they could use their money—no matter how limited—and their time to consolidate power and help those in need through building institutions (churches and community groups), fighting for legislative and policy change, and steering economic development through support of local businesses.[28]

This earlier form of American popular philanthropy is one that was concomitant with African American ways of giving rooted in West African traditions. "Informal giving" such as giving circles—called by variations of the Yoruba term for cooperation, *esusu*—was a part of daily life in precolonial Africa.[29] Concepts such as *ubuntu* (Zulu) or *umuntu* (Xhosa)—indicating a sense of humanity toward others, rooted in the recognition of communal interdependence and a tethered fate—are also common across the continent. Many of these notions of giving to aid the whole survived the Middle Passage and can be observed across the Global South, particularly in the Caribbean and Latin America, and in African American culture.[30] Thus, historian of philanthropy Tyrone Freeman argues that a more appropriate definition of African American philanthropy would be "a medley of beneficent acts and gifts that address someone's needs or larger social purpose that arise from a collective consciousness and shared experience of humanity."[31]

Freeman argues that the narrow white-centered definition of philanthropy is not only limited but harmful in that it "creates an excessive preoccupation with the social and economic elite" and reinforces the notion that Black Americans are necessarily the recipients of others' charitable giving, not agents of change.[32] Research by the Association for the Study of Higher Education (ASHE) has found that much of African American giving centers on "racial uplift," or giving as a means to right centuries of racial oppression and social injustice. In other words, African American forms of philanthropy—that powerful combination of monetary giving and volunteerism—are always already radical acts deeply rooted in the Black radical tradition, a "proactive rather than reactive" form of resistance.[33]

The bulk of African Americans' giving, both historically and today, has been done through Black churches.[34] Tithes and offerings would be made to the church and then distributed to organizations and causes around the globe that the church deemed part of its "kingdom building" mission. Congregants also saw the church as a vehicle through which they could support politicians who advocated for Black causes. Black folks have always given to causes outside their own community, and the post–civil rights generations are even more likely to do so. Yet three-quarters of all African American giving still goes to/through the Black church.[35] This is particularly important to note because historically, Black women have not been allowed to preach from the pulpit, with particular denominations being especially strict. Philanthropy, seen as women's work, therefore became the way for Black women such as Gizelle Bryant to build power within the church structure, acting as program organizers, volunteer coordinators, heads of women's ministries, and building-fund secretaries.

The white philanthropic world has only recently started to recognize Black giving, labeling African Americans as "new and emerging" donors.[36] But as historians such as Evelyn Brooks Higginbotham, Cheryl Townsend Gilkes, Bettye Collier-Thomas, and Martha S. Jones have explored in depth, there's nothing new or emerging about it. The *Chronicle of Philanthropy* has acknowledged that Black-women-led nonprofits have operation budgets nearly 25 percent smaller than those of white-led organizations, requiring them to figure out creative ways to do more with less.[37] The problem is not that African Americans haven't been giving; it is that the philanthropic and nonprofit worlds have not recognized that Black traditions of self-help, mutual assistance, and philanthropy exist in different forms than do white Americans'. African American philanthropists have been overlooked because they employ different methods and have different motivations for giving and fundraising. For example, until very recently, social justice fundraising was considered to be outside the purview of philanthropy proper.[38]

RHOP emerged in this moment when the public conversation around Black giving, and Black women's giving in particular, was finally shifting. The work and power of Black women was gaining more recognition, thanks in large part to the (BLM) movement, the largest social justice–racial justice movement led by young Black people since the Black freedom movement of Gizelle's father's generation. Like that earlier movement, BLM changed the conversation forever. Combining structural approaches similar to those of the 1960s with social media and internet-based crowdsourced fundraising, BLM raised consciousness about systemic racism and police corruption and brutality nationwide. The police murders of Freddie Gray (2015) and Korryn Gaines (2016) brought the movement especially close to home for folks living in the DMV area, where *RHOP* is filmed. To not give attention to the long history of Black philanthropy would have been a real missed opportunity.

The Real Housewives Gets Philanthropic

Real Housewives shows often have one or more philanthropic events per season, but nowhere does philanthropy play a more central role than in season 1 of *RHOP*. Two major plotlines reveal the mechanics of Black women's work in this space in significant detail. Ashley's thread, her quest to befriend the Potomac power brokers, helps viewers learn something about power and how power coalesces around giving. Katie's thread shows how the proverbial sausage is made: what goes into launching a successful (or unsuccessful) foundation or event. Of course, they must remain true to *The Real Housewives* brand—always bringing a heaping of cattiness and shade throwing as they seek to teach something about Black women's generosity.

We meet Ashley Darby in episode 2 ("Divas, Queens and Bubalas") at a Sip with Socialites event held at the Graham in the Georgetown area of D.C. Sip with Socialites is an organization that Ashley cofounded with several of her girlfriends of various ethnicities who aim to be "fashionably charitable." Most of the women work in the media, event planning, public relations, health administration, and tech fields. According to the organization's website: "Sip with Socialites is a group of dynamic women sharing their points of view on all the latest headlines over cocktails."[39] The money the organization raises from these fashionable mixers goes to a cause of the group's choosing. This night, half of the bar tab is going to Touching Heart, a youth-centered group that empowers kids of all socioeconomic backgrounds to become grassroots-minded, philanthropic world changers.[40]

A newcomer to Potomac, Ashley has a different relationship to philanthropy than many of the ladies in that she has been a recipient of charitable giving herself. In episode 2, Ashley shares that for much of her childhood in Sandy Spring, Maryland, she and her siblings experienced housing and food insecurity. Churches and other charitable services helped the family to get by. Ashley was able to attend college and eventually went on to win Miss District of Columbia and compete in the Miss America pageant in 2011. While bartending at a club in the Georgetown neighborhood, she met divorced real estate developer Michael Darby and essentially plotted to get him to marry her. Michael introduces Ashley to a "luxurious lifestyle, a whole other world I hadn't known before," complete with a beach house in Bethany Beach, Delaware, which the girls visit later in the season, and a penthouse apartment in Arlington.

Ashley's interest in philanthropy is twofold. She wants to emulate the efforts of the givers who helped her and her family escape life in tents, cars, and shelters, and she needs philanthropy to help her fit into her new community and her new role as a high society wife. Her Sip with Socialites group represents her success in making friends, but the women are seen by many as philanthropic lightweights—cute millennials in bodycon dresses. It is time for Ashley to upgrade her game and expand her network. Sip with Socialites member Jana, who is described by Katie as being "super connected," invites Katie (who is also eager to expand her rolodex) to the event in Georgetown, and Katie invites Gizelle and Robin to join her.

At this point, Ashley is not even on the Potomac ladies' radar. She is drawn to their group when she learns that Gizelle is from Potomac. She starts trying to connect, but the Housewives are initially unimpressed. Gizelle describes Ashley as "THOT-ish" (That Hoe Over There), "ratchet," and "rough around the edges" and overall does not approve of her youthful, brown-liquor-drinking, free-spirited ways. Robyn comments that Ashley has spent "too much time around white people" because she doesn't know Black girl code (according to Robyn, Black women do not hump on one another on the dance floor). Gizelle says in the confessional, "I'll tell you one thing: she is *not* from Potomac, Maryland," as they show footage of Ashley standing up on one of the lounges at the event, gyrating and yelling "Where's the booty poppin music?! We need to make it twerk up in here!"[41]

Karen and Charrisse are introduced to Ashley in episode 3 ("What a Little Whiskey Can Do") when Katie brings them together on a shopping expedition. Karen sees a little of herself in Ashley, so she "puts her up on game": "It's respect that gets you into the circle. It's a hard circle to get into." Karen is willing to coach Ashley as she attempts to navigate Potomac's treacherous social waters. A Karen Huger co-sign goes a long way. She has built a formidable reputation after arriving as an outsider herself, and in her confessional, Ashley says she aspires to be like Karen. Ashley's strategy illustrates that a successful socialite must also be a successful philanthropist, and a successful philanthropist has to cultivate strategic friendships. Therefore, Ashley is determined to make friends to move up the social hierarchy. By episode 4 ("Desperately Seeking Marriage"), Ashley is also starting to see potential for both strategic and genuine friendships in this group of women.

Episode 3 does a deep dive into Katie's philanthropic work, kicking off an arc that extends into season 2. "To be a socialite is a full-time job. To be a philanthropist is a full-time job," Katie says. "I've been a socialite since I've been in diapers."[42] Now she is ready to commit to philanthropy as her way of life. The episode opens with her doing an interview with *Washington Life* magazine. "During my modeling days, I used my good looks and charm to make money. Now, I use it to raise awareness about the Rost Foundation," she says in her confessional. This magazine feature is a way to amplify her foundation. Having access to and controlling the press is a key element of being a power broker. "To take the Rost Foundation to the next level, I've got to raise more money and more awareness."

Katie's first mission is to establish a signature fundraising event for the foundation. Signature events become the cornerstone of an organization's annual fundraising goal. In a sea of events on the DMV ball-and-gala circuit, it is crucial that a foundation hosts something unique that makes people excited to attend. If successful, they will establish a crowd who will put the event on their annual social-giving calendar. Katie decides on a Casino Royale night. To attract donors to a new event, she needs to get her name (not her mother's) into the social ether. Press helps with that, as does getting invited to the right events. Katie and Andrew attend the Best of Washington gala looking for some "new blood" to invite to Katie's fundraiser. The camera shows Katie literally walking up to people in the predominantly white crowd, introducing herself, and asking if they would be interested in attending a casino night. If this is any indication, it is fair to conclude that, despite her pedigree, Katie is not skilled in schmoozing. The viewer experiences secondhand embarrassment as Katie fumbles her way through the crowd.

In episode 5 ("Error on the High Seas"), Katie decides to turn to the Grande Dame of Potomac for help. She makes a pitch for Karen to join the Casino Royale host committee and help make the event a success. "Karen is a very connected person here in Potomac," Katie observes. Earlier we learned that Katie is hanging out with Karen and Charrisse because they "gotta lotta money, and I need that money."[43] Her goal is to raise $100K for Imagine Stage, an organization that helps youth find their voices and identities through the performing arts. She's got just one month to pull it together.[44] When selecting a fundraising goal, an organizer wants a round figure that is large enough to be impactful (for the cause and for their annual financial goals) and also attainable. Viewers are supposed to quickly surmise that Katie's number is too large for a nascent foundation with an inexperienced leader and an untested signature event.

Katie is desperate to have Karen on her host committee if she has any hope of reaching her outsized fundraising goal. The Grande Dame declines, saying she only commits to things to which she can give her time fully, and she's already stretched thin with the Huger annual charity event. But there's also a subtext: Karen knows her own heft and picks and chooses what she deems worthy to have her name attached to, and she doesn't need Katie's event in her portfolio. The subtle art of shade is at work when Karen says, "Perhaps next year." Viewers have already heard Katie say that she *can't* pull off the event without Karen's guidance, so they can already conclude that this event will be a bust. Katie makes another play, asking for Karen's rolodex, to which Karen replies, "Oh, you not gettin' that!" and then laughs wickedly. Katie looks defeated. She has overplayed her hand, made it too obvious that she is desperate for an alliance.

By the end of the episode, Katie has switched to convincing Gizelle to join the host committee and lend the power of her prominent name to the effort. Though it is not explicitly stated, Katie also needs Gizelle's First Lady planning skills, which again gestures to Black women's long history of civic work through the Black church. In her confessional, Gizelle says that she doesn't know what she is signing up for, but she will help Katie because she is willing to do anything for a good cause. To Katie's face, she emphasizes the importance of her reputation: "If I'm going to help you, which I will, it can't be a hot mess." Katie does her best to reassure Gizelle.

The committee Katie finally succeeds in assembling consists of Gizelle, who has a name and planning skills; Robyn, who has a marketing background; and Ashley, who was easy to recruit because she is also playing the networking game. At this point, it is three weeks out from the event. Katie has not even secured a venue; she does not have a guest list or target number of invitees. When asked, she does not even know how formal she would like the event to be. In the confessional, Robyn says, "Does anyone see the problem here? Because I do!" Gizelle gives it to Katie straight up: "You're tryna raise a hundred thousand dollars in three weeks, and we don't have a venue, no one's been invited." Robyn wants to make it clear that she doesn't want Katie to blame her if she does not reach the fundraising goal. Katie assures Robyn that she has never put on an event that has failed, but it is starting to look like she's never even put on an event.

In a fit of frustration with their questions, Katie kicks Gizelle and Robyn off the committee almost immediately after begging them to join. In the confessional, Katie explains that "there's a lot of pressure to succeed" from her family, so she doesn't need all the girls' negativity. Ashley is the only one left, and she knows that she does not have the experience or the rolodex to help pull off an event of this magnitude on her own. "I think we should tread with caution here, Katie," Ashley says. Katie kicks her off too, says she doesn't need any of their help, and disinvites them all from the event. In the end, Katie is forced to postpone launching the casino night because she just can't pull it together in the allotted time. This is a shocker to no one. She announces in episode 8 ("All Shades of Shade") that the best thing she can do for the Rost Foundation is "be out, be seen, and have my name on the lips of every person who is important in this city." Having failed to hitch her event to an already successful name, she switches focus to just getting her own name out there by emceeing the *Washington Life* swimsuit fashion show fundraiser at D.C.'s Penthouse Pool and Lounge.

Meanwhile, the plot with Karen's foundation event is still rolling ahead. In episode 8, Karen and her assistant, Eny, begin mapping the details of the O Gala event for Alzheimer's awareness, in memory of her mother-in-law, Odessa Huger, who died from Alzheimer's, and in honor of Karen's mother, Georgia Raines Wooden, who has been diagnosed with early onset dementia. Ray tells Karen that he does not want a big loud event because he and his siblings are still grieving. "Let me go to my rsvp list and axe it," she replies. She scales it down from a gala to a cocktail party held in her own home, calling it the "launching party" for the O Gala and asking guests to donate "in Odessa Huger's honor under the O Gala event." Karen states in the confessional, "Even though the scope of it is smaller, it's still gonna be fantastic." She wants every detail to be perfect, right down to the flowers. She can't find cherry blossoms, so she settles on a centerpiece of eighty-nine freedom roses, one for every year Odessa lived. There's valet parking, a jazz band, and half a dozen high-top tables in the foyer. When guests walk in, they are greeted by a server who offers them a glass of wine.

"I cannot believe Karen is calling this a gala and that she's having it in her living room. I'm very unimpressed," says Katie. Karen's planning process looked a lot more professional than Katie's, but Katie still calls it a "Podunk cocktail party," throwing further shade at the fact that this small event was supposedly keeping Karen so busy that she couldn't be on Katie's host committee.[45] Karen's guests surely don't have the appearance of high-net-worth individuals, and it does not quite live up to the Grand Dame hype that viewers had heard so much about—especially if we contrast Karen's cocktail party with the $80,000 fiftieth birthday party Charrisse throws for herself at the Carnegie Library on her estranged husband's dime. These parties are indicators of power and wealth. The Housewives are responsible for not only hosting a certain number of events per season but also covering the bill for the events. The more lux the event, presumably the more disposable income a Housewife has. If this is the case, Charrisse easily wins the battle for queen of Potomac.

Viewers have to wait a whole year to see how the Katie–Rost Foundation arc concludes. She finally has her Casino Royale event in season 2, episode 2 ("All Tea, All Shade"), at the University Club in D.C. Katie's face is all over the invite, which suggests to the girls that it's not really about the cause. And we get more foreshadowing that the event will not be a success when Charrisse explains that, despite being added to Katie's hosting committee, she doesn't really know in which direction the event is moving. Katie seems to be nonplussed about it all, and Charrisse resigns herself to just being on the margins. In the end, Charrisse invites her rolodex (which is what Katie originally wanted from Karen) because Katie has asked her to invite some "high rollers." Charrisse's invited guests show up, dressed to the nines. It is at this event that viewers are introduced to new housewife Monique Samuels (wife of retired Redskins offensive tackle Chris Samuels). Monique shares in the confessional that she and Charrisse recently met at a charity event and instantly hit it off. The Samuelses come to represent new money wisely invested (vs. Robyn and Juan). Charrisse tells viewers in the confessional that Monique and Chris are very prominent in the community. The couple currently lives in Vienna, Virginia, and are looking to buy a home in Potomac. Monique and Chris are jet-setters (they've just returned from Aruba, we learn, after Charrisse asks Monique which of their homes they're currently staying in). Katie's Rost Foundation event does not align with the posh conversation Monique and Charrisse are having about multiple homes and luxury vacays. The event looks low-budget, like it is being held in an inferior hotel's ballroom. Monique says in her confessional that the event was "terrible" and that she "didn't have to throw a gown on for that" because it was more of a cocktail party than a gala. It is a read that is as shady as the episode's title.

Old Money and Champagne Taste 211

Champagne Taste: A Conclusion

As it turns out, no one on the *RHOP* cast is good at hosting large-scale fundraising events. It would have been nice to see what Charrisse might have done if she'd used the $80,000 she spent on her birthday to host a high-society-studded fundraiser. Like the other entries in *The Real Housewives* franchise, their forte is yacht cruises, birthday parties, cocktail-heavy dinners, and girls' trips. And that is fine. It is more in line with what fans of the franchise tune in to see. And, seemingly to capitulate to audience's tastes, subsequent seasons of *RHOP* veered deeper into all things "ratchet."

But it was fun and educational, for me at least, to watch the Housewives explore Black philanthropy—and all its rich grassroots history and entanglements with American capitalism—using the tried-and-true mean-girls formula to bring some conflict. Ashley does eventually make it into the circle and becomes one of the most controversial cast members. She and Michael have been at the center of the show's most salacious plotlines (from threesomes and extramarital affairs to sexual harassment scandals and Ashley's search to find her estranged father). Katie never becomes the philanthropic leader she once dreamed of being. She leaves the show after the first season, credited only as a "guest" in season 2 and as a "friend of the show" in season 4.[46]

The gap that once distinguished *RHOP* from *RHOA* has closed over the seasons. As a cast, all the ladies lose much of the pretentious airs that they had put on in the first season in order to distinguish themselves as a group of refined, educated Black women. Though Karen does still insist on calling herself the Grand Dame (even launching a fragrance called La' Dame), her style and energy becomes younger and fresher. The reads and the clothes remain better over on *RHOA*, but otherwise, you could exchange cast members across the two series and it would not create any real or noticeable difference. In its fifth season, *RHOP* ratings surpassed those of *RHOA*—largely due to a violent confrontation between Monique Samuels (yes, the Monique we were introduced to in season 2 as the epitome of new-money glam) and pageant girl and Howard University alum Candiace Dillard Bassett (who joined the cast in season 3). It seems *RHOP* producers realized that the only way to beat 'em is to engage in the same over-the-top antics as the rest of the reality shows.

It also speaks to a broader shift in *The Real Housewives* brand and friendship-centered reality television writ large. It has all become quite formulaic, relying on the same plot setups and twists and turns to create drama. In that sense, Bravo—which used to rule this soapy-reality domain—is now quite indistinguishable from We TV, VH1, or OWN, which each host competing shows. This is why it is so refreshing to revisit the first season of *RHOP*, when the Bravo folks were trying to do something bold and new that reimagined social politics in the DMV area and offered a new approach to this genre of reality television. The writing was on the wall that this type of philanthropy–high-society angle was not sustainable. However, we are left with a media artifact that could be a useful pedagogical tool in an African American history, media studies, or history of philanthropy course. Let's raise a glass of champagne to that!

Notes

1. Emily Heil, "Why Bravo Picked Potomac for the Newest *Real Housewives*," *Washington Post*, November 20, 2015, https://www.washingtonpost.com/news/reliable-source/wp/2015/11/20/why-bravo-picked-potomac-for-the-newest-real-housewives.

2. For demographics and statistics on Potomac, Maryland, visit the U.S. Census Bureau's online database: https://www.census.gov/quickfacts/potomaccdpmaryland.

3. Latisha Roberson, interview by author, November 22, 2020, Washington, D.C.

4. John Henry, "Prince George's County: How a Community Grappled with Racism to Become a Destination for African-Americans," *WUSA9*, March 15, 2019, https://www.wusa9.com/article/news/local/maryland/prince-georges-county-how-a-community-grappled-with-racism-to-become-a-destination-for-african-americans/65-3a70f85d-9216-4283-9ac7-668b51398b6f.

5. Latisha Roberson, interview.

6. Robert Frank, "10 Richest Neighborhoods in US," CNBC, February 26, 2014, https://www.cnbc.com/2014/02/26/10-richest-neighborhoods-in-us.html.

7. Jean Bentley, "Bravo Announces Two New *Real Housewives* Series, and You'll Never Guess One of the Cities," E! News, November 11, 2015, https://www.eonline.com/news/714967/bravo-announces-two-new-real-housewives-series-and-you-ll-never-guess-one-of-the-cities.

8. Latisha Roberson interview.

9. Heil, "Why Bravo Picked Potomac."

10. Emily Heil and Helena Andrews-Dyer, "What to Expect on *The Real Housewives of Potomac*," *Washington Post*, November 12, 2015, https://www.washingtonpost.com/news/reliable-source/wp/2015/11/12/what-to-expect-on-the-real-housewives-of-potomac.

11. Treva Lindsey, interview by author via phone, August 28, 2020. See also Lindsey, *Colored No More*.

12. Every African American newspaper had one, or several, society columns, which chronicled the lives of the elite men and women in the city, region, or nation.

13. Graham, *Our Kind of People*, 8–9; Taylor, *Original Black Elite*, 67.

14. Betty Granger, "A Society Background Depends on Location," *New York Amsterdam News*, March 20, 1954, 1.

15. For more on the brown paper bag test, see Summers, *Manliness and Its Discontents*; Jenny Berg, "Where Did the Real Housewives of Potomac Go to College?," Bravo, April 26, 2019, https://www.bravotv.com/the-real-housewives-of-potomac/personal-space/where-did-the-real-housewives-of-potomac-go-to.

16. See Taylor, *Original Black Elite*. Taylor discusses how even renowned poet Paul Laurence Dunbar had a difficult time breaking into the D.C. Black elite because of his deep brown complexion. Ultimately, it was decided that his distinguished talent and notoriety were enough to usher him in. Still, we must understand that color was great enough of a barrier that there was considerable hesitation among the gatekeepers of Black high society regarding Dunbar's place in their world.

17. This nickname is a riff on rapper Eric Sermon's moniker. Gizelle uses Green-Eyed Bandits to playfully suggest that she and Robyn are more like sisters than friends. Fans have taken to calling Gizelle and Robyn this name to shade the duo for their regular underhanded acts toward other cast members.

18. *RHOP*, season 1, episode 1, "Mind Your Manners," aired January 17, 2016.

19. For more information on Ray Huger and Paradigm Solutions International, visit https://paradigmsi.com/the-paradigm-team.

20. According to season 5, episode 11 ("Taxing Times and Blurry Lines"), Karen's family was once enslaved on the multiacre plantation before acquiring it and developing the plantation into one of the nation's major suppliers of peanuts. We do not know these details in season 1; instead, viewers are led to imagine Karen being raised on a small destitute family farm.

21. Caroline Gerdes, "'RHOP' Star Katie Rost Is Very Close with Her Mom," *Bustle*, January 31, 2016, https://www.bustle.com/articles/137905-who-are-katie-rosts-parents-the-real-housewives-of-potomac-star-is-very-close-with-her.

22. Janet Bennett Kelly, "On Love: Katie Rost Marries James Orsini," *Washington Post*, January 6, 2012, https://www.washingtonpost.com/lifestyle/style/on-love-katie-rost-weds-james-orsini/2011/12/08/gIQA7CMefP_story.html.

23. *RHOP*, season 1, episode 1, "Mind Your Manners," aired January 17, 2016, on Bravo.

24. For more information on the Ronald F. Rost Foundation, visit https://katierost.wixsite.com/rost-foundation.

25. Freeman, *Madam C. J. Walker's Gospel of Giving*, 3.

26. Carnegie, *The Gospel of Wealth*.

27. McCarthy, *American Creed*, 3; ASHE, "Who Is Philanthropic?," 27.

28. McCarthy, *American Creed*, 3–6. McCarthy offers a deeper examination of philanthropy and the Black church in chapter 5.

29. The term *esusu* shows up variously as *sou-sou*, *susu*, or *su-su*. For more on Black women's giving circles and mutual aid societies, see Valaida Fullwood, Akira Barclay, and Tracey Webb, "The Sweetness of African American Giving Circles: Philanthropy Grows, and More Is Needed," *Charlotte Post*, April 3, 2019, http://www.thecharlottepost.com/news/2019/04/03/opinion/the-sweetness-of-african-american-giving-circles; Lihle Z. Mtshali, "Everything You Ever Wanted to Know

about Those Sou-Sou Savings Clubs African and Caribbean Women Love," *Essence*, December 6, 2020, https://www.essence.com/news/money-career/what-is-a-sou-sou-savings-club-facts.

30. Tyrone McKinley Freeman, "Donors of Color Are Not 'New' or 'Emerging.' We've Been Giving All Along," *Chronicle of Philanthropy*, December 2018, 29.

31. Freeman, *Madam C. J. Walker's Gospel of Giving*, 3–4.

32. Freeman, "Donors of Color Are Not 'New' or 'Emerging.' We've Been Giving All Along," *Chronicle of Philanthropy*, December 2018, 42.

33. ASHE, Who Is Philanthropic?, 27, 29. See also Garrett-Scott, *Banking on Freedom*, chaps. 1 and 2.

34. During the decades between emancipation and the civil rights movement, mutual aid societies and sororal and fraternal orders were popular vehicles of giving. ASHE, "Who Is Philanthropic?," 29; Freeman, "Donors of Color," 42–43.

35. Freeman, *Madam C. J. Walker's Gospel of Giving*, 207; ASHE, Who Is Philanthropic?," 29.

36. Freeman, "Donors of Color," 42. For more on how Black women's historians have written about Black women's philanthropy, see Higginbotham, *Righteous Discontent*; Collier-Thomas, *Jesus, Jobs, and Justice*; Gilkes, *"If It Wasn't for the Women . . ."*; Jones, *Vanguard*.

37. ASHE, "Who Is Philanthropic?," 30.

38. ASHE, "Who Is Philanthropic?," 27–28.

39. The Sip with Socialites website is now inaccessible.

40. For more information, visit the Touching Heart website: https://touchingheart.com/about-us/our-mission.

41. See *RHOP* season 1, episode 2, "Divas, Queens and Bubalas," aired January 24, 2016, on Bravo.

42. *RHOP* season 1, episode 3, "What a Little Whiskey Can Do," aired January 31, 2016, on Bravo.

43. *RHOP* season 1, episode 3.

44. For more information, visit the Imagination Stage website: https://imaginationstage.org/about-us/mission-history.

45. *RHOP* season 1, episode 9, "A Supreme Snub," aired April 16, 2019, on Bravo.

46. Katie's downward spiral in season 4 and on social media was painful to watch. Her mother, Rynthia, blamed Bravo for exploiting Katie. See Tamara Grant, "*RHOP*: Katie Rost's Mom Calls Out Truly Original and Bravo for 'Abusing Her Daughter,'" *Showbiz CheatSheet*, September 10, 2019.

10 Charleston and *Southern Charm*
A Drinking Town with a History Problem

KRISTALYN SHEFVELAND

Owing to the overwhelming success of *The Real Housewives* franchise, Bravo TV branched out to reality programs about groups of friends and the societies in which they live. Each entry in *The Real Housewives* franchise embodies the character and personality of the region or city it inhabits. B-roll for *The Real Housewives of Potomac*, for example, highlights the bucolic cherry blossoms of the capital region, while a stirring soundtrack suggests the discord between the cast members. All of the shows have specific soundtracks that relate to the community they represent, from jazzy urban themes for *The Real Housewives of New York City* to urban hip-hop and pop music for *The Real Housewives of Atlanta*. *Southern Charm* continues these themes; however, unlike *The Real Housewives*, this franchise initially began with a major focus on male relationships and patriarchal power structures. Historically, Charleston has prided itself on being a sophisticated and cosmopolitan city from its earliest settlement. In more recent decades, Charleston boosters have sought to define the city as a cosmopolitan center, with a long history of vibrant social, epicurean, and artistic achievements. Columnist Jim Rutenberg wrote an essay for the *New York Times* Fashion section about Charleston's renaissance as "an international capital of refined culture and distinctive taste," a city that has been featured in *Travel and Leisure, Condé Nast Traveler*, and *Bon Appétit*.[1] Connecting the past to the present and the concepts of honor and kin, this chapter analyzes the portrayals of Charleston and the South Carolina Lowcountry in Bravo TV's *Southern Charm*, which purports to reveal a "world of exclusivity, money and scandal dating back through generations."[2] Many of the cast boast long familial ties to the region, including the patriarchal playboy of the show, Thomas Ravenel (nickname T. Rav), whose family descends from French Huguenot settlers.[3] On display, however, is not a world of exclusivity; rather, for the first six seasons, the show presents clear stereotypes of Charleston's Confederate past, complete with myths about the Lost Cause alongside racial, gendered, and class power structures of Charleston's plantation elite, still present in the modern day.

Charleston's Confederate past and the shadow of the Lost Cause is ever present on Bravo's *Southern Charm*. Through Hollywood films and popular novels, the Lost Cause has captured historical imagination throughout the United States, taking root well into the Deep North, so that tourist attractions like plantations and trinket shops have a steady supply of Confederate memorabilia on hand to sell to Northerners and Southerners alike. The Lost Cause was a deliberate and pervasive effort by Southern historians and heritage groups to reimagine the causes of the Civil War, obfuscating focus from the realities of slavery and instead championing a myth of the bucolic South, an old world of virtue, gentility, and grace filled with white ladies and gentlemen sipping mint juleps on the verandas of their palatial estates. Importantly, the Lost Cause reimagined the war as being fought to preserve the "constitutional principle of states' rights; lauded the courage and sacrifice of soldiers on both sides of the battle; and portrayed Reconstruction as a tragedy that justified disfranchisement and segregation."[4] This phenomena took root not only in the South but throughout the United States, brought to the masses by blockbuster films like *Birth of a Nation* (1915) and *Gone with the Wind* (1939).

In more recent decades, places like Charleston rely on the reimagined South as it contributes to tourist revenue. Outsider scrutiny, however—like the publication of journalist and travel writer Tony Horwitz's *Confederates in the Attic*—coupled with the debates over the Confederate flag at South Carolina's state capitol in Columbia in the late 1990s, has contributed to Charleston's simmering distrust of outsiders. Horwitz writes about the efforts that late twentieth-century Charleston boosters had taken to shed the legacies of the Civil War and the aftermath of the Jim Crow era: "Charleston—Tourist Industry Charleston—preferred to forget the War altogether."[5] In the late twentieth century, Charleston and South Carolina were cast into a national debate about public memorialization of its Confederate past. Thomas Ravenel's father, state senator Arthur Ravenel, publicly spoke out in favor of the Confederate flag at a rally in Columbia in January 2000, calling the NAACP "the National Association for Retarded People." It was within this climate that the Arthur Ravenel Jr. Bridge opened in Charleston, a backdrop B-roll for *Southern Charm* scenes. While Arthur apologized for his remarks in part, he doubled down on his support for the flag: "The NAACP and others—the anti-flag people—describe us as being a bunch of racists." For some Charlestonians, however, the Ravenel bridge acts as a "lasting symbol of unapologetic oppression."[6] While scholars have debated the Lost Cause and its hold on national memory, over the last several decades Charleston has shifted some of its attention away from highlighting only its Confederate past to memorializing and celebrating its connections to the American Revolution in films like *The Patriot* (2000). Colonial Charleston was a diverse space, earning the moniker "the Holy City" for the number of churches within the region as well as its commitment to religious liberty and freedom of belief. Public displays of progressive beliefs, however, belie personal beliefs that at times can still be part of the Lost Cause mythology and the South's racist past. After all, the Ku Klux Klan's reign of terror in South Carolina had multiple waves of violence that has left behind a deeply entrenched systemic racism that continues to inform the politics, economics, and sociocultural dynamics of the region to this day. For the Ravenels and the editors of the first six seasons of *Southern Charm*, there is little desire to face or discuss the realities of racism present in the South or the racist history of the city of Charleston.

When Charlestonians first heard word of the plans for *Southern Charm*, they were opposed. Part of the negative backlash to the show can be connected to lingering resentment toward Sacha Baron Cohen, who came to Charleston in 2002 as the character Borat and proceeded to thoroughly horrify the elite St. Andrew's Society with his lewd and crude behavior and visited the Middleton Place Plantation, lampooning the region for comedic effect in his 2006 mockumentary film, *Borat*. Fears about how outsiders might portray the Holy City are reflected in initial community responses to *Southern Charm* that the show is "a pop culture smear."[7]

Southern Charm is the brainchild of Whitney Sudler-Smith, a Virginia native whose primary residence is in Los Angeles. Previously best known for the 2010 documentary *Ultrasuede: In Search of Halston*, Sudler-Smith was inspired by his friendship with Thomas Ravenel to create *Southern Charm*—originally conceived of as *Southern Gentlemen*—to "deconstruct the myths of the old South but do it in a very funny assertive way."[8] Opening with the jaunty, jazzy tune "It's Easy," performed by Mia Sable, the show is overtly scored to recall the upbeat tunes of the Charleston dance of yesteryear.[9] The *Charleston City Paper* regularly comments on the show, and in anticipation of season 1, columnist Chris Haire wrote an essay titled "H.P. Lovecraft's 'The Call of Southern Charm,'" with the subtitle "T. Rav Lives," in which he proclaims, "There is no language for such abysms of shrieking and immemorial lunacy, such eldritch contradictions of all matter, force, and cosmic order." Commenting on the trailer alone, Haire sees no redeeming qualities to the project and instead describes the endeavor as a horror descending upon Charleston, "a sound of a dire threat . . . only a venomous beast seething for something stronger than sweet tea, spider-legged eyelashes, and a cliff-hanger paternity test." To Haire and other detractors, the show presents more spectacle than substance.[10]

Charleston, the tourist trinkets proclaim, is a drinking town with a history problem. Throughout the show, heavy drinking is a prominent theme. Among the men, there's an emphasis on bourbon, right in line with many takes on the American South, as "bourbon whiskey plays a major role in southern culture, especially in cooking, hospitality, and literature." Bourbon shows up in sweet potato casseroles, bread puddings, and as the main ingredient in classic Southern cocktails like the Hot Toddy, Mint Julep, Old-Fashioned, and, of course, Bourbon and Coke.[11] Patricia Altschul's "medicine" is the perfectly crafted gin martini, and the theme of some of the early seasons surround J.D. Madison's Gentry bourbon business. That J.D. developed a bourbon line signifies the national renaissance of the spirit, moving beyond its Kentucky origins to distilleries all over the nation. Later in the series, Austen Kroll arrives as a beer rep aspiring to create his own beer line. Local response to the show feared the portrayal of the Holy City as a drinking town: "These guys are going to make Charleston look like a city full of drunken, promiscuous snobs and nothing could be further from the truth. . . . Of course we're a completely drunken city, but we don't get drunk on TV."[12]

In the first season (airing in spring 2014), only one of the cast members is from the city of Charleston, though most are from the South. A clear exception is Craig Conover, a College of Charleston law student hailing originally from Delaware, a state that his castmates refer to as "northern." Conover's "Yankee" tendencies, with pretensions to be a Southern socialite, are of frequent comment from castmate Shep Rose. William Shepard Rose III, a native of Hilton Head, South Carolina, is a descendant of the Boykin family, which settled in South Carolina in 1755; were the originators of the state dog, the Boykin spaniel; and whose descendants have a long history of public office. Shep prefers a life of leisure collecting "mailbox money" to a commitment and a steady job.[13] Throughout the series, Craig's aspirations fail to match his work ethic, often leading to clashes with Shep and others. The rivalry between Craig and Shep can be described as jocular with toxic moments, displaying Shep's class antagonism toward men he perceives as lower caste, akin to what political scientist Dolores Janiewski describes as "a common inheritance," whereby certain white men "naturally" dominated those they perceived as subordinate.[14]

The women of *Southern Charm* for seasons 1–6 had a voice in series narrator Cameran Eubanks (later Wimberly), a tenth-generation South Carolinian from Anderson. While Cameran is not a member of the elite upper class of Charleston, her propriety and demeanor help to ingratiate her to Patricia Altschul, the matriarch of the series, and her tacit approval of the shenanigans of the male cast highlight the way that women can be victims of the paternalism present in Southern society and active participants as well. As the voice of morality and reason, Cameran begins the series by giving axioms of the behavior expected of Southern gentlemen, interspersed with the bachelors of the cast breaking all those rules: inappropriate dress, "low class" behavior, cursing, lustful carousing, drinking, and, most of all, exhibiting characteristics of what Cameran calls "Peter Pan syndrome." In many of the seasons, Cameran acts as the straight man to the comedic antics of the series' many male lotharios, most especially Shep.

A foil to the upstanding Cameran is Kathryn Calhoun Dennis. Originally not a full cast member, Kathryn, of Lewiston Plantation near Monck's Corners, appears in conversation with Ravenel's political consultant as a potential romantic partner for Ravenel. Thomas describes her lineage and pedigree similarly to how one might describe a thoroughbred hunting dog or racing horse: "the scion of two major families."[15] Of keen interest to Ravenel, Kathryn is a direct descendant of seventh vice president and South Carolina state senator John C. Calhoun on her mother's side; on the Dennis side, her grandfather was South Carolina state senator Rembert Coney Dennis, who served from 1943 to 1988. When Thomas first meets Kathryn, he is fifty and she is just twenty-one. They spend the night together after a pool party, and the next morning, Ravenel smugly confesses, "A southern gentleman always brings a lady coffee in the morning." Thomas's proclamation and nonverbal body language very clearly implies that he and Kathryn had engaged in sexual activity, a recap at once at odds with the behavior of a gentleman and at the same time completely in line with good ole boy behavior and the paternalism of sexual double standards. In a season 1 exchange with Craig about his crush on Kathryn, Cameran comments that if he married her, he'd be able to live on Kathryn's family plantation, and as *Historians on Housewives* co-creator Jessica Millward has pointed out on the podcast, this "about sums up what you need to know about *Southern Charm*; it's power and privilege, it's southern white masculinity and femininity, and the legacies of slavery in South Carolina are on display." In the case of Kathryn, one can see the legacy of the plantation elite and the potential power of wealthy white women, particularly when it comes to inheritance and family dynasties. While the show in its first six seasons rarely shows the African American descendants of slavery that populate the Lowcountry, the show highlights the presence of enslaved life through the descendants of slaveholders and their wealth, which propagates the mindset of racial inequities and a prowhite ideology.[16]

As the series continues, Kathryn's tumultuous relationship with Thomas is a point of focus, as it turns out that she had a sexual relationship with Whitney prior to Thomas, and a one-night stand with Shep before becoming pregnant with her and Thomas's first child. Later in the season, Thomas meets Kathryn's family at a dinner on their plantation and has a conversation with her father, who comments that he sees no issue about the age difference, laughing with Thomas that his aunt Bee "married a man, Mother told me there was 40 years difference in 'em," opining that Kathryn "always got along better with the older crowd."[17] Throughout the series, Thomas alludes to the political power of the Ravenel name and the legacy of the Huguenot settlement of Charleston. Given his pride in his heritage, it is even more ironic that he has soiled the family name and is a disgraced politician due to his felony conviction for cocaine possession while he was state treasurer. One of the pretexts of the show is Thomas's reclaiming of his political career, and his run as an independent for the U.S. Senate against Lindsey Graham is the main thrust for Thomas's storyline in season 2. Thomas's run for office provides an opportunity for Whitney to direct a misguided campaign commercial that pokes fun at Thomas's wild past, the product of which runs afoul of Kathryn, leading to chaos and rancor between the two camps. In subsequent seasons, Kathryn will lose custody of her two children with Thomas because of her drug use. Fans of the show pay close attention to the gossip blogs and social media as the drama plays out just as much off-screen as it does on-screen.

One can see in the portrayal of the show's cast and its storylines that the producers pursue a legacy of performative Southern gentility that harks back to the popular culture of the slave era. Championed by William Gilmore Simms, a distinctive romantic literature emerged in antebellum South Carolina that focused on family dynasties and lineage in the American South. In Simms's "plantation romance" *The Golden Christmas* (1852), the author tells a story that highlights the social customs of Lowcountry South Carolina. In a discussion with the book's narrator, Dick Cooper, Madame Girardin laments the poor state of Charleston's best families: "It is a hard thing to find any body of pure blood in the city now! Such a mingling of puddles!" In reference to a young woman that the narrator believed was charming, pretty, clever and amiable, Girardin snipes, "It's impossible. As for pretty, that, I suppose, is a matter of taste; and I can hardly allow even that. . . . As for clever—I suppose you means she's smart." When Cooper replies with an affirmation, Girardin continues to scold, "Smartness is vulgar. Rank and family don't need to be smart. . . . Wealth, talent and beauty, even—if all combined—can never supply those graces of manner and character, which are the distinguishing qualities of high birth."[18] Applying this mode of thinking to *Southern Charm*, Thomas Ravenel explains in the opening scene of the first episode, "We have our ways here in terms of being gentile in our customs," yet he makes it a point to consistently remind his cast members (and the audience) of his dynastic claim to the Charleston elite. Whitney Sudler-Smith reveals, "There's a small ruling, entrenched minority of very established old families in Charleston." Dynastic legacies and kin have been a focus within the leading families of Charleston since settlement.[19]

By the mid-eighteenth century, Charleston's interrelated gentry presided over an elaborate, exploitative social order that would last well into the early republic; however, up-country families also created powerful dynastic legacies.[20] A focus for many Southern heritage advocates and elites in the plantation South focused on maintaining a myth of "pure" bloodlines while deliberately ignoring the realities of enslavement, sexual violence, and the mixed communities that play a large role in Southern history.[21] In the late eighteenth century, up-country planters, like the Calhoun family, would join in power with enslaving elites in the Lowcountry as the Cotton kingdom emerged as a new economy.[22] When analyzing *Southern Charm*, it is important to view the gender dynamics not only through the lens of paternalism but also through the lens of race and class, as Southern women can be both victims of the patriarchy and deeply entrenched in the racial and class dynamics of the system, thus becoming perpetrators of discrimination and violence themselves.

Though not from Charleston, Whitney's mother, Patricia, plays the role of Grande Dame and ruling matriarch of the series, explaining rules of conduct with humor but a firm hand. Patricia's role is doling out commentary on the debauched behavior of the miscellaneous cast, frequently in an elaborate caftan with her "medicine," a martini, perched in her hand. Born Madeline Patricia Dey in Jacksonville, Florida, she grew up in Richmond, Virginia, and her public persona both on the show and in her writings is an example of how a white Southern woman uses her lineage to establish herself as a legitimate member of the ruling class in places like Charleston. Educated in art history and archaeology at George Washington University, from which she received both her undergraduate and master's degrees, Patricia lived for many years in Georgetown while lecturing in art history at her alma mater. Her parents were Francis Pearl Sudler Dey and Walter Pettus Dey, a medical doctor. In her book, *The Art of Southern Charm*, Patricia writes that her "Southern roots are strong," including her paternal grandfather, Frank Edgar Dey, a brigadier general in the Confederacy. Her mother, however, was "a beautiful Yankee from Philadelphia" and a divorcée, "something that was so scandalous at the time that I didn't find out until I was in my forties," writes Patricia. That Patricia felt the need to disclose this is intriguing, as she is twice divorced herself and once widowed, making herself a possible target of scorn and judgment for her choices in marriage. Nevertheless, she provides frequent and scathing commentary on the choices of her castmates.

Many of the scenes of *Southern Charm* are set at her home, the historic and architecturally significant Isaac Jenkins Mikell house in Charleston, an 1854 Greek Revival that Patricia purchased in 2008. She redecorated the home with her extensive collection of antiques and art and brought with her a Zuber woodblock-printed panoramic wallpaper depicting a scene from the Revolutionary War, as she claims ancestry to a Patriot soldier who served with George Washington, linking her heritage to the old guard of the American South, with forebears connected to its founding.[23] As the matriarch of the series, Patricia often hosts the rest of the cast at "sophisticated" themed dinners and cocktail hours. Patricia's dinners are frequently a male-only affair, like in season 1 when she hosted a "male chauvinist pig" dinner for the male cast members, in mocking but celebratory jest of the chauvinism present among the male cast.

At these dinners, the editors of the show are harking back to a long tradition of Charleston as a hospitable and epicurean destination. Their efforts are completely in line with the tourism industry of the region as well as documented travel narratives dating back centuries. In an 1832 description of the social scene in Charleston, Mr. John Berkley Grimball, a rice plantation owner, carefully recorded the details of his male-only dinner parties. Entertaining and dining with "men of acknowledged taste," Grimball describes his table as a delightful and bountiful spread, all to highlight his own wealth and position.[24] By the late nineteenth and early twentieth century, Charleston became a popular tourist destination as a home of

Southern hospitality. The tourism industry began a concerted effort to provide a picturesque version of the city's colonial and antebellum past, a vision of moonlight and magnolias. This reinvention of Charleston focused on the Lowcountry's varied and storied culinary heritage, often mythologized with "invented tales of region, race, and food," that appealed to white tourists. This was quite in line with the idea of the paternal slaveholder, thus rebranding slavery and the plantation South by stripping away "any guilt-inducing memories."[25]

In the aftermath of the Civil War, women were a driving force behind the Lost Cause movement as white women "took up the work of public mourning" in the United Daughters of the Confederacy (UDC). The UDC worked side by side with civic leaders to subjugate African Americans as "disfranchisement, segregation, and the battle for memory went hand in hand," and racial violence spread not only through the South but through the whole United States.[26] Missing from *Southern Charm* are the stories of Native peoples and African Americans in the Lowcountry, yet any tourist taking a stroll through the historic Charleston City Market, once the site of the slave market, would find palmetto roses and baskets—heritage pieces connecting the descendants of enslaved peoples to West Africa, particularly Sierra Leone. South Carolina was a unique place in the colonial era, with slave codes borrowed from Barbados by its early white settlers to maintain the slave system, as enslaved persons outnumbered white settlers in some cases three to one. Charleston was the epicenter of the Atlantic slave trade for the American colonies that would become the United States, trading in rice and indigo. The focus on rice led to a unique community of enslaved persons, as South Carolina planters deliberately sought individuals coming from the so-called Windward Coast or Rice Coast, a rice-growing region extending from Senegal to Sierra Leone in West Africa. American colonists had little to no understanding of how to grow rice in the marshlands of South Carolina and Georgia, but the people they enslaved did. Their descendants in the Sea Islands off the coast of South Carolina are called the Gullah, whose English-based creole language has connections to Sierra Leone Krio. In the Charleston City Market, the sweetgrass baskets are a cultural heritage item that connects both to their ancestors and to the rice plantations where enslaved women fanned the rice in large winnowing baskets to separate the grain from the chaff.[27]

The heritage and tourism industry of the twentieth century often steered toward the picturesque and supported themes of the Lost Cause, with a focus on African foodways and culture that ignored the realities of slavery and the violence of the Jim Crow era—a trope that *Southern Charm* has played into from the start. However, in recent years, heritage sites in South Carolina have made progress in their dialogue on systemic racism and the legacy of slavery. To depict the plantation as what it was, a site of horrific injustice, the McLeod Plantation has taken the lead in collaborating with descendant communities and emphasizing a story with a singular focus: the viewpoint of the enslaved African and African American peoples. As a result, more traditional plantation tourism sites, such as Drayton Hall and Middleton Place, have begun shifting their focus to the lives of the enslaved.[28]

Yet like an edition of *Garden and Gun* magazine come to life, in the first six seasons of *Southern Charm*, the editors emphasize palatial homes, plantations, polo matches, and hunting trips—the hallmarks of the upper-class white community in the South. Organized and highly ritualistic hunting events have historical connections to landed elite classes on the European continent, and American Southerners have maintained the tradition as a mark of masculinity as well as class, which one can see in several seasons of the show. Most frequently, the editors emphasize *Gone with the Wind* and broad romanticized views of plantation life and Southern culture, an overt example of nostalgia for the Old South and the Lost Cause. However, the plantation portrayed and romanticized in films was a small-scale industrial society with an enforced racial hierarchy bolstered by the myth of white upward mobility. The first reference to the tumultuous nature of Thomas and Kathryn's relationship occurs near the end of the first episode after Thomas's polo match with a question from Cameran about who a better match for Thomas would be: an audacious Scarlett O'Hara or a moral Melanie Hamilton (Wilkes). Stephanie Barna, columnist for the *Charleston City Paper*, commented on this discussion: "Cameran, please, the game is called Maryann or Ginger. . . . Stop pretending like anybody ever talks about Gone with the Wind in casual dinner conversation. That shit just does not happen without a producer prompting it."[29] Thomas, using hand symbols to indicate his libido, showed a clear preference for the bolder Scarlett. Thomas then opines on Rhett and Ashley, labeling Ashley a "wussy," a "pussy," and a "wimp." While Ashley Wilkes is presented as the perfect gentleman of the Old South in both the novel and the film, Scarlett, her father, and others refer to Ashley's studies as "foolishness." Ravenel, for his part, received pressure from his famous family not to take part in the show and, in an interview with the *New York Times*, also alluded to the seemingly indecisive and unmoored Confederate, Ashley Wilkes: "I'm not going to sit around and listen to what Ashley and his ilk are saying about me."[30] A frequent refrain from Thomas in his confessionals is how little he cares for society types and public perception, a strong libertarian streak that continues with his public persona to this day, especially on his social media, even though Bravo fired him from the show after season 5.

Southern Charm uses references to *Gone with the Wind* frequently to describe their relationships and to describe the South.[31] Among the many themes present in both the book and the film, *Gone with the Wind* is filled with racialized feminine archetypes, and Melanie, Mammy, Ellen, and Scarlett all define different but quintessentially stereotypical Southern women. Scarlett is presented as an "ethnic hybrid," the child of a French Huguenot mother, Ellen Robillard, and a recent émigré Irish father, Gerald O'Hara, the result of which created a "volatile personality" that was bold and often at odds with societal standards and expectations. Mammy, an enslaved woman who also helped raise Scarlett's mother, attempts to rein in Scarlett's tempestuous behavior, acting as a voice of propriety and reason.[32] Critics and scholars describe the character of Mammy as a stereotype from the racist minstrels of the antebellum and postbellum eras. Several elements of the plot serve as examples of the Lost Cause. For example, the enslaved laborers of the O'Hara family are excited to see Scarlett after the war's end, and many stay on with the O'Hara family, a trope of loyal and subservient enslaved people incapable of handling emancipation. Both Mammy and Pork are defenders of the racial and class system, and express sentiments that they are of a higher status than those who work in the field and, in many ways, better than "po whites" like the Slatterys. Class is an important element, as several of the families frequently refer to the Slatterys and others as "white trash."[33] Intriguingly, throughout *Southern Charm*, Kathryn's character is heralded for her pedigree, but her behavior and actions are often the source of much derision and scorn.

Propriety and expectations of feminine behavior are a major theme in *Southern Charm*. While Cameran is open about her desire to be an independent woman who can provide for herself, she is also the first to label an unseemly situation as tawdry and is open about her disdain for the chaos and drama that the Kathryn-Thomas relationship brought to the show in the first several seasons. The expectations placed on white Southern women can be traced back to the rise of the cult of domesticity. Prevalent in popular literature of the era, including *Godey's Lady's Book*, the cult of domesticity had a distinct set of rules for white women to aspire to: piety (Protestant Christian religious belief), purity (chastity of body and mind), submissiveness (to the rule of the patriarch), and domesticity (the caring for one's home and family). To these expectations, the antagonisms of the slave and class systems make the history of Southern women a study apart from the prevailing themes of traditional American women's history, as Elizabeth Fox-Genovese noted: "Southern women's history does not constitute another regional variation on the main story; it constitutes another story."[34]

In *Gone with the Wind*, one can see the archetypes of white Southern womanhood. While Scarlett is often viewed as the stronger of the women, when she returns to Tara to find that the Yankees have destroyed all their food and cotton, Scarlett utters one of the most well-known lines from the film, "As God as my witness, I'm never going to be hungry again," finding strength seemingly from the red clay soil itself. Melanie Hamilton Wilkes is a reserve of strength as well. After Scarlett kills the Yankee soldier, Melanie, although still recovering from childbirth, gathers her strength to immediately help dispose of the body, causing Scarlett to say that she admires Melanie's "thin flashing blade of unbreakable steel."[35] Referencing the cult of white Southern womanhood and its expectations of domesticity, W. J. Cash, in his classic and searing monograph on Southern history, *The Mind of the South*, wrote, "She was the South's Palladium, this Southern woman—the shield-bearing Athena gleaming whitely in the clouds," the standard bearer that led the Confederacy into battle and the New South into a war against Reconstruction and civil rights because "evolution was certain to breed Communism . . . [and] was breaking down Southern morals—destroying the ideal of Southern Womanhood."[36] Identifying the white Southern woman as an embodiment of mythical beauty and connecting her behavior to ideas of sexuality and morality can be seen throughout the history of the American South, even as the Southern ideal of the beautiful woman evolved. It is inscribed in the literature of the South, as in William Faulkner's *The Sound and the Fury*: "I was taught that there is no halfway ground, that a woman is either a lady or not."[37]

As discussed before, this legacy of the Lost Cause is on full display in *Southern Charm*, evident in the choices the production company makes about how the show portrays Charleston. In this case, any discussion of the Civil War, aside from overt Lost Cause nostalgia for antebellum grandeur and pageantry, is largely absent. According to W. J. Cash, the experience of slavery and the loss of the Civil War caused a rigid, defensive mindset for Southerners. In *The Burden of Southern History*, historian C. Vann Woodward wrote: "The South has had its full share of illusions, fantasies, and pretensions, and it has continued to cling to some of them with an astonishing tenacity that defies explanation."[38] In a scene between Thomas and his father, who are discussing Thomas's planned return to politics over oysters and flounder with sweet tea, some insights of Arthur Ravenel's thoughts on gender and the South are made clear. When Thomas mentions that Danni (an artist and trained sommelier, ex-girlfriend of Shep, and friend of Kathryn, who eventually appears regularly on the show) rebuffed his advances because of his conviction and reputation, Arthur jokes that the solution to that is "to get her pregnant . . . and if she has a boy child I'll give the boy $10,000." When discussing the tip, Arthur puts in $5 in cash, quipping, "I like to get rid of those, 'cause there's Ole Lincoln," to which Thomas (who clearly already knows the answer) asks, "You don't like Lincoln?" while laughing. Arthur gives a knowing look to the camera as they leave the table.[39]

The reality of an entrenched hierarchy is ever present in the show. Kathryn and Thomas eventually have two children, a daughter who carries both of their family names, Kensington Calhoun Ravenel, and later a son named specifically for Ravenel's forebears, St. Julien Rambert Ravenel. Cameran mentions their son in her opening monologue as she quips that they have welcomed "the latest Ravenel heir."[40] The most common type of commemorative naming in the South involves the passing on of family names, "like an heirloom, from one generation to another. Often a surname is given as a first or middle name," and this is the case with several of the cast members.[41]

In *Southern Charm*, the rules of respectability are not just related to someone's family lineage, as cast member Landon Clements (seasons 2–4) comments on Kathryn, "Just because somebody came here and had a name 200 years ago, it doesn't mean you have class or breeding now." In the opening episode of season 2, Whitney refers to Kathryn as an "evil sort of white trash. . . . She's like a hillbilly femme fatale," and his mother questions the public way in which Kathryn and Thomas are celebrating the birth of their daughter out of wedlock. This is an example of a classic double standard against the sexual activities of white women, as the rest of the cast holds Kathryn to a different standard than they do Thomas, Shep, and Whitney, all self-confessed lotharios. This double standard, however, carries with it racial connotations in Southern history as well, as demonstrated in a famous toast to Southern white women, quoted in Carl Carmer's *Stars Fell on Alabama*: "To Woman . . . as pure and chaste as this sparkling water, as cold as this gleaming ice."[42] Deconstructing this myth, Florence King in *Southern Ladies and Gentlemen* (1975) makes it clear that this was an excuse for the abuse of enslaved women, that the alleged frigidity of proper white women allowed for "the excuse we needed for messing around down in the slave cabins. . . . We pledge our hearts and our lives to the protection of her virtue and chastity because they are the best political leverage we ever did see."[43] The first several seasons of *Southern Charm* focus on the various women pitted against Kathryn, reinforcing themes of impropriety and ostracization for a character who has not lived up to an ideal of proper womanhood. As Patricia opines, "They say leopards don't change their spots. But I hope that's not correct, because her children need her, and they need her sober."[44] Kathryn is a trope of the femme fatale in these discussions, like a character from central casting for a Tennessee Williams play: unstable, malicious, mercurial, subversive, fragile, and narcissistic—an overwhelming force of nature set to destroy the men around her.[45] Gender roles have proven slower to change in the American South, where "the lady and the gentleman still wield cultural power."[46] And the history of these prescribed roles is deep, with idealized expectations of submissive, domestic, frail, and pious white women.

The realities of life as a woman in the South, from the colonial into the modern era, are starkly different. In the antebellum era, the work of raising large families and working in the home all contributed to the undermining of the Southern woman's own physical and emotional well-being. The Southern climate, with its epidemic and endemic diseases, made things that much worse. Southern women of the elite planter class were also complicit in the violence of slavery, as white women's dedication to the paternalism of the antebellum slave society naturally led them to champion the Lost Cause and continue the racism. Scholarship about the plantation mistress has grown extensively over the last several decades, as has the role of white women in the racial terror of the Jim Crow era.[47]

In later seasons, Kathryn's storyline shifts to a redemptive arc. Kathryn's off-screen issues with Thomas and their custody battle play a key role in seasons 4–6, and the cast shifts its loyalty from Thomas to Kathryn by season 6. In season 4, it is Shep who adamantly defends Kathryn by pointing out to Cameran the double standard of their judgment of Kathryn while Thomas receives a pass (ep. 8), and it is Craig who takes up for her after she comes up in the discussion after a dinner party at Patricia's house (ep. 9). By season 6, the editors have taken a new direction and are highlighting the rise of the new Southern woman led by Chelsea, Danni, and Naomi, who call greater attention to the treatment of Kathryn. As much as the producers have shifted attention away from the Ravenel-focused storyline in season 6, the tone of the show radically changes in season 7, filmed during the height of the COVID-19 pandemic and the Black Lives Matter movement. Thanks to new cast member Leva Bonaparte, a restaurateur of Persian descent, conversations among the cast members include Kathryn's inherited prejudices as a descendant of John C. Calhoun and her off-screen antics as the City of Charleston removes a prominent Calhoun statue from Marion Square in the summer of 2020.[48] These shifts continue throughout season 8, which marks Kathryn's departure from the show, as her off-screen narrative continues to draw tabloid attention, and producers continue to reorient the show to a more general reality television tableau, with less emphasis on Charleston's historic racial and class hierarchy. While the producers of *Southern Charm* attempt to pivot on the narrative arc of their show to highlight a more diverse Lowcountry storyline, the first six seasons have left an indelible mark with class antagonisms, Lost Cause nostalgia, and the mythos of the Old South deeply entrenched and on flagrant display.

Notes

1. Jim Rutenberg, "When Bravo Came to Charleston," *New York Times*, April 18, 2014.

2. Jordan Upmalis, "Meet the Stars of Southern Charm," Bravo, accessed September 16, 2024, https://www.bravotv.com/the-daily-dish/meet-the-stars-of-southern-charm.

3. Van Ruymbeke, *From New Babylon to Eden*; Robert Weir, *Colonial South Carolina*; Hart, *Building Charleston*.

4. Hall, "'You Must Remember This,'" 449.

5. Horwitz, *Confederates in the Attic*, 52.

6. Jeff Wilkinson, "Ravenel's Remark Still Fuels Flag Fight," GoUpstate, January 29, 2000.

7. Rutenberg, "When Bravo Came to Charleston."

8. Rutenberg, "When Bravo Came to Charleston"; Sudler-Smith, *Southern Gentlemen*.

9. Lindsay Denninger, "The *Southern Charm* Theme Song Is Painfully Perf," Bustle, April 13, 2015.

10. Rutenberg, "When Bravo Came to Charleston"; Chris Haire, "H.P. Lovecraft's 'The Call of Southern Charm,'" *Charleston City Paper*, January 16, 2014.

11. Cowdery, *Bourbon, Straight*, 127–29.

12. Harriet McLeod, "South Carolina Reality TV Series Raises Eyebrows in Polite Society," Reuters, March 2, 2014.

13. Shep is also related to Mary Boykin Chesnut, a slaveowner who kept a diary during the Civil War; Boykin Spaniel Society, "History of the Boykin Spaniel," accessed September 13, 2024, https://www.boykinspaniel.org/boykin-spaniel.php;

Jodi Walker, "Shep Rose's Family Gave Him All That 'Southern Charm,'" Bustle, April 27, 2015.

14. Janiewski, "Southern Honor, Southern Dishonor," 72.

15. *Southern Charm*, season 1, episode 1, "Peter Pan Sin-Drome," aired March 3, 2014, on Bravo.

16. Jessica Millward, Kacey Calahane, and Max Speare, "Episode 1: The Pilot," *Historians on Housewives*, August 1, 2019, on Bravo.

17. *Southern Charm*, season 1, episode 7, "The Third Man," aired April 14, 2014, on Bravo.

18. Simms, *The Golden Christmas*, 21–22; Hagstette, *Reading William Gilmore Simms*.

19. Smith, "Family Dynasties."

20. Glover, *All our Relations*; Klein, *Unification of a Slave State*.

21. Bardaglio, *Reconstructing the Household*; Lemire, *"Miscegenation"*; Coleman, *That the Blood Stay Pure*; Lowery, *The Lumbee Indians*.

22. Dattel, *Cotton and Race in the Making of America*.

23. Altschul and Davis, *Art of Southern Charm*; Christopher Mason, "Socialite Patricia Altschul's House in Charleston," *Architectural Digest*, December 16, 2016.

24. Quoted in Ferris, *Edible South*, 28.

25. Ferris, *Edible South*, 216–17.

26. Hall, "'You Must Remember This,'" 7–8. See also Cox, *Dixie's Daughters*; C. R. Wilson, *Baptized in Blood*; L. F. Edwards, *Scarlett Doesn't Live Here Anymore*.

27. Benjamin, *Atlantic World*, 399. See also Wood, *Black Majority*; Carney, *Black Rice*; Littlefield, *Rice and Slaves*.

28. Parker, "Under Scrutiny."

29. Stephanie Barna, "Southern Charm: It's Not a Show It's an Intervention," *Charleston City Paper*, March 5, 2014.

30. Rutenberg, "When Bravo Came to Charleston."

31. Fox-Genovese, "Scarlett O'Hara: The Southern Lady as New Woman"; Higgins, "Tara, the O'Hara's, and the Irish Gone With the Wind"; Cox, "Gone with the Wind as Southern History"; Richardson, "Mammy's 'Mules' and the Rules of Marriage," 52–78; Hale, *Making Whiteness*.

32. Richardson, "Mammy's 'Mules' and the Rules of Marriage," 65–66.

33. Mitchell, *Gone with the Wind*, 408, 420.

34. Fox-Genovese, *Within the Plantation Household*, 42.

35. Mitchell, *Gone with the Wind*, 408, 420.

36. Cash, *The Mind of the South*, 86, 339.

37. Wilson, "Cult of Beauty," 18–19; Roberts, "Ladies and Gentleman, Myth, Manners & Memory," 85–88; Faulkner, *The Sound and the Fury*, 118.

38. Cash, *Mind of the South*; Woodward, *Burden of Southern History*.

39. Cox, *Dixie's Daughters*; *Southern Charm*, season 1, episode 2, "Sh-epic Fail!," aired March 10, 2014.

40. *Southern Charm*, season 3, episode 10, "From Here to Paternity," aired June 6, 2016.

41. Kolin, "Personal Names," 168–71.

42. Carmer, *Stars Fell on Alabama*, 15.

43. King, *Southern Ladies and Gentlemen*, 38.

44. *Southern Charm*, season 4, episode 1, "While the Kat's Away," aired April 3, 2017.

45. Blackwell, "Tennessee Williams and the Predicament of Women," 9–14.

46. Roberts, "Ladies and Gentlemen," 158.

47. Gilmore, *Gender and Jim Crow*; Jones-Rogers, *They Were Her Property*; Clinton, *Stepdaughters of History*; Janney, *Burying the Dead but Not the Past*.

48. Stephen Hobbs, Gregory Yee, Jerrel Floyd, Mikaela Porter, Fleming Smith, and Rickey Ciapha Dennis, "John C. Calhoun Statue Taken Down from Its Perch above Charleston's Marion Square," *Post and Courier*, June 24, 2020.

11 *Real Housewives*, Black Capitalism, and the New South

The Franchise History Behind Dennis "The Hot Dog King of Atlanta"

....

MARCIA CHATELAIN

In the winter of 2015, a group of Atlanta residents were in an uproar over flyers that featured the cast of their city's *Real Housewives* and a play on words: BLACK WIVES MATTER.[1] The riff on the political movement Black Lives Matter—which had come to national prominence the previous summer after the killing of Michael Brown in Ferguson, Missouri—was deemed offensive by some, as its appropriation by a show whose cast members argue over Donkey Booty exercise videos and failed attempts to launch fashion brands appeared to diminish the gravity of the movement's work against police violence. Bravo's representatives distanced themselves from the posters that appeared in shopping malls across Atlanta, and the poster's design company claimed that cast member Kenya Moore—or someone claiming to be the former Miss USA—had commissioned them. Regardless of the origin of the poster, the short-lived controversy sparked by associating the movement with the wives suggested that racial politics had nothing to do with reality television. But an examination of the emergence of *The Real Housewives of Atlanta* (RHOA) in 2008, and the evolution of one of its cast members, Porsha Williams, reveals that racial politics—past and present—has been at the center of the show, even when it is not fully engaged with current events. Williams's political awakening as a Housewife, her romantic relationship with her entrepreneur co-parent, and her grandfather's work in the civil rights movement render her a symbol of the contradictions of a television program that centers Black women's wealth in the South.

Precisely one month before the historic election of the first Black president of the United States, Bravo offered its own entry into the annals of Black history: for the first-time ever, a *Real Housewives* series would be led by a predominately Black cast. With a debut of Tuesday, October 8, 2008, as the nation was deliberating on the possibility of a Black family in the

White House, reality television viewers were welcomed to the sprawling homes of Lisa Wu-Hartwell, DeShawn Snow, NeNe Leakes, Shereé Whitfield, and the only white cast member, Kim Zolciak. In introducing the concept to the public, Bravo explained the show this way:

> Expanding on the success of the original hit series *The Real Housewives of Orange County* and the watercooler sensation *The Real Housewives of New York City*, Bravo is heading South for its newest installment, *The Real Housewives of Atlanta*. An up-close and personal look at life in Hotlanta, *The Real Housewives of Atlanta* follows five glamorous Southern belles as they balance motherhood, demanding careers and a fast-paced social calendar, and shows what life is like in the most exclusive areas of Atlanta. These driven and ambitious women prove that they're not just "housewives," but entrepreneurs, doting mothers and classy Southern women.[2]

By the time viewers came to the Atlanta series, it was clear that cast members were "not just 'housewives,'" as the New York and Orange County stars were also divorcées, single mothers, and bachelorettes. The show's capacious definition of what makes one a Housewife for Bravo's purposes reveals that perhaps the most important distinction among the series versions is place, more so than the marital or employment status of its cast members. Each franchise relies on place to more narrowly define the women, and the choice of the expression "Southern belle" to denote the Atlanta Housewife made it clear that the cast would be understood as defined by the supposed conservatism, specific protocols, and ostentatiousness of Southern femininity. Yet *RHOA*'s disruption of the racial homogeneity of the earlier series compelled viewers to rethink notions of gentility and privilege in the region, which most visibly shows the signs of the nation's birth from the institution of slavery and its Jim Crow era. To suggest that Atlanta is more racist than other Housewives cities, like New York or Washington, D.C., or Miami, would be to ignore the great reach of white supremacy nationally and globally, but the city of Atlanta and the decision to cast the show with mostly Black women forced the franchise to engage the issue of race more explicitly than it had with its other entries in the franchise.

The regional specificities of the Housewives context appear throughout the series in myriad ways, but there are clear standard bearers of a Housewife existence that remain pretty consistent across the franchise. Housewives, regardless of their location, deal with complicated romantic relationships; they host dinner parties that devolve into screaming matches. Housewives work themselves up into a lather over the assignment of accommodations on girls' trips, birthday party budgets often equal the first-year tuition at a liberal arts college, and VIP seating is essential for any and all events. Over the years, the "not just 'housewives'" have become a commodity for in-person appearances and in business through sponsored content deals and the hawking of actual products. Housewives sell signature merchandise in wine shops, open restaurants, resell clothing online, and present their designs to viewers of QVC. The Atlanta Housewives are no different in that their commercial life intersects with the social patterns of their city. The places in which Housewives do their special work is tinged by the distinct differences between the definition of wealth and success as determined by their local community. A gated McMansion in Coto de Caza and the doorman buildings of the Upper East Side are worlds apart, but they are clearly objects of envy across the board. Atlanta Housewives live in sprawling homes that are often the perfect backdrops for poolside parties and outdoor teas, yet they heighten tensions around tardiness because they are only accessible through the clogged arteries of the city. Housewives in Southern California, Atlanta, and New York City discuss traffic as part of their small-talk banter more often than do their Dallas and Potomac counterparts. In these moments, the realest parts of their lives are exposed, but soon more TV-ready drama fills the screen, and audiences are served what they came for: shady comments and spilled tea.

Another Black Housewife would not appear in the franchise until Stacie Turner joined the predominately white cast of *The Real Housewives of D.C.* in 2010, and in press interviews before the show premiered, she often noted the distorted view the show presented of a city with such a large Black population. When asked about being the only nonwhite cast member, she told a local news organization, "D.C. is such a diverse city and it is known as Chocolate City. I expected there to be other nationalities on the show and there weren't. I feel additional pressures and really hope that I represent well."[3] Ostensibly, Bravo could have made a similar choice in casting Atlanta in a manner that focused on the whiteness of the city's elite and framed the story of the Housewives in the tone of Vivian Leigh's performance in *Gone with the Wind* rather than to the beat of a twirling Kenya Moore's "Gone with the Wind Fabulous," one of the many auto-tuned songs birthed from a Housewives' fight. Ultimately, although there was nothing inevitable about the creation of a Black Housewives vehicle by virtue of its location, the representation of the city and its belles has served to structure the ways that the women perform the role of Black Housewife for a television audience.

In its fifteen-season run, not only has *RHOA* distinguished itself as the only series in the franchise to feature a majority-nonwhite cast, but its assembly of Black women is also representative of the economic mobility of the New South. The Great Migration of African Americans transformed cities like Chicago, New York, and Los Angeles between the world wars. The reverse migration of Blacks back to the South beginning in the 1970s set the stage for a wide swath of what is identified on social media and popular culture as Black excellence.

Since the 1970s, upwardly mobile Black people have been flocking to Charlotte, Memphis, Dallas, Houston, and Atlanta to try their hand at the nascent industries—banking, aviation, entertainment production, and energy—that boomed (and occasionally busted) between 1970 and 2000. The economic opportunities in the oil and gas industries in cities like Houston and New Orleans, the growth of the medical economy throughout the South, and the real estate booms of the early 2000s coincided with the educational and career gains of a generation of Black people who were able to benefit from a short window of aggressive affirmative action policies, minority scholarships to college and graduate schools, and diversity hiring programs in corporate America. Before the legal challenges to affirmative action reconfigured college access and the real estate bubble burst, the Black middle and upper-middle class could point to Atlanta as the crown jewel of reverse migration destinations. Atlanta in October 2008 held two truths when we first meet the Housewives: Lehman Brothers, the fourth-largest investment bank in the United States, had filed for bankruptcy, one of many financial disasters that sent shockwaves across the world; and the first Black president was headed toward a historic victory. Throughout the unfolding of *RHOA*, the tensions between Black economic precarity, which was revealed during the Great Recession, and the power of the Black excellence narrative shaped cast narratives on and off the show.

The promises and pitfalls of Black achievement and the New South were illustrated in the romance between Housewife Porsha Williams and her former partner, Dennis McKinley. Williams, who lent her voice and star power to the political movement to end police brutality toward Black people, and McKinley, as a Black business owner focused on expanding his hot dog franchise among a network of other Black businesspeople, represented two interlocking visions of Black progress that were rooted in the civil rights movement that took shape and developed in Atlanta. On the surface, their relationship is just one of many that entertain viewers and provide fodder for entertainment blogs, but their partnership also speaks to why the Atlanta series stands apart from the other links in this chain of cable programs. As Williams adopts the position of previous generations who sought equal access to the franchise for Black people, and Dennis tries to realize Black economic goals by selling franchises, their public-facing work speaks to the racial and economic dynamics portrayed season after season on Bravo.

......

The fifth season of *The Real Housewives of Atlanta*, which premiered days before Barack Obama's second historic election in 2012, introduced Porsha Williams to the Housewives landscape. Among a cohort of *actual* housewives cast for the show, Williams, a Georgia native, presented herself as a prototype of Black Southern royalty: the granddaughter of civil rights activist Hosea Williams. If New York housewife Luann de Lesseps's status as a countess was an indicator of her marriage to a man of pedigree, then Williams's association with the Black freedom struggle was a nod to a different form of social capital in the South, which was measured in historical proximity to the civil rights movement. In the convention of how Housewives are introduced to the series, whether as a friend of an existing Housewife or as a newcomer to the Housewife home base, the introduction montage is where the subject has to lay out her value and worth to the series. In these flashy interstitial segments, the Housewife offers up the social clout she has amassed by virtue of either her marriage to a man of considerable wealth or her own business and professional success. "My husband is" or "I am the owner of" leads the segment. Rarely do Housewives use familial status to define themselves to others. In only rare cases, like New York City alumna Tinsley Mortimer in her conversion from fallen socialite to bachelorette Housewife, does a Housewife place herself in the context of her family of origin.

But as a true Georgia peach, Porsha Williams exists at the intersection of the two most enchanting narratives of Atlanta: (1) the people's fight against white supremacy led by the iconic Dr. Martin Luther King Jr., and (2) an embrace of the monetization of Black opportunity, entertainment, and Black capitalism that characterized the city as the lodestar of the New South of the post-1968 era.[4]

Atlanta historian Maurice Hobson has described the city as "having witnessed both the greatest successes and greatest failures with regard to blacks in the United States," marked by "the sordid racial history of the American South with its riots and rebellions, yet . . . transformed into the South's newest world-class international city by the late twentieth century."[5] This transformation moved beyond the work of the city leaders in attracting business or the 1996 Olympics to the region; equally important to the revival of Atlanta was the film and television industry. By the late 2000s, Atlanta was the setting of countless episodes of MTV's home-and-garden show *Cribs*, which often featured Black musicians, actors, and athletes residing in Atlanta, even if their professional lives took them to New York City or Los Angeles. The state of Georgia's aggressive pursuit of film and television deals created an awareness of Atlanta's affordability, and Black elites often used its historical sites, including King's Ebenezer Baptist Church and the Atlanta University Center, to situate Atlanta into a "sordid racial history" that signaled gravitas but rarely suggested the permanency of racism.

Atlanta's dual identities as a place of serious struggle and bloodshed, and its representation as a place where every day serves up a Black bacchanal, is embodied by Williams's evolution as a Housewife. Williams's evolving storylines on *The Real Housewives*, her relationship to on-again, off-again co-parent Dennis McKinley, and her rise as a racial justice advocate after the summer protests of 2020 represent the complexities of post-1968 Black politics and culture in the South. More so than their colleagues, the Atlanta Housewives have presented television viewers with more insights into interracial dynamics, discussions about the unfinished business of racial justice movements, and glimpses into the psychic pain of living under the threat of racial violence from police. Although the focal point of many of the show's seasons have conformed to the Housewife staples of friend drama, relationship drama, and business drama, the inescapable reality of being Black women whose privileges never fully inoculate them from the scourge of racism has made the entire series unusually real in a format that relies on manipulation by producers and is constantly plagued by rumors of fake and contrived storylines. For Williams, a native of the Atlanta area, her primary identification throughout the series can be understood as her articulation of what it means to be a Black woman in the South. Over the course of eight seasons, she has probably experienced the most change in her personal life and image while still remaining tethered to her status as a descendant of Black political struggle. Williams was first introduced to viewers as eventual ex-husband and former professional football player Kordell Stewart's self-proclaimed "Black Barbie doll." She then joined the ranks of single Housewives and shed her conservative veneer in favor of a more carefree, sex-positive presence on the show. Soon, she entered a relationship with Atlanta businessman Dennis McKinley and gave birth to her daughter Pilar. Williams attributed motherhood with deepening her political awakening. A feature for the *New York Times*—which described her as a onetime "glamorous goofball"—focused on her participation in protests (and subsequent arrest) in Louisville, pleading for justice for Breonna Taylor, a victim of police violence. Williams's activism was described this way: "The resolve to join in arrived swiftly, she said, "because I have a little girl in the house. And it doesn't take but a second for a mother to think about the fact that they want their child to be healthy, well and have a good life."[6]

Although Louisville brought forth Williams's first arrest, she was no stranger to protest. Throughout her appearances on *Real Housewives*, Williams has gestured toward accompanying her grandfather on marches through segregated and racist parts of suburban and rural Georgia. In her one-on-one segments to frame her experiences with community service as her most recent acts of civil disobedience, Williams evokes her grandfather as a source of inspiration as well as a means of laying claim to being the heir to a perch among Atlanta's elite. In the summer of 2020, while the nation mourned the passing of her grandfather's friend Congressman John Lewis and celebrated the voter registration work of local political activist Stacey Abrams, Williams's identity as a Georgian and her use of her celebrity power to align with the Black Lives Movement proved reality television's ability to platform more than just Housewives' pet projects. Williams's political life was integrated into season 13, with castmates jokingly calling her "Porsha Luther King" and gifting Pilar a doll fashioned after Rosa Parks. The inflections and references to civil rights in earlier seasons were used to define Williams's value to Atlanta as a place, but Williams's own articulations about her responsibility to Taylor and other victims of police violence allowed her to center herself as a valuable voice for a new generation. The *Times* wrote of Williams, "Like many millennials who grew up supporting civil rights habitually, if less assertively than the legends of the 1960s (whose exalted peerless-ness became, over time, a self-fulfilling reputation), Ms. Williams felt a radical urgency and responsibility to act after Mr. Floyd's death."[7] Williams's urgency, drawn from her connection to that peerless group through her grandfather but fortified by the millennial formation in the culture of reality television, has allowed her to be both the symbol of joviality and a voice for justice in the reality show world she inhabits.

· · · · · ·

"We have our civil rights, now we're fighting for our silver rights!" Through the 1980s, Jesse Jackson used that turn of phrase to inaugurate a new era in Black progress, in which he argued that marching on a state capitol building would only make sense if it brought economic capital to Black America. For Jackson, who also served by King's side and was a movement regular like Hosea Williams, King's death signaled a shift in Black priority making. As an adherent to the Black capitalism school of change making, the reverend regularly brokered agreements with corporate entities—from Coors Brewing Company to Burger King—to facilitate more Black representation on boards, as vendors and contractors, and as construction workers. Buoyed by his organization Operation PUSH (People United to Save Humanity) in Chicago, Jackson was a frequent visitor to Atlanta to support the city's Black politicians and leaders, and more importantly, his call for Black wealth creation was repeated feverishly among his peers. If Atlanta saw itself as the birthplace of King's leadership of the movement, then King's unfinished work would be resolved by the business class through their victories. Although Hosea Williams continued to walk the path of public service during this period by serving in the Georgia state senate, he agreed with Jackson, who once told a crowd in Indiana, "We're not fighting for social generosity, we're not marching for welfare, we're marching for jobs."[8]

While Porsha Williams expands her presence as Hosea's granddaughter through her activism, her co-parent Dennis McKinley is the manifestation of Hosea and Jesse's work in the 1970s and 1980s, which emphasized the need for Black business to also set forth the path of freedom. Although he is not a Georgia native, McKinley's presence as Williams's companion rounds out the modern Atlanta story their relationship presents to viewers. McKinley entered Williams's life (and the television show) in 2017, and after a whirlwind courtship, the couple got engaged shortly after Williams announced that she was pregnant with her first child. Five years after joining the cast, Williams was fulfilling her dreams of motherhood and marriage on-camera, and McKinley's wealth and his business were featured prominently throughout the seasons that chronicled their relationship. Eventually, the relationship soured, and after a spin-off about the conflict surrounding their breakup titled *Porsha's Family Matters* aired, Williams found a new love in Simon Guobadia. Guobadia is a petroleum company founder who was once married to a *RHOA* supporting cast member; since their relationship was made public, Williams has spent less time on publicizing activism, but she remains in the spotlight by giving interviews about the couples' three wedding ceremonies.[9]

Although he did not enjoy a happily-ever-after life with Williams, McKinley's presence as a representation of Black Atlanta was significant for the show's aims. McKinley, a Detroit native, personifies the second generation of reverse migrants who understood the New South as providing a low cost of living and the Black elite who embraced an entrepreneurial spirit. From what he offers *Real Housewives* audiences, McKinley's fortune was built on hot dogs. Throughout the seasons in which he and Williams are dating, McKinley's Original Hot Dog Company is the preferred caterer for takeout at parties and casual lunches filmed at Williams's country club–adjacent home in suburban Duluth. Hot dogs, on their surface, may not appear to be as weighted by the legacies of fighters for Black freedom as Williams's activism, but fast food has a well-traveled route for civil rights believers who pivoted toward silver rights during the golden age of Black capitalism. During this golden age, roughly between 1968 and 1980, King's Southern Christian Leadership Conference, the NAACP, and Jackson's Operation PUSH promoted fast-food franchising and encouraged using federal Black business ownership programs to bring McDonald's, Burger King, and Kentucky Fried Chicken outlets to the hyper-segregated corners of American cities, where corporations and foundations committed to growing inner-city businesses. Among the various proposals for Black-owned bookstores, food cooperatives, and coffee shops, fast-food franchises were often identified as the best business options because they were backed by the might of established fast-food brands. This strategy of bringing Black franchising to communities in Los Angeles, Chicago, New York City, and Atlanta often relied on using the rhetoric of racial progress, like the fight for the franchise through the ballot, and reinterpreting it to mean that progress could be seen through the opening of a new burger franchise. Beginning with McDonald's granting a franchise to an African American in 1968, just months after King's death, the fast-food industry began to target Black communities and co-opt the language of Black freedom to sell franchising.[10]

Fast-food franchises were sometimes presented as a panacea for all that ailed poor, disenfranchised Black communities: for the struggling and underemployed, it could provide jobs and a pathway to managerial leadership. For the hustling and undercapitalized, it could provide enormous wealth. From the vantage point of the early twenty-first century, when health practitioners became concerned about the diet-based diseases that disproportionately affect African Americans, few today are willing to present fast food as a totalizing social good. But the issue of Black wealth-building continues to shape-shift, and even though Williams is occasionally a vegan on seasons of *The Real Housewives*, McKinley's business acumen is applauded, even if it's enlarged by selling hot dogs. McKinley's forefathers in the movement for Black dollars are the same people who fought for civil rights. With the support of the federal government and a growing recognition of the rising affluence of Black consumers, fast food became the crown jewel of Black capitalism's campaigns. From soul's godfather James Brown, who launched his Gold Platter restaurants in Macon, to a series of Dairy Queens near Morehouse College franchised by Freedom Riders Julian Brown and Hank Thomas, the desire to see Black-owned businesses helped facilitate the frenzy for fast food in Atlanta, as well as other cities that embraced Black capitalism.[11]

McKinley acquired the Original Hot Dog Company in 2015, having retooled the brand established by another entity. Like the men who came before him, McKinley emphasizes that his business provides Black people a mechanism for addressing racial inequality, while still centering the notion that there is endless opportunity provided by Black capitalism. In the spring of 2019, the Original Hot Dog Company announced it was offering franchise opportunities using the type of language that franchising boosters like activist-turned-Congressman Julian Bond used in the 1970s. "'Currently, we are looking for franchisees that are looking to open restaurants, create jobs, boost their city's economy, and do some remarkable things in their community,' says Chief Development Officer, Tarji Carter. 'We are looking to do this on a national level.'"[12]

For the interested franchisee, expanding McKinley's footprint comes at a price, although a relatively accessible one compared to the multimillion-dollar franchise fees associated with the big legacy brands. For the Original Hot Dog Company, an interested party pays a franchise fee of $40,000 and has to show a net worth of $100,000. Franchising a McDonald's or a Burger King can require ten times what McKinley is asking, but the franchise system overall can imperil first-time business owners because the franchisee assumes the liabilities of running a business, while the franchisor merely provides the blueprint. The actual nuts-and-bolts of the system can appear as secondary to the possibility of uplifting Black communities through the business model. And the logics of Black excellence and Black capitalism often focus on that hope, at the detriment of the realities of a business's limited capacity to address the consequence of racism, wealth gaps, and state violence.

In a feature in *Black Enterprise*, the gospel of Black capitalism founded in 1970, McKinley perpetuates the narrative of the magical franchise in an interview highlighting his continued success in fast-food franchising. Despite the disastrous impact of the COVID-19 crisis on restaurants in 2020 and 2021, McKinley managed to open fifteen new locations during the summer of 2020, shortly after the nation experienced the first wave of the virus and restaurants across the country were temporarily shuttered. The success of the Original Hot Dog Company coheres with the hustle-hard ethos of Atlanta's Black business class. In the face of economic devastation caused by the global pandemic, McKinley affirms that his potential franchisees were all seeking ways to outsmart the system. "Even with COVID-19, we've seen a surge in interest from candidates that were laid off and don't want to go through that again, even when the economy recovers."[13] Despite a more COVID-19 favorable take-out model, a hot dog franchise is only as strong as the consumer base that surrounds it, and McKinley's certainty that his business can survive and provide owners autonomy echoes the pro-franchising rhetoric that surrounded the minority franchising initiatives of the late 1960s and the celebrity-backed fast-food restaurants that targeted Black businesspeople. McKinley's Original Hot Dog Company represents Black capitalism 2.0, and he reproduces the fantasy of Black-owned business as a salve for what ails Black communities. "I also want to point out that 100% of our owners are people of color—Black or Brown. I don't think many franchises can say that. And not only that, at least half are women. We're very proud of that fact."[14]

· · · · · ·

Fast-food franchising in the United States has built its reputation on uniformity regardless of location. Every french fry, milkshake, and hamburger sold under the banner of a fast-food brand is expected to taste, feel, and look a certain way. In reality television's take on franchising, similar rules dominate, even when the locations change. Fashion shows, holiday parties, end-of-the-season gatherings, reunion shows, girls' trips, charity events, product launches, and planned confrontations are available on every menu, and the cast is responsible for delivering the item to audiences with only slight variation. Housewives in Dallas may head to the relatively modest lakes of Texas, while New Jersey's ladies enjoy weekends on the edges of the Atlantic Ocean, but the audience recognizes the familiar tropes of these getaways and their explosive finales. All the cities come alive when the women visit cherished institutions, like New York City's Four Seasons, or drop by a Housewives-owned boutique in a suburban mall in Gwinnett County, Georgia, and these visits indicate that a conflict or reconciliation is on the horizon. Yet by placing Black women in a Black mecca at the center of the *Real Housewives of Atlanta*, no matter how much the franchise conforms to the rules of the genre, the weight of the city's history and the way it serves to reflect the vision of Black futures make the peach holders distinct, even as the show suggests that they are not that different from their sisters in other cities. Since the introduction of Atlanta to *The Real Housewives* universe, only franchise newcomer Salt Lake City and its rootedness in the city's Mormon origins replicates some of the lingering historical dynamics of Atlanta. Yet Atlanta still remains both inside and outside the Housewives universe in that the franchise demands that all its cast members adhere to a certain relationship to wealth and gender performance and provide a window into the life of elites as defined by place. Yet the sheer weight of that place—Atlanta—and the weight of Black women's history refuses it and remakes it into something evocative and wholly different. Porsha Williams's status as Hosea Williams's granddaughter has remained a constant referent for her social status and her affinities for the South. Additionally, her proximity to Atlanta's civil rights past provides an opportunity for viewers to understand Williams and all of her castmates as tethered to place in ways that white Housewives—many of whom are transplants or rooted in their respective cities due to their spouse's careers—are not. *The Real Housewives of Atlanta* made history by opening up a Black experience to cable viewers, and the weight of history informed how they looked at themselves, each other, the present, the past, and their imaginings of a future in which Black women's lives could be as entertaining as white women's. It is for these reasons that Porsha Williams as character and Porsha Williams as legacy and Porsha Williams as matriarch of a New South family—alongside her other castmates, whose stories reveal the layers of Black political and economic imagination—may be the most revealing in this reality show world.

With the introduction of a new entry into the series, audiences can be certain of specific elements of storytelling that bring together groups of women—with varying levels of intimacy from previous friendships—and know that they will encounter interpersonal dramatics, displays of wealth, and revelatory gossip. Yet with *The Real Housewives of Atlanta*, audiences must also contend with a world that acknowledges the impact of racism on the perspectives and concerns of privileged Black women, a complexity rarely seen on scripted or unscripted television. Prior to the season capturing 2020, *RHOA* fans were given only glimpses of the ways these Black women interacted with Southern history, their children's encounters with police, and an occasional confrontation with a white cast member's veiled comments about race. The Atlanta vehicle exposes how the Bravo universe captures politics and place in its programming, and how a television series can be simultaneously formulaic and illustrative of how race shapes and informs how the Housewife life is lived. Black wives indeed matter.

Notes

1. "Controversial *Real Housewives of Atlanta* Flyers Appear with Slogan 'Black Wives Matter,'" January 20, 2015, https://abc7.com/bravo-the-real-housewives-of-atlanta-rhoa-reality-tv/483545; "*Real Housewives of Atlanta* 'Black Wives Matter' Promo Poster Riles Some," *Atlanta Journal-Constitution*, January 27, 2015, https://www.ajc.com/blog/radiotvtalk/real-housewives-atlanta-black-wives-matter-promo-poster-riles-some/p8GLVJ5tX13WfuXlWANgON. Incidentally, Kelly Dodd from the *Real Housewives of Orange County* received criticism from social media and some of her castmates for wearing a "Drunk Wives Matter" hat and posting a picture of it on social media in the midst of the protests over the killing of George Floyd in Minneapolis in 2020.

2. "*The Real Housewives of Atlanta*, Season 1," Bravo, accessed December 23, 2020, https://web.archive.org/web/20140415025126/http://www.bravotv.com/the-real-housewives-of-atlanta/season-1.

3. "*Real Housewives* Stacie Turner: I Was 'Surprised' to Be the Only African American Cast," August 5, 2010, https://www.nbcwashington.com/local/real-housewife-stacie-turner-i-was-surprised-to-be-the-only-woman-of-color-on-the-show/2101778.

4. For more on Black capitalism, see Case, *Black Capitalism*; Allen, *Black Awakening in Capitalist America*; Weems Jr., *Business in Black and White*.

5. Hobson, *Legend of the Black Mecca*, 249. For more on Atlanta, see Levy, "Selling Atlanta"; Bullard and Thomas, "Atlanta: Mecca of the Southeast"; "Blacks Played Major Role in City's Economic Development," *Atlanta Daily World*, August 13, 1978; Clark Rozell, "Auburn's 'Sweet' History," *Atlanta Daily World*, June 17, 1979.

6. Caity Weaver, "Porsha in Protest," *New York Times*, August 10, 2020, https://www.nytimes.com/2020/08/10/style/porsha-williams-real-housewives-atlanta.html.

7. Weaver, "Porsha in Protest."

8. "Turnout Small at King Memorial," *Chicago Sun-Times*, April 15, 1983.

9. Emily J. Shiffer, "Who Is Porsha Williams' Husband? All about Simon Guobadia," *People*, March 29, 2023, https://people.com/tv/who-is-simon-guobadia-porsha-williams. Porsha Williams finalized her divorce from Dennis McKinley in February 23, 2024.

10. See Chatelain, *Franchise*.

11. "Franchise Route Looks Good for Blacks—Thomas," *Atlanta Inquirer*, February 24, 1973; William Reed and "Saluting a Champion—Businessman Henry Thomas," *Smithsonian*, November 29, 2017.

12. "The Original Hot Dog Factory Announces Franchising Initiative," April 5, 2019, https://www.qsrmagazine.com/news/original-hot-dog-factory-announces-franchising-initiative.

13. "*Black Enterprise* Feature: Businessman Dennis McKinley on Expanding His Hot Dog Franchise to 15 Locations," July 7, 2020, https://theoriginalhotdogfactory.com/hot-dog-blog/black-enterprise-feature-businessman-dennis-mckinley-on-expanding-his-hot-dog-franchise-to-15-locations.

14. "*Black Enterprise* Feature: Businessman Dennis McKinley on Expanding His Hot Dog Franchise to 15 Locations," July 7, 2020, https://theoriginalhotdogfactory.com/hot-dog-blog/black-enterprise-feature-businessman-dennis-mckinley-on-expanding-his-hot-dog-franchise-to-15-locations.

Bibliography

Primary Sources

Archives

Archivo General de Indias, Seville, Spain
Archivo General de la Nación de México, Mexico City, Mexico
Archivo Histórico de la Nación, Madrid, Spain
Boykin Spaniel Society
South Carolina Department of Archives and History, Charleston, South Carolina

Audio

Latisha Roberson interview, conducted by author, November 22, 2020.
National Public Radio
Pretty Mess Records
Treva Lindsey interview, conducted by author via phone, August 28, 2020.

Published Materials

Beecher, Catherine. *A Treatise on Domestic Economy*. Rev. ed. New York: Harper & Brothers, 1845.
Carnegie, Andrew. *The Gospel of Wealth*. New York: Carnegie Corporation of New York, 2017. First published in 1889 as two articles, "Wealth" and "The Best Fields for Philanthropy."
Carranza, Alonso. *Discurso contra malos trajes y adornos lascivos*. Madrid: Imprenta de Maria de Quiñones, 1636.
Collection de documentos para la historia de la formación social Hispanoamérica, 1493–1810, edited by Richard Konetzke. Vol. 2. Madrid: Consejo Superior de Investigaciones Científicas, 1953.
Ezcaray, Antonio de. *Vozes del dolor: Nacidas de la multitud de pecados, que se cometen por los trages profanos, afeytes, escotados, y culpables ornatos*. Seville: Thomas Lopez de Haro, 1691.
Gage, Thomas. *Travels in the New World*. Edited by J. Eric S. Thompson. Norman: University of Oklahoma Press, 1959.
Hume, Martin A. S. *The Year after the Armada*. London: T. Fisher Unwin, 1896.
Jimenez Patón, Bartolomé. *Reforma de trajes. Doctrina de Frai Hernando de Talavera, primer Arzobispo de Granada*. Baeza: Juan de la Cuesta, 1638.
Le galant qui a fait le coup. In *Recueil de farces (1450–1550)*, vol. 6, edited by André Tissier, 309–66. Geneva: Droz, 1990.

Marqués de Careaga, Gutierre. *Invectiva en discursos apologeticos contra el abuso público de las guedejas*. Madrid: María de Quiñones, 1637.

Novísima Recopilación de las Leyes de España. Madrid, 1805–07.

Passio sanctarum Perpetuae et Felicitatis Opera hagiographica anonyma aetatis partum: Passiones (saec. II-V). The Library of Latin Texts. Turnhout: Brepols, 2010.

Ramón, Tomás. *Nueva prágmatica de reformación, contra los abusos de los afeites, calzado, guedejas, guardainfantes, lenguaje crítico, moños, trajes y exceso en el uso del tabaco*. Zaragoza: Diego Dormer, 1635.

Recopilación de Leyes de Los Reynos de Las Indias. Madrid, 1681.

Sudler-Smith, Whitney. *Southern Gentlemen*, pilot, Vimeo, 2017, https://vimeo.com/203473074?fbclid=IwAR1zOvfut7etCcIG4RcgXdIEN6sB5JEem8f-ojQbp2UADilZI2NB6-wX8Hw.

Tissier, André. *Recueil de farces (1450–1550)*. Vol. 6. Geneva: Droz, 1990.

Trump, Donald J. Remarks to Supporters Prior to the Storming of the United States Capitol Online by Gerhard Peters and John T. Woolley. The American Presidency Project. https://www.presidency.ucsb.edu/node/347341.

Secondary Sources

Allen, Robert L. *Black Awakening in Capitalist America: An Analytic History*. Trenton, NJ: Africa World Press, 1990.

Altschul, Patricia, and Deborah Davis. *The Art of Southern Charm*. New York: Diversion Books, 2017.

Álvarez-Nogal, Carlos, and Leandro Prados de la Escosura. "The Decline of Spain (1500–1850): Conjectural Estimates." *European Review of Economic History* 11, no. 3 (2007): 319–66.

Anderson, Fiona. "Fashion: Style, Identity and Meaning." In *Exploring Visual Culture: Definitions, Concepts, Contexts*, edited by Matthew Rampley, 67–84. Edinburgh: Edinburgh University Press, 2005.

Andrejevic, Mark. *Reality TV: The Work of Being Watched*. Lantham, MD: Rowman & Littlefield, 2004.

Andrejevic, Mark, and D. Colby. "Racism and Reality TV: The Case of MTV's Road Rules." In *How Real Is Reality TV? Essays on Representation and Truth*, edited by David S. Escoffery, 195–211. Jefferson, NC: McFarland, 2006.

Arcy, Jacquelyn. "Affective Enterprising: Branding the Self through Emotional Excess." In *The Fantasy of Reality: Critical Essays on "The Real Housewives,"* edited by Rachel E. Silverman, 75–92. New York: Peter Lang, 2015.

Arnold, Janet. *Queen Elizabeth's Wardrobe Unlock'd*. New York: Routledge, 1988.

Asch, Ronald, and Adolf Birke, eds. *Princes, Patronage, and the Nobility: The Court at the Beginning of the Modern Age, c. 1450–1650*. New York: Oxford University Press, 1991.

ASHE, "Who Is Philanthropic? Philanthropy by Nontraditional Donors." *ASHE Higher Education Report* 37, no. 2 (2011): 27–40.

Aspers, Patrick, and Frédéric Godart. "Sociology of Fashion: Order and Change." *Annual Review of Sociology* 39 (2013): 171–92.

Bardaglio, Peter W. *Reconstructing the Household: Family, Sex, and Law in the Nineteenth Century South*. Chapel Hill: University of North Carolina Press, 1996.

Barker, Deborah E., and Kathryn McKee. *American Cinema and the Southern*. Athens: University of Georgia Press, 2011.

Baron, Ava, ed. *Work Engendered: Toward a New History of American Labor*. Ithaca, NY: Cornell University Press, 1991.

Bass, Laura R., and Amanda Wunder. "The Veiled Ladies of the Early Modern Spanish World: Seduction and Scandal in Seville, Madrid, and Lima." *Hispanic Review* 77, no. 1 (2009): 97–144.

Baudonivia. "De Vita Sanctae Radegundis Libri Duo." In *Monumenta Germaniae Historica: Scriptores Rerum Merovingicarum*, vol. 2, edited by Bruno Krusch. Hannover: Hahnsche Buchhandlung, 1888.

Bell, David, and Joanne Hollows, eds. *Ordinary Lifestyles: Popular Media, Consumption and Taste*. Maidenhead, UK: Open University Press, 2005.

Benjamin, Thomas. *The Atlantic World: Europeans, Africans, Indians and their Shared History, 1400–1900*. Cambridge: Cambridge University Press, 2009.

Bix, Amy Sue. "Equipped for Life: Gendered Technical Training and Consumerism in Home Economics, 1920–1980." *Technology and Culture* 43 (October 2002): 728–54.

Bjelskou, Peter. *Branded Women in U.S. Television: When People Become Corporations*. Lanham, MD: Lexington Books, 2015.

Blackwell, Louise. "Tennessee Williams and the Predicament of Women." *South Atlantic Bulletin* 35, no. 2 (1970): 9–14.

Blight, David W. *Race and Reunion: The Civil War in American Memory*. Cambridge, MA: Harvard University Press, 2001.

Bograd, Michele. "Strengthening Domestic Violence Theories: Intersections of Race, Class, Sexual Orientation, and Gender." In *Domestic Violence at the Margins: Readings on Race, Class, Gender, and Culture*, edited by Christina Pratt and Natalie Sokoloff, 25–38. New Brunswick, NJ: Rutgers University Press, 2005.

Boydston, Jeanne. *Home and Work: Housework, Wages, and the Ideology of Labor in the Early Republic*. Des Moines, IA: Oxford University Press, 1994.

Boylorn, Robin M. "'Brains, Booty, and All Bizness': Identity Politics, Ratchet Respectability, and *The Real Housewives of Atlanta*." In *The Fantasy of Reality: Critical Essays on "The Real Housewives,"* edited by Rachel E. Silverman, 27–42. New York: Peter Lang, 2015.

Brucculieri, Julia. "How Fast Fashion Brands Get Away with Copying Designers." *Huffpost*, September 4, 2018.

Bruna, Denis, ed. *Fashioning the Body: An Intimate History of the Silhouette*. New Haven, CT: Yale University Press, 2015. Published in conjunction with an exhibition of the same title, organized by and presented at the Bard Graduate Center, April–July 2015.

———. "Puffed-Out Chests and Paunched Bellies: The Broadening of Men's Bodies from the Fourteenth to the Sixteenth Century." In *Fashioning the Body: An Intimate History of the Silhouette*, edited by Denis Bruna, 39–45. New Haven, CT: Yale University Press, 2015.

Brzenchek, Alison, and Mari Castañeda. "*The Real Housewives*, Gendered Affluence, and the Rise of the Docusoap." *Feminist Media Studies* 6, no. 1 (February 2017): 1–15.

Bullard, Robert D., ed. *In Search of the New South: The Black Urban Experience in the 1970s and 1980s*. Tuscaloosa: University of Alabama Press, 1989.

Bullard, Robert D., and E. Kiki Thomas. "Atlanta: Mecca of the Southeast." In *In Search of the New South: The Black Urban Experience in the 1970s and 1980s*, edited by Robert D. Bullard, 75–97. Tuscaloosa: University of Alabama Press, 1989.

Butler, Judith. *Gender Trouble: Feminism and the Subversion of Identity*. New York: Routledge, 1990.

Bynum, Caroline Walker. *Holy Feast and Holy Fast: The Religious Significance of Food to Medieval Women*. Berkeley: University of California Press, 1987.

Carmer, Carl. *Stars Fell on Alabama*. Tuscaloosa: University of Alabama Press, 2000.

Carney, Judith Ann. *Black Rice: The African Origins of Rice Cultivation in the Americas*. Cambridge, MA: Harvard University Press, 2009.

Carrera, Magali Marie. *Imagining Identity in New Spain: Race, Lineage, and the Colonial Body in Portraiture and Casta Paintings*. Austin: University of Texas Press, 2012.

Case, Frederick. *Black Capitalism: Problems in Development, A Case Study of Los Angeles*. New York: Praeger, 1972.

Cash, W. J. *The Mind of the South*. New York: Vintage Books, 1991 (1929).

Chakrabarty, Dipesh. *Provincializing Europe: Postcolonial Thought and Historical Difference*. Princeton, NJ: Princeton University Press, 2000.

Chatelain, Marcia. *Franchise: The Golden Arches in Black America*. New York: Liveright, 2020.

Child, Lydia Maria. *The American Frugal Housewife*. 12th ed. Boston: Carter, Hendee, 1833.

Cholakian, Patricia Francis. *Women and the Politics of Self-Representation in Seventeenth-Century France*. Newark: University of Delaware Press, 2000.

Clinton, Catherine. *Stepdaughters of History: Southern Women and the American Civil War*. Baton Rouge: Louisiana State University Press, 2016.

Coakley, John W. "Managing Holiness: Raymond of Capua and Catherine of Siena." In *Women, Men, and Spiritual Power: Female Saints and Their Male Collaborators*, 170–92. New York: Columbia University Press, 2006.

Cohen, Lizabeth. *A Consumer's Republic: The Politics of Mass Consumption in Postwar America*. New York: Alfred A. Knopf, 2003.

Coleman, Arica L. *That the Blood Stay Pure: African Americans, Native Americans, and the Predicament of Race and Identity in Virginia*. Bloomington: Indiana University Press, 2013.

Collier-Thomas, Bettye. *Jesus, Jobs, and Justice: African American Women and Religion*. Philadelphia: Temple University Press, 2013.

Constable, Giles. *Three Studies in Medieval Religious and Social Thought: The Interpretation of Mary and Martha, The Ideal of the Imitation of Christ, The Orders of Society*. Cambridge: Cambridge University Press, 1995.

Corp, Edward. "Catherine of Braganza and Cultural Politics." In *Queenship in Britain, 1660–1837: Royal Patronage, Court Culture and Dynastic Politics*, edited by Clarissa Campbell Orr, 53–73. New York: Manchester University Press, 2002.

Cott, Nancy. *The Bonds of Womanhood*. New Haven, CT: Yale University Press, 1977.

Couldry, Nick. *Media, Society, and World: Social Theory and Digital Media Practice*. Cambridge, UK: Polity Press, 2012.

Cowan, Ruth Schwartz. *More Work for Mother: The Ironies of Household Technology from the Open Hearth to the Microwave*. New York: Basic Books, 1983.

Cowdery, Charles K. *Bourbon, Straight: The Uncut and Unfiltered Story of American Whiskey*. Chicago: Made and Bottled in Kentucky, 2004.

Cox, Karen L. *Dixie's Daughters: The United Daughters of the Confederacy and the Preservation of Confederate Culture*. Gainesville: University Press of Florida, 2003.

Cox, Nicole B., and Jennifer M. Proffitt. "The Housewives' Guide to Better Living: Promoting Consumption on Bravo's *The Real Housewives*," *Communication, Culture and Critique* 5 (2012): 295–312.

Crane, Susan. *The Performance of Self: Ritual, Clothing, and Identity during the Hundred Years War*. Philadelphia: University of Pennsylvania Press, 2002.

Crowston, Claire. *Credit, Fashion, Sex: Economies of Regard in Old Regime France*. Durham, NC: Duke University Press, 2013.

Cruickshanks, Eveline, ed. *The Stuart Courts*. Thrupp, Gloucestershire: Sutton, 2000.

Dattel, Gene. *Cotton and Race in the Making of America: The Human Costs of Economic Power*. Lanham, MD: Ivan R. Dee, Rowman & Littlefield, 2009.

Davidson, Arnold I., and Maggie Fritz-Morkin. "Miracles of Bodily Transformation, or How St. Francis Received the Stigmata." *Critical Inquiry* 35, no. 3 (2009): 451–80.

Davis, Natalie Zemon. *Society and Culture in Early Modern France*. Stanford: Stanford University Press, 1975.

———. "Women on Top." In *Society and Culture in Early Modern France*, 124–51. Stanford: Stanford University Press, 1975.

Deery, June. *Consuming Reality: The Commercialization of Factual Entertainment*. New York: Palgrave Macmillan, 2012.

Deller, Ruth A. *Reality Television: The TV Phenomenon That Changed the World*. London: Emerald, 2019.

DuBois, Ellen Carol. *Feminism and Suffrage: The Emergence of an Independent Women's Movement in America, 1848–1869*. Ithaca, NY: Cornell University Press, 1978.

———. *Woman Suffrage and Women's Rights*. New York: New York University Press, 1998.

Dubrofsky, Rachel E. "The Surveillance of Women on Reality TV: Watching *The Bachelor* and *The Bachelorette*." *Communication Faculty Publications* 21 (2011): 111–29.

———. "Surveillance on Reality Television and Facebook: From Authenticity to Flowing Data." *Communication Theory* 21, no. 2 (2011): 111–29.

Eckstein, Jessica. "Reasons for Staying in Intimately Violent Relationships: Comparisons of Men and Women and Messages Communicated to Self and Others." *Journal of Family Violence* 26 (2011): 21–30.

Edge, John T. ed. *The New Encyclopedia of Southern Culture*. Vol. 7, Foodways. Chapel Hill: University of North Carolina Press, 2014.

Edwards, Jennifer C. *Superior Women: Medieval Female Authority in Poitiers' Abbey of Sainte-Croix*. Oxford: Oxford University Press, 2019.

Edwards, Laura F. *Scarlett Doesn't Live Here Anymore: Southern Women in the Civil War Era*. Urbana: University of Illinois Press, 2004.

Epstein, Barbara Leslie. *The Politics of Domesticity: Women, Evangelism, and Temperance in Nineteenth-Century America*. Middletown, CT: Wesleyan University Press, 1981.

Escoffery, David S. "Domestication Incorporation: *Cribs* and *The Osbournes* as Narratives of Domestication," edited by David S. Escoffery, 97–112. Jefferson, NC: McFarland, 2006.

———, ed. *How Real Is Reality TV? Essays on Representation and Truth*. Jefferson, NC: McFarland, 2006.

Evelyn, John. *The Diary of John Evelyn*. Edited by E. S. de Beer. 6 vols. Oxford University Press, 1955.

Fairchilds, Cissie. *Domestic Enemies: Servants and Their Masters in Old Regime France*. Baltimore, MD: Johns Hopkins University Press, 1984.

Farrow, Ronan, *Catch and Kill: Lies, Spies, and a Conspiracy to Protect Predators*. New York: Little, Brown, 2019.

Faulkner, William. *The Sound and the Fury*. New York: Vintage Books, 1990.

Ferris, Marcie Cohen. *The Edible South: The Power of Food and the Making of an American Region*. Chapel Hill: University of North Carolina Press, 2014.

Fisher, Andrew, and Matthew D. O'Hara. *Imperial Subjects: Race and Identity in Colonial Latin America*. Durham, NC: Duke University Press, 2009.

Fiske, John. *Media Matters: Everyday Culture and Political Change*. Minneapolis: University of Minnesota Press, 1996.

Fiske, John, and John Hartley. *Reading Television*. London: Routledge, 1978.

Fortunatus, Venantius. "De Vita Sanctae Radegundis, Liber I." In *Monumenta Germaniae Historica: Scriptores Rerum Merovingicarum*, vol. 2, edited by Bruno Krusch. Hannover: Hahnsche Buchhandlung, 1888.

Foucault, Michel. *Discipline and Punish: The Birth of Prison*. Translated by A. Sheridan. New York: Vintage Books, 1995.

Fox, Ragan. "Queering *Housewives.*" In *The Fantasy of Reality: Critical Essays on "The Real Housewives,"* edited by Rachel E. Silverman. New York: Peter Lang, 2015.

Fox, Richard Wightman, and T. J. Jackson Lears. *The Culture of Consumption: Critical Essays in American History, 1875–1940.* New York: Pantheon Books, 1983.

Fox-Genovese, Elizabeth. "Scarlett O'Hara: The Southern Lady as New Woman." *American Quarterly* 33, no. 4 (Autumn 1981): 391–411.

———. *Within the Plantation Household: Black and White Women of the Old South.* Chapel Hill: University of North Carolina Press, 1988.

Franklin, Donna L. *Ensuring Inequality: The Structural Transformation of the African-American Family.* Oxford: Oxford University Press, 1997.

Freeman, Tyrone. *Madam C. J. Walker's Gospel of Giving: Black Women's Philanthropy during Jim Crow.* Urbana: University of Illinois Press, 2020.

Friedan, Betty. *The Feminine Mystique.* New York: W. W. Norton, 1963.

Friedman, John Block. "Coats, Collars, and Capes: Royal Fashions for Animals in the Early Modern Period." In *Medieval Clothing and Textiles*, vol. 12, edited by Robin Netherton and Gale R. Owen Crocker, 61–94. Suffolk, UK: Boydell Press, 2016.

Garcia, Venessa, and Patrick McManimon. *Gendered Justice: Intimate Partner Violence and the Criminal Justice System.* Lanham, MD: Rowman & Littlefield, 2011.

Gardiner, Ralph. *Englands Grievance Discovered, in Relation to the Coal-Trade.* London: R. Ibbitson and P. Stent, 1655.

Garrett-Scott, Shennette. *Banking on Freedom: Black Women in U.S. Finance before the New Deal.* New York: Columbia University Press, 2019.

Gates, Racquel J. *Double Negative: The Black Image and Popular Culture.* Durham, NC: Duke University Press, 2018.

Gates, Henry Louis, Jr. *The Signifying Monkey: A Theory of African American Literary Criticism*, new ed. 1988; Oxford: Oxford University Press, 2014.

Gilkes, Cheryl Townsend. *"If It Wasn't for the Women . . .": Black Women's Experience and Womanist Culture in Church and Community.* Ossining, NY: Orbis Books, 2001.

Gillig, Paulette, Nancy Grigsby, Kathleen Malloy, Kathy McCloskey, Marilyn Sitaker, and Orin Strauchler. "Humiliation, Manipulation, and Control: Evidence of Centrality in Domestic Violence against an Adult Partner." *Journal of Family Violence* 19, no. 6 (2004): 339–54.

Gilmore, Glenda. *Gender and Jim Crow: Women and the Politics of White Supremacy in North Carolina, 1896–1920.* Chapel Hill: University of North Carolina Press, 1996.

Ginzberg, Lori. *Women and the Work of Benevolence: Morality, Politics, and Class in the Nineteenth-Century United States.* New Haven, CT: Yale University Press, 1990.

———. *Women in Antebellum Reform.* Wheeling, IL: Wiley-Blackwell, 2000.

Glickman, Lawrence B. *Buying Power: A History of Consumer Activism in America.* Chicago: University of Chicago Press, 2009.

Glover, Lorri. *All Our Relations: Blood Ties and Emotional Bonds among the Early South Carolina Gentry*. Baltimore, MD: Johns Hopkins University Press, 2000.

Glymph, Thavolia. *Out of the House of Bondage: The Transformation of the Plantation Household*. Cambridge: Cambridge University Press, 2003.

Goldstein, Carolyn M. *Creating Consumers: Home Economists in Twentieth-Century America*. Chapel Hill: University of North Carolina Press, 2012.

Graham, Lawrence Otis. *Our Kind of People: Inside America's Black Upper Class*. New York: Harper Perennial, 1999.

Griffey, Erin, ed. *Henrietta Maria: Piety, Politics and Patronage*. Burlington, VT: Ashgate, 2008.

———. Introduction to *Henrietta Maria: Piety, Politics and Patronage*. Edited by Erin Griffey, 1–12. Burlington, VT: Ashgate, 2008.

———. *On Display: Henrietta Maria and the Materials of Magnificence at the Stuart Court*. New Haven, CT: Yale University Press, 2015.

Grindstaff, Laura. *The Money Shot: Trash, Class, and the Making of TV Talk Shows*. Chicago: University of Chicago Press, 2002.

Gyucha, Attila, and William A. Parkinson, ed. *First Kings of Europe: From Farmers to Rulers in Prehistoric Southeastern Europe*. Los Angeles: Cotsen Institute of Archaeology Press, 2022.

Hagstette, Todd. *Reading William Gilmore Simms: Essays of Introduction to the Author's Canon*. Columbia: University of South Carolina Press, 2017.

Hale, Grace Elizabeth. *Making Whiteness: The Culture of Segregation in the South, 1890–1940*. New York: Vintage Books, 1998.

Hall, Catherine. *White, Male and Middle Class: Explorations in Feminism and History*. New York: Wiley, 2013.

Hall, Jacquelyne Dowd. "'You Must Remember This': Autobiography as Social Critique." *Journal of American History* 85, no. 2 (1998): 439–65.

Haralovich, Mary Beth. "Sit-Coms and Suburbs: Positioning the 1950s Homemaker." In *Private screenings*, edited by Lynn Spigel and Denise Mann, 111–41. Minneapolis: University of Minnesota Press, 1992.

Hart, Emma. *Building Charleston: Town and Society in the Eighteenth-Century British Atlantic World*. Columbia: University of South Carolina Press, 2010.

Hartman, Mary S. *The Household and the Making of History: A Subversive View of the Western Past*. Cambridge: Cambridge University Press, 2004.

Hayden, Dolores. *The Grand Domestic Revolution: A History of Feminist Designs for American Homes, Neighborhoods, and Cities*. Cambridge, MA: MIT Press, 1989.

Hayward, Maria. *Rich Apparel: Clothing and the Law in Henry VIII's England*. Farnham, UK: Ashgate, 2009.

Hearn, Alison. "Variations on the Branded Self: Theme, Invention, Improvisation, and Inventory." In *Media and Social Theory*, edited by David Hesmondhalgh and Jayson Toynbee, 194–210. London: Routledge, 2008.

Hesmondhalgh, David, and Jayson Toynbee, ed. *Media and Social Theory*. London: Routledge, 2008.

Higginbotham, Evelyn Brooks. *Righteous Discontent: The Women's Movement in the Black Baptist Church, 1880–1920*. Cambridge, MA: Harvard University Press, 1994.

Higgins, Geraldine. "Tara, the O'Hara's, and the Irish Gone with the Wind." *Southern Cultures* 17, no. 1 (2011): 30–49.

Hill, Annette, *Reality TV: Audiences and Popular Factual Television*. New York: Routledge, 2005.

Hobson, Maurice. *The Legend of the Black Mecca: Politics and Class in the Making of Modern Atlanta*. Chapel Hill: University of North Carolina, 2017.

Hochschild, Arlie Russell. *The Outsourced Self: Intimate Life in Market Times*. New York: Metropolitan Books, 2012.

Horwitz, Tony. *Confederates in the Attic: Dispatches from the Unfinished Civil War*. New York: Vintage Departures, 1999.

Howell, Martha C. *The Marriage Exchange: Property, Social Place, and Gender in Cities of the Low Countries, 1300–1550*. Chicago: University of Chicago Press, 1998.

Inness, Sherrie A. *Dinner Roles: American Women and Culinary Culture*. Iowa City: University of Iowa Press, 2001.

Isenberg, Nancy. *Sex and Citizenship in Antebellum America*. Chapel Hill: University of North Carolina Press, 1998.

Jackson, Nancy Berkaw. *Gender and the Southern Body Politic*. Jackson: University of Mississippi Press, 2000.

Jacobs, Margaret D. *White Mothers to a Dark Race: Settler Colonialism, Maternalism, and the Removal of Indigenous Children in the American West and Australia, 1880–1940*. Lincoln: University of Nebraska, 2011.

Janiewski, Dolores. "Southern Honor, Southern Dishonor: Managerial Ideology and the Construction of Gender, Race, and Class Relations in Southern Industry." In *Work Engendered: Toward a New History of American Labor*, edited by Ava Baron, 70–91. Ithaca, NY: Cornell University Press, 1991.

Janney, Caroline E. *Burying the Dead but Not the Past: Ladies' Memorial Associations and the Lost Cause*. Chapel Hill: University of North Carolina Press, 2008.

Johnson, Rosser, and Rebecca Trelease. "Glocalization, Hard-Won Status, and Performative Femininity: A Case Study of *The Real Housewives* Format." *Journal of Asia-Pacific Pop Culture* 3, no. 2 (2018): 324–41.

Jones, Martha S. *Vanguard: How Black Women Broke Barriers, Won the Vote, and Insisted on Equality for All*. New York: Basic Books, 2020.

Jones-Rogers, Stephanie E. *They Were Her Property: White Women as Slave Owners in the American South*. New Haven, CT: Yale University Press, 2019.

Kantor, Jodi, and Megan Twohey. *She Said: Breaking the Sexual Harassment Story That Helped Ignite a Movement*. Penguin Press: New York, 2019.

Kernsmith, Poco, and Roger Kernsmith. "Treating Female Perpetrators: State Standards for Batterer Intervention Services." *Social Work* 54, no. 4 (2009): 341–49.

King, Florence. *Southern Ladies and Gentlemen*. New York: St. Martin's Press, 1973.

Klein, Rachel N. *Unification of a Slave State: The Rise of the Planter Class in the South Carolina Backcountry, 1760–1808*. Chapel Hill: University of North Carolina Press, 1990.

Knuckey, J. "'I Just Don't Think She Has a Presidential Look': Sexism and Vote Choice in the 2016 Election." *Social Science Quarterly* 100 (2019): 342–58.

Kolin, Philip C. "Personal Names." In *The New Encyclopedia of Southern Culture*, Volume 5: *Language*, edited by Michael Montgomery and Ellen Johnson, 168–71. Chapel Hill: University of North Carolina Press, 2007.

Kosior, Katarzyna. *Becoming a Queen in Early Modern Europe: East and West*. London: Palgrave Macmillan, 2019.

Krause, Kathy M., ed. *Reassessing the Heroine in Medieval French Literature*. Gainesville: University Press of Florida, 2001.

Krusch, Bruno, ed. *Monumenta Germaniae Historica: Scriptores Rerum Merovingicarum*. Vols. 2, 25, and 26. Hannover: Hahnsche Buchhandlung, 1884–1951.

Lancaster, Jane. *Making Time: Lillian Moller Gilbreth—a Life beyond "Cheaper by the Dozen."* Boston, MA: Northeastern University Press, 2004.

Lee, Janet, and Susan Shaw. *Women's Voices, Feminist Visions: Classic and Contemporary*. Mountain View, CA: Mayfield, 2001.

Lee, Michael J., and Leigh Moskowitz. "The 'Rich Bitch': Class and Gender Performance on *The Real Housewives of New York City*." *Feminist Media Studies* 12, no. 4 (March 2013): 1–19.

Lee, Youyoung, and Liat Kornowski. "*The Real Housewives* of Bankruptcies, Businesses and Divorces by the Numbers." *Huffington Post*, January 25, 2013.

Lehfeldt, Elizabeth A. "Ideal Men: Masculinity and Decline in Seventeenth-Century Spain." *Renaissance Quarterly* 61, no. 2 (2008): 463–94.

Lemire, Elise Virginia. *"Miscegenation": Making Race in America*. Philadelphia: University of Pennsylvania Press, 2002.

Leonard, Suzanne. "From Basketball Wives to Extreme Cougar Wives: Niche Marketing the Wife Brand." In *Wife, Inc.: The Business of Marriage in the Twenty-First Century*. New York: New York University Press, 2018.

———. "*The Real Housewives of Beverly Hills*: Franchising Femininity." In *How to Watch Television* (2nd ed.), edited by Ethan Thompson and Jason Mittell, 278–86. New York: New York University Press, 2020.

———. *Wife, Inc.: The Business of Marriage in the Twenty-First Century*. New York: New York University Press, 2018.

Leonard, Suzanne, and Diane Negra. "After Ever After: Bethenny Frankel, Self-Branding, and the 'New Intimacy of Work.'" In *Cupcakes, Pinterest and Ladyporn: Feminized Popular Culture in the Early Twenty-First Century*, edited by Elana Levine, 196–214. Urbana: University of Illinois Press, 2015.

Leppert, Alice. "*Keeping Up with the Kardashians*: Fame-Work and the Production of Entrepreneurial Sisterhood." In *Cupcakes, Pinterest and Ladyporn: Feminized Popular Culture in the Early Twenty-First Century*, edited by Elana Levine, 215–31. Urbana: University of Illinois Press, 2015.

Lesseps, Countess Luann de. Kosior *the Countess: How to Live with Elegance and Flair*. New York: Avery, 2009.

Levine, Elana, ed. *Cupcakes, Pinterest and Ladyporn: Feminized Popular Culture in the Early Twenty-First Century*. Urbana: University of Illinois Press, 2015.

Levy, Jessica Ann. "Selling Atlanta: Black Mayoral Politics from Protest to Entrepreneurism, 1973 to 1990." *Journal of Urban History* 41, no. 3 (May 2015): 420–43.

Lewis, Tania. *Smart Living: Lifestyle Media and Popular Expertise*. New York: Peter Lang, 2008.

Lieber, Emma. "Realism's Housewives." *New England Review* 33, no. 4 (2013): 113–30.

Liebman, Seymour B. *The Jews in New Spain: Faith, Flame, and the Inquisition*. Coral Gables: University of Miami Press, 1970.

Lindsey, Treva B. *Colored No More: Reinventing Black Womanhood in Washington, D.C.* Urbana: University of Illinois Press, 2017.

Littlefield, Daniel. *Rice and Slaves: Ethnicity and the Slave Trade in Colonial South Carolina*. Urbana: University of Illinois Press, 1991.

Lorenzetti, Liza, Lana Wells, Carmen H. Logie, and Tonya Callahan. "Understanding and Preventing Domestic Violence in the Lives of Gender and Sexually Diverse Persons." *Canadian Journal of Human Sexuality* 26, no. 3 (2017): 175–85.

Lowery, Malinda Maynor. *The Lumbee Indians: An America Struggle*. Chapel Hill: University of North Carolina Press, 2018.

Lucken, Christopher. "Woman's Cry: Broken Language, Marital Disputes, and the Poetics of Medieval Farce." In *Reassessing the Heroine in Medieval French Literature*, edited by Kathy M. Krause, 152–79. Gainesville: University Press of Florida, 2001.

Lüthe, Martin, and Sascha Pöhlmann, eds. *Unpopular Culture*. Amsterdam: Amsterdam University Press, 2016.

Magder, Ted. "Television 2.0: The Business of American Television in Transition." In *Reality TV: Remaking Television Culture*, edited by Susan Murray and Laurie Ouellette, 141–64. New York: New York University Press, 2009.

Maldini, Irene, and Ragna Luciana Manz. "From 'Things of Imitation' to 'Devices of Differentiation': Uncovering a Paradoxical History of Clothing (1950–2015)." *Fashion Theory* 22, no. 1 (2017): 69–84.

Martin, Scott C. "'A Star That Gathers Lustre from the Gloom of Night': Wives, Marriage, and Gender in Early-Nineteenth-Century American Temperance Reform." *Journal of Family History* 29, no. 3 (July 2004): 274–92.

Mason, Mary Ann. *The Young Housewife's Counsellor and Friend: Containing Directions in Every Department of Housekeeping, Including the Duties of Wife and Mother*. New York: E. J. Hale, 1875.

Matheson, Sarah A. "The Cultural Politics of *Wife Swap*: Taste, Lifestyle Media, and the American Family. *Film and History* 37, no. 2 (2007): 33–47.

May, Elaine Tyler. *Homeward Bound*. 2nd ed. New York: Basic Books, 1999.

Mazouer, Charles. *Le théâtre du Moyen Âge*. Paris: SEDES, 1998.

Mazzoni, Cristina. *Angela of Foligno's Memorial*. Suffolk, UK: Boydell & Brewer, 1999.

McCarthy, Kathleen. *American Creed: Philanthropy and the Rise of Civil Society, 1700–1865*. Chicago: University of Chicago Press, 2003.

McCurry, Stephanie. "Producing Dependence: Women, Work and Yeoman Households in Low-Country South Carolina." In *Neither Lady nor Slave: Working Women of the Old South*, edited by Michele Gillespie and Susan Delfion, 55–74. Chapel Hill: University of North Carlina Press, 2002.

McGarry, Molly. "Spectral Sexualities: Nineteenth-Century Spiritualism, Moral Panics, and the Making of U.S. Obscenity Law." *Journal of Women's History* 12, no. 2 (Summer 2000): 8–29.

McGlynn, Clare, and Erika Rackley. "Image-Based Sexual Abuse." *Oxford Journal of Legal Studies* 37, no. 3 (2017): 534–61.

McRobbie, Angela. "Notes on *What Not to Wear* and Post-Feminist Symbolic Violence." *Sociological Review* 52, series 2 (2004): 97–109.

Melion, Walter, ed. *The Authority of the Word: Reflecting on Image and Text in Northern Europe, 1400–1700*. Leiden: Brill, 2012.

Messing, Jill Theresa. "Risk-Informed Intervention: Using Intimate Partner Violence Risk Assessment within an Evidence-Based Practice Framework." *Social Work* 64, no. 2 (2019): 103–12.

Miller, Elisa. "In the Name of the Home: Women, Domestic Science, and American Higher Education, 1865–1930." PhD diss., University of Illinois at Urbana-Champaign, 2004.

Mintz, Steven, and Susan Kellogg. *Domestic Revolutions: A Social History of American Family Life*. New York: Free Press, 1988.

Mitchell, Margaret. *Gone with the Wind*. New York: Pocket Books, 2008 (1936).

Montgomery, Michael, and Ellen Johnson, ed. *The New Encyclopedia of Southern Culture*. Vol. 5, *Language*. Chapel Hill: University of North Carolina Press, 2007.

Morgan, Appleton. *A History of the Family of Morgan, from the Year 1089 to Present Times*. New York, 1902.

Moss, Pamela, and Avril Maddrell. "Emergent and Divergent Spaces in the Women's March: The Challenges of Intersectionality and Inclusion." *Gender, Place and Culture* 24, no. 5 (2017): 613–20.

Muessig, Carolyn. "The Stigmata Debate in Theology and Art in the Late Middle Ages." In *The Authority of the Word: Reflecting on Image and Text in Northern Europe, 1400–1700*, edited by Walter Melion, 481–504. Leiden: Brill, 2012.

———. "Signs of Salvation: The Evolution of Stigmatic Spirituality before Francis of Assisi." *Church History* 82, no. 1 (2013): 40–68.

Murray, Susan, and Laurie Ouellette, ed. *Reality TV: Remaking Television Culture*. New York: New York University Press, 2009.

Muzzarelli, Maria Giuseppina. "Reconciling the Privilege of the Few with the Common Good: Sumptuary Laws in Medieval and Early Modern Europe." *Journal of Medieval and Early Modern Studies* 39, no. 3 (2009): 597–617.

Netherton, Robin, and Gale R. Owen Crocker. *Medieval Clothing and Textiles*. Vol. 12. Suffolk, UK: Boydell Press, 2016.

Orbe, Mark P. "Representations of Race in Reality TV: Watch and Discuss." *Critical Studies in Media Communication* 25, no. 4 (2008): 345–52.

Orr, Clarissa Campbell. *Queenship in Britain, 1660–1837: Royal Patronage, Court Culture and Dynastic Politics.* Manchester, UK: Manchester University Press, 2002.

Pascoe, Peggy. *Relations of Rescue: The Search for Female Moral Authority in the American West, 1874–1939.* New York: Oxford University Press, 1990.

Pepys, Samuel. *The Diary of Samuel Pepys*, 11 vols. Edited by Robert Latham and William Matthews. Berkeley: University of California Press, 1971.

Pollino, Madison A. "(Mis)Representations of Sexual Violence: The Brett Kavanaugh and Christine Blasey Ford Testimonies." *Critical Studies in Media Communication* 37, no. 1 (2020): 71–84.

Pozner, Jennifer L. *Reality Bites Back: The Troubling Truth about Guilty Pleasure TV.* Berkeley: Seal Press, 2010.

Pratt, Christina, and Natalie Sokoloff, ed. *Domestic Violence at the Margins: Readings on Race, Class, Gender, and Culture.* New Brunswick, NJ: Rutgers University Press, 2005.

Prior, Markus, and Lori D. Bougher. "'Like They've Never, Ever Seen in This Country'? Political Interest and Voter Engagement in 2016." *Public Opinion Quarterly* 82, no. S1 (2018): 822–42.

Richards, Ellen H. *The Cost of Living as Modified by Sanitary Science.* New York: J. Wiley and Sons, 1899.

———. "Ten Years of the Lake Placid Conference on Home Economics: Its History and Aims," *Lake Placid Conference Proceedings* 10 (1908): 19–20. Accessed via Cornell University's Home Economics Archive Research, Tradition, and History.

Roberts, Diane, "Ladies and Gentlemen." In *The New Encyclopedia of Southern Culture.* Vol. 13, *Gender*, edited by Nancy Bercaw and Ted Ownby, 156–60. Chapel Hill: University of North Carolina Press, 2009.

Rodríguez-Salgado, Mia. "The Court of Philip II of Spain." In *Princes, Patronage, and the Nobility: The Court at the Beginning of the Modern Age, c. 1450–1650*, edited by Ronald Asch and Adolf Birke, 205–44. New York: Oxford University Press, 1991.

Rutherford, Janice Williams. *Selling Mrs. Consumer: Christine Frederick and the Rise of Household Efficiency.* Athens: University of Georgia Press, 2003.

Said, Edward. *Orientalism.* New York: Pantheon Books, 1978.

Schoell, Konrad. *La farce du quinzième siècle.* Tübingen: Gunter Narr, 1992.

Schreiner, Klaus, ed. *Frömmigkeit I'm Mittelalter: Politisch-soziale Kontexte, visuelle Praxis, körperliche Ausdrucksformen.* Munich: Fink, 2002.

Schroeder, Stassi. *Next Level Basic: The Definitive Basic Bitch Handbook.* New York: Gallery Books, 2019.

Schroer, Haley. "Sartorial Subversions: Appearance, Identity, and Sumptuary Legislation in the Spanish Empire." PhD diss., University of Texas at Austin, 2023.

Schwaller, Robert. *Géneros de Gente in Early Colonial Mexico: Defining Racial Difference.* Norman: University of Oklahoma Press, 2016.

Sears, Camilla A., and Rebecca Godderis. "Roar Like a Tiger on TV?" *Feminist Media Studies* 11, no. 2 (2011): 181–95.

Silverman, Rachel E., ed. *The Fantasy of Reality: Critical Essays on "The Real Housewives."* New York: Peter Lang, 2015.

Simms, William Gilmore. *The Golden Christmas: A Tale of Lowcountry Life.* Columbia: University of South Carolina Press, 2005 (1852).

Sklar, Kathrine Kish. *Catherine Beecher: A Study in American Domesticity.* New Haven, CT: Yale University Press, 1973.

Smith, Daniel Blake, "Family Dynasties." In *The New Encyclopedia of Southern Culture*. Vol. 13, *Gender*, edited by Nancy Bercaw and Ted Ownby, 101–3. Chapel Hill: University of North Carolina Press, 2009.

Sotiropoulos, Karen. *Staging Race: Black Performers in Turn of the Century America.* Cambridge, MA: Harvard University Press, 2006.

Stage, Sarah, and Virginia B. Vincent. *Rethinking Home Economics: Women and the History of a Profession.* Ithaca, NY: Cornell University Press, 1997.

Stanley, Amy Dru. *From Bondage to Contract: Wage Labor, Marriage, and the Market in the Age of Slave Emancipation.* New York: Cambridge University Press, 1998.

Stansell, Christine. *City of Women: Sex and Class in New York, 1789–1860.* Urbana: University of Illinois Press, 1987.

Stedman, Beirne. "Right of Husband to Chastise Wife." *Virginia Law Register* 3, no. 4 (1917): 241–48.

Strasser, Susan. *Never Done: A History of American Housework.* New York: Henry Holt, 2002. Originally published in 1982 by Pantheon Books.

Summers, Martin, *Manliness and Its Discontents: The Black Middle Class and the Transformation of Masculinity, 1900–1930.* Chapel Hill: University of North Carolina Press, 2004.

Taylor, Elizabeth Dowling. *The Original Black Elite: Daniel Murray and the Story of a Forgotten Era.* New York: Amistad, 2017.

Townsend, G. F. *The Town and Borough of Leominster.* London: A. Hall, 1863.

Trexler, Richard C. "The Stigmatized Body of Francis of Assisi: Conceived, Processed, Disappeared." In *Frömmigkeit I'm Mittelalter: Politisch-soziale Kontexte, visuelle Praxis, körperliche Ausdrucksformen*, edited by Klaus Schreiner, 463–97. Munich: Fink, 2002.

Trouillot, Michel-Rolph. *Silencing the Past: Power and the Production of History.* Boston: Beacon Press, 1995.

Twinam, Ann. *Purchasing Whiteness: Pardos, Mulattos, and the Quest for Social Mobility in the Spanish Indies.* Stanford: Stanford University Press, 2015.

Udy, Daniel. "Secrets, Lies and *The Real Housewives*: The Death of an (Un)Popular Genre." In *Unpopular Culture*, edited by Martin Lüthe and Sascha Pöhlmann, 95–112. Amsterdam: Amsterdam University Press, 2016.

Underdown, D. E. "The Taming of the Scold: The Enforcement of Patriarchal Authority in Early Modern England." In *Order and Disorder in Early Modern England*, edited by Anthony Fletcher and John Stevenson, 116–36. Cambridge: Cambridge University Press, 1985.

Van Deusen, Nancy. *Global Indios: The Indigenous Struggle for Justice in Sixteenth-Century Spain*. Durham, NC: Duke University Press, 2015.

Van Ruymbeke, Bertrand. *From New Babylon to Eden: The Huguenots and Their Migration to Colonial South Carolina*. Columbia: University of South Carolina Press, 2006.

Vilches, Elvira. *New World Gold: Cultural Anxiety and Monetary Disorder in Early Modern Spain*. Chicago: University of Chicago Press, 2010.

Vincent, Susan. *Dressing the Elite: Clothes in Early Modern England*. New York: Berg, 2003.

Weems, Robert E., Jr. *Business in Black and White: American Presidents and Black Entrepreneurs in the Twentieth Century*. With Lewis Randolph. New York: New York University Press, 2009.

Weigley, Emma Seifrit. "It Might Have Been Euthenics: The Lake Placid Conferences and the Home Economics Movement." *American Quarterly* 26, no. 1 (March 1974): 79–96.

Weir, Robert. *Colonial South Carolina: A History*. Columbia: University of South Carolina Press, 1997.

Welch, Evelyn. Introduction to *Fashioning the Early Modern: Dress, Textiles, and Innovation in Europe, 1500–1800*. Edited by Evelyn Welch. Oxford: Oxford University Press, 2017.

Welter, Barbara. "The Cult of True Womanhood: 1820–1860." Pt. 1. *American Quarterly* 18, no. 2 (Summer 1966): 151–74.

West, Candace, and Don H. Zimmerman. "Doing Gender." *Gender and Society* 1, no. 2 (June 1987): 125–51.

Wilson, Charles Reagan. *Baptized in Blood: The Religion of the Lost Cause, 1865–1920*. Athens: University of Georgia Press, 2009.

———. *The New Encyclopedia of Southern Culture*. Vol. 4, *Myth, Manners, and Memory*. Chapel Hill, University of North Carolina Press, 2006.

Wilson, Elizabeth. "Fashion and the Postmodern Body." In *Chic Thrills: A Fashion Reader*, edited by Juliet Ash and Elizabeth Wilson, 3–16. London: Pandora, 1993.

Wood, Peter. *Black Majority: Negroes in Colonial South Carolina from 1670 through the Stono Rebellion*. New York: W. W. Norton, 1996 (1966).

Woodward, C. Vann. *The Burden of Southern History*. Baton Rouge: Louisiana State Press, 2008 (1960).

Wright, Daniel S. *"The First of Causes to Our Sex": The Female Moral Reform Movement in the Antebellum Northeast, 1834–1848*. New York: Routledge, 2006.

Wu, Judy Tzu-Chun. "Interchange: Women's Suffrage, the Nineteenth Amendment, and the Right to Vote." *Journal of American History* 106, no. 3 (December 2019): 662–94.

Wunder, Amanda. "Women's Fashions and Politics in Seventeenth-Century Spain: The Rise and Fall of the Guardainfante." *Renaissance Quarterly* 68, no. 1 (2015): 133–86.

Wynne, Sonya. "The Mistresses of Charles II and Restoration Court Politics." In *The Stuart Courts*, edited by Eveline Cruickshanks, 171–90. Thrupp, Gloucestershire: Sutton, 2000.

Contributors

NICOLE L. ANSLOVER is an Associate Professor of History at Indiana University Northwest. Anslover specializes in twentieth-century American History, with an emphasis on the modern presidency, politics, and international relations. She is the author of *The Transfer of Power between Presidential Administrations: Trouble with the Transition* and *Harry S. Truman: The Coming of the Cold War*, both with Routledge. Because of her expertise in the presidency, she was invited to appear on C-SPAN's series "First Ladies: Image and Influence." Professor Anslover was featured in the episode on Bess Truman, which inspired her to begin working on projects involving the First Ladies and other American women in politics. As an avid Housewives fan and scholar, Anslover tends to look at the women on Bravo through a political lens.

Tagline: I'm a presidential historian. I'm an expert in political power, plot twists, and pettiness.

MARTINA BALDWIN is a full-time lecturer in the Department of Cinema Television Arts at California State University, Fullerton, teaching courses in media literacy, critical media studies, and critical writing. She received her PhD in Media Studies from the University of Illinois at Urbana-Champaign. Her dissertation—"Buzz by Bravo: A Trendsetting Niche Network's Place within Contemporary Television"—combined TV, audience, and production studies. Recent publications include "Bravo: Branding, Fandom and the Lifestyle Network," in *From Networks to Netflix: A Guide to Changing Channels* (Routledge, 2nd ed.).

Tagline: I'm an enigma wrapped in a blanket and watching TV.

EMILIE M. BRINKMAN is a lecturer and historian of early modern Europe, specializing in material culture, politics, and gender. She graduated from Purdue University in 2018 with her PhD in Early Modern European History. She holds an MA in History from Miami University, as well as a BA in History and AA in Art History from Thomas More University. Her research areas include seventeenth-century political culture, queenship, fashion and dress, cosmetic culture and beauty, and the intersection of Renaissance history and modern pop culture. Her work on the history of royal weddings and the British monarchy have been featured in the *Washington Post*. She is currently working on her first monograph, which examines how fashion and material objects served as a site for political discourse and agency during seventeenth-century England.

Tagline: I may be an expert on queenship, but I'm no drama queen.

KACEY CALAHANE is an Associate Professor of History at Chaffey College, and she's the writer and co-host of the *Historians on Housewives* podcast. Specializing in women's gender, and social movement histories, Kacey has co-authored pieces about the *Real Housewives* and history in the *Journal of Women's History* and *Feeding the Elephant*, and she is a co-author of the *Empire Suffrage Syllabus* published with Alexander Street Press in 2021. Kacey's work with *Historians on Housewives* has been featured in *Orange Coast Magazine* and *Thrillist*.

Tagline: *I don't just name 'em, I source 'em too.*

MARCIA CHATELAIN is Presidential Penn Compact Professor of Africana Studies at the University of Pennsylvania. She is the author of *Franchise: The Golden Arches in Black America* (Liveright, 2020), winner of the 2021 Pulitzer Prize for History. She is also the author of *South Side Girls: Growing Up in the Great Migration* (Duke University Press, 2015). Chatelain has discussed Housewives and other pop culture topics while a host for the *Slate* podcast, *The Waves*. Chatelain holds a PhD in American Civilization from Brown University and degrees in Journalism and Religious Studies from the University of Missouri.

Tagline: *I'm a historian; I always have receipts, proof, timelines, screenshots.*

JENNIFER C. EDWARDS is Professor of History at Manhattan College in Riverdale, NY, where she teaches courses on medieval and ancient history. She is the author of *Superior Women: Medieval Female Authority in Poitiers' Abbey of Sainte-Croix* (Oxford, 2019) and *Daily Life of Women in Chaucer's England* (ABC-CLIO, 2022). She is currently working on a book project, "Holy Healing: Saints and Leprosy in the Middle Ages," and a Reacting to the Past role-immersion game, "Christine de Pizan and the Querelle des Femmes." She earned her PhD and MA from the University of Illinois at Urbana-Champaign and her BA from the University of Massachusetts at Amherst. She is general editor of *Medieval Feminist Forum: A Journal of Gender and Sexuality* and serves on the Advisory Board of the Society for Medieval Feminist Scholarship.

Tagline: *You're going to have to work to pass this Jen-Ed, and that's Jen-Ed with a "J"!*

JENNIFER M. FOGEL is an Associate Professor of Broadcasting and Mass Communication at SUNY-Oswego. Her research examines contemporary popular culture, particularly the way that gender is represented on television. Her previous work has analyzed the gendered marketing of *Star Wars* toys, the complicated celebrity of Carrie Fisher, television portrayals of the history of women in medicine, cognitive dissonance in fandom, and articulations of family life in contemporary television series.

Tagline: *Diamonds may be a girl's best friend, but mine is my DVR.*

TANISHA C. FORD is Professor of History and Biography and Memoir at the CUNY Graduate Center. She is the author of *Our Secret Society: Mollie Moon and the Money, Glamour, and Power behind the Civil Rights Movement* (Amistad/HarperCollins, 2023), which was named one of *Vanity Fair*'s and *Ms. Magazine*'s Best Books of 2023. *Our Secret Society* was also nominated for a 2024 NAACP Image Award for Outstanding Literary Work of Biography/Autobiography. Ford has also written three other books: *Liberated Threads: Black Women, Style, and the Global Politics of Soul* (UNC Press, 2015), winner of the OAH Liberty Legacy Foundation Award for Best Book on Civil Rights History; *Dressed in Dreams: A Black Girl's Love Letter to the*

Power of Fashion (St. Martin's, 2019); and *Kwame Brathwaite: Black Is Beautiful* (Aperture, 2019). She writes regularly for public audiences, with stories in the *Atlantic*, the *New York Times*, *Time*, *Elle*, and *Harper's Bazaar*, among others. In 2019, Ford was named to *The Root's* 100 Most Influential African Americans list for her innovative, public-facing scholarship. Her research has been supported by such institutions as the New America/Emerson Collective, the Institute for Advanced Study, the Smithsonian Museum of American History, the Harvard Radcliffe Institute, the Ford Foundation, Andrew W. Mellon Foundation, and the Schomburg Center for Research in Black Culture. Ford is currently writing an experimental biography of sculptor and institution builder Augusta Savage, which will be published by Penguin Press as part of Henry Louis Gates Jr.'s Significations series. For more information, visit her website: tanishacford.com.

Tagline: *Some try to test me, but I've got a PhD in tea and shade.*

NOAH D. GUYNN is Professor of French and Comparative Literature at the University of California, Davis. His work includes two monographs—*Allegory and Sexual Ethics in the High Middle Ages* (Palgrave, 2007) and *Pure Filth: Ethics, Politics, and Religion in Early French Farce* (University of Pennsylvania Press, 2020)—as well as essay-length publications on a range of genres, from courtly romance to crusade chronicles to mystery plays. He has recently co-edited a volume of essays on Bruno Latour titled *Category Crossings: Bruno Latour and the Medieval Modes of Existence* (Romanic Review/Duke University Press, 2020).

Tagline: *I didn't say "middle-aged." I said, "Middle Ages."*

ROSEMARIE JONES holds a Master of Public Policy Administration, with an emphasis in Gender and Policy, and a Graduate Certificate in Gender and Sexuality Studies. She has served as a crisis intervention specialist, court advocate, and programs manager for a domestic and sexual violence agency outside St. Louis, Missouri. Additionally, she is a Women, Gender, and Sexualities adjunct instructor at several local universities. Her research interests include pop culture and feminism, constructions of menstruation, and intimate partner violence. Her work on domestic violence as a form of terrorism has been published in the two-volume set *Misogyny and the US: Causes, Trends, and Solutions*. She has found great comfort, enjoyment, and relaxation in watching the Housewives series after challenging days working with survivors of abuse and trauma. She is thankful for the entertainment Bravo provides and its ability to help her recharge and practice self-care.

Tagline: *I don't play the victim; I help empower them!*

JESSICA MILLWARD is an inaugural Black Thriving Term Chair at UC Irvine. An Associate Professor in the Department of History and Core Faculty member of African American Studies, Millward is an expert on African American history, Black Women's history, and slavery. Dr. Millward's first book, *Finding Charity's Folk: Enslaved and Free Black Women in Maryland* (University of Georgia Press, 2015), was published as part of the Race in the Atlantic World series. An award-winning scholar, she has published in the *Journal of African American History*, the *Journal of Women's History*, *Frontiers*, *Souls*, and the *Women's History Review*, as well as op-eds in the

Chronicle of Higher Education, the *Feminist Wire,* and the *Conversation.* A media-savvy historian, Millward specializes in bringing a historical perspective to modern times. To her frustration (but ultimately a blessing for the sake of her career), her partner, who is from Ghana, refuses to appear with her on *90 Day Fiancé.*

Tagline: I write history but I READ celebrities. I am J-M-Z.

HALEY SCHROER is a Visiting Assistant Professor at Texas Lutheran University. She received her PhD in Latin American history from the University of Texas at Austin in August 2023. Her dissertation, "Sartorial Subversions: Appearance, Identity, and Sumptuary Legislation in the Spanish Empire," examines the rise of racialized clothing laws in the Spanish Empire throughout the sixteenth and seventeenth centuries. Her research has received support from P.E.O. International, the Fulbright Program, the Social Science Research Council's International Dissertation Research Fellowship Program, and the Conference on Latin American History's James R. Scobie Award.

Tagline: Hello, Fashion Police? Just call me the Joan Rivers of the early modern era.

KRISTALYN SHEFVELAND is an Associate Professor of American History at the University of Southern Indiana and a specialist in Colonial Southeast, Native American, and Southern Studies. She is the creator of the River Cities Oral History Project and co-director of the Community Collaboration and Reparative Justice Project for Southwest Indiana. Shefveland is the author of *Anglo-Native Virginia: Trade, Conversion, and Indian Slavery in the Old Dominion, 1646–1722* (University of Georgia Press, 2016) and *Selling Vero Beach: Settler Myths in the Land of the Aís and Seminole* (University of Florida Press, 2024).

Tagline: My family motto is Quid Non, Why Not? Fortune favors the bold!

MAX SPEARE is an Associate Faculty in the History Department at Saddleback College. His research focuses on the roles that slavery and death practices played in shaping social, cultural, and labor relations in eighteenth-century New York City. He is the sound engineer for the *Historians on Housewives* podcast.

Tagline: You better come with sources because I always check footnotes.

SERENITY SUTHERLAND is an Associate Professor of Broadcasting and Mass Communication at SUNY-Oswego. Her research intersects American women's history, science and technology studies, digital humanities, and media studies. She has published on television portrayals of the history of women in medicine, women in science and technology, and pedagogy in the digital humanities. She is also a co-author of the digital project "Visualizing Women in Science and Technology."

Tagline: Always find joy in the journey, even if it's at a repair shop.

Index

Italic page numbers refer to illustrations.

Abrams, Stacey, 239
abuse. *See* intimate partner violence (IPV)
accessories and conspicuous consumption, 46, 49, 71, 72–74; in early modern Europe, 52–53, 61–62; on *Real Housewives of Beverly Hills* (RHOB), 54–58
activism: Black contrasted with white cast members, 7–8, 179; cult of domesticity and moral reform, 7; "performative activism," 15–16; *The Real Housewives of Atlanta* and Porsha Williams, 169–70, 178, 179, 182, 239–40; after 2016 election, 105
Adams, Catherine Frances Lovering, 77
Adams, John, 77
Adams, John Quincy, 77
The Adventures of Ozzie and Harriet (television series), 132, 140
advertising markets, 27, 131, 134; Clorox campaign, 119–20
African American cast members, 13, 193, 194. *See also* Black Americans; *The Real Housewives of Atlanta* (RHOA); *The Real Housewives of Potomac* (RHOP)
African American culture: charitable giving, 203–4, 214–15n29; "signifying," 84, 96, 98, 102
All My Children (television soap opera), 71
allyship and LGBTQ+ rights, 13–14
Altschul, Patricia, 159–60, 219, 220
Amador, Xavier, 36

An American Family (television series), 114, 124
The American Frugal Housewife (Child), 126
Anderson, Fiona, 50
Angela of Foligno, Saint, 38–39
Anslover, Nicole L., 12, 106, 168–85
anthropology, functionalist, 86
antifeminism, 8, 94
appearance and beauty: branding and entrepreneurship, 117–18, 139, 141; and martyrdom, 36; and power in relationships, 150; as self-representation, 80, 227. *See also* clothing; cosmetic procedures
The Apprentice (television series), 171
Arcy, Jacquelyn, 138
Armstrong, Taylor, 3, 72, 145, 150–54, 164
The Art of Southern Charm (Dey), 223
asceticism, 25, 33, 37–39, 42
Asian American cast members, 15, 183
Aspers, Patrick, 50
Association for the Study of Higher Education (ASHE), 204–5
Atlanta, GA, 237–38. *See also The Real Housewives of Atlanta* (RHOA)
Augustine of Hippo, Saint, 39–40
Ayers, Brooks, 30–32, 33, 41

The Bachelor (television series), 67
The Bachelorette (television series), 67
Bailey, Cynthia, 161, 182
Baldwin, Martina, 11, 105, 107–20

baptism, 30, 31. *See also* Christian themes
Barlow, Lisa, 73
Barna, Stephanie, 225
Barney, Simon, 30
Baron Cohen, Sacha, 218
Bassett, Candiace Dillard, 200
Baudrillard, Jean, 143n50
Beador, Shannon, 10, 30–31, 43, 141
beauty. *See* appearance and beauty
Beauvais, Garcelle, 10
Beecher, Catherine, 123, 125, 126–27
Bell, W. Kamau, 182
Bellino, Alexis, 10, 41
Below Deck (television series), 16, 156–57
Below Deck Down Under (television series), 157–58, 165
Berman, Marc, 119
Bethenny Ever After (television series), 36
Biden, Joe, 13, 168
Birth of a Nation (film), 217
Bitch Media, 176
Bix, Amy Sue, 129
Bjelskou, Peter, 133–34, 137, 140
Black Americans: capitalism, 237–43; churches, 205; entrepreneurship and business, 240–43; color caste system, 200–201, 214n16; economic opportunities in South, 236, 237–38; Great Migration, 236; old money and power, 195–96; slavery and emancipation, 96–97; women, 77–78, 238–39. *See also* activism; African American cast members
Black Enterprise (magazine), 243
Black Lives Matter movement, 14, 169, 181–82, 183, 205–6, 233
Black philanthropy, 202–11. See also *The Real Housewives of Potomac* (RHOP)
Boccaccio, Giovanni, 89, 91
Boleyn, Anne, 77–78
Bonaparte, Leva, 183, 230

Bond, Julian, 242
Bonds of Womanhood (Cott), 7
Borat (film), 218
Bouvier, Lee, 76
Boylorn, Robin, 97, 102
Bradley v. The State of Mississippi, 147–48
Branded Women in U.S. Television (Bjelskou), 140
branding: for African American casts, 12–13; of "Bravolebrities," 74, 114–18; self-branding, 125, 133, 136, 138, 140
Bravo cable network, 124; background, 107–8; "Bravolebrities," 74, 107–20; fiction vs. reality, 195; hiring and firing, 183; luxury, importance of, 50; overview, 118–19; as primary source material, 2; ratings and viewers, 109–10. *See also* The Real Housewives cast members; reality television; unscripted television
BravoCon (convention), 1, 107–8, 119–20, 121n4
Brinkman, Emilie, 11, 22, 28, 65–80
Britto, Romero, 78
Brockovich, Erin, 71
Brown, James, 242
Brown, Julian, 242
Brown, Michael, 233
Bryant, Gizelle, 74, 139, 193, 200–201, 202–3, 209–10
Bryant, Jamal, 193
BStrong foundation, 179
The Burden of Southern History (Woodward), 227–28
Burruss, Kandi, 11, 182
Butler, Judith, 136

Calhoun, John C., 220, 230
cancer scam (*RHOC*), 30, 31–32, 33, 61
capitalism: Black, 237–43; and Black freedom struggles, 84, 191; and charitable giving, 203–4; fashion industry, 61; and reality TV, 134. *See*

also conspicuous consumption; consumerism; wealth
Capitol insurrection (January 6, 2021), 168–69, 183–84, 185–86n4
Carmer, Carl, 228
Carnegie, Andrew, 203–4
Carter, Tarji, 242
Cartwright, Brittany, 14
Casey, Ryan, 42
Cash, W. J., 227
caste systems, 200–201, 214n16
Catherine of Braganza (queen), 68, 69–70, 78
Catherine of Siena, Saint, 39, 40
The Celebrity Apprentice (television series), 171, 176
celebrity/fan relationships, 136–37
Chakrabarty, Dipesh, 5
charitable giving and philanthropy, 12–13, 203–4, 214–15n29. *See also* philanthropy and charitable giving
Charles I (king), 67
Charles II (king), 67, 68, 69–70, 75, 78
Charleston, SC, 13, 216–30; heritage and culture, 223–24; Isaac Jenkins Mikell house, 223; overview, 216–18; slavery, legacy of, 224–25; tourism, 224–25; William Gilmore Simms, 221–22
Charles V (Holy Roman Emperor), 76
Chastain, Kate, 157, 164
Chatelain, Marcia, 13, 192, 233–45
Cheaper by the Dozen (Gilbreth), 129
Child, David Lee, 126
Child, Lydia Maria, 123, 126
Chlothar I (king), 38
Cholakian, Patricia, 73
Christianity: asceticism, 37–39; baptism, 30, 31–33; imitatio Christi, 21, 25, 33, 37, 39; martyrdom, 11, 21, 33–37, 42–43; Passion of Jesus Christ, 32–33; patriarchal frameworks, 155; penitential justice, 29; in Spanish Empire, 53; stigmata, 39–41. *See also* hagiography

Chronicle of Philanthropy, 205
Clements, Landon, 228
Clinton, Hillary, 170, 173–74, 175, 178, 187n22
clothing, 22; fashion and glamour excess on *RHOBH*, 54–60; and identity formation, 11, 46–62; imperial Spanish fashion, 47–48, 50–54; materiality and belonging, 50; as medium for expression, 50, 68–69; role in public life, 47; as surveillance, 22, 53. *See also* fashion industry
Cohen, Andy, 11, 14, 25, 56, 71, 105, 107–8, 110–13, 133, 156, 181, 195; COVID-19 pandemic, 182; criticism of, 183
Cohen, Lizabeth, 125
Collier-Thomas, Bettye, 205
colonial dynamics. *See* settler colonialism
Colored No More (Lindsey), 198
The Comeback (HBO series), 111
Confederacy: flag, 217; legacy of, 191, 216–18, 224, 227
Confederates in the Attic (Horwitz), 217
Congressional Record, 13
Conover, Craig, 219
conspicuous consumption, 59–60, 71–73, 125, 129, 133–34; and accessories, 72–73; and jewelry, 73; and pets, 72
consumerism: Black consumers, 242, 243; consumer experiences, 105; and group identification, 49, 84; and housewifery, 124–32, 133–34; and hyperconsumption, 140–41. *See also* capitalism
Consuming Reality (Deery), 134
consumption: and class mobility, 139; hyperconsumption, 140–41; as performance, 139. *See also* conspicuous consumption
cosmetic procedures, 3, 36, 41, 111; and stigmata, 41. *See also* appearance and beauty

Index 269

Cott, Nancy, 1–2, 7, 125, 130
COVID-19 pandemic, 168, 181, 182–83, 185, 243
Cowan, Ruth Schwartz, 131
Cox, Nicole B., 27
Crane, Susan, 77
Cribs (television series), 238
cross-dressing, 86, 95
Crowston, Claire, 59
cult of domesticity, 7, 226–27
Cutburth, Jamie, 120

D'Agostino, Tom, Jr., 76
Damian, Peter, 40
Darby, Ashley, 74, 193, 206–8
Darby, Michael, 193, 207
Davidson, Eileen, 55, 57
Davis, Natalie Zemon, 86, 95, 101
Decameron (Boccaccio), 89, 91
Deery, June, 134
de Lesseps, Alexandre (count), 75
de Lesseps, Ferdinand, 75
de Lesseps, Luann (countess), 4, 7, 25, 75, 78, 79, 172, 237
de Lesseps, Mathieu, 75
Deller, Ruth, 171–72
Dennis, Kathryn Calhoun, 6, 159–60, 220–21, 228, 229–30
Dennis, Rembert Coney, 220
"deputy husbands," 94–95
Desperate Housewives (television series), 133
Dey, Francis Pearl Sudler, 223
Dey, Frank Edgar, 223
Dey, Madeline Patricia, 222–23
Dey, Walter Pettus, 223
Difficult People (television series), 111
diversity: among cast members, 183; diversity training and hiring, 183, 236; regional in United States, 2; in Spanish Empire, 48–49
Dixon, Juan, 193, 201
Dixon, Robyn, 193, 200–201
Dodd, Kelly, 182–83
Dolce, Domenico, 79

domesticity, cult of, 7, 226–27
Doute, Kristen, 14, 183
drug use and abuse, 28, 221
DuBois, W. E. B., 198
Dubrow, Heather, 3, 36
Dunbar, Paul Laurence, 214n16

Edwards, Jennifer C., 11, 21, 25–43
elitism: on *The Real Housewives of Potomac* (RHOP), 199. *See also* wealth
Elizabeth I (queen), 73
Emmett, Randall, 15
Entertainment Weekly, 111
Escoffery, David, 136
Eubanks, Cameran, 220
Evelyn, John, 74–75
Ezcaray, Fray Antonio de, 46, 51

Fallon, Jimmy, 111
Family Karma (television series), 16
family patterns, 93–96; enslaved families, 96–97; as presented on early television, 142–43n28
farce: as genre, 83–84; heroines and women's agency, 85–89; medieval France, 11, 89–93; and *The Real Housewives* franchise, 85–89
fashion industry, 61; fashion names and labels, 74; haute couture, 74. *See also* clothing
fast-food franchising, 241–44
Father Knows Best (television series), 142–43n28
Faulkner, William, 227
feminism: and abusive relationship research, 151; collective action, 99; critiques of functionalism, 86; feminist movement, 131–32; group consciousness as foundation, 2; history of and competing images, 8; intersectional analysis, 149–50, 164–65; second wave (1960s), 148; white womanhood as basis of, 8; and women's agency, 83. *See also* women's movement

femme fatale trope, 85, 228, 229
Fields, Kim, 178
Fiske, John, 132, 143n50
Flicker, Siggy, 184
Floyd, George, 12, 169, 181, 182
Flynn, John, 72
Fogel, Jennifer M., 11, 105–6, 123–41
Ford, Christine Blasey, 180
Ford, Tanisha, 12–13, 191, 193–213
Foster, Yolanda (Hadid), 36
Foucault, Michel, 115
Fox, Ragan, 136
Fox-Genovese, Elizabeth, 127, 227
Francis of Assisi, Saint, 39, 40
Frankel, Bethenny, 36, 78, 138–39, 141, 172; abuse, 145; BStrong foundation, 179; and intimate partner violence (IPV), 154–56
Franklin, Donna, 96
Frederick, Christine, 123, 130–31
Freeman, Tyrone, 204–5
Friedan, Betty, 131
Friedman, John, 72
friendship, female: betrayed confidence, 43–44n13; drama and conflict, 112, 117–18; and factionalism, 28; homosocial aggression, 101; idealized, 1–2; prioritization of vs. self promotion, 57–59; "sisterhood" (women's group consciousness), 1–2, 83. *See also* gender roles
Fulgham v. The State of Alabama, 148
functionalist anthropology, 86
FX Entertainment, 108

Gabbana, Stefano, 79
Gage, Thomas, 52
Gaines, Korryn, 206
Garcia, Monica, 5, 13
Garcia, Robert, 13
Gates, Bill, 203
Gates, Henry Louis, Jr., 98
Gates, Raquel, 170–71
Gay, Heather, 5, 13
Gay, Roxanne, 8

gender roles: enslaved women, 96; femininity and interior spaces, 167n38; femme fatale trope, 229; gender hierarchies, 86; gender politics in *RHOA*, 96–101; masculinity, Southern white models, 220–21; motherhood, 6–7, 124, 133–34, 135, 136, 159; punishment of women, 88; social constructs of and power, 147–48, 156; Southern femininity, 226–27; stereotypes, 102; women and group consciousness, 1–2; women's agency, 86–89, 87. *See also* patriarchal frameworks
Gennari, Benedetto, 78
Gentileschi, Orazio, 78
Gilbreth, Lillian, 123, 129–30
Gilker, Cheryl Townsend, 205
Ginella, Katie, 3
Girardi, Erika (Jayne), 10–11, 22, 42, 54–57, 60; conspicuous consumption, 71; and haute couture, 74; "Pantygate," 69, 70. *See also* Jayne, Erika (Girardi)
Girardi, Tom, 11, 13, 42, 55, 71
Giudice, Teresa, 138, 139, 141, 176–77
giving circles, 204, 214–15n29. *See also* philanthropy and charitable giving
Glanville, Brandi, 54
Glickman, Lawrence, 125
Glymph, Thavolia, 84, 127
Godart, Frédéric, 50
Godderis, Rebecca, 115
The Golden Christmas (Simms), 221–22
Goldstein, Carolyn M., 125, 129
Gone with the Wind (film), 217, 225–26; and white Southern womanhood, 227
Gone with the Wind (Mitchell): metaphors from, 191–92
Gorga, Joe, 147
Gorga, Melissa, 147
Gospel of Wealth (Carnegie), 203
Graham, Lawrence Otis, 194–95
Graham, Lindsey, 221
Grammer, Camille, 59, 72, 180–81

Graves, Curtis, 200, 202–3
Gray, Freddie, 206
Great Migration, 236
Grimball, John Berkley, 223
Grindstaff, Laura, 114
Guobadia, Simon, 240–41
Gunvalson, Vicki, 1, 21, 29–37, 41; Christian rhetoric of, 26; political issues, 177; stigmata, 39–40; suffering and martyrdom, 25–26
Gunvalson, Donn, 30
Guynn, Noah D., 11, 22–23, 28, 83–102
Gwyn, Nell, 75

Hadid, Yolanda (Foster), 36
hagiography, 11, 21; medieval traditions of saints' vitae, 28–29; suffering and martyrdom, 25, 33–34
Haire, Chris, 218–19
hairstyles and wigs, 36, 54–55, 60
Hall, Catherine, 125
Hamlin, Harry, 180
Hampton University, 200
Haralovich, Mary Beth, 142–43n28
Hartley, John, 132
Hartman, Mary, 93–94, 95, 96, 101
haute couture, 74. *See also* fashion industry
Hearn, Alison, 116
Heil, Emily, 197
Henrietta Maria (queen), 67, 78
Henry VIII (king), 78
heraldic crests, 77, 81n32
Hernandez, Rocio, 157
heteronormativity, 8–9
Higginbotham, Evelyn Brooks, 205
Historians on Housewives (podcast), 10, 27
historically Black colleges and universities (HBCUs), 200, 202
history: accessibility of concepts to public, 4–5; historical methodologies and reality programming, 5–6, 21;
unscripted television as teaching tool, 9
Hobson, Maurice, 237–38
Hochschild, Arlie, 135
Holder, Eric, 178
home economics training, 128–29, 131. *See also* housewifery
Horwitz, Tony, 217
households: Hartman's model, 96; as political space, 84; theatrical depictions, 83–84
housewife, the: definition of, 8, 234; idealization of, 123–25; as public figure, 123–26; whiteness, 123
housewifery: commodification of, 124, 137–40; and consumerism, 126–32; housewife as consumer, 134; idealization of femininity, 130–31; privatization of for profit, 135; television's role in evolution of concept, 132–36; women as entrepreneurs, 136–37
Howell, Martha, 94
Huger, Karen, 74, 193, 201–2, 207–8
Huger, Odessa, 210
Huger, Ray, 201–2
Hutchinson, Cassidy, 184
Huysmans, Jacob, 78

identity formation: and alternative identities, 55–56; Black, 200, 239; Black identity in South, 238–39; clothing, 50–54, 55–57, 60, 68–69; complexity of, 97; in early modern Europe, 46, 48–54, 78; and entrepreneurship, 117–18; hairstyle, 54–55; in Spanish Empire, 50–54; U.S.-centric values, 4; in South, 127
I Love Lucy (television series), 134
immigrant narratives, 3, 16
intimate partner violence (IPV), 12, 105, 106; Taylor Armstrong, 150–54; Kathryn Dennis, 159–60; Bethenny Frankel, 154–56; legalization of abuse, 147–48; LGBTQ+ relationships, 156–58; myths concerning, 164;

patriarchal frameworks and power, 146–50, 157, 160–61; *The Real Housewives* and social change, 161–65; *The Real Housewives of Atlanta*, 161–63; resources for survivors, 165; Stassi Schroeder, 158–59; social constructions of gender, 156; and social norms on Bravo, 145–46
Iowa State College, 129
Isaac Jenkins Mikell house, 223

Jackson, Jesse, 240, 241
Janiewski, Dolores, 219–20
Janssen, John, 10
Jayne, Erika (Girardi), 10–11, 42, 55, 60; as alter ego, 69, 70; and conspicuous consumption, 71. *See also* Girardi, Erika (Jayne)
Jenner, Kendall, 72
Jenner, Kylie, 72
Jesus Christ, Passion of, 26, 32–33. *See also* Christianity; suffering
jewelry and conspicuous consumption, 52, 68, 72–73
Jezebel (media organization), 177
Johnson, Rosser, 29
Jon and Kate Plus 8 (television series), 124
Jones, Martha S., 205
Jones, Rosemarie, 12, 106, 145–65
Jordan, Charrisse Jackson, 193, 211
Jordan, Eddie, 193, 201
Judaism, 53–54
Judge, Tamra, 3, 30, 31, 33, 41, 43, 80; political views, 188n44

Kardashian, Kim, 199
Katz, Martin, 73
Kavanaugh, Brett, 179–80
Kemsley, Dorit, 10, 46, 54, 57–59, *58*, 60, 74, 79, 180; "Pantygate," 69
Kemsley, Paul "PK," 69
Kennedy, Jacqueline, 76
Kérouaille, Louise de, 75, 78

Kimmel, Jimmy, 111
King, Florence, 228–29
King, Martin Luther, Jr., 182, 199, 237, 241; fundraising, 202–3
Kroll, Austen, 219
Ku Klux Klan, 218

Landgraf, John, 108–9
Leakes, Gregg, 10
Leakes, NeNe, 23, 156, 161, 194, 199, 234
Leave It to Beaver (television series), 132, 134–35, 140, 142–43n28
Lee, Billie, 13, 14
Le galant qui a fait le coup (The cad who pulled a fast one; play), 23, 89–93, 95–96, 102
Lely, Peter, 78
Leonard, Suzanne, 28, 133, 137, 138–39
Leviss, Rachel, 13, 107
Lewis, John, 239
Lewis, Tania, 135, 137
LGBTQ+ relationships and rights, 8–9, 13–14, 156–58
Lichy, Erin, 184
Lieber, Emma, 29, 36, 42
lifestyle experts, 135, 137, 138
Lindsey, Treva, 198
Locken, LeeAnne, 25
Lost Cause mythology, 6, 13, 191, 217, 218, 224–26
Louis XIII (king), 67
Louis XIV (king), 67–68
Lucken, Christopher, 85

Madison, J. D., 219
Madix, Ariana, 107
MAGA supporters, 183–84. *See also* Trump, Donald J.
Maria Theresa (Holy Roman empress), 67–68
Marks, Meredith, 5
martyrdom, 11; of Real Housewives, 42–43; in *RHOC*, 21; theme of, 33–37. *See also* Christian themes
Mary of Oignies, Saint, 40

masculinity, Southern white models, 220–21. *See also* gender roles; patriarchal frameworks
Maslavi, Jacob, 79
Mason, Mary Ann, 127–28
material culture, 21–22, 50, 68–69, 80. *See also* clothing
Mazouer, Charles, 86
McCarthy, Kathleen, 203
McCord, Alex, 12
McCurry, Stephanie, 127
McKinley, Dennis, 13, 192, 236, 238, 239, 240, 241–43
McKinley's Original Hot Dog Company, 241–43
McSweeney, Leah, 182
Medley, Dorinda, 77, 79, 173, 174, 175–76, 187n26
Mellencamp, Teddi, 3, 56, 180
#MeToo movement, 164–65, 180, 181
Miller, Elisa, 128
Million Dollar Listing (television series), 16
Millward, Jessica, 220
The Mind of the South (Cash), 227
misogyny, 89–93, 160–61. *See also* gender roles; patriarchal frameworks
The Money Shot (Grindstaff), 114
Moon, Tiffany, 15, 183
Moore, Kenya, 139, 145, 161, 233, 235
Morgan, Henry Sturgis, 77
Morgan, John Adams, 76–77
Morgan, J. P., 77
Morgan, Sonja, 3, 76–77, 78, 173
Mortimer, Tinsley, 237; pet dogs, 72
motherhood, 6–7, 124, 133–34, 135, 136, 159
Moylan, Brian, 73, 185
Moynihan Report (1965), 97
Muessig, Carolyn, 39
Murray, Susan, 171
Myers, Seth, 111

NAACP (National Association for the Advancement of Colored People), 217–18, 241
National Coalition Against Domestic Violence, 146
National Domestic Violence Hotline, 165
National Sexual Assault Hotline, 165
Negra, Diane, 138–39
Next Level Basic (Schroeder), 159
Nguyen, Jennie, 15
19 Kids and Counting (television series), 124

Obama, Barack, 170–71, 237
Operation PUSH (People United to Save Humanity), 240, 241
Orange County, CA, 2–3
Osefo, Wendy, 200
Ouellette, Laurie, 171
Our Kind of People (Graham), 194–95

Palmer, Barbara, 69–70, 75
Palmer, Roger, 69–70
"Pantygate" scandal (1662), 22, 66, 69
"Pantygate" scandal (*RHOBH* season 7), 22, 57, 69
Parker, Nina, 14
Parker, Sarah Jessica, 112
Parks, Phaedra, 25, 80, 170, 177, 178
Passion of Jesus Christ, 26, 32–33. *See also* Christianity; suffering
patriarchal frameworks, 132, 155, 220–21; and intimate partner violence (IPV), 160–61; *The Real Housewives of Atlanta* (RHOA), 98–101
The Patriot (film), 218
patronage in royal courts, 67, 78–79
"peak TV," 108–9, 119
Pence, Mike, 168
Pepys, Samuel, 70
"performative activism," 15–16. *See also* activism
Perpetua, Saint, 34–36
Peterson, Lauri, 1

pets and conspicuous consumption, 72
philanthropy and charitable giving, 12–13, 203–4, 214–15n29
Pierce, Sara McArthur, 183–84
piety, 7, 92, 226
Pippen, Larsa, 80
plantations, 217, 225; plantation households, 84
plastic surgery, 3, 36, 41, 111
police brutality, 181–82, 183, 236
popular culture, 8, 9, 11–12, 105, 113, 114–15, 119, 179
Potomac, MD, 195; demographics, 197–98. See also *The Real Housewives of Potomac* (RHOP)
Pozner, Jennifer, 101, 102
Prince George's County, MD, 195–96
private/public spaces, 84, 106, 148–49, 153, 154, 167n38
Proffitt, Jennifer M., 27
Progressive Era, 128
public health, 185
public/private spaces, 84, 106, 148–49, 153, 154, 167n38
purity, 7, 39, 226

Queen for a Day (television series), 124, 142n3
queerness, 8–9. *See also* LGBTQ+ relationships and rights

Race in America (television series), 14
"racial uplift," 191, 205
racism: Black minstrel theater, 85; Bravo series' controversies, 14–15; racial stereotypes, 102; in *RHOA*, 101; as social issue, 182; systemic, 183; whiteness and "morality," 7. *See also* slavery
Radegund, Saint, 21, 37–39
Radziwill, Anthony, 76
Radziwill, Barbara, 76, 81n29
Radziwill, Carole, 75, 76, 170, 172–76
Radziwill, Ludwika Karolina, 76
Radziwill, Mikolaj, 81n29

Radziwill, Stanislaw Albrecht, 76
"ratchet respectability," 97, 101, 198
Ravenel, Arthur, 217, 228
Ravenel, Thomas, 6, 157, 159, 216, 217, 220–21, 222, 228
Raymond of Capua, 40–41
The Real Housewives cast: family patterns, 93–96; gender roles and femininity, 133; getaway trips and finales, 3–4, 56, 243–44; image formation, 118; penance and apologies, 29; performative aspects, 65–66; self-branding, 125–26, 133; self-display, 85; self-promotion, 135–36; suffering and sympathy, 25; traits and interests, 196–97; women as entrepreneurs, 136–40
The Real Housewives franchise: conspicuous consumption, 71–73; emotional conflict, 114; fan appeal, 3; formulaic qualities, 212–13; heteronormativity, 8–9; housewifery, 124; international markets, 2; launch and success of, 27; and martyrdom, 42–43; minstrelsy, 83, 84–85, 102; plotlines and construction, 27–28; political issues, 168–85; on racial issues, 14–16; reform activism, 7–8; regional diversity and specificities, 2, 234–35; 2016 presidential election, 171–76, 178
The Real Housewives of Atlanta (RHOA), 27, 84, 233–45; Atlanta, history of civil rights, 236–37; Black entrepreneurship and business, 240–43; cast members and racial issues, 236; creation and launch, 233–34; gender politics, 96–101; and intimate partner violence (IPV), 161–63; Jamaica visit (2022), 4; medieval French farce, 22–23; moral reform work, 8; political issues, 169, 176, 177–78, 182; *Porsha's Family Matters*, 240; racial issues and Black activism, 179; wealth, 194–95; Porsha Williams, 237–40

Index 275

The Real Housewives of Beverly Hills (RHOBH): Berlin cast visit (2018), 56; clothing and social stratification, 50, 60; contrasted with Orange County, 2–3; fashion and glamour excess, 46–47, 54–60; intimate partner violence (IPV), 150; moral reform work, 7; political issues, 180–81; Rinna Beauty launch, 117–18; Spanish Empire, 60–62; wealth and social status, 2–3

The Real Housewives of Dallas (RHOD), 176

The Real Housewives of D.C. (RHODC), 195, 198, 235

The Real Housewives of New Jersey (RHONJ), 176–77; ancestry and family background, 3; and intimate partner violence (IPV), 147; political views of cast members, 184

The Real Housewives of New York City (RHONY), 15; conspicuous consumption, 76–78; cosmetic procedures, 36; intimate partner violence (IPV), 154, 156; Morocco visit (2011), 4; patronage of art, 78–79; and political issues, 172–76, 177, 184, 187n26; titles and social status, 75–76; 2016 presidential election, 169–70; wealth and social stratification, 3

The Real Housewives of Orange County (RHOC): "Baptism by Fire" episode, 30–37; BravoCon awards, 1; Christian rhetoric, 26; contrasted with Beverly Hills, 2–3; COVID-19 pandemic, 182–83; creation and goals of, 27, 133; martyrdom and suffering, 21; political views of cast members, 188n44

The Real Housewives of Potomac (RHOP), 176, 193–213; and Black philanthropy, 194, 202–11; cast members, 199–202; moral reform work, 8; old vs. new money, 201; overview and history of geographic place, 193–99

The Real Housewives of Salt Lake City (RHOSLC), 15, 73; political views of cast members, 183–84; scriptedness vs. spontaneity, 5

reality television: basic formula, 134; celebrity/fan relationships, 136–37; "fakeness" of unscripted programming, 4–5; scriptedness vs. spontaneity, 4–5; use of surveillance, 115–16. *See also* Bravo cable network; unscripted television

Redmond, Brandi, 187n29
revenge porn, 158–59
Rhimes, Shonda, 170–71, 195
Richards, Ellen Swallow, 123, 128–29
Richards, Kim, 55
Richards, Kyle, 7, 46, 55, 57–59, 72, 79, 153, 176, 180; "Pantygate," 69
Richards-Ross, Sanya, 4
Rinna, Lisa, 54–55, 56, 57, 60, 79, 117–18, 139, 176, 180–81; Rinna Beauty launch, 118
Roberson, Latisha, 195, 196–97
Rockefeller, John D., 203
Rodríguez-Salgado, Mia, 66
Rose, Whitney, 15, 183–84
Rose, William Shepard, III, 219
Roseanne (television series), 140
Rost, Katie, 193, 202, 208–11, 215n46
Rost, Ronald, 202
Rost, Rynthia, 202
Rost Foundation, 202, 208
royal courts: conspicuous consumption, 72; overview, 65–66; patronage, 78; scandal and drama, 67–68; structure and function, 66–67; women and competition, 74–75
Rutenberg, Jim, 216
Rutherford, Janice Williams, 130–31

Sable, Mia, 218
Sainte-Croix, Abbey of, 37–38
saints. *See* hagiography
Samuels, Chris, 211, 212
Samuels, Monique, 211, 212

Sandoval, Tom, 13, 15, 107
Saturday Night Live (television series), 111, 112
Save Our Sons organization, 177, 179
#Scandoval, 13, 107
Schadenfreude, 29
Schoell, Konrad, 86, 95
Schroeder, Stassi, 14, 145, 158–59, 183
Schroer, Haley, 11, 22, 46–62
Schwartz, Tom, 13
Sears, Camilla A., 115
Sebenico, Giovanni, 78
Seinfeld, Jerry, 112
Selling Mrs. Consumer (Frederick), 130
settler colonialism: and Real Housewives cast trips, 3–4; Spain in Western hemisphere, 48–49; and white moral reform movements, 7–8
Shah, Jen, 5
Shahs of Sunset (television series), 16
Shallow, Parvati, 80
Shefveland, Kristalyn, 13, 191–92, 216–30
Sigismund II Augustus (king), 76
Simmons, D'Andra, 187n29
Simmons, Russell, 202
Simms, William Gilmore, 221–22
Simulacra and Simulation (Baudrillard), 143n50
Singer, Ramona, 4, 15, 78, 138, 154, 173–74, 182, 187n26
"sisterhood" (women's group consciousness), 1–2, 83. *See also* friendship, female
$64,000 Question (television series), 114
Sklar, Kathryn Kish, 126–27
slavery: Charleston, SC, 224–25; labor of enslaved women, 127; legacy depicted on *Southern Charm*, 5–6; legacy of, 196, 217, 221, 234. *See also* racism
Slonem, Hunt, 78
Snow, DeShawn, 234
social media: and alternative identities, 55; Bravo cast members, 114–15, 116–17; Andy Cohen, 113; and infighting, 57
socioeconomic stratification: in early modern Europe, 48, 51, 52–53; fashion's role in, 49; and material culture, 68–69; on *The Real Housewives of Potomac* (RHOP), 199; in South, 97. *See also* wealth
Sontag, Susan, 111
Soros, George, 203
Sotiropoulos, Karen, 85, 102
The Sound and the Fury (Faulkner), 227
Southerland, Serenity, 11, 105–6
Southern Charm (television series), 5–6, 13, 157, 159, 160–61, 183, 191–92, 216–30; alcohol use, 219; gender dynamics, 222–23; *Gone with the Wind* references, 225–26; planning stages and backlash, 218–20; and plantation culture, 225; Southern femininity, 226–27; and Southern heritage, 222–23; women cast members, 220
Southern Christian Leadership Conference, 241
Southern domesticity, 127–28
Southern Ladies and Gentlemen (King), 228–29
Spanish Empire: clothing and identity, 50–54; clothing laws, 60–62; imperial Spanish fashion excess, 46; sumptuary laws, 49
Spears, Britney, 72
Stars Fell on Alabama (film), 228
status. *See* socioeconomic stratification; wealth
Steinem, Gloria, 83, 98, 99, 101, 102
Stewart, Kordell, 239
stigmata, 39–41. *See also* Christianity
St. James, Emily, 184
Stracke, Sutton, 3, 7, 73, 74, 79
Strasser, Susan, 131
submissiveness, 7, 10, 94–95, 96, 156, 227, 229. *See also* gender roles

subscription video on demand (SVOD), 108–9
Sudler-Smith, Whitney, 218, 222
suffering: and asceticism, 37–39; cosmetic procedures as performance, 36, 41; medieval narratives of, 26; *Schadenfreude*, 29; as self-promotion, 21; suffering narratives in *RHOC*, 31–33
suicide, 153
sumptuary laws, 22, 49, 50–51, 61; and socioeconomic aspects, 52–53
Superior Women (Edwards), 28
surveillance: clothing as, 22, 53; in reality television, 115–16; and self-branded womanhood, 135, 141; as tool of social regulation, 116, 136
Survivor (television series), 80
Sutherland, Serenity, 123–41

Taylor, Breonna, 169, 181, 182
Taylor, Jax, 14, 15
television: background and overview, 108–10; late-night talk programming, 110–11. *See also* Bravo cable network; reality television; unscripted television
Television Critics Association (TCA), 108
Texicanas (television series), 16
Thomas, Clarence, 180
Thomas, Hank, 242
Thomas, Peter, 23
Thurman, Tracey, 148
Todd, Ken, 69, 147, 150
The Tonight Show (television series), 114
The Traitors (television series), 79–80
trauma: childhood abuse, 152, 155–56; COVID-19, 181; racial capitalism, 84
Treatise on Domestic Economy (Beecher), 126–27
Trelease, Rebecca, 29
Trouillot, Michel-Rolph, 6
Trump, Donald J., 14, 106, 168–77, 182, 184, 187n26, 187n29; Brett Kavanaugh's Supreme Court nomination, 179; MAGA supporters, 183–84
Trump, Melania, 178
Tunney, Peter, 78
Turner, Stacie, 235
Two Ts in a Pod (podcast), 3

Ultrasuede (documentary), 218
United Daughters of the Confederacy (UDC), 224
unscripted television, 4–5; authenticity vs. "fakeness," 79–80; popularity of, 26–27; as teaching tool for history, 10. *See also* Bravo cable network; reality television

Vanderpump, Lisa, 7, 13, 25, 42, 147, 150, 152–53, 159, 176; "Pantygate," 69; pet dog, 72
Vanderpump Rules (television series), 13, 107, 120n1; racism, 183; revenge porn, 158–59
Vibia Perpetua, 21, 34–36
Vincent, Susan, 69
violence. *See* intimate partner violence (IPV)

Wainstein, Jules, 156
Wakile, Kathy, 138
Washington Wizards (NBA team), 201
Watch What Happens Live (television series), 11, 14, 107, 110–13, 176–77; political issues, 182
wealth: conspicuous displays of, 3, 50; old money and Black communities, 193–94; old vs. new money, 3, 194–95, 201; and philanthropy, 203–4; regional differences in United States, 199–200; and status, 133–34. *See also* conspicuous consumption
"Wealth" (Carnegie), 203
Weinstein, Harvey, 180
The Wendy Williams Show, 71
West, Kim Kardashian, 72

whiteness: and "morality," 7; and moral reform movements, 7–8; white supremacy, 8; white womanhood as basis of women's movement, 8
Whitfield, Shereé, 80, 145, 161, 162–63, 178, 234
Wifetime Achievement Awards, 1
wigs and hairstyles, 36, 54–55, 60
Wilkey, Dana, 72
Williams, Eboni K., 15, 183
Williams, Hosea, 169, 182, 192, 199, 240
Williams, Josiah, 14
Williams, Porsha, 13, 14, 169–70, 178–79, 185, 192, 199, 233, 236–40, 244; political activism and arrest, 182

Wilson, Frederica, 178
Women's March (2017), 174–75
women's roles. *See* gender roles
Wooden, Georgia Raines, 210
Woodward, C. Vann, 227–28
Wu-Hartwell, Lisa, 234

Young, Andrew, 200
The Young Housewife's Counsellor and Friend (Mason), 127

Zarin, Jill, 12, 25
Zeitchik, Steven, 109, 120
Zolciak, Kim, 234
Zolciak-Biermann, Kim, 139, 141

www.ingramcontent.com/pod-product-compliance
Lightning Source LLC
Chambersburg PA
CBHW032019230426
43671CB00005B/137